Jewish Imaginaries of the Spanish Civil War

COMPARATIVE JEWISH LITERATURES

Bloomsbury's **Comparative Jewish Literatures** series creates a new venue for scholarship and debate both in Jewish Studies and Comparative Literature as it showcases the diversity of a nascent field with unique interdisciplinary footprints. It offers both a new way of looking at Jewish writing as well as insights into how Jewish literature is looked at by scholars indifferent to or sympathetic with these texts. Through its focus on the diversity of these groups' perspectives, the series suggests that disciplinary location informs how comparative Jewish literatures are understood theoretically, and it establishes new sectors that abut and intersect with the field in the twenty-first century.

Series Editor
Kitty Millet, San Francisco State University, USA

Advisory Board
Agata Bielik-Robson, University of Nottingham, UK
Sarah Phillips Casteel, Carleton University, Canada
Bryan Cheyette, University of Reading, UK
Nan Goodman, University of Colorado at Boulder, USA
Vivian Liska, University of Antwerp, Belgium
Orly Lubin, Tel Aviv University, Israel
Susan McReynolds, Northwestern University, USA
Paul Mendes-Flohr, University of Chicago, USA
Anna Parkinson, Northwestern University, USA
Na'ama Rokem, University of Chicago, USA
Maurice Samuels, Yale University, USA
Axel Stähler, University of Kent, UK
Ilan Stavans, Amherst College, USA

Volumes in the Series:
Jewish Imaginaries of the Spanish Civil War: In Search of Poetic Justice, edited by Cynthia Gabbay
Derrida's Marrano Passover: Exile, Survival, Betrayal, and the Metaphysics of Non-Identity, by Agata Bielik-Robson (forthcoming)
Kabbalah and Literature, by Kitty Millet (forthcoming)
Holocaust Literature and Representation: Their Lives, Our Words, edited by Phyllis Lassner and Judith Tydor Baumel-Schwartz (forthcoming)

Jewish Imaginaries of the Spanish Civil War

In Search of Poetic Justice

Edited by
Cynthia Gabbay

BLOOMSBURY ACADEMIC
NEW YORK • LONDON • OXFORD • NEW DELHI • SYDNEY

BLOOMSBURY ACADEMIC
Bloomsbury Publishing Inc
1385 Broadway, New York, NY 10018, USA
50 Bedford Square, London, WC1B 3DP, UK
29 Earlsfort Terrace, Dublin 2, Ireland

BLOOMSBURY, BLOOMSBURY ACADEMIC and the Diana logo are trademarks of
Bloomsbury Publishing Plc

First published in the United States of America 2022
This paperback edition published 2024

Copyright © Cynthia Gabbay, 2022

Each chapter © of Contributors

For legal purposes the Acknowledgments on p. x constitute an extension
of this copyright page.

Series design: Eleanor Rose
Cover credit © Classic Image / Alamy

All rights reserved. No part of this publication may be reproduced or transmitted
in any form or by any means, electronic or mechanical, including photocopying, recording,
or any information storage or retrieval system, without prior permission in writing
from the publishers.

Bloomsbury Publishing Inc does not have any control over, or responsibility for, any third-party websites referred to or in this book. All internet addresses given in this book were correct at the time of going to press. The author and publisher regret any inconvenience caused if addresses have changed or sites have ceased to exist, but can accept no responsibility for any such changes.

Library of Congress Cataloging-in-Publication Data
Names: Gabbay, Cynthia, 1978-editor.
Title: Jewish imaginaries of the Spanish Civil War: in search of poetic justice /
edited by Cynthia Gabbay.
Description: New York: Bloomsbury Academic, 2022. | Series: Comparative Jewish
literatures | Includes bibliographical references and index.
Identifiers: LCCN 2022015461 | ISBN 9781501379420 (hb) | ISBN 9781501379413 (pb) |
ISBN 9781501379437 (eBook) | ISBN 9781501379444 (ePDF) | ISBN 9781501379451
Subjects: LCSH: Jewish literature–20th century–History and criticism. |
Jewish literature–21st century–History and criticism. | Spain–History–Civil War,
1936-1939–Literature and the war. | Jews–Intellectual life–20th century. |
Jews–Intellectual life–21st century. | LCGFT: Essays.
Classification: LCC PN842.J45 2022 | DDC 809/.9335846081–dc23/eng/20220623
LC record available at https://lccn.loc.gov/2022015461

ISBN: HB: 978-1-5013-7942-0
PB: 978-1-5013-7941-3
ePDF: 978-1-5013-7944-4
eBook: 978-1-5013-7943-7

Series: Comparative Jewish Literatures

Typeset by Deanta Global Publishing Services, Chennai, India

To find out more about our authors and books visit www.bloomsbury.com and
sign up for our newsletters.

For my father: Gracias ve-merci

Beware of the poets
whose fists strike on the tables of the executioners!
("Harangue on the Death of Chaim Nachman Bialik," Cesar Tiempo, 1934).

The poem is the fact, memory fails
under and seething lifts and will not pass
("Mediterranean," Muriel Rukeyser, 1938)

Contents

List of Figures ... ix
Preface and Acknowledgments ... x
A Note on Translations and Transliterations ... xiii
Abbreviations ... xiv

Introduction: The Spanish Civil War and Its Jewish Cultural Phenomenon *Cynthia Gabbay* ... 1

Part One Textualities of War in Journalism, Epistolaries, and Music

1 León Azerrat Alias Ben-Krimo: A Moroccan Jew in the Spanish Civil War *Asher Salah* ... 23
2 Beyond Music: Hanns Eisler (1898–1962) *Antonio Notario Ruiz* ... 41
3 Simón Radowitzky: Revolution, Exile, and a Wandering Jew Imaginary *Leonardo Senkman* ... 56
4 Max Aub, the Exile Who Returns to the Diaspora *Mauricio Pilatowsky Braverman* ... 76
5 The Holy War on Fascism *Deborah A. Green* ... 92

Part Two Textualities of Memory and Postmemory in Contemporary Literature and Thought

6 Jewish Argentine Perspectives and Intellectual Mission around the Spanish Civil War: The Cases of Alberto Gerchunoff and Enrique Espinoza *Melina Di Miro* ... 111
7 "The World Exists and We Are Part of It": The Inzikh's Poetic Response to the Spanish Civil War *Golda van der Meer* ... 127
8 A Better Earth: Spain's Land and Inquisition in Jewish Canadian Spanish Civil War Literature *Emily Robins Sharpe* ... 142
9 A Novel That Never Was: Ruth Rewald's *Vier Spanische Jungen* *Tabea Alexa Linhard* ... 157
10 Using the Kabbalah to Make Sense of the Spanish Civil War: Angelina Muñiz-Huberman's *War of the Unicorn* (1983) *E. Helena Houvenaghel* ... 172

11 A Jewish-Spanish Outlook on the Civil War: *La canción de Ruth* by
    Marifé Santiago Bolaños *Rose Duroux*   184

Conclusion: Poetic Justice for the Lost Spain: Deciphering Jewish Keys in
    Modern and Contemporary Imaginaries *Cynthia Gabbay*   200

Notes on Contributors   225
Index   228

Figures

2.1	Instrumental introduction and beginning of the "March of the Fifth Regiment," from *Cancionero Revolucionario Internacional 2*, 1937	49
2.2	Opening bars of "Einheitsfrontlied" (Song of the United Front), by Hanns Eisler, in *Lieder und Kantante*, Band 2, © 1956 by Breitkopf & Härtel, Leipzig, 1972, assigned to Deutscher Verlag für Musik Leipzig, 178	50
2.3	Bar 9 of "Einheitsfrontlied" (Song of the United Front), by Hanns Eisler, in *Lieder und Kantante*, Band 2, © 1956 by Breitkopf & Härtel, Leipzig, 1972, assigned to Deutscher Verlag für Musik Leipzig, 178	51
2.4	Melody and harmony of *Spanisches Liedchen*, by Hanns Eisler, in *Lieder und Kantante*, Band 2, © 1957 by Breitkopf & Härtel, Leipzig, 1972, assigned to Deutscher Verlag für Musik Leipzig, 177	52
2.5	Quote from "Dies Irae" in bars 10–11, by Hanns Eisler, in *Lieder und Kantante*, Band 2, © 1957 by Breitkopf & Härtel, Leipzig, 1972, assigned to Deutscher Verlag für Musik Leipzig, 177	52
5.1 and 5.2	Original letter by Emmanuel Mink included in David Diamant 1967, 426	100
6.1	Alberto Gerchunoff, unknown photographer. Courtesy of Jorge F. Payró	114
6.2	Samuel Glusberg and his wife Catalina Talesnik in the gardens of Hampton Court Castle, London. Courtesy of Centro de Documentación e Investigación de la Cultura de Izquierdas (CeDInCI), Buenos Aires	120
7.1	Glatstein's poem "Shtile Shpanie" (*Inzikh* June 1938: 145). YIVO's Archive	133
7.2	A fragment of Leyeles's poem "*Shpanishe balade*" (*Inzikh*, March 1939: 20). YIVO's Archive	136
7.3	A fragment of Leyeles's poem "*Shpanishe balade*" (*Inzikh*, March 1939: 20). YIVO's Archive	137
7.4	A fragment of Leyeles's poem "*Shpanishe balade*" (*Inzikh*, March 1939: 20). YIVO's Archive	138
9.1	The original cover of Rewald's *Vier Spanische Jungen* (Köln: Pahl Rügenstein Verlag, 1987). Cover design by Reinhard Alff. Courtesy of Dirk Krüger	158
9.2	Ruth Rewald and her daughter Anja in 1937, reproduced in *Vier Spanische Jungen* (Köln: Pahl Rügenstein Verlag, 1987). Courtesy of Dirk Krüger	161
11.1	Rose Duroux as a refugee child from the SCW in Orléans (France), and wearing a pullover donated by the Quakers, April 26, 1940. Courtesy of Rose Duroux	190

Preface and Acknowledgments

This work was written and achieved during a pandemic that obliged its contributors, editors, and readers to isolate and endure challenging changes and uncertainty. Some of them experienced the deaths of their loved ones, others suffered from the illness, and many carried unprecedented burdens. Therefore, and because it has been a time of worry, confusion, and sorrow embedded in discoveries and new beginnings, I would like to open these folia with deep reverence to all the people involved in the production of this volume: for their constant reflection, research, and writing, and for building collaborative work across geographies, despite the vivid sensation of being witnesses of an unimagined dystopia.

I do not know if the *shekhinah* lives among our insular existences and connected the dots to enable this dialogue, or if it is *Mosaic enthusiasm* that pushes us ahead. The fact is that we survived and have entered, it seems, into a new phase of the Anthropocene. Howbeit, alas, this new era has been inaugurated by a new devastating war in Europe; one that, from its first week, has awakened a resistance, also recruiting international volunteers. A war in which, once again, the history and stories of the Jewish people resonate. I wonder if the bizarre context of our writing has had an impact on our understanding of the memory of the Spanish Civil War and on the thinking of the Jewish textualities it produced. It turns, at the very least, uncanny to write down the final period of this volume, precisely at the moment where time seems to loop its curl, tapping with its tail on the back cover of the book.

In 2001, I was first exposed to world literatures of the Spanish Civil War with Prof. Niall Binns at Universidad Complutense de Madrid (UCM). He later became my PhD co-tutor, and, eventually, the director of the international research group "The Impact of the Spanish Civil War in the Intellectual Life of Spanish America" (PGC2018-098590-B-I00), financed by the Ministry of Science, Innovation, and Universities of Spain, which I joined in 2016. It is the Department of Hispanic Literatures and Bibliography of the UCM—one of my academic homes—that funded the copyediting of my introduction and conclusion to this volume. I would like to thank the department, as well as Miranda Cooper (assistant editor of *In geveb*) who, *Englishly*, helped me shape my ideas related to the Jewish literatures of the Spanish Civil War.

I am very particularly grateful to Niall Binns who has encouraged my work for twenty years, reading and commenting, transmitting his knowledge with devotion and joy. To him and his research team, my colleagues, especially Olga Muñoz Carrasco, Jesús Cano Reyes, and Bethania Guerra de Lemos, goes my recognition for having enriched my knowledge of the literatures of the SCW, for the warm exchanges, and for the generosity when sharing their *savoir* and their research materials.

When this path started, I was a funded associate researcher at the Latin American Unit of the Harry S. Truman Institute at the Hebrew University of Jerusalem (HUJI)—my base and home for many years. I also worked then as a postdoctoral researcher of the interuniversity program Daat HaMakom, while my research in Jewish studies was based at the Elyachar Center for Studies in Sephardi Heritage and the Center for the Study of Conversion and Inter-Religious Encounters, both at Ben-Gurion University of the Negev. I am thankful to Prof. Haviva Pedaya and Prof. Chaim Hames, directors of those centers, respectively, who welcomed my first project related to the Jewish feminist memory of the Spanish Civil War.

The collaborating spirit and the conceptual framework of this volume were also inspired by Prof. Louise Bethelehem's (HUJI) ERC project, "Apartheid—The Global Itinerary: South African Cultural Formations in Transnational Circulation, 1948–1990," and her outstanding team, with which I worked as a senior researcher between 2015 and 2018. In the field of memory studies, my work was enriched by an additional global perspective that I acquired while working as a postdoctoral investigator and coordinating the young researcher team of the ISF project "Forgetting and Remembering the Great Flu: Laying the Foundations for a Global-Transnational History of Cultural Amnesia and Rediscovery," directed by Prof. Guy Beiner at Ben-Gurion University of the Negev, Israel, between 2017 and 2018.

In the framework of my research at the Harry S. Truman Institute, the doctoral student Talia Huss remotely assisted me with research in archives in Buenos Aires. She was my eyes in Argentina while I was away and I am grateful for her help and devoted work.

In 2018, thanks to the support of Prof. Ruth Fine (HUJI) and Prof. Susanne Zepp (FU), I was awarded a fellowship for experienced researchers at the Freie Universität Berlin (FU) by the Alexander von Humboldt Foundation. Thanks to the AvH Foundation, I obtained the resources for further research on the feminist Jewish literature of the SCW. My stay in Berlin also enabled me to connect with new researchers working both on topics related to the SCW and on Jewish studies. It was while writing the manuscript of the intellectual biography of the POUM's militia captain, Micaela (Feldman) Etchebehere, when I realized the dimensions of the Jewish phenomenon related to the Spanish war, as well as the extended oblivion under which it has been hidden for the last eighty-five years. My hope is that this volume will unveil not only the Jewish literature of the SCW but also the context, causes, and historical absurdity that silenced such an important cultural phenomenon in Jewish history and writing.

Finally, I developed the project of this volume—which goes beyond the gender focus of the previous one—devoted to the Jewish imaginaries of the SCW in world literatures and other textualities initially at the Department of Jewish and Religious Studies at Potsdam Universität and mostly at the Centre/Zentrum Marc Bloch in Berlin (Humboldt University). I am grateful for this new refuge and the exchanges it provided during the pandemic period. Yet, I am writing these final words in my new research home, as a Le Studium research fellow at the University of Orléans, France.

This acknowledgment wouldn't be complete without mentioning the numerous archives and libraries in Berlin, Paris, London, Amsterdam, Madrid, Barcelona, Salamanca, Ávila, Buenos Aires (and very particularly CeDInCI), and their workers who helped me unveil and collect materials. The colleagues who invited me and/or welcomed me to lecture on these topics: Niall Binns, Raanan Rein, Diego Santos, Claudia Nikel, Allison Taillot, Christine Lavail, Zoraida Carandell, Antolín Sánchez Cuervo, Esther Bendahan, Michaela Wolf, Jonathan Schorsch, Brigitte Natanson, Sina Rauschenbach, Aurelio Major and the organizers of the literary event "Barcelona. Novel·la Històrica" (2019), Casa Sefarad (Madrid, 2019), Marcel Odina and the organizers of the Jewish Book Festival "Sefer" Barcelona (2020), as well as the Museo Interactivo Judío de Chile (2020), the Núcleo de Estudios Judíos at IDES (Buenos Aires, 2020), and the Centro Judío Progresista de Chile (2021); the programs that hosted my research at UCM (ERASMUS+, 2017; VR, 2019), Université d'Orléans (VR, 2020), and Potsdam Universität (Bridge Program, 2020), and those that supported my travel to the University of Oxford ("Gendering Jewish Internationalism," 2018) and Graz Universität ("Interpreting and Translating during the SCW," 2019). I cannot name all the colleagues with whom I exchanged thoughts on the topics related to the SCW and the Republican exile but they were also a source of knowledge: I am grateful for the opportunity to read and discover their work, especially the groundbreaking fields developed by Niall Binns, Manuel Aznar Soler, Mari Paz Balibrea, and Gerben Zaagsma. In the field of Jewish studies, I am grateful for having discovered the illuminating voice of Haviva Pedaya who opened the window to so many more.

On a personal note, the most important of my gratitude goes to two special people who inspired me along the way: Aviv and Maayan, my children, who accompanied me across countries, sat by me at the archives, trusted me while I was away, strengthened me along this journey, and mostly, listened to my stories and learned with me. Together they constitute the *hevruta* of my soul. Thanks to their radiant regards, I confirmed that I was walking through a meaningful pathway. I thank them most because all my discoveries are illuminated by their looks and there is no *savoir* without their joy.

Finally, I would like to thank my friends across the globe who are a source of comfort and hope. I am dearly grateful to my father, Zacco, and my sister, Miriam, for, unfailingly and lovingly, encouraging me from a geographical distance; and to my mother, Anita *z'l*, for accompanying me from Above.

C. G. Berlin, September 2021 and Orléans, March 2022

A Note on Translations and Transliterations

Translations belong to the contributors unless otherwise indicated.
Transliterations from Yiddish follow the YIVO model.

Abbreviations

FJC:	Federación Juvenil Comunista/Communist Youth Federation
FACA:	Federación Anarco-Comunista Argentina/Anarcho-Communist Argentinian Federation
CNT-FAI:	Confederación Nacional del Trabajo-Federación Anarquista Ibérica/National Confederation of Labor-Iberian Anarchist Federation
FORA:	Federación Obrera Regional Argentina/Workers' Regional Argentinian Federation
SCW:	Spanish Civil War
PC:	The Communist Party
POUM:	Partido Obrero de Unificación Marxista/Worker's Party of Marxist Unification
S. R.:	Simón Radowitzky
SM:	Salvadora Medina Onrubia
WU:	*The War of the Unicorn* by Angelina Muñiz-Huberman

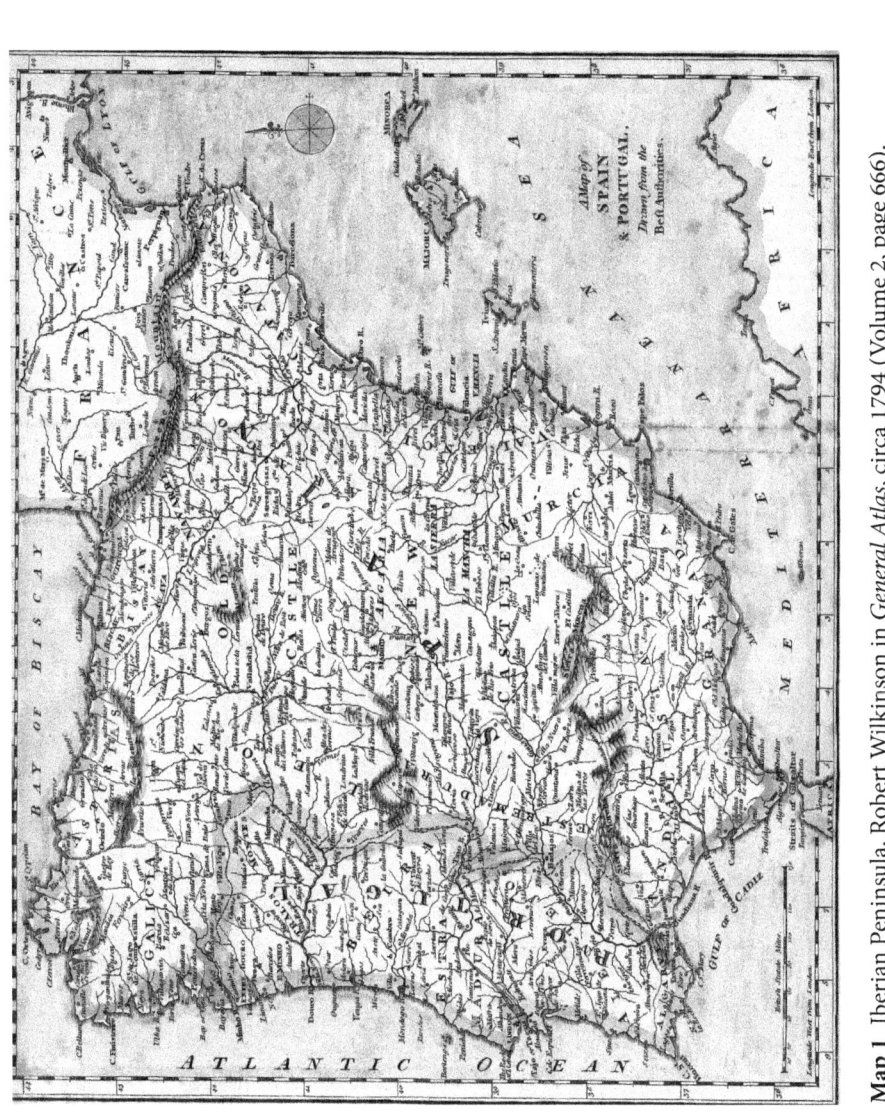

Map 1 Iberian Peninsula, Robert Wilkinson in *General Atlas*, circa 1794 (Volume 2, page 666).

Introduction

The Spanish Civil War and Its Jewish Cultural Phenomenon

Cynthia Gabbay

In order to imagine a Jewish Library of the Spanish Civil War—an internationalist literature written in Jewish languages and/or uttered in Jewish poetic modes—one must first define "Jewish." To define "Jewish," in turn, is to confront one of the most awkwardly veiled, blurred, contested, and misunderstood notions in Western history. Indeed, to say that a cultural artifact is *Jewish* implies also *Polish*, *American*, *Arab*, or *Portuguese*, to name just a few: Jewish identity is a hyphenated phenomenon (Sosnowski 1987) and it demands an action; *to be* Jewish is *to be part of* the non-Jewish world (Norich 2008: 1–4), to create alliances, to miscegenate languages, to incarnate *otherness* and embrace chameleonic tactics of survival. Especially difficult, then, is to broadly identify Jewish cultural manifestations in the twentieth century, the century that eschatologically bludgeoned, throttled, dismembered, cremated, gobbed, and discarded the Jewish people and its Judaism, intending to leave no more than crackling cinders. Given the century's atrocious conditions, who would openly engage in writing self-defined "Jewish literature" after the Shoah (1939–45)—which is to say also, after the Spanish Civil War (1936–9)? In fact, in addition to authors such as Anna Seghers, Primo Levi, and Isaac Bashevis Singer, who were recognized as "Jewish authors" beyond the language in which they wrote (German, Italian, Yiddish)—and despite their self-definition as writers, anti-fascists, and/or Jews—we will discover in this volume more than just a few writers and creators who represented, semiotically or mimetically, Jewish experiences of the Spanish war between 1936 and 1940.

It is also important to note, though, that most writers, poets, and musicians who experienced the war from the inside or the outside (beyond the seas, living under its impact) faced the memory of the Spanish war *long after* the Shoah. Many of the histories depicted processes that inconclusively reverberate between Jewish/non-Jewish (Deutscher 1968) *belonging* and *becoming* internationalists (Gabbay 2020a). These histories were covered under the alluvium of texts devoted to mourning murdered poet Federico García Lorca (Binns 2020: 235–96), as well as under forefront contemporary representations of the war. These representations include fiction—such as *L'Espoir* (Man's Hope) (1937) by André Malraux (Binns 2009: 306–25), *Homage to Catalonia* (1938) by George Orwell (Binns 2009: 379–88), or *For Whom the Bell*

Tolls (1940) by Ernest Hemingway—and poetry—such as Pablo Neruda's *España en el corazón* (Spain in Our Hearts) (1937) (Barchino 2013: 464–72), César Vallejo's *España aparta de mí este cáliz* (Spain, Take This Chalice from Me) (1939) (Muñoz Carrasco 2013: 493–540) or the works of Stephen Spender (Binns 2009: 487–92), Langston Hughes (Binns 2009: 234–42), and W. H. Auden (Binns 2009: 58–63)—devoted to Republican Spain. Such texts became canonical in post–Spanish Civil War world literature.

The anti-fascist defeats in the Spanish Civil War and the Shoah triggered new political, sociological, and psychological knowledge concerning the Western world. These two historical milestones together represent what I call a devastating *epistemic event* (Gabbay 2022a). They did not only cause the deaths of several million people; they also provoked mass exile, the extermination of cultures and languages, and the annihilation of relationships, networks, economies, and exchanges. The twin defeats also altered the witnesses' faces and voices, their fears and their hopes, and often eroded the witnesses' passions, dispositions, and abilities to experience love. They modified *our* perception—three and four generations later—of good and evil. Nevertheless, they were unable to erase the characteristic *Mosaic enthusiasm* of the Jewish people, their deepest conviction in the possibility of repairing the "broken vessel" of the world (Gabbay 2020b). Their pursuit of *tikkun olam* is,[1] in fact, what enables us researchers, today, to identify and define "the Jewish literature of the twentieth and twenty-first centuries" as a living multiple organism.

Since this volume rejects outright essentialist demarcations of "Jewish literature," we shall avoid the definition of Jewish writing as reliant *only* on the Jewish origins of the authors *or* on pure identity categories. If our hypothesis is that "Jewishness" is translated in some way into text, while Dan Miron affirms that "the most stable characteristic of the modern Jewish identity is its permanently being in a state of crisis" (2010: 406), we can recognize then that "Jewishness" may manifest itself in texts and other cultural artifacts incalculably to the rationalist eye and the tonic ear, because these artifacts will be constantly representing crisis! Thus, our goal is to unveil the cultural products of the multifaceted Jewish experience that led to writing on the Spanish Civil War *even* after and *despite* the Nazi genocide that followed. Imagine Noah writing on the despicable world before the deluge, *after the deluge*. Who would have been left to read his words? Imagine Miriam writing about her unraveling of the infant Moses' survival *after* crossing the Red Sea. Writing about a traumatic past or a

---

[1] Regarding *tikkun olam*, Michael Löwy adopts Gershom Scholem's (1968: 268–86) mystical definition and identifies it in the works of Jewish German thinkers and writers: "For the cabbalists—notably Isaac Luria and the Safed school—the *Tikkun* re-establishes the great harmony that was disturbed by the Breaking of the Vessels ('*Shevirat Ha-Kelim*') and later by the fall of Adam. As Scholem notes, 'the *Tikkun*, the path to the end of all things, is also the path to the beginning.' The *Tikkun* implies 'restoration of the original harmony'; in other words, 'the re-institution, the re-integration of every original thing.' The coming of the Messiah is the accomplishment of *Tikkun*, the Redemption is the 'return of all things to their original contact with God.' This 'World of *Tikkun*' ('*Olam Ha-Tikkun*') is, therefore, the utopian world of messianic reform, of the removal of the blemish, the disappearance of evil. // In libertarian thought, there is clearly an analogous duality between restoration and utopia" (Löwy [1992] 2017:16).

revolutionary life-changing event is a complicated task because, among other reasons, it is hard to identify possible interlocutors. It is essential, then, to take into account that Jewish memory and postmemory of the Spanish Civil War are pierced by the devastating impact of the Shoah: in the first place, the Shoah covered Jewish memory of the war in Spain[2] with a veil of traumatic oblivion[3] for those who suffered it. This veil of traumatic oblivion constituted another added layer of trauma for those among them who survived pogroms and persecution or inherited the memory of those who did survive—as well as for the second and third generations that followed, in the stage of postmemory (Hirsch 2012: 1–25). This postmemory was reconstructed by voices that neither were involved in these two wars, nor were contemporaneous to them; the Jewish experience appears either questioned and re-elaborated or, in radical contrast, merely erased. Research must therefore take into consideration the cultural context determined by historical trauma (Gabbay 2022b).

But why juxtapose the words "Jewish" and "Spanish Civil War" in the first place, you may ask? This book will answer: because the Spanish Civil War was supremely important to the history of the Jewish people. As a crisis within the wider crisis of tradition (Mosès 2006: ch. 8) that produced the "Jewish century"—as Yuri Slezkine imagines it (2004)—the Spanish war had an enormous impact on the lives of Jewish intellectuals, as well as internationalist thinkers and artists as a whole (Pérez and Aycock 2007; Binns 2009; Binns 2020; Robins Sharpe 2020; Sánchez Zapatero 2021). Indeed, the results of this war were the defeat of the free and progressive world and subsequently the success of fascism: one of the direct precedents that enabled the Holocaust of the Jews, the Sinti, the Roma, the LGBTQ+, and the disabled to be modernity's most devastating event. How did the Spanish Civil War affect Jewish intellectuals? And why did we not know before about its centrality for the Jewish people? Why? Because the West was predisposed to forget: an oxymoronically passive action that the Jewish people can only disobey, Jewish survivors being really bad at forgetting; Jews—much like Jorge Luis Borges' Funes "the Memorious"—are driven to remember by the "eleventh commandment," *Zakhor* (Gabbay 2020b). How then? Why the forgetting? Well, that is a longer story, and in many ways, a story neglected and sidelined by mainstream historiography on the Spanish Civil War,[4] as is the case for other aspects related to race and religion (Esenwein 2005: 133–56). Historiography is nevertheless currently reconsidering the relation between the SCW

---

[2] Gerben Zaagsma (2017: "Introduction," 1–14 and "Part Three," 109–57) demonstrates how the Shoah and the foundation of the State of Israel interfered in reconstructing the discourse on Jewish involvement in the Spanish Civil War and modulated the perception of a new Jewish masculinity.

[3] On *the lethomechanisms of oblivion* in another traumatic context, see Gabbay (2022d).

[4] See its absence in Paul Preston's *La guerra civil española* (2003), for example, or the inquiry into the antisemitic rebels' imaginary in *The Spanish Holocaust: Inquisition and Extermination in Twentieth-Century Spain* (Preston 2012), which identifies the hatred against imaginary Jews in Spain, but simultaneously ignores the massive participation of Jewish volunteers in the SCW. We shall say that in a way, the Jewish phenomenon of the SCW, passed under the historiographical Western radar. The original causes of this "forgetfulness" cannot be explained without a deep understanding of the history of the West rooted in an early-age obsessive cultural appropriation of Judaism, as well as in inherited medieval anti-Judaism.

and the Holocaust (Brenneis and Herrmann 2020; Senkman and Milgram 2020). In fact, there are Jewish historians (a mostly modern phenomenon, except for a very few examples, following Yerushalmi 1996) who wrote about the participation in the (Republican) International Brigades and militias of volunteers of Jewish origins while the Spanish war was still going on. It started with testimonial voices like the *in situ* chronicle by American journalist Gina Medem (1937, 1998), and continued with those of fighters and/or historians of the Jewish experience such as Luigi Longo (1966), Sygmunt Stein ([1961] 2012), Joseph Toch (1973), Alberto Fernández (1975), David Diamant (1979), Arno Lustiger (1989), Jacobo Maguid (1994), Raanan Rein (2000), Ephraïm Wuzek and Larissa Wuzek-Gruszow (2012), Martin Sugarman (2015), Jerónimo Boragina and Ernesto Sommaro (2016), and Gerben Zaagsma (2017). In that sense, writing *Jewishly* or *on Jews* in the Spanish war and after it entailed a counter-writing. Other perspectives focused on the relation between Spain and the Jews, integrating the Jewish participation in the Civil War (González 2009; Rozenberg 2010; Garzón 2020: 83–99). While the imaginaries of the Spanish war are intrinsically related to a historical event we will not, nevertheless, refer to literature or music as historical genres. However, our objects of study are traversed by the historical experience.[5]

The Spanish Civil War erupted on July 18, 1936, in the midst of "volcanic" activity of humanist cultural ferment across the Western world.[6] Freedom discourse and anti-fascist discourse were ubiquitous. Spain was in the midst of the Second Spanish Republic; meanwhile, both communism and fascism were on the rise in Europe. The Civil War began in earnest when Spanish nationalist rebels led by Francisco Franco attempted a *coup d'état*. What followed was nearly three years of war, and then the nationalist forces succeeded in gaining control of Spain. During the conflict—in which left-wing subjects transcended individual affiliation (communists, unionists, socialists, and anarchists found themselves allied) and fought against the openly fascist Falange Española and General Franco's supporters—volunteers from all over the world traveled to Spain. Some enlisted in the communist-organized International Brigades (Castells 1974; Skoutelsky 2005; Tremlett 2020) to bolster the democratic government; others in anarchist and Trotskyite militia groups opted to support social revolution (Trotsky 1973; Durgan 2004). The International Brigades comprised around 40,000 volunteers from fifty-three countries.

Those volunteers, who came to Spain from all over the West between mid-1936 and mid-1938 in order to fight fascism, were well aware that the Spanish Civil War was, for the rest of Europe, a political, military, and strategic experiment toward a World War that was waiting to explode. From Lodz to Buenos Aires, from Jerusalem to Toronto, they knew that a devastating wave of hatred was about to control territories,

---

[5] My study applies literary and cultural research methods on Jewish textualities of the SCW and therefore does not focus on the differences between historical and fictional texts. For a study on fusion of the fiction and historical genres in Spanish literature see Sara J. Brenneis (2014).

[6] See, for example, the First International Anti-Fascist Writers Congress in Defense of Culture held in Paris in 1935 (Aznar Soler 1987).

politics, and thoughts; and it was in the clear interest of Jewish communities to try and prevent this tragedy. However, most of those volunteers were, at the time—after a history of pogroms and antisemitism exerted on the Jewish communities of East Europe and Germany especially since 1881—*converted* to *internationalism* (Bertolo 2008; Namli et al. 2014), and as such, they did not always identify themselves as "Jewish." Rather, they shared the anti-fascist discourse on freedom and socialism with gentile proletarians and intellectuals from all over the world. Michael Löwy explains this historical crossroad as allowed by the "elective affinity" between Jewish and Christian messianism together with socialist revolutionary programs (Löwy 2017: chs. 1–2).

From a different perspective, Amelia M. Glaser interprets the choice of the Yiddish (penned and gunned) fighters at the time in the framework of a double counternarrative, both in relation to world and Jewish traditional narratives on the Jewish people's alliances:

> The Yiddish poets whose verse filled Communist Party journals during the long 1930s offer a counternarrative to the story of Jewish religious and ethnic insularity. These revolutionary writers were proposing a radically new understanding of community: if their parents and grandparents had identified as Jews, they chose instead to identify as workers of the world. And yet their vocabulary for describing group belonging came from Jewish tradition and Jewish collective memory. (2020: 2)

Nevertheless, many Jewish authors wrote in non-Jewish languages. This volume demonstrates the modes through which those authors wrote *Jewishly* even when they used different registers.

From a gender perspective, it is central to point out that many women also explored and, to some degree, achieved feminist emancipation while participating in combat and in political decision-making (Ackelsberg 1991; Coignard 2017; Gabbay 2020a, 2020b; Lines 2012; McGee Deutsch 2010; Usandizaga 2007; Nash 2006). Several authors of Jewish origins such as Anna Seghers (Germany), Simone Weil (France), Margarita Nelken (Spain), Agniya Barto (Russia) (on all of them, see Taillot 2016), Ilya Ehrenburg (Russia), and Hanan Ayalti (alias of Daniel Klenbort, Palestine-South America-USA) took part in the itinerant Second International Anti-Fascist Writers Congress in Defense of Culture, which was held in July 1937 in Valencia, Barcelona, Madrid, and Paris (Aznar Soler 2018; Binns 2020: 203–34); Gerda Taro participated as one of the photographers of the event (Arroyo 2018: 945–77). As had occurred with modern Jewry, their hyphenated condition ironically contributed to the dimming of their particularities as Jews living and contributing to building a new West.

Indeed, out of the more than 40,000 anti-fascist volunteers (brigadists and militiamen and women) who arrived in Spain, between 15 percent and 25 percent were identified by historians as being of Jewish origin. Most of them were scattered across the different International Brigades and transnational militias (Rozenberg 2010). While the numbers are still being discussed, they are nevertheless outstandingly high for a population that represented in the West only between 1 percent and 2 percent (Zaagmsa 2017: 22–4). These numbers certainly point to an ongoing Jewish crisis. A socialist Jewish unit called the "Naftali Botwin Company," the second company of the Palafox Battalion, was formed as part of the International Brigades in 1937. The Naftali Botwin Company comprised 150 Jews from Europe and Palestine, including a group of Jewish women and two Palestinian Arabs (Zaagsma 2017: ch. 2: 37–58). The Palafox Battalion had a Yiddish anthem—composed by Olek Nus—and produced the journal, *Botvin*, in Yiddish (Zaagsma 2017: 56–7).[7]

In September 1938, the International Brigades were dissolved and almost all surviving volunteers left Spain, while a very small portion of militiamen and women stayed until they were forced out, along with the almost half a million Spanish Republicans who escaped the country in the Retirada of January 1939. For many, it was the beginning of decades of exile in France, the Soviet Union, or the Americas.

It is important to remember that the volunteers were not only proletarians but also intellectuals and artists (writers, journalists, poets, musicians, photographers). In fact, in addition to the crafts of arts and literature, the mediating métiers—like those of reporters, translators, and interpreters—started to be valued more highly during the war (Brenner 2022; Kölbl et al. 2020; Preston 2009), and their words and images shaped our knowledge of the Spanish war.

Both the war and the anti-fascist struggle in Spain had a huge impact on the internal conversation of Jewish communities across the world; especially in Europe (Zaagsma 2017: chs. 3–5: 60–105) but also in Palestine (Rein 2016; *Madrid before Hanita* 2006) and the Americas. This is particularly evident during the war in the organization of aid-to-Spain committees in Jewish communities (Kersffeld 2012; Zaagsma 2017) and in the uncountable op-eds and articles in the Jewish press. For example, from the first days of the war, on July 19, 1936, one of the most important Yiddish journals in Argentina, *Di Presse*, gave thorough information on the fascist rebellion and the ensuing Civil War in Spain, always highlighting the bravery of Republican resistance and working toward a particular imaginary of the Spanish war. Throughout the three years of warfare, the news related to Spain occupied a key space on the front page with op-eds such as "Fashistisher Oyfshtand in Shpanisher Maroko" (Fascist Uprising in Spanish Morocco) (July 19), "Blutike Shlakthn in Ganz Shpanie" (Bloody Battles across Spain) (July 22), or "Di Folks-Armeyen Ringlen Arum Saragusa, Cordove un Sevilie" (The Popular Armies Besiege Zaragoza, Cordoba and Seville) (July 29). Once a week, they offered a section with the "Events of Spain in Pictures" (Di Geshenishn in Shpanie in Bild). Indeed, in that year in Spain, 1936, a new aesthetic genre was born: *photojournalism*, and those responsible for this development were the couple signing their photos under the heteronym of "Robert Capa," that is, Gerda Taro (Pohorylle) and Endre Ernő Friedmann, a Polish-German and a Hungarian, both

---

[7] Also the Thälman Battalion had its own war song in Yiddish, "Af Leb'n un Toit a Farband" (Notario Ruiz, this volume, chapter 2).

of them photographers of Jewish origins, who met in Paris and signed their romantic, artistic, and journalistic alliance in Spain (Maspero 2006; Arroyo 2011).[8]

In September 1936, *Di Presse* started publishing a series of articles titled "Vos ikh hob gezen un gehert in Shpanie" (What I Saw and Heard in Spain), signed in Paris by "L. Weiss"—Leo Weiss, also known as Leo Katz (following Gerben Zaagsma 2017: 62 and 71). The first article of the series (September 16, 1936), "Spetsyel far *Di Presse*" (Especially for *Di Presse*), described the Spanish Republic's situation across the country and privileged the impressions of the author above any possible analysis of the bellicose situation:

די ארטיקל סעריע, וואס איך שרייב דא, איז א רעזולטאט פון א פערצנטעגיקער רייזע איבער שפאניע. איך וויל דא נישט געבן קיין אנאליז וועגן דער פאליטישער, מיליטערישער און עקאנאמישער סיטואציע. איך וויל דא איבערגעבן די אוממיטלבארע איינדרוקן וועגן דעם, וואס איך האב פאר די 14 טעג געזען און געהערט אין שפאניע. איך האב זיך פאר די 14 טעג אויפגעהאלטן אין בארצעלאנא, מאדריד, וואלענסיא, אין עטלעכע אנדערע שטעט, איך האב באזוכט דעם פראנט און די קאזארמעס פון די מיליצן, איך האב געהאט די מעגלעכקייט צו ריידן מיט פארשידענע פערזענלעכקייטן פון די פארטייען פון פאלקספראנט און מיט פארטרעטערס פון די פראלעטארישע מאסנארגאניזאציעס, מיטן פרעזידענט פון דער רעפובליק או מיטן שף פון דער מעלוכע.(13)

This can be translated as:

> The series of articles I am writing here is the result of a fourteen-day journey through Spain. Here, I will not give any analysis relating the political, the military or the economic situation in the country. I will convey immediate impressions of what I have seen and heard in Spain during the last two weeks. I spent 14 days in Barcelona, Madrid, Valencia, and in several other cities; I visited the front and the militiamen's barracks, I had the opportunity of speaking to important figures from the different parties comprising the Popular Front and representatives of the proletarian mass organizations, as well as with the President of the Republic and the chief[9] of the Monarchy.

---

[8] Gerda Taro created "Robert Capa" as part of a professional and commercial strategy in order to sell both her photographs and those of her partner to journal agencies outside Spain. "Robert Capa" is, therefore, an aesthetic *signature* and does not represent a real person. There is still debate regarding the authorship of the photos signed by "Capa" in Spain before Taro's death in Brunete on July 26, 1937. Unknown photographic negatives by Gerda Taro, Endre Friedmann, and David Seymour were retrieved seventy years after the war in what is today known as "the Mexican suitcase" (Ziff 2011). Historically, Taro has been invisibilized and largely forgotten; firstly, because she died very early during the war, and secondly, because Friedmann continued to use the *nom de plume* for his own photography after her death, thus profiting individually from their acquired and shared fame in Spain. This project was so effective that he was remembered as "Robert Capa," and not as Friedmann. His later valuable work, of course, helped bury the "prehistory" of the name. Feminist historians and cultural researchers are nowadays examining the role Taro played in relation to Friedmann and "Capa," and are revindicating her groundbreaking figure.

[9] Weiss possibly refers to Antonio Goicoechea, leader of Renovación Española, advocate of the return of the Spanish Monarchy. The King of Spain himself, Alfonso XIII, was in exile in Rome since 1931 when the Second Republic of Spain was founded.

The series was published in eight consecutive issues until September 30. Later on, *Di Presse* gave steadily greater attention to the relation between the war in Spain and the growth of Nazism in Germany and its economic and military intervention in the Peninsula.[10] The Spanish Civil War started to acquire forms and tones in the collective imagination. The eye of the reporter, aided by his Jewish tongue, surveyed the Spanish landscape after 500 years of seeming Jewish absence, observing it from the dual perspective of belonging and from what progressively became a metonymical claim to Spain's territory via the internationalist discourse. This gaze was verbalized during and after the conflict through semantic fields identified with the exilic imagination of the lost Sepharad (Gabbay 2020c: 153–78; Glaser 2020: 139–73; Robins Sharpe, this volume; Duroux, this volume).

In these press articles, I would also like to highlight the imperious need for direct testimony and for telling the history of the Spanish war from a firsthand perspective, a tendency that is strongly present both in the fiction and nonfiction literature of the Spanish Civil War and has found ample expression in "the genres of commitment" such as epistolaries, autofiction, autobiographies, memoirs, chronicles, and personal diaries (for examples in the Latin American field, see Binns 2020: 71–140). The chapters that follow allow a glimpse into some of these genres. Indeed, the witness's perspective became central during this period (Herrmann 1998) and prepared future world literature for testimonial and memory accounts which, throughout the twentieth century and in the context of other conflicts, slowly acquired legitimation thanks to institutions devoted to the struggle for human rights and to the growing importance of the witness in public debate (Givoni 2016).

On January 14, 1937, T. Elski, a volunteer in the Thäelmann Group, known also as the Jewish Militia (Zaagsma 2017: 67–8, 71), author of *Af di frontn fun shpanye, reportazhn* (At the Spanish Fronts, Reportage Pieces) (1939), and who had participated in Barcelona's Popular Olympiad (Rein 2017), published in *Di Presse* "a brivu fun Shpanien" (a letter from Spain) under the title "Vos ikh hob itst getrafn in Madrid" (What Just Happened to Me in Madrid) where he contrasts "the unprecedented fascist barbarians" (di umderherte fashistishe barbaryen) with "the magnificent spirit of the people of Madrid" (di glentsendike shtimung bam madrider folk). This kind of testimony, which was read in the Jewish press—both L. Weiss and T. Elski usually wrote for the Parisian Yiddish *Naye Prese*—as well as the international press, had a huge impact on intellectuals, especially among those who were committed to anti-fascism and the proletarian cause. Following the European avant-garde artistic experience related to the First World War, and in Spain to the Generation of '27 (Schammah Gesser 2016), many artists and writers during the 1930s were involved in surrealism or existentialism; simultaneously, politically engaged forms of socialist realism were especially adopted by Soviet intellectuals. Throughout the decade, the tense aesthetic and ideological dispute between artists and intellectuals preluded the

---

[10] Just as an example, the Nazi Air Force bombarded the city of Gernika in the Basque country on April 26, 1937, and massacred its population. The world was informed of this event through the famous painting by Pablo Picasso, *Guernica*, which was painted in May and June 1937.

varied aesthetics to be produced by the Spanish Civil War (Aznar Soler 1987: 11–75). In the case of Jewish writers, they found "a reason to address via communist revolution a history of trauma dating back to the fifteenth century. With this poetic return to Spain came a Comintern-inspired Jewish aesthetics that merged past, present, and future" (Glaser 2020: 140).

From the literary perspective, which is one of this volume's main focuses, the decision to concentrate on *Jewish imaginaries* of the Spanish Civil War responds, on the one hand, to the need to avoid essentializing the poetics in question to the presupposed ethnic conditions of the authors studied—in fact, not all of them have Jewish origins, although we propose to study their works in the framework of Jew*ish* poetics. On the other hand, the interest in these *Jewish imaginaries* enables the examination of the mingling of linguistic, structural, and figurative characteristics playing altogether in the objects of study. This examination engages in measuring the harmonies and contradictions these characteristics might provoke when merging and producing new fields of imagination around the events in Spain. In effect, the call for chapters inviting authors to participate in this volume proposed a diversity of perspectives so as to understand the notion of "Jewish poetics." It was a call for reflection at the crossroads of several phenomena which, through my own reading of Jewish texts and research in Jewish studies, I had identified as "Jewish modes." Indeed, I had often found in aesthetic and literary Jewish fields, examples of polyglossia and diglossia, cosmopolitanism, and converse identities (Gabbay 2020d), topics related to exile and migration (Gabbay 2022c), Jewish semantic fields and topics, a focus on ethics, law, and/or messianic ethos (Gershom Scholem Spring and Summer 1934's letters on Kafka to Walter Benjamin 1989; Scholem 1995: 1–36), epistemic disobedience (Slabodsky 2014: ch. 5 on Albert Memmi), humour and irony, structural or thematic focus on memory and oblivion (Rothberg 2009), mythic or archetypic dimensions (Houvenaghel, this volume), Talmudic-like dialogues and constructions, experiences of translation and self-translation (Gabbay 2022a, 2022c), Jewish intertextuality or modern Jewish thought, anti-Catholicism (Joskowicz 2014), matriarchal perspectives and anti-patriarchal discourses (Gabbay 2020a, 2020d), the use of Jewish poetic rhythms (Harshav 2014), Jewish literary structures and interrogative sequences, Jewish liturgy and culinary tradition, and structural or thematic horizontalism (Gabbay 2022c). As I see it, none of these characteristics can separately define a Jewish text; however, the intersection of some of these "Jewish modes" produces particularities that can be attributed to Jewish writing because Jewish culture constitutes "a matrix for Jewish literary texts" (Wirth-Nesher 1994: 3). And with this statement, I would like to introduce the possibility of a feminist perspective that takes into account Jewish culture indeed, as a *matrix* and enables non-linear and non-homogeneous discussions on Jewish *textualities*.

The authors of this volume replied to the call for chapters with a variety of intersections but the examples here, of course, do not fulfill the infinite possibilities of what a Jewish text or artifact would be able to offer, as an exemplary volume could do in the Borgesian "library of Babel" (Gabbay 2016a). I would like to start by defining Jewish literature through Dan Miron's proposal of a "new Jewish literary thinking" able to comprehend the nature of *a complex* or *a galaxy* of literatures both in Jewish and non-Jewish languages (2010), minor and major literatures (Deleuze and Guatarri 1975; Casanova [1999] 2008), but also literatures in between (Miron 2010: ch. 10). I may add that this *galaxy* is not only infinite to human perception and understanding, but it also owns unpredictable variables, an expert camouflaging talent, and the ability to absorb black holes (new undefined phenomena), thus creating large territories of "undecidability" and the rhizomatic never-ending question in regard to the definition of what Jewish literature might be. For all these reasons and those that will follow, the collected results of this inquiry are highly heterogeneous. The chapters of this interdisciplinary volume, each of them, represent, therefore, a twist in the Jewish kaleidoscope.

Here, these questions arise from authors' discussions of the Jewish imaginaries produced in the works written by writers such as Charles Yale Harrison (Canada), Lan Adomian (USA-Mexico), Simón Radowitzky (Argentina-Mexico), Hanns Eisler (Germany-USA-Austria), León Azerrat (Morocco), Alberto Gerchunoff (Argentina), Samuel Glusberg alias Enrique Espinoza (Argentina), Max Aub (Spain-Mexico), Miriam Waddington (Canada), Ted Allan (Canada), Ruth Rewald (Germany), Marifé Santiago Bolaños (Spain), Angelina Muñiz-Huberman (Mexico), Jacob Glatstein (Poland-USA), and Aaron Glanz-Leyeles (Poland-USA). These are some of the many authors who, from our point of view, produced Jewish cultural products—or *Jewish textualities*, as I prefer to read them—in relation to the war in Spain; nevertheless, they are only a small portion of the writers and creators who have written on the SCW in the context of "the Jewish century" and beyond. In my conclusion, I will refer to other names that can allow us to map more accurately the Jewish imaginaries of the Spanish war. Figures like Rubén Sinay (Argentina), Yankev Glantz (Mexico), Peretz Markish (Ukraine-Russia), Eduardo Samuel Calamaro (Argentina), Aaron Kurtz (USA), Margarita Nelken (Spain-Mexico), César Tiempo (Argentina), Ilya Ehrenburg (Russia), Bernardo Kordon (Argentina-Chile), Micaela Feldman Etchebehere (Argentina-France), Máximo José Kahn (Germany-Spain-Argentina), Hanan Ayalti (Russia-Palestine-France-Uruguay-USA), Adelina and Paulina Abramson (Argentina-Russia), Ephraim Rachman (Palestine-Israel), H. E. Kaminski (Germany-Argentina), and the more recent authors Bárbara Jacobs (México), Robert Cohen (Switzerland-USA), and Graciela Mochkofsky (Argentina), among other references, can lead us to greater knowledge of the *poetic justice* that this *open corpus* entails as a whole (and as a *galaxy* itself) when it becomes an archive of poetic memory. Some I have written on in previous works; others will be only recalled or given an uncomfortable corner in the labyrinth of Jewish literature of the Spanish Civil War.

While the general scope of this volume covers the phenomena happening in the West (in centers like New York, Barcelona, and Paris, and marginal centers such as Buenos Aires or Mexico City), you will discover that some topoi concentrate more literary Jewish manifestations than others. The explanation is related to the distribution of Jewish authors across the globe but also to the history of the Spanish Civil War and its ensuing exiles (Aznar Soler and López García 2017; Balibrea 2017; Garzón 2009; Schwarzstein 2001). Therefore, I propose to observe this literary phenomenon in the context of a historical wave of *temporal migration*—which in many ways is similar to the one we are experiencing today.[11] The political pilgrimage to Spain was also an intellectual pilgrimage, and implied not only a movement away from home but, in many cases, also the search for a place to hold on to after expulsion or persecution—especially in the cases of German (Nelles et al. 2019) and Eastern European intellectuals—a temporal home, then, to be followed by another exile, sometimes with shorter or longer spells in concentration camps (Nickel 2019; see also the case of Simón Radowitzky by Leonardo Senkman and the case of Max Aub by Mauricio Pilatowsky, both in this volume) or even in hiding under Francisco Franco's nose (see Micaela Feldman's case in Gabbay 2022b). So, while many authors writing on the Civil War from abroad were concentrated in Argentina, the USA, and France, those who actively participated in the conflict left Spain for exile in countries like Mexico (Muñiz-Huberman 2006: 99–111; Staroporlsky Nowalski 2018) and Russia because historically, Mexico was the product of the 1910–20 revolution, and Russia represented the center of the communist world. Indeed, both countries opened up their frontiers and welcomed the Republican exiles, as well as the persecuted brigadists, militiawomen, and militiamen. This happened in the context of a mostly general rejection of the exiles by other Western countries. However, Mexico, for example, was not eager to receive Jewish refugees (Gleizer 2014).

As I stated earlier, this volume examines genres that are especially representative of this period, such as letters, memoirs, and other personal accounts. The volume is divided into two parts. The first part, "Textualities of War in Journalism, Epistolaries, and Music," presents genres that can be understood as prevailing cultural products of the war and in most cases were produced during the war; some of them were uttered as part of the general Republican effort to fight Francisco Franco and the Falange's fascist insurrection. The representation of the Spanish Civil War presented in these chapters is accompanied by testimonies given through different kinds of aesthetic mediations. This part is reserved for the study of textualities that might eventually have served as literary resources for the construction of the forthcoming cosmopolitan imaginaries. Jewish journalism, as well as epistolaries (collections of letters), has much to tell about the encounter between old traditions and new experimentations, framed by urgency, migration, and messianic hope. Epistolaries allow us to enter the inner world of fighters and volunteers in order to understand the relationship between writing, gender, and struggle. Some of them served later on as resources that nurtured these representations. Meanwhile, journalism played in the war an important and pioneering role (Núñez Díaz-Balart 2012; Cano Reyes 2017). Journalists, men and women, not only participated in the International Brigades but also traversed the hierarchies and enmities imposed by the conflict and were subsequently able to unveil a diversity of realities. Their work was crucial to supporting the call for more volunteers (many of them intellectuals) as well as the performance of new aesthetics (short forms, minimalism, appellative discourses, agitprop) that would influence world literature

---

[11] On the "transnationalisation of habitus" of political militants and intellectuals following this specific wave of temporal migration, see Zaagsma (2017: 33).

and journalism long after the defeat. We will observe, therefore, the aesthetic relation between different kinds of writing genres and the construction of secular *imaginaries* embedded nevertheless in Jewish topics and performed through the intersection of "Jewish modes."

The volume opens with a chapter by Asher Salah, who presents the figure of León Azerrat (1910–97?), alias Ben-Krimo, a revolutionary writer and anarcho-syndicalist originally from the Maghreb. Ben-Krimo's reflections on the Jewish question in Spain, European colonialism in Morocco, and Spanish popular theater are scattered in a motley journalistic production across the 1930s. His activity is of interest because of the still largely unknown contributions of Sephardic Jews from North Africa to the Republican cause during the Civil War. The chapter shows the contingencies within Ben-Krimo's writing and raises the debates of the time relating to antisemitism and philo-Sephardism in Spain. From another perspective, the field of music during the war and its relation to the temporal migration of Jews in Spain is an under-investigated field. Probably, only the case of Lan Adomian (1905–79) has received some attention. The second chapter, by Antonio Notario Ruiz, situates the engaged music of the German communist composer Hanns Eisler (1898–1962) and his aesthetical proposals on *listening* as characteristic of the Jewish musical field when entangled with related theories by his friend Theodor Adorno and his teacher Arnold Schönberg. Notario Ruiz brings to the fore the exilic stay and musical participation of Eisler in the Spain of 1937. In the background of Eisler's Jewish and anti-fascist exilic experience, he recalls his imprint in the "sentimental memory" of Republican Spain. In the third chapter, Leonardo Senkman presents Simón Radowitzky's (1891–1956) epistolary from Spain and later exile in Mexico to his friend, Salvadora Medina, like him, an important anarchist figure from Argentina. From a cultural-historical perspective, Senkman connects the dots between Radowitzky's participation in the revolution in Spain, his forced exile to Mexico, and the wandering Jewish imaginary he reclaims in his letters. This works enables a reevaluation of the epistolary genre and the possibilities it opens in the study of the Jewish imaginary projected *in* but also produced *following* the Spanish war. In the fourth chapter, Mauricio Pilatowsky Braverman examines the paradoxical Jewish self-definition of the Spanish writer Max Aub (1903–72) and confronts it with his dramatic play *San Juan* where Aub offers an unspoken identification between the Republican and the Jewish exiles through the flight across the Mediterranean Sea of Jewish refugees escaping Nazism. His analysis opens the debate on the contiguity and discontiguity of the Jewish experience and anti-fascist intellectualism in Europe under the progressive Nazi invasion. The fifth and last chapter of this first part offers a series of translations by Deborah A. Green who, through independent research, has gathered dozens of letters from Yiddish-speaking volunteers of the International Brigades relating their experiences of the war. Green presents some of her translations, adding some metacultural and metalinguistic context which allows us to understand the outstanding dimension of Yiddish in the Spanish war.

After the Spanish conflict, when the Nazi invasion of Europe expanded, it became clearer that the anti-fascist fight and its literary expression were not only a Spanish issue, nor just a European one, but indeed a clue to surviving the Second World War, as well as later navigating the Cold War. Indeed, world literatures and the arts built "a Noah's ark" that carried and protected the archive of Jewish histories and languages as they related to anti-fascist Spain. Literature became a polyglossic living archive able to negotiate past and present identities and languages. The Jewish adventure in Spain was often romanticized, highlighting the image of both new Jewish (Westernized) masculinities and emancipated women, in apparent harmony with modernity. These languages and memories were incorporated as tools in order to redefine Jewish identity after the Shoah while building new *imaginaries* and exchanging the notion of "transnational and polyglot Jewishness" for "cosmopolitanism," incarnated in national citizens, usually bilingual but not polyglots anymore. Cosmopolitanism was a shared home that found its object of desire in new exotic horizons: the recent past or the translatable unknown cultures. The literature of the Spanish Civil War, just as the literatures of the Shoah, the Latin American "Boom," the Middle East, and North Africa, started to nurture new resources for Western literature, which invested in the task of translation and integrated them into its cosmopolitan imaginary. Postmemory literatures then arrived, often camouflaged among memory narratives and devoting renew thoughts on Jewish belonging. Postmemory literatures started an important task when opening the archive of the Jewish histories and languages. This cultural process is not yet complete.

The second part of this book, "Textualities of Memory and Postmemory in Contemporary Literature and Thought," offers six case studies from Argentina, the USA, Canada, Germany, Mexico, and Spain. Five of the cases involve authors who reacted to the war and the anti-fascist revolution from a distance, either geographical or temporal. The imaginaries they constructed allow us to understand the role of fiction from a postmemory perspective and in contraposition (but not necessarily *in opposition*) to the genres enacted by the case studies of the first part of this volume. The first chapter, by Melina Di Miro, presents the cases of Alberto Gerchunoff (1883–1950) and Enrique Espinoza (pen name of writer and publisher Samuel Glusberg, 1898–1987), two of the most outstanding Jewish intellectuals from Argentina, a site where secular Jewish life at the time was simultaneously traversing a cultural peak and intensively confronting reactionary and conservative opponents (both in the regime and in the streets of Buenos Aires). Di Miro's text examines the imaginary of Spain in the context of the Argentinian debate at the intersection of socialism, Judaism, and nationalist Catholicism, and shows how the war in Spain affected Jewish Argentinian politics. At the same time, this analysis puts to the front the question relating the role of Jewish Argentine writers, which was of significance in Argentina throughout the twentieth century.

In the second chapter, Golda van der Meer introduces the New Yorker Yiddish poetic and avant-garde journal *Inzikh* and its role in the debate on the anti-fascist struggle contemporary to the Spanish war. Through the case studies of the poets Aaron Glanz-Leyeles (1889–1966) and Jacob Glatstein (1896–1971)—*Introspectivist* poets in exile—van der Meer examines the impact of the Spanish war on the modernization of Yiddish and the Yiddish lyrical rhythms. Yiddish-American poetry confirms through the *Inzikh*'s poets, its intrinsic engagement with both progressive politics and experimental poetry. Emily Robins Sharpe, in the following chapter, brings a broad corpus of Canadian literature and poetry of which the Jewish writers are numerous in connecting Spain's cause to Canada's future and Jewish history. Robins Sharpe examines the case studies of first-generation and second-generation exilic poets such as Abraham Moses Klein (1909–72), Miriam Dworkin Waddington (1917–2004), and Sonja Ruth Greckol (1946–), and the writers Ted Allan (1916–95), Matt Cohen (1942–99), and Mordechai Richler (1931–2001). The analysis focuses on the spatial imaginary evoked regarding Spain in comparison to the Canadian landscape which allows Jewish writers to confirm their belonging to the nation of reception and, simultaneously, a transnational commitment to anti-fascism as representative of the Canadian progressive identity. Nostalgia for a lost Sepharad enables these authors to utter a reminder of the long anti-Jewish and anti-Muslim history rooted in medieval Spain. The fourth chapter, by Tabea Alexa Linhard, is the only one in this section devoted to tracing the biography of a book written by an author, the German Ruth Rewald, who was in Spain during its war. The Jewish experience of exiled Rewald was eventually shared with other six million people decimated in Nazi concentration camps. In this context, her manuscript *Vier Spanische Jungen* (Four Spanish Boys) was lost for decades and rediscovered to be published postmortem in German. Linhard situates this novel (which modern publishing criteria might deem "young adult") in its historical context and retraces the story of the manuscript across France, Russia, and Germany where it was finally unveiled. The Jewish destiny of the manuscript itself and its embedding in translation and polyglot circumstances add new reflections to our discussion on the Jewish imaginaries of the Spanish Civil War, as well as to the *poetic justice* a postmortem publication might allow. In the fifth chapter, E. Helena Houvenaghel also adds a different perspective to our subject. Houvenaghel analyzes the metaphors discussing good and evil inscribed in Angelina Muñiz-Huberman's (1936–) novel *The War of the Unicorn* (1983) and contributes with the examination of a kabbalistic representation of the Spanish Civil War. She also focuses on the significance of genre hybridity in the corpus of the Hispano-Mexican author, who played an important part in the introduction of Sephardic knowledge in Latin American literature. Finally, Rose Duroux studies the transhistorical intersection of the Sephardic and Republican exiles in the imaginary built in the novel *La canción de Ruth* (2010) by the Spanish author Marifé Santiago Bolaños (1962–). Duroux focuses on the construction of exilic memory from a gender perspective and interrogates the definition of *Jewish poetics* and the integration of philo-Sephardic literature, a mode which counts several renowned Spanish writers in the literature of the twenty-first century.

The volume closes with a final discussion by Cynthia Gabbay (editor of this volume and voice of this same introduction), which attempts to problematize the definition of Jewish secular literature of the Spanish Civil War by linking, comparing, and debating the various conclusions reached by the authors in this volume. It also confronts the cases studied throughout the chapters with additional case studies. The conclusion seeks to complete the perspective that identifies *poetic justice* in the construction of

Jewish Imaginaries of the Spanish Civil War in contrast and as an answer to the defeat of anti-fascism in the mid-twentieth century while also unmasking the romanticizing cosmopolitan imaginaries related to this historical event. Subaltern and non-canonical poetic voices might unveil different expressions of Jewish poetics.

We are perfectly aware, of course, that this volume does not exhaust the subject of Jewish representations of the Spanish Civil War—a field of research almost totally ignored until now.[12] Because, in its collectiveness, our work is pioneering both in its topics and in its interdisciplinary theoretical frame, readers might identify significant differences between the chapters, in terms of topics, studied genres, methodologies, and theoretical perspectives. As the icebreaker of the *epistemic event* discussed, we have navigated in the Noah way, without a compass, deprived of canonical lines to pursue. As the first major study to address this world literary topic, then, we can only hope to inspire other researchers and writers to follow, in the future, new lines of research in this field.

References

Ackelsberg, M. A. (1991), *Free Women of Spain: Anarchism and the Struggle for the Emancipation of Women*, Bloomington: Indiana University Press.

Arroyo, L. (2011), *Documentalismo técnico en la Guerra Civil española. Inicios del fotoperiodismo moderno en relación a la obra de Gerda Taro*, Castellón: Universidad Jaime I.

Arroyo, L. (2018), "Gerda Taro, la fotógrafa del Congreso de 1937," in M. Aznar Soler (ed.), *Segundo Congreso Internacional de Escritores para la Defensa de la Cultura (València-Madrid-Barcelona-París, 1937). Actas, discursos, memorias, testimonios, textos marginales y apéndices*, 945–77, Valencia: Institució Alfons el Magnànim/Centr Valencià d'Estudis i d'Investigació.

Aznar Soler, M. (1987), *I Congreso Internacional de Escritores para la Defensa de la Cultura (París, 1935)*, 2 vols, Valencia: Conselleria de Cultura, Educació i Ciència de la Generalitat Valenciana.

Aznar Soler, M. (ed.). (2018), *Segundo Congreso Internacional de Escritores para la Defensa de la Cultura (València-Madrid-Barcelona-París, 1937). Actas, discursos, memorias, testimonios, textos marginales y apéndices*, Valencia: Institució Alfons el Magnànim/Centr Valencià d'Estudis i d'Investigació.

Aznar Soler, M. and J. R. López García (eds.). (2017), *Diccionario biobibliográfico de los escritores, editoriales y revistas del exilio republicano de 1939*, 4 vols, Sevilla: Renacimiento.

Barchino, M. (2013), *Chile y la Guerra Civil española. La voz de los intelectuales*, Valencia: Calambur.

Balibrea, M. P. (ed.). (2017), *Líneas de fuga: hacia otra historiografía cultural del exilio republicano español*, Madrid: Siglo XXI.

---

[12] Besides my own research (Gabbay 2022b, 2022c, all 2020, 2016b), see also Robins Sharpe (2020), Glaser (2020: ch. 4, 139–73), and Garzón (2003: 151–66).

Benjamin, W. and G. Scholem. (1989), *The Correspondence of Walter Benjamin and Gershom Scholem, 1932–1940*, trans. G. Smith, New York: Schocken Books.
Bertolo, A. (ed.). (2008), *Juifs et anarchistes*, Paris: Editions de l'Eclat.
Binns, N. (2009), *Voluntarios con gafas. Escritores extranjeros en la guerra civil española*, Madrid: Mare Nostrum.
Binns, N. (2020), *"Si España cae –digo, es un decir–". Intelectuales de Hispanoamérica ante la República Española en guerra*, Valencia: Calambur.
Boragina, J. E. and E. R. Sommaro. (2016), *Voluntarios judeo-argentinos en la Guerra Civil Española*, Buenos Aires: Ediciones CCC.
Brenneis, S. J. (2014), *Genre Fusion. A New Approach to History, Fiction, and Memory in Contemporary Spain*, Indiana: Purdue University Press.
Brenneis, S. J. and G. Herrmann. (2020), "Introduction," in S. J. Brenneis and G. Herrmann (eds.), *Spain, the Second World War and the Holocaust. History and Representation*, 3–26, Toronto: University of Toronto Press.
Brenner, A. (2022), *Hoy las barricadas (Crónicas de la revolución española, 1933–1937)*, Critical Edition by E. San José, Sevilla: Renacimiento.
Cano, J. (2017), *La imaginación incendiada. Corresponsales hispanoamericanos en la Guerra Civil Española*, Madrid: Calambur.
Casanova, P. (2008 [1999]), *La République mondiale des Lettres*, Paris: Editions du Seuil.
Castells, A. (1974), *Las Brigadas Internacionales de la guerra de España*, Esplugues de Llobregat, Barcelona: Ariel.
Coignard, C. (2017), *Las militantes del POUM*, Barcelona: Laertes.
Deleuze, G. and F. Guattari. (1975), *Kafka. Pour une littérature mineur*, Paris: Editions de Minuit.
Deutscher, I. (1968), *The non-Jewish Jew and Other Essays*, Oxford: Oxford University Press.
Diamant, D. (1979), *Combattants Juifs dans l'Armée Républicaine Espagnole*, Paris: Editions Renouveau.
Durgan, A. (2004), "International Volunteers in the POUM Militias," *Fundación Nin*, Available Online: https://web.archive.org/web/20090108182707/http:/www.fundanin.org/durgan1.htm (accessed March 15, 2020).
Elski, T. (1939), *Af di frontn fun shpanye, reportazhn [At the Spanish Fronts, Reportage Pieces]*, Paris: A. B. Tserata.
Esenwein, G. R., ed. (2005), "Race, Religion and Gender," in *The Spanish Civil War: A Modern Tragedy*, chapter 6, 133–56, New York and London: Routledge.
Fernández, A. (1975), *Judíos en la guerra de España*, Madrid: Tiempo de Historia.
Gabbay, C. (2016a), "Worlds of Libraries: Metafictional Works by Arlt, Borges, Bermani and De Santis," in *Canadian Review of Comparative Literature*, 43.2: 241–262, https://doi.org/10.1353/crc.2016.0019.
Gabbay, C. (2016b), "Identidad, género y prácticas anarquistas en las memorias de Micaela Feldman y Etchebéhère," *Forma. Revista d'estudis comparatius. Art, literatura, pensament*, 14: 35–57.
Gabbay, C. (2020a), "(Jewish) Women's Narratives of *Caring* and Medical Practices during the Spanish Civil War," in Miriam Offer (ed.), *Nashim: A Journal of Jewish Women's Studies and Gender Issues, 36, Jewish women medical practitioners in Europe before, during and after the Holocaust*, 205–33, Bloomington: Indiana University Press.
Gabbay, C. (2020b), "El onceavo mandamiento: memoria del fuego en la literatura judía y feminista de la guerra civil española," in E. Kahan, A. Raber, and W. Wechsler

(eds.), *Hacer Patria. Estudios sobre la vida judía en Argentina*, 31–67, Buenos Aires: Teseo.

Gabbay, C. (2020c), "Una cuestión de espacio: promesas de liberación y utopía en la poesía yidis e hispana de la guerra civil española," in P. Molina Taracena (ed.), *Poesía de la guerra civil española: una perspectiva comparatista*, Chapter 9, 153–78, Bern: Peter Lang.

Gabbay, C. (2020d), "Babilonia y Revolución en España: Prácticas de escritura cosmopolita de una miliciana/ Mika Feldman Etchebehere," in J. Kölbl, I. Orlova and M. Wolf (eds.), *¿Pasarán? Kommunikation im Spanischen Bürgerkrieg. Interacting in the Spanish Civil War*, 82–99, Vienna: New Academic Press.

Gabbay, C. (2022a), "*Neodjudezmo* en la lírica latinoamericana disidente: la construcción de registros intersticiales entre la autotraducción y el glosario," M. L. Spoturno and R. Grutman (eds.), *Mutatis Mutandis 15 (1)'s special issue, Self-translation and/in Latin America and the Latina diaspora*, 65–94, https://doi.org/10.17533/udea.mut.v15n1a05.

Gabbay, C. (2022b), "Iterología de Micaela Feldman/Etchebehere tras la guerra civil española: entre el insilio melancólico y el exilio de imaginación cosmopolita," in C. Nickel and D. Santos Sánchez (eds.), *Women in Exile: Female Literary Networks of the 1939 Republican Exile*, Special Volume in *Journal of Spanish Cultural Studies* 23 (1), 51–70, https://doi.org/10.1080/14636204.2022.2033430.

Gabbay, C. (2022c), "L'autotraduction de Mika Feldman Etchebehere ou écriture à deux plumes pour un pacte cosmopolite," in C. Lavail and A. Taillot (eds.), special issue in *Crisol* 26, forthcoming.

Gabbay, C. (2022d), "Traces in the Archive of a Great Oblivion: Ibero-American Representations of the 'Spanish' Flu," in G. Beiner (ed.), *Re-Awakenings: The Forgotten and Unforgotten Influenza Pandemic of 1918–1919*, Chapter 18, 314–32, Oxford: Oxford University Press.

Garzón, J. I. (2003), "Judíos y temas judíos en la literatura española del exilio republicano," in N. Rehrmann (ed.), *El legado de Sefarad en la historia y la literatura de América latina, España, Portugal y Alemania*, 151–66, Salamanca: Amarú.

Garzón, J. I. (2009), *El exilio republicano español y los judíos*, Madrid: Hebraica.

Garzón, J. I. (2020), "Spain and the Jews during the Holocaust," in S. J. Brenneis and G. Herrmann (eds.), *Spain, the Second World War and the Holocaust. History and Representation*, 83–99, Toronto: University of Toronto Press.

Givoni, M. (2016), *The Care of the Witness: A Contemporary History of Testimony in Crises*, Cambridge: Cambridge University Press.

Glaser, A. M. (2020), *Songs in Dark Times. Yiddish Poetry of Struggle from Scottsboro to Palestine*, Cambridge: Harvard University Press, Chapter 4, 139–73.

Gleizer, D. (2014), *Unwelcome Exiles. Mexico and the Jewish Refugees from Nazism, 1933–1945*, Boston: Brill.

González, I. (2009), *Los judíos y la Guerra Civil española*, Madrid: Hebraica Ediciones.

Harshav, B. (2014), *Three Thousand Years of Hebrew Versification: Essays in Comparative Prosody*, New Haven & London: Yale University Press.

Herrmann, G. A. (1998), "The Self Writing War: Memory Texts of the Spanish Civil War and the Antifascist Resistance," Cornell University, PhD dissertation.

Hirsch, M. (2012), *The Generation of Postmemory: Writing and Visual Culture after the Holocaust*, New York: Columbia University Press.

Joskowicz, A. (2014), *The Modernity of Others: Jewish Anti-Catholicism in Germany and France*, Stanford: Stanford University Press.

Kersffeld, D. (2012), *Rusos y rojos. Judíos comunistas en los tiempos de la Comintern*, Buenos Aires: Capital intelectual.

Kölbl, J., Orlova, I. and M. Wolf (eds.). (2020), *¿Pasarán? Kommunikation im Spanischen Bürgerkrieg. Interacting in the Spanish Civil War*, Vienna: New Academic Press.

Lines, L. M. (2012), *Milicianas: Women in Combat in the Spanish Civil War*, Plymouth: Lexington Books.

Longo, L. (1966), *Las Brigadas Internacionales en España*, Mexico City: Ediciones Era.

Löwy, M. ([1992] 2017), *Redemption and Utopia: Jewish Libertarian Thought in Central Europe: A Study in Elective Affinity*, Stanford: Stanford University Press.

Lustiger, A. (1989), *Schalom libertad! Juden im spanischen Bürgerkrieg*, Frankfurt a.M.: Athenäum.

Madrid Before Hanita: Jews from Palestine in the Spanish International Brigades (2006), [Film] Dir. Eran Torbiner, Israel, 58 min.

Maguid, J. (Jacinto Cimazo). (1994), *La revolución libertaria española (1936–1939)*, Buenos Aires: Reconstruir.

Maspero, F. (2006), *L'ombre d'une photographe: Gerda Taro*, Paris: Le Seuil.

McGee Deutsch, S. (2010), *Crossing Borders, Claiming a Nation: A History of Argentine Jewish Women, 1880–1955*, Durham and London: Duke University Press.

Medem, G. (1937), *Los judíos luchadores de la libertad: Un año de lucha en las Brigadas Internacionales*, Madrid: Ediciones del Comisariado de las Brigadas Internacionales.

Medem, G. (1998), "Jewish Fighters in the Battlefields of Spain," in Z. M. Baker (ed.), *From a Ruined Garden: The Memorial Books of Polish Jewry*, 116–72, Bloomington and Indianapolis: Indiana University Press.

The Mexican Suitcase (2011), [Film] Dir. Trisha Ziff, Mexico-Spain: 212 Berlin, Mallerich Films, and Alicorn Films Productions, 86 min.

Mosès, S. (2006), *L'Ange de l'Histoire*, Paris: Gallimard.

Miron, D. (2010), *From Continuity to Contiguity: Toward a New Jewish Literary Thinking*, Stanford: Stanford University Press.

Muñiz-Huberman, A. (2006), "Exilios olvidados: los hispanoamericanos y los hispanojudíos," in M. Aznar Soler (ed.), *Escritores, editoriales y revistas del exilio republicano de 1939*, 99–111, Sevilla: Renacimiento.

Muñoz Carrasco, O. (2013), *Perú y la Guerra Civil española. La voz de los intelectuales*. Valencia: Calambur.

Namli, E., J. Svenungsson and A. M. Vincent. (eds.). (2014), *Jewish Thought, Utopia, and Revolution*, Amsterdam and New York: Editions Rodopi.

Nash, M. (2006), *Rojas: las mujeres republicanas en la guerra civil*, Barcelona: Taurus.

Nelles, D., Linse, U., H. Piotrowski and C. García. ([2010] 2019), *Antifascistas alemanes en Barcelona. El grupo DAS: sus actividades contra la red nazi y en el frente de Aragón*, Barcelona: Virus.

Nickel, C. (2019), *Los exiliados republicanos en los campos de internamiento franceses*, Sevilla: Renacimiento.

Norich, A. (2008), "Introduction," in A. Norich and Y. Z. Eliav (eds.), *Jewish Literatures and Cultures. Context and Intertexts*, Brown Judaic Studies, Vol. 349, 1–7, Providence: Brown University.

Núñez Díaz-Balart, M. *La prensa de guerra en la zona republicana durante la guerra civil española*, Madrid: Ediciones de la Torre, 1992.

Pérez, J. and W. Aycock. (2007 [1990]), *The Spanish Civil War in Literature*, Texas: Tech University Press.

Preston, P. (2003), *La guerra civil española*, Madrid: DeBolsillo.

Preston, P. (2009), *We Saw Spain Die: Foreign Correspondents in the Spanish Civil War*, London: Constable.

Preston, P. (2012), *The Spanish Holocaust. Inquisition and Extermination in Twentieth-Century Spain*, London: Harper Press.

Rein, R. (ed.). (2000), *They Shall Not Pass: The Spanish Civil War, 1936–1939*, (Hebrew) Tel Aviv: Zmora-Bitan.

Rein, R. (2016), "Tikkun Olam and Transnational Solidarity: Jewish Volunteers in the Spanish Civil War," *Contemporary Judaism and Politics*, 2 (10): 207–30.

Rein, R. (2017), "El desafío a los juegos olímpicos de Berlín: los atletas judíos de Palestina en la frustrada olimpíada popular de Barcelona," *Historia Contemporánea*, 56: 121–55.

Robins Sharpe, E. (2020), *Mosaic Fictions: Writing Identity in the Spanish Civil War*, Toronto: University of Toronto Press.

Rothberg, M. (2009), *Multidirectional Memory: Remembering the Holocaust in the Age of Decolonization*, Redwood City: Stanford University Press.

Rozenberg, D. (2010), *La España contemporánea y la cuestión judía: retejiendo los hilos de la memoria y de la historia*, Madrid: Casa Sefarad-Israel/Marcial Pons.

Sánchez Zapatero, J. (ed.). (2021), *La trinchera universal. Los voluntarios internacionales y la literatura de la Guerra Civil española*, Granada: Comares literatura.

Schammah Gesser, S. (2016), *Madrid's Forgotten Avant-garde: Between Essentialism and Modernity*, Sussex: Sussex Academic Press.

Scholem, G. (1968), *Major Trends in Jewish Mysticism*, London: Thames and Hudson.

Scholem, G. (1995), "Toward an Understanding of the Messianic Idea in Judaism," in *The Messianic Idea in Judaism: And Other Essays on Jewish Spirituality*, 1–36, New York: Schocken Books.

Schwarzstein, D. (2001), *Entre Franco y Perón. Memoria e identidad del exilio republicano español en Argentina*, Barcelona: Crítica.

Senkman, L. and A. Milgram (eds.). (2020), *Cultura, ideología y fascismo. Sociedad civil iberoamericana y Holocausto*, Madrid/Frankfurt: Iberoamericana/Vervuert.

Skoutelsky, R. (2005), *Novedad en el frente. Las brigadas internacionales en la guerra civil*, Madrid: Temas de hoy.

Slabodsky, S. (2014), *Decolonial Judaism: Triumphal Failures of Barbaric Thinking*, New York: Palgrave Macmillan.

Slezkine, Y. (2004), *The Jewish Century*, Princeton: Princeton University Press.

Sosnowski, S. (1987), "Latin American-Jewish Writers: Protecting the Hyphen," in J. Laikin Elkin and G. W. Merkx (eds.), *The Jewish Presence in Latin America*, Chapter 16, 297–308, London: Routledge.

Staropolsky Nowalski, M. (2018), *Presencia judía en el exilio español en México. Por vuestra libertad y la nuestra*, México: Ateneo Español.

Stein, S. (2012), *Ma guerre d'Espagne. Brigades internationales: la fin d'un mythe*. Paris: Seuil.

Sugarman, M. (2015), *Against Fascism: Jews Who Served in the International Brigade in the Spanish Civil War*, Self-published, Available online: https://www.marxists.org/subject/jewish/spanjews.pdf (accessed March 15, 2020).

Taillot, A. (2016), *Les intellectuelles européennes et la guerre d'Espagne: De l'engagement personnel à la défense de la République Espagnole*, Nanterre: Presse Universitaire de Paris Ouest.
Toch, J. (1973), *Juden im spanischen Krieg 1936–39*, Vienna: Zeitgeschichte.
Tremlett, G. (2020), *The International Brigades. Fascism. Freedom and the Spanish Civil War*, New York: Bloomsbury Publishing.
Trotsky, L. (1973), *The Spanish Revolution (1931–39)*, New York: Pathfinder Press.
Usandizaga, A. (2007), *Escritoras al frente. Intelectuales extranjeras en la Guerra Civil*, San Sebastián: Nerea.
Wirth-Nesher, H. (1994), "Introduction. Defining the Indefinable: What is Jewish Literature," in H. Wirth-Nesher (ed.), *What is Jewish Literature?*, 3–12, Philadelphia: Jewish Public Society.
Wuzek, E. and L. Wuzek-Gruszow. (2012), *Combattants Juifs dans la Guerre d'Espagne: La compagnie Botwin*, Paris: Editions Syllepse.
Yerushalmi, Y. H. (1996), *Zakhor. Jewish History and Jewish Memory*, Seattle and London: University of Washington Press.
Zaagsma, G. (2017), *Jewish Volunteers, The International Brigades and The Spanish Civil War*, London: Bloomsbury.

Part One

Textualities of War in Journalism, Epistolaries, and Music

1

León Azerrat Alias Ben-Krimo

A Moroccan Jew in the Spanish Civil War

Asher Salah

The first time I ran into the protagonist of this chapter, I was assailed by doubt. Could different people be hidden behind the name of an individual, whose existence had been so erratic and contradictory that it was difficult to assemble the puzzle of the available information within the bounds of a single human experience? And indeed, the life of León Azerrat Cohen, also known under the literary pseudonym of Ben-Krimo, bore an uncanny resemblance to the biographies born out of Max Aub's literary imagination. Azerrat could have been a sort of Jewish replica of Jusep Torres Campalans, the fictitious Catalan Cubist painter of Aub's homonymous novel (Aub 1958), or a Moroccan counterpart of the writer Luis Álvarez Petreña, Aub's apocryphal alter ego (Aub 1973). The story of León Azerrat was also the chronicle of an artist involved with the modernist avant-gardes and engaged with the left, who, after a sudden desertion of his previous ideals at the end of the war, reappeared under a new disguise, beneath the camouflage of the political credo of his former enemies.

As with Álvarez Petreña, León Azerrat's literary endeavors were also not those of a professional writer, crowned with his peers' recognition and acclaimed by the public. Azerrat was rather an amateur wordsmith, involved in intense, albeit chaotic, activity as a newspaper correspondent, as a radical pamphleteer, and even as a lyricist of popular tunes. Like his fictional companions Álvarez Petreña and Torres Campalans, Azerrat's multiple identities disclosed the profile of a generation shattered by a decade-long war—the Spanish internecine conflict and the Second World War—which found its literary reflection in the inner dissociations of the modernist subject.

Azerrat was a dissident not only in the political meaning of the term but first and foremost to the extent that his unpredictable biography defied any attempt at categorization. It was punctuated by repeated exiles and political instability, dwelling at the borderline of various languages and cultures, Arabic, Spanish, Catalan, French, English, and perhaps even Yiddish.

The existence of León Azerrat Cohen has eluded the attention of most of the history books devoted to the Jews of the Spanish protectorate in Morocco or to the Spanish Civil War. However, his off-beat personality stars in the witty testimony of Rafael Cansinos Assens in 1950, who devoted an entire chapter of his book, *Los Judíos de Sefarad*, to León Azerrat, under the rather explicit alias of León Azenbat:

> A terrible young man named León Azenbat fell upon the small Jewish community of Madrid as an apocalyptic meteor. He called himself an "avant-garde Hebrew poet." He came from Morocco, from that dark African continent, whence the Almohads, the Almoravids, and the Benimerins once stormed like devastating plagues. León Azenbat was just another one of those terrible plagues. When they saw him arrive, the naive and fervent Israelites of the small Sephardi community trembled with dread and their beards shivered. He was a sort of a Jewish Antichrist, the last calamity, the Azenbatic plague, announced for the end of time. León Azenbat condensed in himself an entire cocktail of revolutionary explosives: an atheist, a Bolshevik, and above all an "avant-garde poet." Could a descendant of the prophets, of the psalmists of the Bible, be involved in that absurd kind of poetry called "Dada"? (Cansinos Assens 1950: 149–50)

César González-Ruano (1903–65), a foremost Spanish journalist, closely associated with the Ultraísta movement, and also an antisemitic writer who collaborated with the Nazis in Paris during the war (Sala Rose and Garcia-Planas 2014), recalled in his memoirs having been in touch during his sojourn in Tetuan in 1935 with "A cunning Jew called León Azerrat who later roamed a bit in Madrid. León Azerrat had been a barber and pretended to have a certain knack for journalism" (González-Ruano 1951: 242).

León Azerrat could have gained more fame as the author of the lyrics of some very successful boleros such as "Tanger" (1961), sung by Charles Sananès alias Charles Danvers, or "Lecciones como la vida" (1973), interpreted by Fosforito and Paco de Lucía. But his contribution as a lyricist was eclipsed by the popularity of the performers of these songs.

Of his poetic endeavors, almost nothing is left. Only fifteen poems remain out of a harvest that may have been more copious. The first known poem was published when Azerrat was just eighteen in the first issue of the bimonthly journal of Tangier, *Adelante* (Azerrat 1929: 2). This journal was founded by a group of young Jewish intellectuals, under the direction of Rabbi Moisés Azancot, an important Zionist intellectual of Tangier born in 1880 who initiated him to freemasonry.

Twelve years later, ten other poems were published, again in Tangier, in what appears to be the only extant printed collection of his works, under the title of *El alba inquietante*.[1] Of his later production, in the archive of the pianist Pilar Bayona

---

[1] I would like to thank Julian Gómez and Antonio Bayona for bringing to my attention the existence of this publication.

(APB) in Zaragoza are preserved four typewritten poems from an otherwise unknown cycle, *Romances de la moreria*, that were offered by Azerrat to the pianist during her tour of performances in Tetuan in the summer of 1945. From the extant evidence, Azerrat's poetry is characterized by a naive emphasis and a substantially conventional sentimentality, abusing late romantic and crepuscular tropes with a layer of modernist aesthetics. Azerrat's fondness for orientalist clichés appears for instance in verses such as these from his "Balada de los vientos": "¡Qué sensación la de ahora, / nirvana en el pensamiento, / droga de la tarde mora! / . . . Arenales y palmeras, / sed de meharis sedientos, / espejismo en el calor / del color de los desiertos."

In the Spanish press of the 1930s, Azerrat is presented as the distinguished author of *Rosas negras* (*Diario de Córdoba* 1934: 2), although it is dubious whether these poems were ever printed. Cansinos Assens (1950: 147) mentions another collection of poems under the title *Dioses sin dios* where Azerrat exposed his pacifist and egalitarian creed.

Nor did he succeed better as a playwright. Together with Ángel Villatoro, who was later involved in cinematographic productions for the Spanish Republic, Azerrat allegedly authored a comedy in three acts, *La desdeñosa*. Two other titles are known from the following announcement in the gossip column of one of the main liberal daily newspapers in Spain, *El heraldo de Madrid* (1936: 8):

> The young and distinguished writer León Azerrat lost seven or eight days ago the original manuscripts of two of his comedies. One was titled "Azrayatyh, the smoke woman, comedy of oriental setting" and the other "Enemy Night," also in three acts, but written in prose. Its plot, with a pacifist aim, takes place in a political and colonial setting, against the backdrop of the war in Morocco.

However, there is no evidence supporting that these theatrical pieces were ever performed on stage. This inability to have any of his works published became a sort of a hallmark of his literary persona in the intellectual milieu of Madrid in the 1930s (Cansinos Assens 1950: 149).

Yet, despite his slight fortune as a poet and a playwright, León Azerrat had been much more felicitous as a political columnist and a reporter. His career spanned almost seven decades, witnessing the history of Spain from the Second Republic to the recovery of democracy, through the Civil War and the Francoist regime. His multifaceted and contradictory intellectual and political trajectory deserves a careful examination since it runs against some general assumptions concerning the history of the Jews in contemporary Spain. Azerrat's biography sheds new light upon at least two issues that need to be revisited: the simmering antisemitism of some segments of the Spanish Second Republic's left, despite the philo-Sephardi stances of many of their leaders, and the role played by Moroccan Jews in the Republican struggle, despite their alleged support of Franco during the Civil War.

Azerrat's Beginnings and His Literary Persona between Morocco and Spain

Azerrat, son of Abraham and Miriam, was born in 1910, two years before the assignment to Spain of the protectorate over the northern area of Morocco, in Alcazarquivir, a city with a community of approximately 1,500 Jews who retained Judeo-Spanish (Haketia) as their native language (Margolin 2010; Akrif 2018). Azerrat most likely received his education in one of the many Alfonso XIII schools, established by the Spanish government in Morocco to foster Spanish cultural influence among the local population (Valderrama Martínez 1959; Calderwood 2019).

Here he worked as a hairdresser and may have lived for a period in Tangier, participating in the cultural activities of the local Jewish youth. In June 1929 Azerrat, entangled in debts, enlisted in the Spanish army stationed in the Rif as "escribiente jalifiano," a clerk in charge of the contacts with the local indigenous population. He was discharged in March of the next year for his incompatibility with the disciplinary requirements of military life (AGA 64, 29). At the age of twenty, in 1930, he left Morocco and landed in Madrid with the intention of finding his way into its thriving intellectual life. At the time of his arrival, the Jewish community of the capital, officially established only a decade earlier in 1920, counted 130 members and had a small synagogue, the Midras Abrabanel founded in 1917.

In the Spanish capital, he attended the in-crowd of Rafael Cansinos Assens and was encouraged to pursue his poetic vocation by the dramatist and Nobel Prize in Literature laureate Jacinto Benavente (1866–1954) (Cansinos Assens 1950: 152). Azerrat's first steps in the literary circles of Madrid were guided by his extremely self-conscious character, fashioning his image as a celebrated poet and a highly demanded lecturer, prior to giving any proof of his talent. His avowed literary models were disparate, ranging from Calderón de la Barca (Ben-Krimo 1937b: 7, 1937d: 2) to Pierre Benoit (Azerrat 1934a: 2, 1934b). In journalism, he claimed to have drawn inspiration from two figures close to Carlist and reactionary circles. One was González-Ruano, with whom he had been acquainted at least since 1931 (*El pueblo* 1931: 2), and the other Federico García Sánchiz (1886–1964), whose model of "charlas líricas" Azerrat tried to imitate (*El heraldo de Madrid* 1930: 5). But prior to being able to write for more prestigious journals, his fledgling ambitions had first to undergo an apprenticeship in popular tabloids such as the *¡Tararí!* (1930–6).

Azerrat made no secret of his Jewishness, outspokenly exposing his identity as a Sephardi Jew. In Madrid, he promoted a journalistic campaign in favor of a "Hispano-Sephardic" rapprochement (*El imparcial* 1930: 6; *El sol* 1930: 5). Among his ideas, there was the program to "address to all the representatives of the left and of the right this interesting question: what do you think of the expulsion of the Jews in 1494 [sic]?" (*La libertad* 1930: 4). His project partially failed but he was able to get responses from personalities of all the Spanish political spectrum such as Santiago Ramón y Cajal, Ángel Osorio y Gallardo, José María Gil Robles, and Manuel Azaña (Ben-Krimo 1938: 13).

His stay in Madrid had to be interrupted around 1933 when he came back penniless to Morocco to his mother and sisters. Upon his return to Spain two years later, he engaged in radiophonic readings of his works and spent several months as an itinerant lecturer on Moroccan issues in various towns of Andalucía. In May 1935, different newspapers announced Azerrat's comeback to Madrid. Here he met Federico Garcia Lorca (1898–1936), introduced by the dramatist Agustín de Figueroa (1903–88) during a concert by Arthur Rubinstein on November 28, 1935 (Morla Lynch 2008: 501).

From this moment on, Azerrat pushed his condition as a Sephardi to the background, insisting instead on being more generically a Moroccan. He became increasingly committed to encouraging a better knowledge of the social reality in Spanish Morocco, calling for a stronger involvement of Spain in its colonies (Azerrat 1935a, 1935b).

The political models for Azerrat at this time were two antithetical figures, the Rifian warrior 'Abd-el-Krim (1882–1963) and the Indian pacifist Mahatma Gandhi (1869–1948), both fighters for the independence of their countries. Azerrat admired 'Abd-el-Krim as a freedom rebel icon, father of modern guerrilla warfare, and leader of the independent Republic of the Rif in the 1920s (Ben-Krimo 1938c: 31). This is why during the Spanish Civil War León Azerrat signed his political articles under the pen-name of Ben-Krimo, that is to say, the son of 'Abd-el-Krim. This did not prevent Azerrat from being also a follower of the pacifism and strict vegetarianism of Gandhi, to whom he dedicated some lectures in 1931 at the Theosophical Athenaeum of Madrid (*La libertad* 1931: 9; *El sol* 1931: 5). Azerrat's connections with the theosophical circles in the peninsula could also point to his involvement with Freemason circles in the capital (Penalva Mora 2013).

In 1932, Azerrat was wounded by a saber slash by the police while attending a meeting of the CNT, the anarchist trade union, in Madrid (*El sol* 1932: 8). His early political commitment to the left is also attested by Cansinos Assens (1950: 152), who recalls his fights for the liberation of Ernst Thaelmann (1886–1944), arrested by the Gestapo in 1933, and Georgi Dimitrov (1882–1949), probably during his trial in Leipzig in the same year.

From Azerrat the Poet to Ben-Krimo the Journalist

The Spanish Civil War marks a watershed in Azerrat's biography, opening a new phase in his life, that of the activist and of the political leader. He put aside his dreams of becoming a poet and a playwright and engaged his pen in the service of the social revolution. His writing became drier, purged of the rhetorical excesses of the past, and his articles grew closer in style to war briefings. The dissipated and naive youngster turned into a man of action. Ben-Krimo took over León Azerrat.

In anarchism Azerrat found a congenial ideology inspired by the works of Emma Goldman, whom he personally met and interviewed when she visited Spain in 1937 (Ben-Krimo 1937c). During the Civil War, Azerrat reported from the Madrid front (Vives 1938: 23), later moving to Valencia, in the steps of the Republican government which had installed its headquarters there in November 1936, prior to their transfer to Barcelona in October 1937. His articles were published in the Spanish and the Catalan press. He strongly identified with the Catalan culture and political self-government, being acquainted with Lluís Companys (1882–1940), the president of the Generalitat, and with the Commissar for Propaganda of the Catalan Government, Jaume Miravitlles (1906–88) (Ben-Krimo 1938o, 1938p: 4).

Ben-Krimo contributed to the efforts of war against fascism with intense journalistic activity. He was the correspondent and editor of some of the main anarchist newspapers of the time. In the first year of the war, he wrote for *CNT*, the daily newspaper of the anarchist trade union, published first in Gijón and later in Barcelona. In 1937, his signature appears in two other anarchist daily newspapers of Valencia. One was *Nosotros* (1936–9), organ of the Federación Anarquista Iberica (FAI), where he was in charge of the section "Magrebinas," and the other *Fragua social* (1936–9), of the Regional Committee of Levante of the CNT. For *Nosotros* Ben-Krimo wrote also on theater together with the mysterious Russian Oscar Blum (1886–1938?), a chess master and a revolutionary suspected of being a czarist spy, who had been the artistic director of the Scholem Aleichem theater in Moscow in 1922 (Dennis and Peral Vaga 2009: 44, 96).

Azerrat's political columns on trade union issues from Valencia were mostly published by *Solidaridad obrera*, the historical newspaper of the anarchist movement, between 1937 (Ben-Krimo 1937e: 4) and 1938 (Ben-Krimo 1938a: 6). His participation in the foundation of the anarchist mural journal, *Esfuerzo* (*Acracia* 1937: 6), conceived as the organ of the anarchist youths in Barcelona and whose publication was interrupted in May 1937, may indicate Ben-Krimo's direct involvement with the anarchist insurgency in that month and its repression by the Stalinist elements in the Communist Party.

In early 1938, Ben-Krimo moved from Valencia to Barcelona. In Barcelona, he integrated the staff of *Umbral* (Threshold), a magazine linked to anarchism, and of *Mi revista*, a bimonthly directed by the CNT syndicalist Eduardo Rubio Fernández. Here he continued to write about Morocco (Ben-Krimo 1938b: 47–9, 1938c: 31) and published his first cinematographic critiques (Ben-Krimo 1938: 106). On September 10, 1938, he was invited to lecture at the Federación de Juventudes Libertarias on "Luces amarillas: los barbaros en pie contra la cultura," probably a reading of poems with musical intermezzos (*El diluvio* 1938: 2).

From this quick overview of his journalistic endeavors, Azerrat alias Ben-Krimo appears to have been actively engaged in multifarious social as well as political and cultural activities. However, his main concerns were Jewish and Moroccan issues, sensitive to the plights of his persecuted brethren "for many sentimental reasons that still vibrate in my soul, which feels and suffers for all the humiliations that one of the greatest races in history has endured and still is enduring with barbarous furor" (Azerrat 1938: 12). In his quixotic defense of these causes, the emphatic and verbose Azerrat reappears at the surface, beneath the militant Ben-Krimo.

Ben-Krimo and Leftist Antisemitism

Azerrat succeeded in making for himself a name as an expert on Jewish affairs in anarchist circles in Republican Spain and in particular in Catalonia. Marian Vives, a regular contributor to the Catalan press, devotes a long interview to Ben-Krimo in *Catalans! El magazine popular*, a journal directed between 1938 and 1939 by Josep Roig i Guivernau, and says:

> We have among us a Jewish writer, León Azerrat Cohen, who is more known under his pen-name "Ben-Krimo" and is considered an authority in this question. Ben-Krimo, an anti-fascist, a revolutionary writer, works indefatigably in favor of our cause, which is also his. A fine connoisseur of the Jewish and the Muslim worlds, his articles in Yiddish and Arabic addressed to these two races have greatly benefited our cause. (Vives 1938: 22)

In this interview, Ben-Krimo estimates the number of Jewish volunteers fighting in the International Brigades to be 6,000. This became one of the main sources for subsequent attempts to calculate the number of Jews who participated in the military effort on the Republican side during the Spanish Civil War (Diamant 1979; Lustiger 1991; Rein 2000).

The Jewish question appears recurrently in Ben-Krimo's articles. In his columns dealing with North African politics, he often focused on the situation of the Jews in Morocco (Ben-Krimo 1938b: 47–9). He engaged his interviewees to condemn antisemitism, as he did with the reluctant sheriff Sidi Mohammed ben Abesalam El Wazzani, who had been in September 1936 at the head of a delegation of French Moroccan nationalists in Barcelona to obtain the support of the Catalan workers' organizations in proclaiming the autonomy of the territories of the Spanish protectorate under the sultan's aegis (Alcolea Escribano 2012). The defeat of the German boxer Max Schmeling by the African American Joe Louis offered Ben-Krimo the opportunity to mock the Nazi "myth of racial purity" (Ben-Krimo 1938i). He praised the engagement of Marlene Dietrich and Greta Garbo against fascism and antisemitism (Ben-Krimo 1938m). In reporting about Freud's exile to England, Ben-Krimo wrote a passionate defense of Freudian psychoanalysis against Jung's connivance with Nazism (Ben-Krimo 1938f: 4).

In an article published by *La humanitat*, Ben-Krimo recalled the conversations he had in Madrid in 1936 with the Rumanian rabbi Sabetay De Jaen (1883–1947) on the strong cultural and spiritual bond linking Sephardi Jews to Spain, and with the Catalan poet Gabriel Alomar (1873–Cairo 1941) on Zionism (Ben-Krimo 1938h: 3). Ben-Krimo appreciated Alomar's philo-Semitism. However, he disagreed with him when Alomar both opposed the national claims of Zionism on Palestine, on the basis that they were supported "by the international bank," and disapproved of the possibility of allowing the Jews to settle again in Spain "because very few would favorably perceive such an initiative" (Pérez i Ventayol 2010).

Ben-Krimo faced similar prejudices when he drafted a project to convince Mariano Rodríguez Vázquez, also known as Marianet (general secretary of the CNT of Catalonia from 1936 until 1939), to give shelter in Republican Spain to persecuted European Jews. This was in early May 1938, a few months prior to the Evian conference when the question of Jewish refugees fleeing the German Reich was brought to the attention of an international forum (CDMH/PS-BARCELONA, 811,12). The correspondence with Marianet could have also been triggered by the upcoming Sephardic World Congress, which was to be held in Amsterdam on May 15, 1938, and saw the participation of one of Azerrat's closest friends, Menachem Coriat Bendahan, rabbi of the Barcelona Jewish community (González 2004: 282).

Ben-Krimo presented to the attention of the leader of the Anarchist National Committee the outline of a program concerning what he called "the Sephardi problem." This was a subject that Ben-Krimo deemed to be of the utmost urgency and should have been included as a priority in the agenda of the Republican government. After some notes on the historical background of the Sephardi diaspora, Ben-Krimo described the failed attempts in the recent past to make possible the return of the Sephardim to Spain.

According to Ben-Krimo, Republican Spain should have opened wide its doors, not only to Sephardim but also to all Jews persecuted by fascist regimes, repealing once and for all the expulsion edict of 1492. The idea of abrogating the edict of the Catholic monarchs had already been defended by the fascist author Ernesto Giménez Caballero in 1929 (Marquina Barrio 1987). It had been discussed in the Spanish Parliament during the government of the radical Republican Alejandro Lerroux in 1933 but did not result in any tangible action (Lisbona 1993: 51). However, for Ben-Krimo the time was ripe to act since antisemitism was "one of the cornerstones of fascism" and every true antifascist should have been uncompromisingly fighting against it. Therefore, by inviting persecuted Jews to settle in Spain, the Spanish Republic would have contributed to the struggle against reactionary forces worldwide.

Marianet agreed with Azerrat about "the importance of operating in that direction to gain support for our cause and struggle" and appointed him responsible for the antifascist propaganda within the Propaganda Department of the Ministry of Education. However, he vehemently rejected Azerrat's request to abolish the expulsion edict. Even stronger was his opposition to opening the doors of Spain to Jewish immigration. These were his arguments:

> To open Spain's doors to all the Jews who wish to come here is impossible because it would undoubtedly be one of the most counterrevolutionary decisions that we could take. We are sure that [the admission of the Jews] would mean the immediate revival and strengthening of capitalism and the old exploitation. It is very likely that we will go back in social progress and re-establish something of the regime existing prior to the proclamation of the Republic.

Marianet's misunderstanding of Ben-Krimo, due to his perception of the Jews as being inherently capitalists, demonstrates that not all the sectors of the Republican left in Spain were necessarily sympathetic with the Jewish cause, and antisemitic biases were not limited to the fascist and Catholic circles. Among these groups, the image of the Jew still provoked a rejection motivated by its association with usury and exploitation (González 2004: 26). Among the Republicans and within the libertarian movement, antisemitic stereotypes were widespread. For example, *Solidaridad obrera*, on January 31, 1937, accused Franco of being a "Jewish traitor" and criticized "Jewish plutocrats" for collaborating with Hitler (Seidman 1991; Eiglad 2015: 214). According to Danielle Rozenberg (2006: 162), this is one of the reasons behind the reticence of the Spanish Second Republic to grant shelter to Jewish refugees. Only on November 16, 1938, two months prior to the entrance of the Francoist troops in Barcelona, Manuel Azaña's government offered political asylum to anyone who had suffered persecution for his political and religious credo (Lisbona 1993: 89).

The debate between Marianet and Ben-Krimo echoes the heated exchange of letters between Emma Goldman and Reginald Reynolds regarding Zionism, which the latter considered a movement to be fought as an expression of the Jewish plutocracy (*British Imperialism* 1989: 24–7). Goldman retorted with the importance of the right of asylum for the Jewish persecuted masses who wished to settle in Palestine and with the existence of a Jewish proletarian movement also present and active in Palestine (Goldman 1938).

The simplistic and Manichean vision concerning the Jewish question emerges in another public intervention of Marianet when he wrote that "in Spain two economic powers existed: one of the Jews and the other of the Jesuits. That of the Jews was based almost exclusively on foreign capital. That of the Jesuits appeared in most cases as a national capital" (Mintz 1970).

On June 5, Ben-Krimo responded briefly to Vázquez's antisemitic imaginary and with this letter ended their correspondence. This did not prevent Ben-Krimo, in the aforementioned interview with *Catalans* magazine, from denouncing the stereotype of the Jewish attachment to money, responding, albeit belatedly and obliquely, to Vázquez's prejudices as follows:

> Against Jewish capitalism—which is important—you can find also poverty. . . . Gold is always conservative, whether Jewish, Chinese or hundred percent Aryan. Gold is gold . . . and let's not forget that Jews are inherently anti-fascist. (Vives 1938: 24)

The strongest argument against antisemitism for Ben-Krimo was to be found in the blood tribute Jews were ready to offer for the Republican cause. While visiting the Madrid front, he related the following episode. Next to a machine gun, two men were conversing in Yiddish. One of them said that he had promised his mother to leave Spain only when there would no longer be any German or fascist left. The other added that this war would be the occasion to prove to the eyes of the world that Jews would never betray the cause of freedom. Ben-Krimo could not restrain his tears and joined the conversation in Yiddish! The next day, when he returned to the front, one of them was killed (Vives 1938: 24).

Azerrat also advanced another argument to convince the Republican side to support the Jews: the possibility of using the support of North African Jews, especially those of Spanish Morocco, in the struggle against fascism.

An Imaginary Jewish and Muslim Alliance in the Anti-Fascist Fight in Morocco

And this brings us to the second aspect of Ben-Krimo's public activity during the Civil War, which is the question of the position of the Jews of the Spanish protectorate toward the rebel side.

It has been often repeated that the communities of the Moroccan protectorate favored Franco and the national movement (Lifschitz 1984: 16; González 2004: 290). This was notwithstanding the attacks against synagogues, the boycott of Jewish businesses, the obligation to pay huge "voluntary" contributions, and the murder of Jews, such as the mayor of Ceuta, José Alfon, who died beaten by fascists soldiers in the summer of 1936 (Salafranca Ortega 1990; Lisbona 1993: 63). According to Danielle Rozenberg (2006: 154), "the economic support of the Jews to Franco was not only due to ideological affinities, but to the personal relations that the Jews had established with the commanders of the Spanish Navy stationed in North Africa after the Rifian war."

Against this historiographical consensus, Maite Ojeda (2013: 180s) and Eloy Martin Corrales (2002) have revealed the existence of several hundred Moroccan Jews affiliated with Freemason lodges and many others who were actively supportive of the Republican fight. Ben-Krimo himself had in mind these North African Jews favorable to the Republic, who went underground in Spanish Morocco occupied by Franco's troops, when he mentioned to Marianet his program of political agitation against the fascists, directed at both Jews and Arabs.

The anarchist movement was at the time spearheading the fight against European colonialism and favored the creation of an alliance between European and African workers to defeat fascism. Ben-Krimo was a member of the Asociación Antifascista Hispano Marroquí, founded by the Palestinian communist Mustafa Ibn Jala in 1936, and actively fostered its goals, writing and lecturing on Moroccan issues. Ben-Krimo's conference for the association of the Catalan press on September 4, 1938, on the topic "What I Can Report about Morocco," was attended by a packed audience and was repeatedly interrupted by standing ovations (*La humanitat* 1938: 3; *El diluvio* 1938: 5).

Although no account of the content of this or other lectures is extant, his program very likely coincided with the vision of Juan García Oliver (1901–80) (López Agudín 1982: 48) and the geographer Gonzalo de Reparaz Rodríguez (1860–1939), who considered propaganda work in Morocco to be a foremost geopolitical challenge to win the war (Ferretti and Garcia-Alvarez 2018). Reparaz and Ben-Krimo authored a series of newspaper and radiophonic appeals addressed to the Moroccan and Arab populace in Spanish and Arabic, which were published in *CNT* during the war (Ben-Krimo 1938e: 2).

In these appeals, Ben-Krimo claimed that Morocco ought to be freed from the imperialist grip and returned to its true children, that is, Jews and Muslims (Ben-Krimo 1936a; 1937a). Azerrat defended the Rif inhabitants against those among the Republicans who considered them either barbarians or dreadful mercenaries on the side of the fascist insurgents (Ben-Krimo 1936b: 3). In 1938, he called the Moroccan soldiers fighting among Franco's troops to rebel "against the treason they are the victims," insisting on the shame for a good Muslim to fight side by side with Catholic fanatics such as those who considered the war against the Republic to be a crusade (Ben-Krimo 1938e: 2).

Azerrat was optimistic about the chances of organizing a Moroccan rebellion against fascism and he reported that in Tangier the situation could be ripe for such an event: "Morocco, with its base in Tangier, has become the powder keg that could result in the death blow for the invading and treacherous fascism" (Ben-Krimo 1938g: 4). In October of that same year, he was dispatched to Casablanca by the Republican government on a propaganda mission among the Arab population (AGA 81, 02062).

However, these hopes were destined to remain frustrated. In his vision of Judeo-Arab-Berber solidarity promoted by the Spanish progressive forces, Ben-Krimo did not apparently understand the potential for conflict that could be triggered by the clash of Zionism and the emerging Arab national movements, aggravated by the Arab uprising in Palestine under the British mandate in 1936. On the contrary, he was convinced that the troubles in Palestine were prompted by provocateurs financed by the fascist regime of Mussolini, such as Mulay Abd-el Aziz (1878–1943) (Ben-Krimo 1938n: 4). In addition, he did not seem to have been aware of the growing interethnic tensions that jeopardized the coexistence of Jews and Muslims in Morocco (Martin Corrales 2013: 100–1).

On January 1, 1939, a few weeks before the capitulation of Barcelona, the newspaper linked to the moderate intellectual sectors of Catalan republicanism, *La publicitat*, announced the departure of Ben-Krimo to the territories of French Morocco in order "to continue his campaign of propaganda among the Arabs for the cause of the Republic" (*La publicitat* 1939: 3).

From Anarchist Intellectual to Writer for the Falangist Press

The years of exile after 1939 and of the Second World War were a particularly troubled period in Azerrat's life. He settled in Oran for seven months in the entourage of the Republican general Julio Mangada (1877–1946), giving lectures and trying to reorganize fighting militias against the Spanish government. With the consent of the French authorities and at the behest of the Comité de Acción Republicana he moved in October 1939 to Casablanca for a financial mission related to the former Spanish consul in French Morocco, Ramón González Sicilia (1885–1963) (AGA 64, 813). From there, he joined his mother and four brothers in Tangier, then under international sovereignty.

However, after the Spanish occupation of the city in June 1940 and the Ley de Responsabilidades Políticas, whose application was extended to the inhabitants of the city by a decree of May 31, 1941 (*Boletín oficial* 1941: 3984), he was imprisoned in Ceuta for a short time. In January 1942, he was assigned to confinement in his birthplace Alcazarquivir. Azerrat eluded this restriction and from 1942 he lived between Tetuan, working as a freelance journalist for the local newspaper *Marruecos*, and Tangier, where he ran a food shop in the harbor with one of his brothers.

Outspokenly showing his support for the allies fighting against Nazi Germany, he remained under strict surveillance by Franco's secret police, at least till 1946. He was suspected of keeping contact with subversive elements in the Spanish Protectorate and with Moroccan nationalists, such as Mekki El Nasiri (1906–94), and of being an agent of the British and French intelligence services (AGA 81, 5674). All this did not prevent him from regularly asking for help from the Spanish authorities to get travel permits and official accreditation as a journalist. Being a Moroccan subject, together with his social and economic marginality, his eccentricities, and perhaps some services given to the Spanish authorities, as it appears from the nickname "el cotorro" (chatty bird) in the secret files concerning him, may explain why his past record of Republican activism did not expose him to heavier repressive measures.

His state of mind in these difficult years appears in the collection of poems published in Tangier in 1941 with unequivocal titles such as "On the roads that are not of fire anymore [*Por las rutas que ya no son de fuego*]" or "Now that I am walking like a dead body [*Ahora que ando como un muerto*]," he writes, "who is waiting for me? Whom am I waiting for? In which remote islands have now settled those friends of mine?" asking himself, "I would like to know why am I living this life of a dead man" (Azerrat 1941).

In the aftermath of the Second World War, Azerrat was able to resume his work as a journalist in the Spanish press, writing correspondences from Morocco for Falangist newspapers such as *Los sitios*, *Fotos*, *La falange*, *Yugo*, and *El alcázar*. Perhaps, Azerrat's expertise in Moroccan affairs and his knowledge of languages helped him to cause the authorities to gloss over his previous commitment to the radical left during the Civil War. The right-wing specialist on colonial affairs, José María Cordero Torres (1909–77), praised Azerrat as one of the prominent Jewish intellectuals in Tangier "in favor of the modernization of Sephardism" (Cordero Torres 1949: 100). In the Spanish press yearbook, Azerrat is listed as the correspondent in Madrid for a bilingual journal, in Spanish and Arabic, *El día* of Tetuan (*Anuario* 1955–6: 32). His journalist activity reached a peak in the first half of the fifties.

However, an abrupt interruption occurred in 1956. This may be related to the warning sent on June 11, 1956, by the Ministry of Information and Tourism to the editorial board of the *ABC*, a daily newspaper for which Azerrat occasionally wrote, where his name was listed as a person banned from writing in the Spanish press (Iglesias 1980: 370–1).

In 1951 he sought to resume relations with the literary gatherings of the capital, frequenting the Café Gijon, a famous establishment in Madrid for his literary reunions (Ordóñez 2007: 55), dominated at the time by César González-Ruano, an old acquaintance of Azerrat but also one of his sternest disparagers. Juan Perez Creus, a regular participant of the in-crowds at the Café Gijon in the fifties, wrote an epigram about Azarrat at the time. It confirms that the appreciation of his pathetic figure had not changed since the 1930s in the intellectual milieu of Madrid: "Here comes, don Leon, with his dark hair, his moustache and his walking stick. He claimed without flinching to be a prince of Zion but he was a barber in Larache. What a sucker!" (Perez Creus 1996: 88).

At that time, Azerrat had already abandoned his youthful avant-garde tastes, apparently adapting to the ideological line of the Franco regime. Thus, he was among the fiercest critics of the eccentric sketches for the theatrical mise en scène of Jose Zorrilla's *Don Juan Tenorio*, created by Dalí in 1949 (Pardo 1996: 192). These scornful remarks against modernist excesses may sound hilarious for someone like Azerrat who used to introduce himself as a "pretender to the throne of Sion" and who professed to be a painter influenced by surrealism (Morales 1951: 22).

However, more than theater and poetry (Salama Benarroch 1997: 86), now, his main field of interest was cinema. In his collaborations with *Primer plano*, the Falangist film culture magazine founded in 1940, Azerrat posed as a guide and friend of the various Spanish and international stars passing through Tangier, such as Luis Mariano, Imperio Argentina, Joan Fontaine, and Errol Flinn. He even played a small role in the 1950 movie *L'homme de la Jamaïque* by the French filmmaker Maurice de Canonge.

Azerrat boasted a collaboration with Orson Welles as a literary adviser on the set of *Othello*, shot in Morocco. He also pretended to be working on a script for one of Welles's next films that should have been titled *Quartier nord* inspired by life in the foreign legion (Morales 1951: 22). In 1952, the Galician newspaper, *La noche*, introducing Azerrat as a sort of celebrity, announced that he has just finished writing a comedy titled *La noche enemiga* and had begun the scenario for a film that should have been directed by Cesáreo González (1903–68), called *La ruta desconocida* (The Unknown Path) about the slums of Algiers. His cinephile tastes were oriented to the French film noir of the 1930s and to American melodramas, while he abhorred the neorealistic experience (Morales 1951: 22). Although almost no evidence exists concerning Azerrat's literary endeavors in this period, these preferences seem to point to the absence of any aesthetic development since his earlier romantic poems on the mysteries of the Orient.

In 1956, the year of Morocco's independence and the Suez crisis, Azerrat wrote some reportages demonstrating a deep knowledge of the corridors of power in Morocco (Martínez Milán 2017: 192). He was unquestionably favorable to the independence of North African countries and a staunch critic of French hesitations to grant it (Azerrat 1956b: 5). He praised Spain's recognition of Moroccan independence and in the Spanish press some photographs were published of Azerrat accompanying Ahmed Balafrej, then minister of foreign affairs, on his first visit to Madrid (Azerrat 1956a: 25). Azerrat's exclusive interviews with Sultan Mohamed V during his state trip to Spain in April 1956 suggest a personal relationship with the Moroccan sovereign, whom Azerrat had already met in Tangier in 1947 (Azerrat 1956a: 3). His sympathies for Arab nationalist claims also emerge in his positive appreciation for Nasser's politics (Azerrat 1956d: 13–14).

From various journalistic sources, it appears that he often traveled to Madrid. In 1960, we find him talking in the capital about "the world of the Sephardies" (*ABC* 1960b: 66) and at the Mangold Institute about "the mistery of Atlantis" (*ABC* 1960a:

63). He was active in the Judeo-Christian Friendship Association, for whose newsletter he collaborated in the 1970s (Azerrat 1972: 4).

In the wake of the incorporation of Tangier to the Kingdom of Morocco in 1956, Azerrat definitely left Tangier, like many other Jews, and settled in Marbella. He occasionally collaborated with the local press and signed the preface to the collection of poems by the poet Manuel Perez-Piaya y Campos from Malaga (Manuel Perez-Piaya y Campos 1967). Rafael de Loma Rodríguez (1940–2014), the last director of *El sol*, a newspaper published in Malaga, gives this rather gloomy portrait of Azerrat in his old days:

> I remember well a Sephardi called León Azerrat, who, in some moment of his life, should have been an important journalist, but who had already lost his brightness with only some poses of bohemian with which he had to survive in Marbella. Some fiancée chosen from the noble lot of his housekeepers often saved the Sephardi from starvation. (De Loma Rodríguez 2014: 150)

The last article in the Spanish press signed by Azerrat is for El Día de Santa Cruz de Tenerife on May 27, 1997. In the new Spain, after the transition from dictatorship to democracy, the struggles and contradictions of León Azerrat Cohen had lost any interest, condemning him to a destiny of oblivion.

The entire existential trajectory of Azerrat is marked by a double condition of marginality, as a Jew in a Spain still fundamentally marked by antisemitic imagery, and as a Moroccan, an object of colonial condescension among the ruling classes of the dominant power. His political choice in favor of anarchy made him share the fate of his comrades in struggle, ousted from the centers of power of Republican anti-fascism in 1937, and then obliged to exile after the defeat of the Republic in 1939. His attempts to reconcile himself to the representatives of the new Francoist regime did not allow him to obliterate his revolutionary past, nor did his constant support for Moroccan national claims spare him exile from Morocco after its independence in 1956.

This constant inadequacy for the situations in which he evolved is reflected in a literary output that rarely managed to pass the design stage. Like his numerous theatrical and cinematographic ideas, most of his poetic production has been lost and has never been published. At ease in different languages, his skills as a cultural and political mediator were mostly limited to conveying images of his native Morocco and Sephardic Judaism that supported orientalist stereotypes.

It was only as a journalist for the Republican press that Azerrat enjoyed public recognition. And it is precisely under his heteronym of Ben-Krimo, engaged in an intense campaign for the rights of his Jewish brethren and Moroccan countrymen, that his many literary personae as a Jew, a Sephardi, a Moroccan coexisted harmoniously for the first and perhaps only time in his long intellectual journey. In a space free from the traditional boundaries of genres and languages, he developed his transnational and polyglot character. Paradoxically, it was precisely during the three years of the Spanish Civil War that Azerrat was able to bridge the inner conflict that had relegated him to the margins of the literary avant-garde of Madrid in the 1930s, whereas, with the victory of Franco, he was condemned to play the role of a wretched eccentric.

References

ABC. (1960a), October 29: 63.
ABC. (1960b), November 10: 66.
Acracia. (1937), July 19 and July 26: 4.
Akrif, M. (2018), *Les juifs de Alcazarquivir, du paradis de la coexistence a l'enfer de la séparation et de la haine. Approche historique*, Rabat: Matbaa Alamnia.
Alcolea Escribano, J. (2012), "¿Moro invasor o hermano revolucionario?," *Cahiers de civilisation espagnole contemporaine*, 1. Available online: http://journals.openedition.org/ccec/4047; https://doi.org/10.4000/ccec.4047 (accessed September 24, 2020).
Anuario de la prensa española (1955–1956), Madrid: Ministerio del Turismo.
Aub, M. (1958), *Jusep Torres Campalans*, Mexico: Texontle.
Aub, M. (1973), *Vida y obra de Luis Álvarez Petreña*, Barcelona: Seix Barral.
Azerrat, L. (1929), "¡Sigue Bohemio!," *Adelante*, February 1: 2.
Azerrat, L. (1934a), "L'Atlantide," *El sur: diario de la tarde*, September 5: 2.
Azerrat, L. (1934b), "Antineo o la atracción de Marruecos," *La Actualidad*: 23.
Azerrat, L. (1935a), "La política que debe desarrollar España en África," *España y Marruecos*, 3, July 7: 6.
Azerrat, L. (1935b), "Deberes de política africanista," *España y Marruecos*, 4, August 7: 11.
Azerrat, L. (1938), "España y los sefardíes bajo el signo de la República," *Umbral*, April 23: 13.
Azerrat, L. (1941), *El alba inquietante (Viaje a la muerte). Poemas*, Tanger: Imp. Henry Tellier.
Azerrat, L. (1956a), "Así es el monarca que nos visita: Sidi Mohamed ben Yussef sultán de Marruecos," *Fotos*, April 7.
Azerrat, L. (1956b), "Argelia nueva Indochina en el Norte de África. Un imperio que se derrumba a pesar de las ametralladoras," *La hora*, August 4: 5.
Azerrat, L. (1956c), "La Arabia Saudí y la custodia de los Santos lugares del Islam," *Los Sitios, diario de FET y de las JONS*, August 5: 10.
Azerrat, L. (1956d), "El río Nilo y el canal de Suez," *Línea*, August 12: 13–14.
Azerrat, L. (1956e), "Pequeña historia de la interdependencia," *Fotos*, September 1: 25.
Azerrat, L. (1972), "El museo sefardí de Toledo," *Boletín informativo amistad judeocristiana*, 39: 4.
Azerrat, L. (1973a), *Diario de las Palmas*, July 13: 15.
Azerrat, L. (1973b), October 10: 10.
Azerrat, L. (1973c), November 2.
Ben-Krimo. (1936a), "Appel pour un Maroc libre," *L'Espagne Antifasciste*, December 11: 2.
Ben-Krimo. (1936b), "Encore au sujet du Rif," *L'Espagne Antifasciste*, December 18: 3.
Ben-Krimo. (1937a), "La conciencia honrada del mundo. ¡Marruecos! ¡Marruecos! ¡Marruecos!," *Fragua Social*, January 16: 1.
Ben-Krimo. (1937b), "El teatro de ayer y de hoy," *Nosotros*, February 25: 7.
Ben-Krimo. (1937c), "Emma Goldman a su regreso a Madrid," *Solidaridad Obrera*, September 30.
Ben-Krimo. (1937d), "Por un teatro revolucionario," *Nosotros*, March 8: 2.
Ben-Krimo. (1937f), *Mi Rivista*, April 15: 31.
Ben-Krimo. (1937e), "Soli en Levante. La CNT dice su palabra cordial y sensata," *Solidaridad Obrera*, September 21: 4.

Ben-Krimo. (1938a), "Los delegados hablan para Solidaridad Obrera," *Solidaridad Obrera*, January 18: 6.
Ben-Krimo. (1938b), "Marruecos bajo el signo infamante de la cruz gamada," *Mi revista*, March 15: 47–9.
Ben-Krimo. (1938c), "La sombra de Mohamed Abd-el-Krim, enemigo mortal de los generales imperialistas y caudillo de la independencia del Rif," *Mi revista*, April 15: 31.
Ben-Krimo. (1938e), "Subleveu-vos contra la traicio. L'escriptor marroqui Bem Krimo s'adreca novament a tots el musulmans del nord Africa," *La Humanitat*, May 26, 1949: 2.
Ben-Krimo. (1938f), "Freud i l'omosexualisme nazi," *La Humanitat*, June18, 1969: 4.
Ben-Krimo. (1938g), "Tanger, la ciutat cosmopolita del vell imperi xerifia, escenari actual d'intriges, espionatge i propaganda feixistes," *La Humanitat*, 7, 1979, June 30: 4.
Ben-Krimo. (1938h), "Sota el signe de la Republica. Israel a Espanya," *La Humanitat*, July 8: 3.
Ben-Krimo. (1938i), "Lo negro contro lo ario," *Mi revista*, July 15: 106–7.
Ben-Krimo. (1938l), "Poemas de h-oy," *Tiempos Nuevos*, July 19, 1938.
Ben-Krimo. (1938m), "Llums i ombres del mon," *Catalans!*, July 20, 16.
Ben-Krimo. (1938n), "Les terribles maniobres del feixisme, l'ex solda del Marroc, Muley Abd El Aziz utlizat com element provocador," *La Humanitat*, 7, 2003, July 28: 4.
Ben-Krimo. (1938o), "L'estyl Catalunya," *La Humanitat*, August 28, 2030.
Ben-Krimo (1938p), "Un home i un poble," *La Humanitat*, September 27, 2055: 4.
Boletín Oficial del Estado. (1941), June 3: 3984.
British Imperialism & The Palestine Crisis: Selections from the Anarchist Journal 'Freedom' 1938–1948. (1989), London: Freedom Press.
Calderwood, E. (2019), "Moroccan Jews and the Spanish Colonial Imaginary, 1903–1951," *The Journal of North African Studies*, 24 (1): 86–110.
Cansinos Assens, R. (1950), *Los Judíos de Sefarad: episodios y símbolos*, Buenos Aires: Editorial Israel.
Cordero Torres, J. M. (1949), *El africanismo en la cultura hispánica contemporánea*, Madrid: Ediciones Cultura Hispánica.
De Loma Rodríguez, R. (2014), *La Aventura del Sol: la transición en Málaga a través del diario "Sol de España" (1967–1982)*, Málaga: Cedma.
Dennis, N. and E. Peral Vaga. (2009), *Teatro de la guerra civil: el bando republicano*, Madrid: Fundamentos.
Diamant, D. (1979), *Combattants juifs dans l'armée républicaine espagnole 1936–1939*, Paris: Renouveau.
Diario de Córdoba. (1934), September 2: 2.
El Diluvio. (1938), September 6: 5.
El Diluvio: diario político de avisos, noticias y decretos. (1938), September 3, 203: 2.
Eiglad, E. (2015), "Anti-Zionism and the Anarchist Tradition," in A. H. Rosenfeld (ed.), *Deciphering the New Antisemitism*, 206–42, Bloomington: Indiana University Press.
Ferretti, F. and J. Garcia-Alvarez. (2018), "Anarchist Geopolitics of the Spanish Civil War (1936–1939): Gonzalo de Reparaz and the 'Iberian Tragedy,'" *Geopolitics*. Available online: doi10.1080/14650045.2017.1398143.
Goldman E., (1938), "Palestine and Socialist Policy," *Spain and the World*, August 26, 1938.
González I. (2004), *Los judíos y la segunda república (1931–1939)*, Madrid: Alianza Editorial.

González-Ruano, C. (1931), *El Pueblo*, October 3: 2.
González-Ruano, C. (1951), *Memorias: mi medio siglo se confiesa a medias*, Madrid: Renacimiento.
González-Ruano, C. (1952), *Diario íntimo*, Barcelona: Noqer.
El Heraldo de Madrid. (1930), September 19: 5.
El Heraldo de Madrid. (1936), February 24: 8.
La Humanitat. (1938), September 6, 2037: 3.
Iglesias, F. (1980), *Historia de una empresa periodística. Prensa Española. Editora de ABC y Blanco y Negro (1891–1978)*, Madrid: Editorial Prensa Española.
El Imparcial. (1930), August 10: 6.
La Libertad. (1930), August 15: 4.
La Libertad. (1931a), May 13: 9.
La Libertad. (1931b), October 31: 9.
Lifschitz, C. (1984), *Franco, Spain, the Jews, and the Holocaust*, New York: Ktav.
Lisbona, A. (1993), *Retorno a Sefarad a política de España hacia sus judíos en el siglo XX*, Zaragoza: Riopiedras.
López Agudín, F. (1982), "La Segunda República y la cuestión marroquí," *Tiempo de historia*, 90: 48.
Lustiger, A. (1991), *Shalom libertad!: les Juifs dans la guerre civile espagnole*, Paris: Cerf.
Margolin, J. (2010), "Ksar el-Kebir," in N. A. Stillman (ed.), *Encyclopedia of Jews in the Islamic World*, Boston: Brill, https://referenceworks.brillonline.com/entries/encyclopedia-of-jews-in-the-islamic-world/ksar-el-kebir-SIM_0007310?s.num=10&s.au=%22Aomar+Boum%22&s.f.s2_parent_title=Encyclopedia+of+Jews+in+the+Islamic+World.
Marquina Barrio, A. (1987), "La acción exterior de España y los judíos sefarditas en los Balcanes," in F. Ruiz Gómez and M. Espadas, Burgos (eds.), *Encuentros de Sefarad*, 418–40, Ciudad Real.
Martin Corrales, E. (2002), "Represión contra cristianos, moros y judíos en la Guerra Civil en el protectorado de Marruecos, Ceuta y Melilla," in F. Rodríguez Mediano (ed.), *El protectorado español en Marruecos. Gestión colonial e identidades*, 111–38, Madrid: CSIC.
Martin Corrales, E. (2013), "Tensiones judeo-musulmanas en el protectorado español de Marruecos en tiempos de la II República (1931–1936)," in E. Martin Corrales and M. Ojeda Mata (eds.), *Judíos entre Europa y el norte de África (siglos XV–XXI)*, 100–1, Barcelona: Bellatierra.
Martínez Milán, J. (2017), "Tan cerca pero tan lejos: Canarias y Marruecos en la segunda mitad del siglo XX," in E. Martin Corrales and J. Pich Mitjana (eds.), *España frente a la independencia de Marruecos*, 191–205, Barcelona: edicions Bellaterra.
Mintz, F. (1970), *L'autogestion dans l'Espagne révolutionnaire*, Paris: Bélibaste.
Morales, S. (1951), "León Azerrat escribe un guión para Orson Welles. Entrevista con el más dinámico periodista del Norte de África," *Primer Plano*, October 28, 576: 22.
Morla Lynch, C. (2008), *En España con Federico García Lorca*, Madrid: Renacimiento.
La noche: único diario de la tarde en Galicia. (1952), August 11.
Ojeda Mata, M. (2013), *Identidades ambivalentes. Sefardíes en la España contemporánea*, Madrid: Sefarad Editores.
Ordóñez M., (2007), *Ronda del Gijón: una época de la historia de España*, Madrid: Aguilar.
Pardo, J. (1996), *Autorretrato sin retoques*, Barcelona: Anagrama.

Penalva Mora, V. (2013), "El orientalismo en la cultura española en el primer tercio del s. XX. La Sociedad Teosófica Española (1888–1940)," PhD Thesis, Barcelona: Universitat Autònoma de Barcelona.

Pérez, J. (2005), *Los judíos en España*, Madrid: Marcial Pons.

Perez Creus J., (1996), *El extramundi y los papeles de Iria Flavia: revista trimestral fundada y dirigida por Camilo José Cela*, 5–8: 88.

Pérez i Ventayol, J. (2010), *L'exemple dels jueus: el catalanisme d'esquerres i la seva visió del poble jueu, del sionisme i del conflicte a Palestina (1928–1936)*, Barcelona: Promociones y Publicaciones Universitarias.

Perez-Piaya y Campos, M. (1967), *Mi voz hacia el soneto*, Málaga: Imp. Tip. Salesiana.

La Publicitat. (1939), January 1: 3.

Reiner R. (ed.). (2000), *Ha-Fascism Lo Yaavor: Milhemet Ha-Ezrahim Bi-Sfarad*, Tel Aviv: Zmura-Bitan.

Rozenberg, D. (2006), *L'Espagne contemporaine et la question juive : les fils renoués de la mémoire et de l'histoire*, Toulouse : Presses Universitaires du Mirail.

Salafranca Ortega, J. (1990), *La población judía de Melilla (1874–1936)*, Caracas: Asociación Israelita de Venezuela.

Salama Benarroch, R. (1997), *Rosario: aquella danza española*, Granada: Manigua.

Sala Rose, R. and P. García-Planas (2014), *El marqués y la esvástica. Cesar González-Ruano y los judíos en el Paris ocupado*, Barcelona: Anagrama.

Seidman, M. (1991), *Workers Against Work: Labor in Paris and Barcelona during the Popular Fronts*, Berkeley: University of California Press.

El Sol. (1930), July 6: 5.

El Sol. (1931a), May 13: 4.

El Sol. (1931b), October 29: 5.

El Sol. (1932), March 1: 8.

Valderrama Martínez, F. (1956), *Historia de la acción cultural de España en Marruecos, 1912–1956*, Tetuán: Editora Marroquí.

Vives, M. (1938), "L'etern problema del jueu en relació a la guerra espanyola," *Catalans!*, July 30: 22–5.

Archival Resources

CDMH—Centro Documental de la Memoria Historica, Salamanca
AGA—Archivo General de la Administración, Alcalá de Henares
APB—Archivo Pilar Bayona, Zaragoza

2

Beyond Music

Hanns Eisler (1898–1962)

Antonio Notario Ruiz[1]

I wanted to express something new and, for that, I needed new listeners.

(Eisler 1990: 53)

Prelude

There is an artistic genre that inextricably links music and literature: the song. In many cultures, in many eras, under different names, the song has been present. The Spanish Civil War is no exception. And among the musicians of Jewish origin who traveled to Spain to collaborate in the fight against fascism and contribute their songs, three musical protagonists stand out: Lan Adomián (Jakob Weinroth Waisman, Moguiliov Podolsk, 1905–Mexico City, 1979), Otto Mayer-Serra (Otto Heinrich Michael Philipp Mayer, Berlin, 1904–Mexico City, 1968), and Hanns Eisler (Leipzig, 1898–Berlin, 1962). At that time, they already shared the experience of exile. Adomián collaborated with the poet Miguel Hernández (1910–42), who died in Franco's prison. Eisler composed songs of combat and struggle in collaboration with José Herrera Petere (1909–77).[2] Mayer-Serra devoted himself to musicology from a social point of view and edited some of the songbooks that collected the compositions sung during the

---

[1] This work is part of the results of the GIR of Aesthetics and Theory of the Arts (Instituto de Iberoamerica, University of Salamanca), as well as of the research projects *Aesthetics Hybrids of the Moving Image: Spanish Video Art and Identity Dynamics on the Global Map* (PGC2018-095875-B-I00, MICIU 2017–20) and *Modern and Contemporary Spanish Thought: Study and Edition of Unpublished Texts* (USALIB1).

[2] It is highly recommended to listen to the music mentioned in this chapter. For this purpose, phonographic recordings can be used, or they can be easily found on the internet in different versions.

war by Adomián, Eisler, and many other composers.[3] All three shared with millions of women and men the Jewish experiences of exile, anxiety about an uncertain future, militancy in various Marxist or emancipatory tendencies, and persecution.

Although both Adomián and Mayer-Serra will reappear in this essay, I will focus on the contributions of Hanns Eisler for several reasons—firstly because, besides sharing a brief time with musicians and poets in Spain in January 1937 (Schebera 1998: 145–50), his compositional trajectory before and after the Civil War, his collaboration with philosophers such as Theodor Wiesengrund Adorno (1903–69) or Ernst Bloch (1885–1977), and his compositional, film, and theatrical collaboration with Bertolt Brecht (1898–1956) are very relevant. Secondly, his theoretical writings are of great importance and relevance for our matter. Eisler considered music as a political tool (Goehr 1994). His songs are the expression of his commitment to the transformation of society. He sought new music to build a new society and a socialist musical culture (Eisler 1990: 178). He proposed to put an end to "bourgeois sentimentalism," "musical illiteracy," and "the anarchy and chaos of bourgeois music" that he diagnosed in the 1920s and 1930s (Eisler 1990: 133, 183, 336). One of his most important artistic contributions is to be found in his songs. Through the song genre, especially in the German Lied tradition, musicians and poets created a new artistic field that goes beyond music and poetry. It is a specific artistic territory: musical sounds and words are united through common features such as meter or through sound evocations of meanings. In this way, an artistic product is achieved in which music and poetry can no longer be thought of separately. Eisler composed songs throughout his life. Another important feature of Eisler's output is the central role he assigns to listening. One could even say that there is a proposal in his texts to think of a freedom that is achieved in listening and from listening. In this sense, he distinguishes between music to be performed and music to be listened to: "The first demand that the class struggle demands of political songs is that they should be easily understandable, easily intelligible and express an energetic and precise attitude" (Eisler 1990: 133). On the other hand,

> Music composed only to be listened does not need to be as comprehensible as political songs. Its conception is oriented according to the respective contents, and within this it is possible to develop broader and more demanding musical forms. (idem: 202)

Eisler's interest in listening is also found in Adorno and has long been part of my research (Notario Ruiz 2009a, 2009b, 2014,2015). On the other hand, I propose to consider Eisler's concern with listening, texts, and their indispensable comprehensibility (Eisler 1990: 131) in relation to the Jewish heritage in Western culture. This concern is also present in other authors of Jewish origin such as Schönberg, Adorno, or Bloch and, although I consider that it does not need to be argued, two references will suffice. Beyond the possible

---

[3] José Herrera Petere, pen name José Herrera Aguilar, was a poet and novelist belonging to the generation of 1936 and an admirer of Pablo Neruda and surrealism. Very committed to communism, he went into exile at the end of the Civil War. He was also very active in literature during his exile.

musicological value of Leon Schidlowsky's contributions, let us consider the importance he attaches to listening: "Jewish religion is auditory and not visual" (Schidlowsky 1961: 24). This auditory character is inherited, from religion, in culture in general and particularly in literature. We find it, for example, in Kafka, as Benjamin mentions to Scholem in a letter on June 12, 1938: "Kafka listened attentively to tradition, and he who sharpens his ear does not see" (Benjamin/Scholem 1987: 248). In a complementary way, in another sense, one can take into consideration what the writer Edmond Jabès states (Jabès 2000: 41):

> Jewish psalmody has remained attached to the text. It remains quite distinct from the Western conception of chant, whose main aim is to exalt religious sentiment, to magnify [...] in the synagogue it is the very words of the sacred text, immutable, which make its chant heard, which offer us nothing more than the word, than the infinite of the letter, to hear, to see.

The very sonority of the words allows the composer a sonorous asceticism centered on the importance of the word: the musician does not need to embellish, adorn, or, in short, add anything to the words. He can therefore concentrate on finding the musical expression of what the words say and what they do not say but evoke. In my opinion, beyond the musicological problems that can be raised around the definition of Jewish music or the Jewish in music (Seroussi 2020), Eisler maintains a relationship with words and with music in which listening is essential. Before I continue, I will present some aspects that I consider relevant to Eisler's biography and his understanding of music.

The "Karl Marx of Music"

During the process known as the "Cold War witch hunt," which was intended to put an end to the presence of communist infiltrators on American territory, Eisler was referred to as "the Karl Marx of communism in music" during the interrogations (Betz 1994: 191). Beyond the anecdote, what is important to note is that since the composition of the "Comintern Song" in the 1920s, Eisler had achieved international notoriety among the workers' movement for his musical contributions. In that context, his trip to Spain in 1937 had a special significance.

Johannes (Hanns) Eisler was born in Leipzig in 1898, although he soon became attached to Vienna. The son of the Jewish-born philosopher Rudolf Eisler, a specialist in Kant, Hanns Eisler received a strong socialist impulse from his Lutheran mother. His musical training was self-taught, due to the family's precarious financial situation, and after a brief period at the New Vienna Conservatory, he was admitted as a private pupil of the composer Arnold Schönberg (1874–1951) in 1919. Eisler was already composing works with social content and conducting workers' choirs. Thanks to Schönberg's strict methodology—thorough analysis and study of the works of Bach, Beethoven, Schubert, and Brahms intended to master the structures and functions of tonal language—he became deeply acquainted with the tradition of bourgeois music before he began to compose avant-garde works. Eisler soon made a name for himself as a composer.

Moreover, in Vienna, he met Theodor Wiesengrund Adorno, with whom he maintained an almost fraternal friendship (Claussen 2005: 96). He always retained a deep respect for Arnold Schönberg's human and musical qualities. But they were separated by abysmal sociopolitical differences (Eisler 1990: 58, 324, 361). That is why he left Vienna to devote himself to music with a political and revolutionary vocation.

In Berlin, he met Bertolt Brecht. From then until Brecht's death, their friendship and artistic collaboration continued. Eisler, without completely abandoning his knowledge of avant-garde language, composed fight songs such as those discussed in this chapter, theater music—*The Measures Taken* (1930), *The Mother* (1931)—and film music—*Hell on Earth/No Man's Land* (Trivas 1931), *Kuhle Wampe* (Brecht 1931), *Youth Speaks* (Ivens 1932), *New Earth* (Ivens 1933), and *Dans les rues* (Trivas 1933). Through all these compositions he gradually created his own technique, which was as foreign to conventional bourgeois music as it was to the Viennese avant-garde dialect. At the same time, he was consolidating his theoretical perspective. During the 1930s he traveled several times to Moscow, working in the orbit of the German Communist Party and communist organizations such as Das Rote Sprachchohr (Betz 1994: 75). In Berlin, he set up a working group with young musicians that included Jewish artists and intellectuals such as Otto Mayer—whom he would meet again in Barcelona—and Ernst Hermann Meyer. Like so many millions of people, Nazism forced him into a long exile that would never end. He traveled to various countries—Austria, Czechoslovakia, Denmark, the United States, France, the Netherlands, the United Kingdom, and the Soviet Union—carrying out intense communist activity before moving to Spain in January 1937. In Madrid and Murcia, he collaborated with Ernst Busch, Herrera Petere, and Ludwig Renn. At that time, he composed for the international brigadistas and militiamen some of the songs that came to be performed alongside those that had already brought him fame a few years earlier.

After his stay in Spain, he continued his exile, traveling first to the United States and then, for a few months, to Mexico, the host country for so many Republican exiles. It was precisely in Mexico that Adomián and Mayer-Serra ended up finding refuge. Eisler taught there. Back in New York, he worked at the Film Music Project of the Rockefeller Foundation from November 1939 and developed his theories of film music (Gall 2006; Viejo 2008). From New York, he moved to Los Angeles in 1942, where he reconnected with Schönberg and Adorno. There, he regained his relationship with the former, who by then had already returned to Judaism also musically through his operas *Moses and Aaron* (1932) and *Kol Nidre* (1938). He collaborated with Adorno on the book *Composing for the Film* (1942–4). He also took advantage of this period to compose film music for Fritz Lang and Bertold Viertel, among others—*Hangmen Also Die!* (Lang, 1943), *None but the Lonely Heart* (Odets, 1944), *Deadline at Dawn* (Odets, 1946). The highlight of this period is the composition of numerous songs, forty-six of which are collected in *The Hollywood Songbook* (1943). A new level of production had begun. Without abandoning either avant-garde language or political commitment, he wrote works based on other poets' words and even on his own texts. He shifted toward a more intimate poetic language with texts by Heinrich Heine, Friedrich Hölderlin, Eduard Mörike, Blaise Pascal, Arthur Rimbaud, and William Shakespeare. Thanks to the experience he had acquired, his intense work, and his sensitivity, Eisler had a very deep relationship with the texts of the songs he composed. In many cases, it was he who chose the poems and texts and recomposed them, as in those mentioned by Pascal or with the verses of Shakespeare or Hölderlin (Betz 1994: 184). Even more illustrative is what Betz states in relation to some of Brecht's poems: several of Brecht's poems received their final form only after discussion with Eisler. In this case, the composer contributed to the final creation of the poems. In fact, Brecht himself claimed that Eisler read with enormous precision (Betz 1994: 183). But it is in what Brecht considered only reading that, in my hypothesis, the fundamental aesthetic and creative element I have been mentioning is introduced: *listening*. This is confirmed by many of the statements in his writings (Eisler 1990: 134, 392).

The end of the war and the defeat of Nazism did not bring calm. In 1947 Eisler was forced to leave the United States when the persecution of anyone suspected of being close to communism began. He first settled in Vienna but soon traveled to the eastern sector of Berlin, where he lived for several years. After composing the anthem of the new German Democratic Republic, he gradually distanced himself from official cultural policy. During this period, he completed his *German Symphony* (1959), a large-scale work for orchestra and choir that is a sonorous manifesto against fascism. But his disagreement with the authorities grew. The most important clash came when he conceived the project for an opera about Faust in 1952 (Eisler 1996). In the libretto, Eisler distanced himself from the bourgeois interpretation of Faust. Through the famous character, Eisler denounced artists who turned their backs on the people. In addition, he removed any possible antisemitic bias from some of the historical versions. However, due to the cultural guidelines in force in the German Democratic Republic at the time, which defended classicism and tried to recover authors such as Goethe for the new society that was being created, the authorities discarded Eisler's project. The frustration of the project was soon added to the death of his friend Brecht in 1956. This resulted in depression and voluntary exile in Vienna. He died in 1962, during one of his visits to Berlin.

Echoes of the Spanish Civil War

The presence of Jewish communities in Spanish history is unavoidable. Most of what is described as Spanish is incomprehensible without the profound Jewish imprint. In many cases, such as in music or poetry, this imprint is intertwined with other cultural contributions and it is practically impossible to discern what corresponds to each thread of the heritage. The appreciation of this phenomenon is relatively recent, with brilliant moments in the 1920s and 1930s. In the musical field, the contributions of Alberto Hemsi[4] and Máximo José Kahn,[5] among many others, are unforgettable.

---

[4] Alberto Hemsi (1898–1975) was a Sephardic composer and ethnomusicologist born in Turkey; he died in France. He collected Sephardic melodies around the Mediterranean and composed ten volumes of Sephardic couplets from them, *Coplas Sefardíes*. He maintained friendships with Spanish composers and theorists as early as the 1930s.
[5] Máximo José Kahn (1897–1953) was a German-Jewish essayist and writer, naturalized Spanish in 1934 and exiled to Argentina at the end of the Civil War. In 1937, he started a Sephardic Romancero project.

The Civil War was experienced by Jewish communities all over the world as a tragedy of their own that presented the real possibility of fighting fascism. The call to defend democracy and freedom was unhesitatingly heeded by its members. At the same time, the Spanish Civil War remains the founding event in the contemporary history of this country. Nothing that has happened since has been able to avoid reference to that brutal confrontation: not the long Franco dictatorship, the transition to a democratic form of political and social organization, nor even the current moment of institutional and political reconsideration. Ideas, beliefs, memories, symbols, and values of the opposing sides and of the numerous political and social groups that made up each of them continue to hang over the Spanish present to one degree or another. But so does the plural and complex imaginary of those who fought, died, won, and were defeated in that fratricidal conflict.

The Spanish Civil War has given rise to hundreds of literary works (Sánchez Zapatero 2020). The same literature includes the numerous echoes of the musical presence in the Civil War. Let us recall Alejo Carpentier's novel *Consagración de la primavera* (The Rite of Spring), for example (Carpentier 1998: 255–91). In addition to taking the title of a famous work by the composer Igor Stravinsky for his novel, he portrays scenes featuring the singer Paul Robeson,[6] a volunteer in the International Brigades, as well as some of the most common songs among the left-wing combatants, such as "The Internationale" and "La Marseillaise." In one way or another, thanks to literature, musicology, and the printed press from that period, we know what was listened to and sung during the war. A very important part of the memory of the Civil War and of its sentimental and sonorous image is linked to the songs, couplets, and hymns that were sung during the three years it lasted. Analysis of all this music indicates that its origin was, to a large extent, popular. In fact, this origin meant that the melodies traditionally sung in the villages were used as a support for different texts, sometimes even on both sides (Díaz Viana 1986)—for example, "Si me quieres escribir" and "¡Ay, Carmela!". Other melodies belonged to some hymns of left-wing parties or regional anthems: "Els segadors," "Eusko gudariak," "Himno de riego," etc.

A third group of songs that were sung during the war were pre-war and they were related to political parties, trade unions, or Republican institutions: "La Marseillaise," "To the Barricades," "The Internationale," etc. But there is a fourth group made up of songs that were composed during the war. These have survived in the collective lore thanks to the compilations: the *Cancionero revolucionario internacional*, compiled by the musicologist Otto Mayer-Serra in 1937 (Mayer 1937), of which only two volumes appeared; the *Cancionero de las brigadas internacionales* by Ernst Busch in 1938 (Busch 1938); and the *Canciones de lucha* by Carlos Palacio (1911–97)[7] (Palacio 1939).

---

[6] Paul Robeson (1898–1976), an African American actor and baritone with close ties to civil struggles and solidarity, traveled to Spain during the Civil War and gave concerts in different places. He popularized the song "Old Man River" (1927).

[7] The composer Carlos Palacio was incessantly active in cultural activities during the war, especially in the field of music through Altavoz del Frente, one of the initiatives of the Republican side that permanently encouraged both the civilian population and those fighting on the front line, with a central role for radio broadcasting (Peral 2012).

The songbook, published by the composer Carlos Palacio in 1939, was reissued in a facsimile edition in 1980 and was recorded in 2001, thanks to the musicologist and pianist Ana Vega Toscano, preserving the title of Palacio's compilation. Both the aforementioned songbooks and the disc include Eisler's contributions: "Marcha del 5º Regimiento" and "¡No pasarán!" both with text by the writer José Herrera Petere, "La Comintern" with text by Franz Jahnke and Maxim Valentin, and "Canción del Frente Popular," with text by Bertolt Brecht but adapted to the Spanish situation by Félix V. Ramos. As I have already mentioned, there is also a group of songs composed by Lan Adomián: "Las puertas de Madrid," "La guerra, madre: la guerra," and "Canción de la Sexta División" with text by Miguel Hernández, and "Todos camaradas" and "Madrid y su heroico defensor" with text by Plá and Beltrán. Many years later, in 1978, Arthur London included in the reissue of Busch's songbook a Yiddish song: "Af Leb'n un Toit a Farband," sung by the Jewish volunteers of the Thälmann Battalion (Labajo 2004).

Songs for a War

Although Palacio includes three songs by Eisler, the ideological and personal constellation linked to the Civil War allows us to add others. I will limit myself, however, to the songs that exemplify the aforementioned difference that Eisler established in his texts between music to be performed and music to be listened to.

The songs recorded on the album *Songs of Struggle*—which were part of the Palacio songbook, with the exception of "Song of the Popular Front"—meet this demand in full, especially the energetic character, essential at a time of extreme suffering such as that experienced by the Spanish people in that conflict. The songs that I contemplate within this requirement are: "The Comintern" (1926), "Song of the Popular Front" (Canción del Frente Popular, 1935), "They Shall Not Pass!" (¡No pasarán!, 1937), "March of the Fifth Regiment" (Marcha del 5º Regimiento, 1937), and "All or Nothing" (O todo o nada, 1934–5).

There are two other songs in the Spanish constellation that fulfill a different requirement: music to be listened to. In this group would be "Spanisches Liedchen"— with text by Brecht—and "In dem Spanischen Land," musicalizing Ludwig Renn's text (collected in Ernst Busch's songbook in 1938). They are not songs of struggle, although they are linked to what happens in the war. Therefore, from a musical point of view, the affirmative, martial elements that make up fight songs are absent: marching rhythms, very optimistic and easily remembered melodies. These two, on the contrary, belong to what Eisler called "listening songs": a more leisurely rhythm, slightly freer melodies. The texts, on the other hand, mention tragedy and death, and the music underlines this presence.

I present here a selection of the texts of the songs and some comments and approaches to the music of the songs.

1. "They shall not pass!" (1937). The slogan "They shall not pass!" became famous in the defense of Madrid at the beginning of the war. With little time to organize a military defense, the volunteers, together with the efforts of the entire citizenry, contributed to resisting the rebel attacks. Eisler composed "music to be performed" (Eisler 1990: 131), a song to be played on the radio and sung to bolster the spirits of those fighting and those living in the rear. The public was experiencing the rigors of war but was confident of victory against fascism. And it was necessary to support the spirit of resistance with music. Eisler's music, inevitably, has a simple structure and is articulated with motifs that are very easy to sing and remember. As in many of his songs, it has a syllabic character and is simply adapted to the structure of verse and refrain. At the end of the text, the Fifth Regiment is mentioned, one of the most important on the Republican side, and to which a march composed by Eisler was dedicated, which I comment on next. Apart from this composition, the people sang to the Fifth Regiment by changing the lyrics of popular songs.

2. "March of the Fifth Regiment" (Marcha del 5º Regimiento, 1937) (Mayer-Serra 1937: 8–9).

    Forward, battalions;
    Onward, heroes of Steel.

    According to Diego Alonso Tomás (Alonso 2019: 282), this march is composed of the same music that Eisler used for the "Himno de la Olimpíada Popular" organized in Barcelona in 1936 (Rein 2017: 129). Eisler's friendship with Otto Mayer-Serra led him, according to Alonso, to travel to the Catalan capital in April 1936. Eisler was later commissioned to compose the anthem for the Olympiad, based on a text by Josep María Segarra (1894–1961). The opening ceremony was to be held on 19 July. But the *coup d'état* had already taken place on that day and so the Olympiad never took place.

    As in the previous song, Eisler thinks in terms of music to be sung, and therefore the harmonic, melodic, and rhythmic structures are simple. This makes it easy to be identified by the rhythm and the melody easy to memorize. In other words, it is a song that invites you to sing along, follow the rhythm, and be contaminated by the energy and optimism that it communicates.

    The Fifth Regiment was one of the most important in the early stages of the Civil War. Eisler was already working in Madrid and knew how the militiamen and soldiers for whom the march was intended could sing. He renounced any harmonic or melodic complexity. In contrast to the usual absence of an introduction in most of Eisler's songs, in this case, there are some initial bars of a martial character—without a frame, below the indication *Tempo di Marcia*—which facilitate the entrance of the voice, equally martial and surrounded by a red line. This voice, which has the syllables of each word below it, is the melody of this song. The notes contained in the grey brackets form the accompaniment, which in this case corresponds to a piano (Figure 2.1).

Figure 2.1 Instrumental introduction and beginning of the "March of the Fifth Regiment," from *Cancionero Revolucionario Internacional 2*, 1937.

The grey vertical ellipses indicate chords—i.e., simultaneous superpositions of several sounds. These chords advance as if each one corresponded to a step, one after the other, in a regular way. It should be remembered that the tonal laws of academic music establish which relationships between these chords are possible and which are not. They also establish which notes can be part of the melody depending on which chords are used. In this case, both the chords and the melody respect these rules. Finally, marked in black is a rhythmic and melodic motif that is very characteristic of wind instruments such as the trumpet and is widely used in military music. Eisler uses it to reinforce the martial character of this song. The syllabic character of the song makes it easy to play and memorize. The general structure is strophic.

3. "The Comintern" (1926).[8] This is one of the best-known songs in the workers' movement. Eisler himself reports in a short autobiography that it was already popular in the late 1920s. The text expresses the main ideas of Soviet communism, which at that time was hegemonic (Mayer-Serra 1937: 28–9):

Proletarian legion, peasant legion
in compact ranks let us march to the front.

4. "Song of the Popular Front."[9]

Slaves of the world, rise
Prepared to annihilate fascism.

---

[8] Performed by the Freedom Choir, listen here: https://open.spotify.com/track/5ZayMtocRFRi7X9GeT6vvi?si=xSNM9BG6Rx60mCWp1VvmDg.
[9] Performed by Germán Coppini and Los Monstruitos, listen here: https://open.spotify.com/track/25dYvdQRLcNuMmSABINuvM?si=xgB4Iz5xSye1nnpSno92GA.

Figure 2.2 Opening bars of "Einheitsfrontlied" (Song of the United Front), by Hanns Eisler, in *Lieder und Kantante*, Band 2, © 1956 by Breitkopf & Härtel, Leipzig, 1972, assigned to Deutscher Verlag für Musik Leipzig, 178.

There is an earlier version of this song that does not mention Spain. This is the English version by Eric Bentley (1967). The "Popular Front" policy was the strategy set by the Communist Party throughout Europe. Eisler even devoted a lecture to it in his writings (Eisler 1990: 246–57). In Spain, this policy proved successful in the elections of February 1936. Eisler and Brecht's song was already popular in the workers' movement before the Civil War, and its incorporation into the repertoire of the Republican side, reinforced by the International Brigades, made it easy for it to become one of the songs included in the songbooks of the time. Eisler begins this song respecting the formal conventions of tonal language that we have already seen in the previous song (Mayer-Serra 1937: 30–1) (Figure 2.2).

Both melody and harmony move along classical lines. But Eisler leaves one of his typical disruptive elements and a few bars further on there are the barely perceptible dissonances that produce the sense of unease born of social inequalities and aggravated by the war situation (Figure 2.3).

This clash between two notes or similar ones is repeated in bar 13. And, in any case, the marching character of this song limits the disruptive interventions that even then characterized the new style created by the composer. But they are there, barely perceptible to the listener, explicit enough to disturb the listener and raise awareness of human suffering.

5. "Spanisches Liedchen."[10]

My brother was a pilot
His papers came one day

The original German text belongs to Brecht. It is a much more musically elaborate song without a tonal character. It consists of thirty-three bars. The structure is A-B-A, i.e., two identical parts—beginning and end—and a different one in the

[10] The English translation is by the poet David Sutton. The German text says: "Mein Bruder war ein Flieger / Eines Tags erhielt er eine Kart' / er hat seinen Koffer eingepackt und südwärts ging die Fahrt." Listen here: https://open.spotify.com/track/77s3RVOzgWN3eZ1Ru4fBY6?si=mRR7t-VkQW-_TAGlgX7e2w, sung by Roswitha Trexler. Piano, Jutta Czapski.

Figure 2.3 Bar 9 of "Einheitsfrontlied" (Song of the United Front), by Hanns Eisler, in *Lieder und Kantante*, Band 2, © 1956 by Breitkopf & Härtel, Leipzig, 1972, assigned to Deutscher Verlag für Musik Leipzig, 178.

middle of the song. This song is a perfect example of Eisler's way of working: diverging from the tonal language of the bourgeois period and the language of Arnold Schönberg. On the contrary, he uses a new relationship to words that is not unpleasant for the listener but offers an alternative in the service of the poem.

The visual aspect of this song is very similar to that of the "Fifth Regiment March," discussed earlier. If there I marked the chords with grey ellipses, here I mark them with black lines (Figure 2.4). They imply a continuous movement as if they were steps, that is, the march implied by the word *Marschtempo*. But listening to this song shows that it does not sound like that march. The relationship between the accompaniment—the two lower staves—and the melody is unconventional, and although it is not unpleasant, it does create a sense of unease and disquiet in the listener. Finally, a very peculiar feature of this song is that, unlike the previous songs, there is a brief musical solo interlude that quotes the opening notes of the Gregorian "Dies Irae"—bars 10–11 and 12–13—a thirteenth-century Latin hymn that evokes the Last Judgment since it was used by the composer Hector Berlioz in the *Symphonie Fantastique* (1845)[11] (Figure 2.5). It is a literal quotation although partially blurred by the accompaniment. It corresponds to the tragic "conquest" of the poem's protagonist: a tomb in the Sierra del Guadarrama.

---

[11] Performed by the London Symphony Orchestra, conducted by Sir Colin Davis. Listen here: https://open.spotify.com/track/7FdFPOWkgArNIjozJogBP2?si=SJ1gYK-aRZKp_Kh4qoaWeA.

Figure 2.4 Melody and harmony of *Spanisches Liedchen*, by Hanns Eisler, in *Lieder und Kantate*, Band 2, © 1957 by Breitkopf & Härtel, Leipzig, 1972, assigned to Deutscher Verlag für Musik Leipzig, 177.

Figure 2.5 Quote from "Dies Irae" in bars 10–11, by Hanns Eisler, in *Lieder und Kantate*, Band 2, © 1957 by Breitkopf & Härtel, Leipzig, 1972, assigned to Deutscher Verlag für Musik Leipzig, 177.

6. "In dem Spanischen Land."[12] The original text was written in German by Arnold Friedrich Vieth von Golßenau, who took the literary name Ludwig Renn. He was an officer in the International Brigades. He met Eisler in Madrid in 1937 and years later in Berlin. Eisler composed a simple melody with accordion accompaniment for these verses. The overall musical structure is very elementary, but no longer martial or warlike in character. It is closer to the elegiac genre to which Eisler devoted himself in a special way during his exile in the USA.

In opposition to Hanns Eisler's aesthetic and musical approaches, we find in Adomián a very specific awareness of musical Judaism, even if this may be a matter of musicological debate, as Adomián himself recalls later, in his symphony, of his father's role as cantor (*hazan*) in a Ukrainian synagogue. He himself recalls this later, in his Symphony No. 2, *La Española*, which he composed long after the end of the war, in 1966:

> I have used what could be called an inner projection of *cante jondo*, which, combined with my experience of the war, represented Spain and Spanishness for me. Besides,

---

[12] Sung by Ernst Busch here: www.youtube.com/watch?v=7zqpMmpSlbQ.

I have always had *cante jondo* in me, from my childhood in the Ukraine and my adolescence in the United States; my father was a synagogue cantor and I have always felt a kinship between *cante jondo* and Hebrew religious songs. Perhaps because of this and because of my Jewish ancestry, I immediately found myself in Spain as if I were in my own land. (Toral y Fernández de Peñaranda 1996: 2043)

In the songs that Adomián composed during the Civil War, we do not perceive these echoes, but we do perceive a popular character and a delicate treatment of the musical elements. Miguel Hernández's texts are far from the warlike and military epic of the songs we have just discussed, but they express the depth of the painful experiences caused by the war.

Coda

Hanns Eisler shares many of the common experiences of the international Jewish community: the Marxist-rooted revolutionary commitment to a more just world, exile, uprooting, persecution, the anti-fascist struggle, and, in his case, a literary and musical commitment. His songs are part of that experience and helped many other people to find a way of communicating and expressing similar yearnings to his own. As the writer Buero Vallejo would say much later, the songs of composers like Adomián and Eisler "resounded in Spanish prisons, on all the fronts of the European resistance and in the Nazi concentration camps" (Téllez 2018: 81). In that sense, Eisler's contribution to the musical imaginary of the Spanish Civil War is unavoidable. His songs belong to *the sentimental memory* of several generations and continue to illustrate his concept of new music for a better society that remains to be achieved. In addition to his work on songs, which he did not interrupt during his exile, Eisler composed the music for the soundtrack of Alain Resnais' film *Nuit et Brouillard* (1955), which was so important in the fight against antisemitism and in the construction of the permanent memory of the victims of Nazism. In short, his songs, the rest of his compositions, and his texts are not only past: they are waiting to be brought to the present through interpretation, listening, and reading.

References

Alonso, D. (2019), "From the People to the People. The Reception of Hanns Eisler's Critical Theory of Music in Spain through the Writings of Otto Mayer-Serra," *Musicologica Austriaca: Journal for Austrian Music Studies*, Available online: https://www.musau.org/parts/neue-article-page/view/76 (accessed October 11, 2021).
Benjamin, W. and Scholem, G. (1987), *Correspondencia 1933–1940*, Madrid: Taurus.
Bentley, E. (1967), *The Brecht-Eisler Song Book*, New York: Oak Publications.
Betz, A. (1994), *Hanns Eisler, Música de un tiempo que está haciéndose ahora mismo*, Madrid: Tecnos.

Busch, E. (1938), *Cancionero de las Brigadas Internacionales*, Barcelona: Tipografía catalana.
Canciones de lucha, 1936–1939. (2000), Alboraia: EG Tabalet.
Carpentier, A. (1998), *La consagración de la primavera*, Madrid: Castalia.
Claussen, D. (2005), *Adorno. Uno de los últimos genios*, Valencia: Publicaciones de la Universidad de Valencia.
Díaz Viana, L. (1986), "Canciones populares de la Guerra Civil: Un estudio de oralidad literaria," Available online: http://www.cervantesvirtual.com/nd/ark:/59851/bmc447g4 (accessed October 11, 2021).
Eisler, H. (1990), *Escritos teóricos: materiales para una dialéctica de la música*, La Habana: Editorial Arte y Literatura.
Eisler, H. (1996), *Johann Faustus Oper*, Leipzig: Faber und Faber.
Gall, J. C. (ed.). (2006), *Adorno, Theodor Wiesengrud and Eisler, Hanns, Komposition für den Film, mit einem Nachwort von J. C. Gall und einer DVD "Hanns Eislers Rockefeller Filmmusik-Projekt 1940–42,"* Frankfurt am Main: Shurkamp.
Goehr, L. (1994), "Political Music and the Politics of Music," *The Journal of Aesthetics and Art Criticism*, 52: 99–112.
Jabès, E. (2000), *Del desierto al libro. Entrevistas con Marcel Cohen*, Madrid: Trotta.
Labajo, J. (2004), "Compartiendo canciones y utopías: el caso de las Brigadas Internacionales de la Guerra Civil española," *Trans: Transcultural Music Review*, 8. Available online: https://www.sibetrans.com/trans/articulo/201/compartiendo-canciones-y-utopias-el-caso-de-los-voluntarios-internacionales-en-la-guerra-civil-espanola (accessed October 11, 2021).
Mayer-Serra, O. (1937), *Cançoner Revolucionari Internacional / Cancionero Revolucionario Internacional*, Barcelona: Comissariat de Propaganda de la Generalitat de Catalunya.
Notario Ruiz, A. (2009a), "La vigencia de los planteamientos estéticos y musicales de Hanns Eisler," *Constelaciones. Revista de Teoría Crítica*, 1: 102–4.
Notario Ruiz, A. (2009b), "Todavía Adorno y Eisler," in M. Olarte (ed.), *Reflexiones en torno a la música y la imagen desde la musicología española*, 119–33, Salamanca: Plaza Universidad Ediciones.
Notario Ruiz, A. (2014), "L'émancipation de l'écoute ou pourquoi lire – et jouer – encore Adorno et Eisler," *Filigrane. Musique, esthétique, sciences, société*, 17. Paris. Available online: http://revues.mshparisnord.org/filigrane/index.php?id=634 (accessed October 11, 2021).
Notario Ruiz, A. (2015), *"…nothing but listen…" Escuchar con Miguel de Cervantes, Santiago Ramón y Cajal y Ángel González*, Salamanca: Nueva Graficesa.
Peral Vega, E. (2012), "Altavoz del frente: una experiencia multidisciplinar durante la Guerra Civil española," *Hispanic Research Journal*, 13 (3): 234–49.
Rein, R. (2017), "El desafío a los Juegos Olímpicos de Berlín 1936: los atletas judíos de Palestina en la frustrada Olimpiada Popular de Barcelona," *Historia Contemporánea*, 56: 121–55.
Sánchez Zapatero, J. (2020), *Arde Madrid. Narrativa y Guerra Civil*. Sevilla: Espuela de Plata.
Schebera, J. (1998), *Hanns Eisler. Eine Biographie in Texten, Bildern und Dokumenten*, Mainz: Schott.
Schidlowsky, L. (1961), "Introducción al estudio de la música judía," *Revista Musical Chilena*, 15 (77): 24–38.

Seroussi, E. (2020), "Art. Jüdische Musik, Schreiben über Jüdische Musik," in Laurenz Lütteken (ed.), *MGG Online*, Available online: https://www.mgg-online.com/mgg/stable/372635 (accessed October 11, 2021).

Téllez, E. (2018), "La música comprometida de Hanns Eisler: un itinerario europeo," *Quodlibet: revista de especialización musical*, 69: 31–81.

Toral y Fernández de Peñaranda, E. (1996), "Glosa de los hermanos muertos," *Boletín del Instituto de Estudios Giennenses*, 162 (3): 2033–53.

Viejo, B. (2008), *Música moderna para un nuevo cine: Eisler, Adorno y el Film Music Project*, Tres Cantos: Akal.

3

Simón Radowitzky

Revolution, Exile, and a Wandering Jew Imaginary

Leonardo Senkman

Confession is the language of someone who has not erased his condition of subject; it is the language of the subject as such. The confession is the discovery of who wishes to write, and is out of him or herself in flight.

(María Zambrano, 1995)

Dear Salvadora, Sister, Cheers, As you see, I have become a wandering Jew.

(S. Radowitzky to Salvadora Medina, Brussels, May 1, 1939)

The memory of the Spanish Civil War is a revisited narrative matrix that allows us to rethink the imagined Jewishness of some Argentine communist *brigadistas* and libertarian volunteers alike. Noteworthy are the letters to Salvadora Medina Onrubia (1894–1972) sent by the famous young Ukrainian anarchist Simón Radowitzky (1891–1956), who killed the Buenos Aires chief of police in 1909 and was confined for twenty-one years in Ushuaia. His letters were written in different places and times; first, during his deportation to Uruguay immediately after his life imprisonment sentence was commuted in 1930; later, in Barcelona, as a volunteer in the Spanish Civil War; and finally, on the road to exile (Marti 2011).

Salvadora Medina Onrubia, recipient of the letters from her protégé, the stateless Simón Radowitzky, was a respected feminist anarchist, married to the powerful owner of the newspaper *Crítica*. During the Civil War, the deported Radowitzky shared his libertarian international ideal with other volunteers identified as "Rioplatenses"; this collective identity at the front and in the Catalan rearguard helped erase differences of nationality and religion among Italians, Spaniards, and Russian volunteers. Like many international volunteers, the libertarian Radowitzky unwittingly erased evidence of his origin, nationality, and ethnicity within that heterogeneous transnational community.

Radowitzky's fourteen letters (written between October 1935 and February 1941) not only provide information about his personal experience in Spain and what happened after his decision to go into exile, but they also unveil both epistemic and ideological dissent against the rigid thinking of communist and anarchist *brigadistas*.

The letters to Salvadora Medina are completely different from the memoirs written by Jewish Argentine communists who enlisted in the Civil War. Unlike the interlocutors in texts of communist *brigadistas*, Radowitzky's interlocutor is not only an ideologically anarchistic "sister"; Salvadora is his "little sister," whom he platonically loves even before she helps free him from prison. She is the unique woman to whom Simón is willing to reveal his adult intimacy, and finally, she is the confidant of Simón's secrets and the serious decisions he took, such as going into exile. In Simón's hybrid texts, the reader grasps his tenderness inscribed in loving words but juxtaposed into sentences of ideological nature, written out of his need for Salvadora's advice.

Before analyzing these letters, it is necessary to inquire into four paradigmatic tropes that make up the imagery of Jewish brigade members and volunteers in the Spanish Civil War: 1. internationalism, 2. memoir and epistolary genres, 3. homeland repatriation, and 4. the post–Civil War imaginary of exile and of the wandering Jew.

The ideologically motivated libertarian River Plate volunteers traveled to Spain, not only to help the besieged Republic but also to rehearse the ideal of transnational fraternity. Such a goal would only be possible to achieve if the dreamed-about social revolution could be carried out, testing new ways of living anarchistic life. Enlisting to fight for the Republic at the front, or helping in the rear, however, was nurtured by an anarchist internationalism different from that of the communist *brigadistas*. Anarcho-communists such as Radowitzky believed that transnational brotherhood would be possible through living together in a community made up of multiethnic, multilinguistic, and cosmopolitan comrades in Aragon and Catalonia. Local anarchists and native River Plate volunteers also joined such a community.

Some Jewish communist comrades who wrote testimonies about their Spanish experience express an internationalist note. They do not hide their purpose of legitimizing awful national and international developments according to the political position of the Communist Parties of Argentina (PCA), Spain (PCE), and the USSR (PCUS) (Boragina and Somaro 2016: 179–236). Conversely, texts by Argentine anarchists show marks of transnational circulation, connections, and crossings beyond hierarchical proletarian internationalism, with their center in Moscow. Herein lies the difference between the transnational *ácrata* (libertarian) spirit and communist political internationalism. The first deals with aspects agreed upon from below, and much less with international labor relations structured from above; instead, anarchists preferred to deal with issues such as transnational migration, world strike waves, and militant travels by heterodox (writers, educators) and Orthodox (activists) intellectuals. In addition, they connected with networks of anarchist exiles and their publications in cosmopolitan cities like Paris, London, Berlin, New York, as well as Buenos Aires, Montevideo, and São Paulo. Such cities served as centers for the circulation of democratic ideas. This was the anarchist way of understanding internationalism on the local, regional, and global levels (Bantman 2006: 969; Bantman and Altena 2017). These transnational networks may have influenced the writing of the anarchists: unlike the communists, they preferred to publish short and easy-to-read texts according to the *ácrata*-style agitprop that included epistolary publications.

Conversely, young Argentine communists who joined the worldwide brigades adopted the internationalist paradigm of the Communist Youth Federation (FJC), which also operated as a cadre school. Similarly, in terms of the most common literary genre, the memoirs of those communists who were drafted by their PC hierarchical superiors as International Brigade members used a variety of rhetorical resources to build credibility on the Soviet narrative,[1] according to an inflexible discipline imposed by the Communist International (Kirschenbaum 2015: 181–236).

Moreover, Radowitzky's formal break with the genre of memoirs written by communist *brigadistas* suggests an unequivocal epistemic dissent in his epistolary texts. Memory was a discursive genre adopted not only by communist *brigadistas*, but also by anarchists who montaged selective personal and collective events into an orderly grouping of political experiences woven into their private lives. Instead, the intimacy in Simón's letters to Salvadora reveals a man in love who does not constantly recall his anarchist militancy.

The anarchist volunteer writes private letters. However, the public space always appears in Radowitzky's enunciation, provoking the effect of presence and immediacy rather than the effect of distance (Violi 1987: 94–7). In his private letters to Salvadora, the social subject overlaps the textual subject and can be heard in his enunciation as a figure of speech.

Conversely, in the autobiographies and memoirs of José Maguid and Fanny Edelman (Gabbay 2020a: 31–67), which also recall the Spanish Civil War, there is a sharp separation between the individual writer and the "textual subject." They also display a problematic relation between the figure of the *memorator*, which, to a certain extent, intends to be identical in every case, and the configuration of the remembered subject, which is different in each case and does not always display the same attitude toward the *memorator*. Simón's letters feature twists of colloquial language, and elocutive expressions lacking ideological rhetoric; despite Simón's colloquial speech, we hear how the act of his enunciation is transformed into a figure of speech. Explained through Patrizia Violi's theoretical concepts, the real subject of his letters is inaccessible and can only be grasped in the simulation of his writing (Gabbay 2020a: 96).

This unattainability becomes more significant because we ignore the responses to Simón's letters: the textual corpus to be analyzed is made up only of letters from the sender; we know some of Salvadora's responses only by reading Simón. This absence of sender–recipient exchange frustrates reading of "the couple's" intimacy. Moreover, the letters unveil two differences between Radowitzky and his other comrades who fought the Civil War. The first is the impossibility of Radowitzky being repatriated to Argentina after the Republican defeat, due to the conditions of his release from prison, in contrast with other Jewish anarchist comrades from Argentina and Uruguay who came back home. The other difference *vis-à-vis* those repatriated comrades was Radowitzky's identification with being "a wandering Jew," on the eve of, and during, his escape to Mexican exile. The account of the experience of the defeated Radowitzky, before and

---

[1] It is estimated that 35,000 men and women from across the globe responded to the call by the Communist International—the Comintern.

during his political exile, makes it possible to highlight an impediment that is largely ignored in texts of communist brigade members who managed to return to their native country. While the figure of the Spanish Republican exile has been studied in works on the escape to Latin America since 1939, much less attention has been dedicated to the different fates experienced by volunteers and *brigadistas* with Argentine or Uruguayan nationality than to non-naturalized foreigners like the deported Radowitzky.² His case is illuminating because, unlike Jewish Argentine anarchists Jacobo Maguid and José Grunfeld, and Jewish communist *brigadistas* Fanny Edelman and Benigno Moskovich, who managed to be repatriated, the expelled Ukrainian Jewish Radowitzky had no option other than exile.

In her posthumously published book *Los bienaventurados* ([1979] 2004), María Zambrano differentiates between being an exile and being a *desterrado*—an outcast. The exile is differentiated from the *desterrado* because he/she has no hope of ever returning to his/her homeland, but at the same time suffers from the impossibility if living anywhere. However, the Spanish poet and philosopher believed that the exile nurtures, at least, his/her hope of ceasing to be an exile and returning sometime to his/her land (Zambrano 2004: 36-9; Sánchez Cuervo and de Blas 2011: 268-322). Simón Radowitzky simultaneously represented both Zambrano's definitions of the figure of an exile and an outcast. But his exile condition was closer to the Spanish philosopher Adolfo Sánchez Vásquez's testimony following his arrival in Mexico aboard the legendary steamer *Sinaia* (June 1939): "The exile always lives separate from his own, from his land, from his past. And on the shoulders of a permanent contradiction: between an aspiration to return and the impossibility of achieving it" (Sánchez Vázquez 1997: 37).

Radowitzky did not experience such a split: he had simply always lacked a land and a free past. Nor did he suffer exile as Sánchez Álvarez and other exiles understood it: "With his roots cut off, he cannot take root here; caught in the past, dragged by the future, he does not live the present. Hence, his idealization of the lost, a nostalgia that envelops everything in new light [. . .]. Idealization and nostalgia nurture constant comparison" (Sanchez Vazquez 1997: 39).³

Such sentiment sensed among numerous Republican exiles was not experienced by Radowitzky: neither as the anarchist Jewish teenager threatened in Russia, nor by the avenging anarchist for whose crime he was confined for twenty-one years in the penal colony in Ushuaia, nor when he was deported to Uruguay and imprisoned during the dictatorship of José Terra (1933-4). Finally, after the defeat of the Spanish Republic, he lost revolutionary hope during his Mexican exile. Even though Radowitzky did not feel

---

² It is unknown whether the more than twenty-eight Spanish anarchist volunteers with extensive residence in Argentina, as well as five Italians, one French, and one Russian, could be repatriated to their pre-war land of reception.
³ The original says: "Cortadas sus raíces, no puede arraigarse aquí; prendido del pasado, arrastrado por el futuro, no vive el presente. De ahí su idealización de lo perdido, nostalgia que envuelve todo en una nueva luz. [. . .] Idealización y nostalgia nutriendo la comparación constante" (Sánchez Vázquez 1997: 36-7).

nostalgic for the past, he nevertheless idealized the libertarian brotherhood with which he continued to envision a future inhabited by free humanity.

Not only were Radowitzky's transnational linguistic codes different from the internationalist codes of communist brigade members, but the surprise of having discovered that he had become a "wandering Jew" meant something completely different than being "a non-Jewish Jew," a cosmopolitan identity coined years later by Isaac Deutscher (1968). This last alternative was incarnated by numerous former volunteer militiamen and revolutionary brigade members. Perhaps this ambiguous cosmopolitism during voluntary exile in Europe occluded all ethnic difference and national belonging, in the spirit of the ideological canon on the "Jewish question" framed by the Third and Fourth Communist International.

Meanwhile, where, and how, can we find traces and shreds of Jewish motivation (positive or negative) among internationalist communist Argentine volunteers who enlisted in the Spanish Civil War? A shortcut that could perhaps shed light is to confront testimonies about Jewish motivation (negative or positive) in autobiographical texts of both Argentine and European communist Jews, especially those who had immigrated to France from Poland and Belgium, and who were later recruited by the French Communist Party to fight in the Civil War (Van Doorslaer 1993: 148). However, unlike the European brigade members, almost none of the Argentine Jews analyzed suffered antisemitic discrimination; furthermore, the anti-fascist ideology of those internationalist Argentines did not harbor any project for solving "the Jewish question," as has been shown by some recently studied European testimonies (Rueda Laffond 2019: 252).

Of course, internationalism was not the exclusive ideology of Jews in the 1930s. But the fact that the notion of "homeland" did not exist in the legacy of traditional Jewish political culture in Poland (where many Jewish brigade members had grown up with and then rejected it) would not explain that some Jewish volunteers experienced their libertarian anarchist internationalism with incomparable intensity. The endangered Spanish Republic became the homeland icon of the whole anti-fascist world for waging a global battle against Franco's nationalists as well as advancing the Social Revolution in Spain. More precisely, Catalonia was the scenario of Bakunin's "here and now" in the imagery of the *libertarian* Radowitzky.

Raquel Ibáñez Sperber brings an anecdote in her seminal research which problematizes the absence of a homeland for the Polish Jewish brigade member. David Diamant, quoting Ilex Beller, describes a Polish volunteer who spends his free time cleaning his machine gun, explaining to his Jewish comrade in arms that a "Maxim" has to be able to "sing a rhymed song." To prove it, he shows his Jewish comrade that every time he touches it, the machine gun "utters a syllable of the Polish national anthem: Poland is not dead as long as we live." Ibáñez Sperber reflects, "It is difficult to imagine such an anecdote starring a Jewish *brigadista* from Eastern Europe. Without land that they can feel their own, without a national anthem, those Jews of the International Brigades give the impression of having been either pure internationalists, or belonging to a group more ethnic than national" (Ibáñez Sperber 2006: 110).

We lack texts of Radowitzky himself referring to his own notion of homeland and ethnicity. But there is evidence of certain ethnic and cultural Jewish anarchist circles which he frequented in 1909, months before he executed the chief of police. From the beginning of the anarchist-communist movement where the young immigrant Radowitzky became a militant, immigrants did not consider Argentina as their adoptive homeland. They rejected its representative parliamentary and electoral system, a direct consequence of their rejection of the state. An early informational campaign against Argentina as a "liberal and tolerant country" launched by the anarchist daily *La protesta* in 1905 denounced the Residency Law that deported Italian, Spanish, and Jewish trade unionists from Russia.

It should be taken into account that, despite their rejection of religion, anarchist Jews in Argentina set up unions and ethnocultural associations through which they expressed their militancy in Yiddish. Radowitzky frequented one of them in 1909. Javier Díaz's pioneering research, "Anarchism in the Jewish Labor Movement in Buenos Aires" (2016: 119–40), identifies six anarchist Jewish groups that emerged between 1905 and 1909. The last to appear, at the end of May 1908, was the Burevéstnik nucleus, and Simón Radowitzky was its only known member. The objective was to spread libertarian ideas among Russian-speaking workers, complementing the already existing circles that did the same in Yiddish. In addition, Radowitzky also frequented the Yiddish cultural activities of the Arbeiter Fraind that brought together almost all anarchists and played a very important role in the unions of Jewish workers, as well as in their cultural lives (Katz 1946, 1980: 164). In 1908, the Arbeiter Fraind inaugurated the Idishe Populere Bibliothek, the headquarters of the Burevéstnik group, whose books were also consulted by Simón Radowitzky.

Thanks to the Idishe Abteilung, *La protesta* was read as the second Yiddish daily in Argentina. This was the only case in Argentine history of a non-Jewish daily with a section in Yiddish.[4] Radowitzky did not have any affinity for Yiddish language and culture, as was the case of another Argentine Jewish libertarian, Jacobo Maguid, who wrote letters in Yiddish to his mother narrating anarchist actions. However, despite Simón Radowitzky's transnational labor-class consciousness and Leon Tolstoy's ethos for unceasing examination of the self, it is not improbable to suppose that he did not reject his family's Jewish ethnic identity. Moreover, he also possibly knew how to read Yiddish and wrote letters in that language to his mother who had emigrated to the USA.

In letters to his friend Salvadora Medina, before, during, and after the Civil War, Simón Radowitzky confesses his profound objection to the notion of a national homeland, as well as his disagreement with anti-fascist internationalists who completely erased their Jewishness. Simón Radowitzky felt much more than an expatriate when he

---

[4] The page was published daily from March 15 to June 7, 1908. The section revealed the collaboration between the group Arbeiter Fraind and *La protesta*. *La protesta* was ideologically characterized as Tolstoyan anarcho-individualist, while Arbeiter Fraind grouped around him almost all the other anarchists. One of its leaders, Moishe Shutz, was appointed in 1909 as the group's secretary; previously, in Russia together with Simón Radowitzky, he would have belonged to an *acrat* group (Díaz 2016: 126–7).

lived through three consecutive dramatic crossroads: first by being exiled to Uruguay, then by fleeing—physically and morally defeated—from Spain, and third, when, on his way to exile, he finally declared himself a "wandering Jew."

Letters from the Anarchist "Wandering Jew" Simón Radowitzky to Salvadora Medina

Very few letters from International Brigade members have been recovered, and even fewer from Latin Americans. The Association of Friends of the International Brigades (AABI) has received on numerous occasions—mainly celebrations of tributes and anniversaries—legacies of brigade members belonging to relatives living in Latin American countries. From Argentina, private donations belonging to two known authors of stories and memoirs were received: Luis Alberto Quesada and Jesús Castilla Latorre. In addition, interviews were recorded with Quesada and communist leader Fanny Edelman. However, there are no letters from Argentine brigade members.

Conversely, correspondence of Spanish Republicans written in exile is preserved; there is a repository of thousands of letters from Republicans who, through the Mexican embassy in Paris and later at the consulate in Marseille, requested asylum and refuge beginning in 1939. The archive of the Ministry of Foreign Relations of Mexico managed to safeguard some 7,000 letters from Republican exiles seeking asylum and refuge, which are preserved in eighteen boxes in its diplomatic historical collection.[5]

In this completely uneven panorama, the fourteen letters written by Simón Radowitzky stand out for their documentary importance—and not only those written during the years of the Civil War. Even before Radowitzky enrolled as a volunteer in Spain, his letters anticipated future dissents and questioning. However, the letters, supposedly written in a "minor epistolary genre," reveal a special significance for better understanding the Civil War contradictions in his life.

According to Maria Zambrano, literary genres in letters are distinguished not by their stylistic form, nor even by their subject matter, but because of "the necessity of life that has given rise to them and seeks to express itself" (Zambrano 1995: 25). It is this necessity of Radowitzky's life that determines his form of epistolary expression, a genre of confessional writing that reveals a lot about his life (Zambrano 1995: 82–4; Llevadot 2001: 60–7). The richness of the letters, precisely, does not emerge from the debris of his poor daily survival but in Radowitzky's attempt to allude to a "pure time" when he longed to break through the confines of his life. In his letter to "Sister Salvadora" on August 22, 1936, from Montevideo, on the eve of his embarkation as a volunteer to Spain, intimate life and the anarchist behavior "that make[s] me love life and Struggle" share similar sentimental and ideological valences in Simón's writing:

---

[5] See the series "Las cartas del exilio Republicano en México," *El país,* Madrid, November 2012, https://elpais.com/tag/c/9bd6c58eee4150abdfba52bca4df98b8.

I work more for your satisfaction than mine and I can assure you, as I have always done before, that wherever I find myself and the friendly ties I have, my behavior has always been as Anarchists should be [sic].

But I owe more to you than to anyone in my intimate life, you have encouraged me and brought me out of childhood illusions. Today I look at life with a little more serenity, I no longer have so many illusions, *I live for our ideal and for my little sister, these are the two causes that make me love life and Struggle.* (my emphasis) (August 22, 1936, Montevideo)[6]

On September 8, 1936, Simón wrote to Salvadora again, and confessed that out of so much joy at receiving her last letter, he had forgotten to tell her about his father's death:

For my part I can tell you, as usual, I'm fine, I'm working and . . . you said that work will change me a bit, well, you're right, but . . . I'm more rebellious now . . . despite everything, I am already very happy with the joy it has caused you. *I can already see that your joy has flowed over me, because when I received your letter and when I wrote you the answer, I did not even remember [to] give you news about my family, that my old dad died 11 months ago.* (my emphasis) (September 8, 1936)[7]

In the same letter, Simón becomes impatient for not receiving news from Diego Abad de Santillán[8] who was coordinating his shipment from Montevideo to Spain with the anarchist group headed by the printing worker Roberto Cotelo; the letter makes explicit his internationalist anarchist ideal inspired by Bakunin and is very different from the rival internationalism version shared by the communist brigade members.

I imagine, dear little sister, how anxious you will be to have to go there, not only because Spanish blood runs through your heart, but also because of your humanitarian feelings to be able to help them in their gigantic struggle for our

---

[6] S. R. to Salvadora Medina, Montevideo, August 22, 1936, "Trabajo más para satisfacción tuya que la mía y te puedo asegurar, como siempre he hecho antes, que en cualquier lugar [que] yo me encontrara y las relaciones que tengo, mi conducta siempre ha sido como deben ser los Anarquistas. Pero a vos debo más que a nadie en mi vida íntima, que me ha alentado y me sacó de las ilusiones infantiles. Hoy miro ya la vida con un poco más [de] serenidad, ya no me hago tantas ilusiones, *vivo para nuestro ideal y para mi hermanita, son dos causas que hace amar la vida, y la Lucha*."

[7] S. R. to Salvadora Medina, Montevideo, September 8, 1936: "De mi parte te puedo decir, como de costumbre, estoy bien, trabajo y . . . vos decías que el trabajo me modificará un poco, pues tenés razón, pero . . . soy más rebelde ahora . . . a pesar de todo, ya estoy muy contento de la alegría que te ha causado. *Ya puedo ver que tu alegría ha influido sobre mí, pues cuando recibí tu carta y cuando te escribí la contestación, ni siquiera me acordé [de] darte una noticia de mi familia, que mi viejo hace 11 meses que murió*."

[8] The Spanish Diego Abad de Santillán (1897–1983), author, editor, and translator of classics of anarchist thought, led the Iberian Anarchist Federation. He was the first to write a book about the Jewish anarchist convict, *Simón Radowitzky* (Abad de Santillan 1927); in 1924 and 1925, Abad de Santillán regularly published in *La protesta*, "The monthly news about the martyr of Ushuaia" (1940).

Ideal. The Freedom and Well-being of humanity, as Kropotkin used to say. I dream of going to Spain.[9]

Anarchists imagined that the Civil War not only had to wage a decisive battle against fascism but should be the historic opportunity to carry out the humanist social revolution betrayed by the Bolsheviks in the USSR. Consequently, the anarchists went mainly to Catalonia to reinforce the popular and autonomous power of the National Labor Confederation led by Buenaventura Durruti. The participation of the Argentine volunteers was well organized by two great anarchist organizations based in Buenos Aires: FORA (anarcho-syndicalist) and FACA (anarchist-communist). The anarchist-communist volunteers Jacobo Prince, Jacobo Maguid, and José Grunfeld, who held important political and military positions in FAI-CNT., brought FACA representation (the volunteer writer Rodolfo González Pacheco very suggestively identified them as "the Jews of the FACA").

In a similar way, women's anarchist organizations in Argentina were mobilized to help Republicans. The female anarchist group in Uruguay was asked to help by knitting woolen clothes to be shipped to the CNT and FAI. Yet, Simón's request to Salvadora in his letter of September 28 was significantly different, asking her to "tear" raw wool from the clothes of the rich bourgeoisie who frequented the Buenos Aires mansion of the anarchist wife of the millionaire businessman Natalio Botana. The *anarchist*, Radowitzky reminded his protector, shared the ideological support of expropriating anarchists while other comrades condemned them as thieves:

> We hope to send some clothes next month. Here, most of the colleagues take their winter clothes to send them to Spain, but despite goodwill it is not enough and, talking with Luce, we remember you. We know very well that you, on your part, will collaborate in Buenos Aires, but it is said that a direct steamer, the "San Antonio," is coming from Barcelona as they say to buy food or clothes. I think you will be able to find out in B. A. [Buenos Aires] the day the steamer arrives to agree to send even raw wool but you can do that alone or, with the help of some of your friends, tear the wool from the clothes of some of the bourgeoisie who go to your house to eat or drink vermouth. We hope that as usual you will do it, or rather, you will have already done it.[10]

---

[9] S. R. to Salvadora Medina, Montevideo, September 8, 1936: "Me imagino, querida hermanita, qué ansias tendrás de ir allí, no solamente porque por tu corazón corre sangre española, sino por tus sentimientos humanitarios para poder ayudarlos en su lucha gigantesca por nuestro Ideal. La Libertad y el Bienestar de la humanidad, como decía Kropotkin. Yo sueño con ir a España."

[10] S. R. to Salvadora Medina, Montevideo, September 28, 1936: "Esperamos para el mes que viene mandar algo de ropa, aquí casi a la mayoría de los compañeros les sacamos la ropa de invierno para mandarla a España pero a pesar de la buena voluntad es bastante poco y, conversando con Luce, nos acordamos de vos. Sabemos muy bien que vos, de tu parte, colaborás en Buenos Aires, pero como se dice que viene un vapor directo de Barcelona, el San Antonio, según dicen para comprar víveres o ropa, creo vos lo podrás averiguar en B. A. el día que llegue para ponerse de acuerdo para mandar aunque fuera lana en bruto, pero para eso vos podrás hacer sola o con ayuda de algunas de tus amistades de arrancar la lana a la ropa a algunos de los Burgueses que van por tu casa a comer

Simón Radowitzky's last letter before leaving for Spain juxtaposes criticism of a new theatrical drama of Salvadora's and a memory from his youth in Ukraine. Simón's first comments focus on the drama, *A Man and His Life, Under the Invocation of the Fiery Moment of Spain*, which Salvadora Medina sent him a few weeks before it premiered in 1936. The second act of the drama reminds Radowitzky of "[the] underground Russia [of] the Nihilist times that I have known"; a *memory* that carries with it a host of associated words drawn from predominantly Russian revolutionary discourses that Radowitzky thought could resonate in Salvadora's ears. He reminds her of the young nihilists who assassinated Tsar Alexander II in 1881 and were famous throughout Europe as advocates of the use of violence to achieve political change. Radowitzky had quite possibly been influenced by the ideas of Bakunin, an admirer of Nechayev's zeal, and the triumphalist stories of the Russian section of the World Revolutionary Alliance, which turned out to be a fictitious organization. Simón enthusiastically writes about his youthful memories of Kyiv:

> I read your book with great enthusiasm because it reminds me of that beautiful time when I knew the Nihilists, that is, the Revolutionaries of the time of Tsarism. I met many and I treated them intimately; you truly describe them as [if] you were a *Rusita* [a young Russian woman].
>
> [...] The only thing that seems to me is that Sonia is too human, because she had the courage to commit suicide without taking out the traitor with another shot.
>
> [...] When reading the second act, the Machiavellian conversations of the diplomats, I think of Spain with the farce of neutrality, and ... even Revolutionary Russia ... it is also neutral, while maintaining trade with German and Italian fascism.[11]

Such indignant reflection against the neutral position of European democracies had anticipated the repudiation, two years earlier at the end of August 1939, by both anarchists and anti-Soviet Trotskyists of the Stalin–Hitler non-aggression pact, signed by their foreign ministers Molotov and Ribbentrop.[12]

After commenting on Salvadora Medina's play,[13] Simón Radowitzky expresses his irresistible desire to have already arrived in Republican Spain, although he does not

---

o tomar el vermut. Esperamos que como de costumbre que tú lo harás, o mejor dicho, lo estarás ya haciendo."

[11] S. R. to Salvadora Medina, Montevideo, September 30, 1936: "Con mucho entusiasmo leo tu libro pues me hace recordar ese hermoso tiempo cuando conocía los Nihilistas o sea los Revolucionarios del tiempo del zarismo, conocí mucho y los traté íntimamente y verdaderamente los describís como [si] vos fueras Rusita... Lo único que me parece es que Sonia es demasiado Humana, pues tuvo valor de suicidarse sin llevarse con otro tiro al traidor.

[...] Al leer el segundo acto, las conversaciones Maquiavélicas de los diplomáticos, pienso en España con la farsa de la Neutralidad, y ... hasta la Rusia Revolucionaria ... también es Neutral, mientras tanto mantiene comercio con el fascismo Alemán y Italiano [*sic*]."

[12] On the impact of the Hitler–Stalin pact on different Latin American communist militants, see Senkman and Milgram (2020: 787–809).

[13] Salvadora Medina had successfully premiered feminist plays in previous years (Escales 2020: ch. 3).

hide his fear of a military defeat of the Republic. However, the "rebellious spirit of the proletariat is not defeated":

> I plan to read your work again and I think I will read it several more times, because even though I read it, my imagination is in Spain, since I cannot and do not have the means to be there. The latest news was not very encouraging, but despite everything, I hope in our triumph, all the blood poured out by the Spanish people must triumph, because [the] rebellious spirit of the proletariat is not defeated.[14]

Both topics in Radowitzky's letter—his assessment of Russian revolutionary nihilism in Salvadora Medina's play, and his feeling of the Republican defeat perceived before even arriving in Spain—are reading keys for grasping epistemic and ideological dissents. Radowitzky apologizes in the postscript (perhaps suspecting the incomprehensibility of both dissents?), and ends his letter distraught: "Excuse me this time for my letter so incomprehensible, *I already tore up a lot of written pages, I don't know what's wrong with me, everything comes out the other way around*" (my emphasis).[15]

However, in the nearly two years he spent in Spain, Radowitzky continued to turn out the opposite of what he thought to tell his "dear little sister." Just after arriving in Barcelona, he was appointed to liaison tasks, but his discontent at not sharing the fate of his companions in the front led him to disobey and participate in the battle of Teruel, where he almost lost his life. Radowitzky was forced to work in the rear and when the moment of urgent withdrawal arrived, he received the important mission of safeguarding the historical archive of the CNT-FAI (Marti 2011: 291–3).

Two months after the end of a fierce battle that has been called the "Spanish Stalingrad," he relates to Salvadora in a letter from Barcelona dated April 18, 1938, that "we, despite everything, live with optimism and faith in our triumph. As long as there is an anti-fascist standing, we will fight. 'Never Defeated' is the general cry of all Spanish people and Catalonia. You have to see, little sister, with what enthusiasm they are now going to the front and everyone, all united like a steel pad."[16]

Unlike the Communist International Brigades, the anarchist volunteers marched mainly to Catalonia to reinforce the popular and autonomous power of the National Labor Confederation led by Buenaventura Durruti: "Being able to say [to] the whole world at this time in Spain that we defend not only the freedom of the world but also

---

[14] S. R. to Salvadora Medina, Montevideo, September 30, 1936: "Pienso leer otra vez tu obra y creo que la leeré varias veces más, pues a pesar que lo leo mi imaginación está en España, ya que yo no puedo ni tengo medios para estar allí, las últimas noticias no eran muy alentadoras, pero a pesar de todo espero en nuestro triunfo, toda la sangre vertida por el pueblo español tiene que triunfar, pues [el] espíritu rebelde del proletariado no está vencido."

[15] S. R. to Salvadora Medina, Montevideo, September 30, 1936: "*Disculpame esta vez por mi carta tan incomprensible, rompí ya muchas hojas escritas, no sé lo que me pasa, me sale todo al revés.*"

[16] S. R. to Salvadora Medina, Barcelona, April 18, 1937: "nosotros a pesar de todo, vivimos con optimismo y fe en nuestro triunfo, mientras haya un antifascista en pie, pelearemos. Vencidos Nunca es el grito general de todo el pueblo español y principalmente Cataluña. Hay que ver, hermanita, con qué entusiasmo ahora van al frente y todos, todos unidos como un bloc de acero."

its independence, so as not to be an Italian-German colony." His internationalism is an accusation against the European democracies from whom "we once expected help . . . But today we are convinced, with or without their help, we will crush Italian-German fascism."[17] Confidence in the Republican forces themselves, and not in Soviet aid, arises from the anguished optimism written in the first lines of the letter: "And I can assure you as long as there is a man standing in loyal Spain, they will not pass. We live here with optimism and with confidence in our own strength."[18] Unfortunately, many anti-fascists knew early on that their own forces were not enough and the Republican defeat was inevitable. However, the Spanish experience was called a moral defeat by Radowitzky.

The exiled communist-anarchist, canonized before the age of forty as a mythical stateless person and vindicated martyr, had possibly suspected upon arrival in Spain that he was going to become an exile after fighting in the 28th Division of Gregorio Jover, composed mainly of anarchists. It was precisely at the Aragon Front where Radowitzky experienced not a break with his past, but the beginning of a painful process of epistemic dissent, fed by ideological dissent. The moral defeat in Spain was a painful experience for Radowitzky that led him to question the nature and origin of knowledge as well as the understanding of everyday life. At the same time, it also was a disappointing experience because of ideological dissent *vis-à-vis* political decisions by many of his own anarchist comrades, during decisive episodes of the Civil War.

Both reasons for dissent began months before the defeat. The first started when Radowitzky befriended Antonio Casanova, a Galician emigrant to Argentina who had been among the founders of the Argentine Anarchist-Communist Federation, and the second, after ten months of stubborn fighting at the front when, for health reasons, Radowitzky's comrades forced him to stay in Valencia and work in culture and propaganda for the National Confederation of Labor. His dissent deepened even more when the dissolution of the anarchist militias was decided and he witnessed the violent confrontations in Barcelona between communists and anarchists in May 1938.

The military defeat and profound ideological dissent influenced Radowitzky's progressive certainty about Republican isolation and the failure of the Spanish social revolution. At the same time, he discovered the extent of the courage and faith of the men and women fighting for their libertarian ideal in the face of uncertainty. Undoubtedly, his confidence grew as he became increasingly convinced that true revolutionaries should act with human responsibility and make ethical decisions in everyday life (Tarcus 2005: 140).

---

[17] "un tiempo esperábamos una ayuda . . . Pero hoy día estamos convencidos con ayuda de ello o sin su ayuda, aplastaremos al fascismo Ítalo-Alemán" (Letter by S. R., Barcelona, July 30, 1938).
[18] S. R. to Salvadora Medina, Barcelona, July 30, 1938: "y te puedo asegurar mientras haya en la España Leal un hombre en pie No pasarán. Nosotros aquí vivimos con optimismo y con confianza en nuestras propias fuerzas."

In summary, after unsuccessful episodes of struggling, a strong epistemic uncertainty affected Radowitzky's ability to understand his world and his life. Radowitzky did not leave a testimony of his anarchist practices before and after the confinement in Ushuaia; his letters are the only testimony that was written by the mythical "Saint of Ushuaia," imprisoned for life and speaking about himself as a fiery avenging revolutionary. The absence of such a record is barely compensated by descriptions of comrades during Radowitzky's militancy in the CNT-FAI house in Barcelona:

> He was modest, shy, intense, he never talked about anything and less about himself. In the midst of the intellectuals and the prominent militants, Simón was modest, silent, and went unnoticed. It was necessary to find him in a moment of loquacity, to lead him imperceptibly toward the field of trust and confidence so that he would reveal himself and show himself to the extent that he perceived and penetrated with his spirit . . . I asked him and Simón would answer me . . . I remember I spent hours listening to him, without interrupting him, letting him express himself with his slow voice dragging the syllables, sometimes looking for the words that best expressed his thought without hurting anyone. (Montseny 1956: 83–4)[19]

Radowitzky managed to leave Spain, but before his departure, he helped to transport the archive of the National Confederation of the Labor-Iberian Anarchist Federation (CNT-FAI) by truck, preventing it from falling into Francoist hands. Today, these files can be viewed at the archive of the Institute of Social History in Amsterdam.

The first letter after Radowitzky's flight is dated May 1, 1939, from Brussels. It opens with a significant confession that goes beyond a metaphor: it refers to his new identity as "a wandering Jew." It does not allude to either the Republican defeat or his resignation from participating in anti-German actions in occupied France, as these involved other Argentine *brigadistas* in prison. His first confession as a fugitive volunteer after suffering horribly in the Saint Cyprien concentration camp and crossing half of France on foot[20] is that he had "become" a "wandering Jew." This is a meaningful confession, written by a defeated volunteer who cannot be understood solely through his feeling of insecurity, loneliness, and powerlessness:

---

[19] "Como era modesto, tímido, reconcentrado, nunca hablaba de nada y menos de sí mismo. En medio incluso de los intelectuales, de los militantes destacados, Simón modesto, silencioso, pasó inadvertido. Era preciso encontrarle en un momento de locuacidad, llevarle insensiblemente hacia el terreno de la confianza y de la confidencia para que se descubriera y mostrase hasta dónde su espíritu percibía y penetraba . . . Yo le preguntaba y Simón me contestaba . . . Recuerdo que pasé horas escuchándole, sin interrumpirle dejándole manifestarse con su voz lenta arrastrando las sílabas, buscando a veces las palabras que expresasen mejor su pensamiento sin herir a nadie" (Montseny 1956: 83–4).

[20] The defeated Republicans and fugitive volunteers across the French border were concentrated in camps where 275,000 Spaniards passed, guarded by "Moors and Senegaleses" from the French colonial forces. José Maguid and Jacobo Prince ended up in French concentration camps, from which they managed to escape with the help of French anarchists. Others, such as José Grunfeld and Arturo T. García, escaped and took refuge in London before repatriation in Argentina (Ortiz 2015: 327–43; Boragina 2015: 327–43).

Brussels, May 1, 1939
Dear Salvadora, Sister, Cheers,

As you see, I have become a wandering Jew, after having traveled almost half of France by car and a little bit by foot. I am now in Brussels having become a Cuban citizen, as you see.[21]

Having accepted an apocryphal identity, disguised as a tourist with a false Cuban passport to travel to Mexico, Radowitzky felt like much more than an undocumented foreigner. He describes himself as a Foreigner with capital letters:

I will tell you [that] when you receive the present, [it is] very likely [that] I will be already traveling to Mexico. I have everything arranged, the documentation and the visas, so I hope, if there are no obstacles, to write to you soon from Mexico. At last I was able to rest a little bit after having crossed the border. As you know, I was in the concentration camp, you cannot imagine how much we have suffered there during the first 15 days. If they told me, I would have doubted that in the middle of the twentieth century, civilized France could have treated us so inhumanly. The first time, I escaped from the concentration camp and they caught me in Perpignan; the second time, I left the concentration camp despite the Senegalese and their gendarmes, *because I was without documentation and they were herding every field bug that smelled like a Foreigner*. But despite everything, I was lucky: I arrived in Paris and the companions sent me to Brussels, and now I am waiting for the steamer to leave and I have everything ready to embark as a tourist. (my emphasis)[22]

The letter from the fugitive Foreigner shows another clue into the Jewish imaginary of Simón Radowitzky: assuming that his radical foreignness (made invisible by his libertarian cosmopolitanism), wouldn't conclude the story of Radowitzky, confined in the Saint Cyprien concentration camp "in the twentieth century in civilized France." Stateless and exiled, a defeated volunteer and fugitive, a "Foreigner" with capital letters, Radowitzky does not confess by chance that "I have become a wandering Jew." Certainly,

---

[21] "Querida Hermana Salvadora, Salud, // Como me ves, *me he hecho un judío errante*, después de haber recorrido casi la mitad de Francia casi todo en auto y un poco a pie, me encuentro ahora en Bruselas hecho un ciudadano como ves cubano."

[22] Letter by SR to SM, Bruselas 1.5.1939: "Te diré [que para] cuando recibas la presente, [es] muy probable [que] estaré yo ya de viaje para México. Tengo ya todo arreglado, la documentación y las visaciones, así espero, si no hay obstáculos, escribirte pronto de México. Al fin pude descansar un poco después de haber pasado la frontera, como sabrás estuve en el campo de concentración, no puedes imaginar lo que se ha sufrido allí los primeros 15 días, con contarlo dudo que lo crea que en el pleno siglo XX en la Francia civilizada nos hayan tratado tan inhumanamente, la primera vez que escapé del campo y me agarraron en Perpiñán y la segunda vez me fui del campo a pesar de los senegaleses y sus gendarmes, *lo que sí como andaba sin documentación y andaban arriando a todo bicho viviente que se sentía olor a Extranjero*, y a pesar de todo tuve suerte, llegué a París y los compañeros me mandaron a Bruselas y ahora espero la salida del vapor y ya tengo todo listo para embarcarme como turista."

he does not allude to the mythical Christian figure of the wandering Jew—Ahasveros, the iconic Foreigner condemned to perpetual wandering to purge the deicide of Jesus Christ. Simón's wandering Jew is not a phantasmagoric Christian condemnation, but the reappearance of his nomadic being in *galut* (exile), the no-place of the wandering exile; the pariah described by Enzo Traverso in "The Sons of Ahasvero," whose Jewish wandering "became a metaphor for a minority living on the margins of society, sometimes by choice, sometimes forced" (Traverso 2014: 41).

A religious and cultural ethnic minority whose otherness was marked for centuries in the *galut* has become unrecognizable in modernity, thanks to its mobility, exchanges, acculturation, revolutionary stands, and the multilingualism of the Jewish diaspora. Furthermore, Traverso recalls the stereotypical literary construction of the figure of the wandering Jew in the Christian imagination; however, the figurative language for remembering the legend in the Jewish imagination was symmetrical but completely inverted.

The defeat of the Spanish Republican cause, after much suffering, also convinced the anarchist volunteer Simón Radowitzky to accept exile in Mexico, as did many Spanish Republicans and fugitive brigade members in 1939. The path of exile was the only possible option for Radowitzky to save his life after the defeat. Perhaps that is why he did not try to join the anti-Nazi struggle or the French Resistance against the collaborationist Vichy regime, as the Argentine *brigadista* Luis Alberto Quesada attempted to do.[23] When Quesada fled to the Pyrenees, Radowitzky was interned in the Gurs concentration camp, huddled in the Argentine barracks with fifty to sixty compatriots. No other Jewish anarchist felt that he was a "wandering Jew," because the *desterrado* (outlaw) Radowitzky could never dream of one day returning to his non-existent homeland. Despite having shared a diaspora of political exile with other defeated Spaniards in México, he felt that he had a different fate than a deterritorialized man. Unlike the exiled Sánchez Vásquez, alienated from the Mexican present, Radowitzky would probably have felt closer to the "diasporic life" of the "desterrado," a condition that María Zambrano described as the stage before the advent of a universal homeland:

> The defeat that gave rise to the exile, mine and that of millions of people, for many years, was, I have already said, diaspora: [. . .] The exile has been, above all and more than anything else, diaspora: the lost friends, the frustrated occasions. The always open attempt of a new homeland that embraces them all [. . .]. A "there" that is, paradoxically, the place of exile itself transformed into a kind of universal homeland, into a homeland with capital letters. (2004: 36)

---

[23] The son of Andalusians returned to Spain, six-year-old Luis Alberto Quesada retained Argentine nationality. A combatant at age 16 as a member of the Socialist Youth, at the end of the war he was division commissioner in the 104th Brigade. Gino Baumann (1979: 46) infers that many Spanish-Argentines with dual nationality in the Civil War had a "precarious nationality consciousness": they felt more Spanish than Argentine; this was the case of Quesada. However, the Argentine citizenship helped him not to be deported to the concentration camps; finally, the sentence was commuted to life imprisonment, and he was able to return to Argentina.

In his comments on Zambrano's notion of diaspora, Antolín Sánchez Cuervo alludes to a symbolic relationship: "From the diaspora, exile becomes a form of existence that makes the Jewish translation of the promised land its own and more universal transforming the material relationship with blood and land into a symbolic relationship" (Sánchez Cuervo 2014: 141–2).

The first letter to Salvadora from México, dated February 12, 1941, begins with another significant confession written by the stateless Radowitzky: "I am now an authentic Mexican citizen." But he immediately regrets being unable to achieve the main objective of acquiring the Mexican nationality: crossing the border with the United States to visit his mother and brothers.

> I'm fine now, I am an authentic Mexican citizen, but even though I have all the documentation as a nationalized Mexican, the Consul of North America denied me the visa to enter, [but] I have a certain friendship with the Secretary of the Ministry of Foreign Affairs, I asked to find out why, and yesterday he told me that they have denied me because I am an Anarchist, because in the consulate they have the list of all the Spaniards who have arrived . . . but I will go anyway, I have friends at the border, plus a deputy also goes there and very likely I will go with him, so when you receive this letter, very likely I will be next to my Mother.[24]

Mexican exile Raúl Gómez Saavedra—the pseudonym used by Simón Radowitzky from the time of his arrival in 1941 until his death in February 1956 in Mexico City—aims to finally exorcise the legendary but spectral images of Simón Radowitzky: the "avenger and martyr," coined by Diego Abad de Santillan in 1927, and the "expropriating anarchist" mentioned by Osvaldo Bayer. The exiled and nationalized Mexican Raúl Gómez Saavedra changed his identity to put an end to his previous long years as a doomed outcast that deprived him of all personal documentation. In the country of exile, he was helped by the Uruguayan consul and poet Ángel Falco, who provided him with employment in the legation, and by Ricardo Mestre Ventura, Spanish anarchist and founder of the Social Library Reconstruir. Raul Gomez Saavedra (Radowitzky) collaborated in the International Section of Aid to refugees in Mexico, conflicted by divisions and quarrels among Spanish exiles. Until the end of his life, he worked in a toy factory, a metaphoric work for his life as an exile.

"Despite the fact that I have a relatively good time," Simón Radowitzky writes to Salvadora that "I feel deep nostalgia for *allí* [there]," similarly to other Argentine and Uruguayan melancholic exiles in Mexico. Indeed, he attached "some photos where I

---

[24] Letter by S. R., Mexico, February 12, 1941: "Estoy bien ahora, soy auténtico ciudadano Mexicano, pero a pesar que tengo toda la documentación como nacionalizado como Mexicano, el Cónsul de Norte América me negó la visación para entrar, como tengo cierta o [*sic*]? amistad con el Secretario del Ministerio de Relaciones Exteriores, yo hice averiguar y ayer me dijo que me lo han negado por ser Anarquista, porque en el consulado tienen la lista de todos los españoles que han llegado . . . pero yo voy lo mismo, tengo amigos en la frontera, a más un diputado va también para allí y muy probable[mente] yo voy con él, así que al recibir la presente muy probable[mente] estaré yo al lado de mi Madre."

think you will recognize me when I was doing the barbecue, [and] Falco called me the 'Gaucho in Pajamas.'" But predictably, in the same letter to his beloved Sister, Radowitzky also tells "how beautiful México is," and that "as a Mexican . . . I have to do propaganda for my new *Homeland*" (Simón Radowitzky to Salvadora Medina, Mexico, December 2, 1941).[25]

During his Mexican exile, the lonely "wandering Jew" missed only two women: Salvadora and his mother. He could not meet his mother because he could not cross the Mexico–US border without a visa. We do not know in which language he wrote his letters (Yiddish? Russian?) or if he told her about his bond with Salvadora; however, we do know that to his beloved protector of all life, he wrote, "I do not lose hope of having the pleasure of drinking *mate* with you."

In light of the anarchist-feminist free love ideology shared by almost all their comrades who venerated free union, according to Bakunin's book *Woman, Marriage and Family*, the platonic love of Simón and Salvadora seems an anachronistic bond. However, this is the only love bond that ex-convict number 155 wanted to hold in life with his protective friend. Moreover, the Simón–Salvadora couple has been fictionalized by Alicia Dujovne Ortiz in her novel *La más agraciada* (The Most Graceful) (2015). Dujovne Ortiz describes only one moment of their long relationship when both dear "siblings" met for the first time in Montevideo:

> The meeting disappoints her. Not for an instant does it occur to Salvadora to think of what Simón feels when he sees her in front of him: a woman with red hair, with that silver glow of the miserable little animal wrapped around her neck . . . Just one feature of that face reminds her of the emotion of his letters. A feature that moves former prisoner 155, a childish feature: the tip of her nose, flat and rounded, a blunt nose. He looks away from her pulpy lips, just as he would like to separate himself from that perfume that he has never had the opportunity to smell, neither in prison nor outside, never, that perfume—should you say it, can you think about it?—not of a companion but of a bourgeois lady. (2015: 148)[26]

The narrative irony of Alicia Dujovne Ortiz seems to remind us sarcastically that Salvadora's feminist fidelity to anarchism, which promised the emancipation of

---

[25] Letter by S. R. to Salvadora Medina, Mexico, February 12, 1941: "Pero a pesar de que yo me la paso relativamente bien siento nostalgia de allí . . . México es un país muy hermoso, va progresando mucho, el clima es muy variable en los pueblos, ahora hace un poco [de] frío y a 50 kilómetros de México estamos en pleno verano, te aseguro que te va a gustar muchísimo, a más como Mexicano . . . yo tengo que hacer propaganda para mi nueva Patria . . . adjunto van unas fotos que creo que me reconocerás cuando hacía el asado, Falco me llamó el Gaucho en Pijama."

[26] "Ni por un instante se le ocurre pensar a Salvadora en lo que siente Simón al vérsela adelante: una mujer de pelo rojo, con ese resplandor plateado del mísero animalito enroscado alrededor de su cuello . . . Apenas un rasgo de esa cara le recuerda la emoción de sus cartas. Un rasgo que al ex penado 155 lo conmueve, un rasgo infantil: la puntita de su nariz, chata y redondeada. Roma, una nariz roma. De los labios pulposos aparta la vista, así como desearía apartarse todo él de ese perfume que jamás ha tenido la ocasión de olfatear, ni en la cárcel ni afuera, nunca, ese perfume—¿debe decirlo, puede pensarlo?—no de compañera sino de señorona burguesa."

women, implied the transformation of affectionate and sexual relationships as an inherent part of a general social revolution.

Conclusion

Radowitzky's letters may be read on an individual level as the micro-history of an anarchist volunteer who took part in the Spanish Civil War. They illuminate the "official story" told in history books. I share the interpretation of Horacio Tarcus on Radowitzky's imaginary longings:

> Simón has two wishes: one, to rediscover his mother; two, to see Salvadora again, to share, once more, a few *mates*. He sends his photos, asks for images of her, which he carries with him wherever his life as a "wandering Jew" takes him, just as Salvadora preserves his objects as fetishes. She even dies surrounded by his *polin* (prisoner's hat number 155 of the Ushuaia prison) and other memories that Simón sent her. (Tarcus 2005: 140)

Radowitzky imagined himself as a non-biological son of a large labor family. Much more imaginative are his notions of consanguinity as told to a special envoy of the newspaper *Crítica*, during an interview with Radowitzky in the Ushuaia prison in January 1930. According to the widespread account of Osvaldo Bayer, the interviewer, Eduardo Barbero Sarzabal, first wrote of his admiring surprise upon hearing the speech of prisoner number 155: "When Radowitzky speaks, it seems that he chews the words. And they come out, brief and concise, like a firing pin" (Bayer 1975: 80).

Likewise, both exile and Jewishness overlap imaginatively in Radowitzky's notion of belonging to an expanded, non-biological family. Indeed, identification with the revisited "wandering Jew" in Radowitzky's letters sheds light on the invisible Jewishness in an all-embracing firmament of anarchist, cosmopolitan, and internationalist imaginary. However, the firmament of the anarchist cosmopolitan imaginary of Radowitzky is vastly different from his proletarian internationalism (Traverso 2006). The first term is now pervaded by a persistent diasporic sense of non-belonging, as the Republican defeat in Spain has made the ideal of internationalist becoming more difficult (on Jewish belonging into internationalist becoming, see Gabbay 2020b: 207–9).

Meanwhile, the icon of "the wandering Jew" that embodies an atavistic sentiment of *galut*—displacement and exile—transforms the defeated volunteer of the Spanish Civil War into a Jewish exile. This character is condemned to survive not within the imaginary of an internationalist, oriented toward a "geography of escape" (Gabbay 2022, 61–6), but, rather, as a rootless cosmopolitan Jew returning to an extraterritorial diaspora of exiles, whose intimacy of a being in love is revealed when Simón writes his letters to Salvadora, without ever attempting to create literature.

References

Abad de Santillán, D. (1927), *Simón Radowitzky, el vengador y mártir*, Buenos Aires: FORA.

Abad de Santillán, D. (1940), *Por qué perdimos la guerra. Una contribución a la historia de la tragedia española*, Buenos Aires: Imán.

Bantman, C. (2006), "Internationalism Without an International? Cross-Channel Anarchist Networks, 1880–1914," *Revue belge de philologie et d'histoire*, 84: 969.

Bantman, C., and B. Altena (eds.). (2017), *Reassessing the Transnational Turn. Scales of Analysis in Anarchist and Syndicalist Studies*, Oakland: PM Press.

Baumann, G. F. (1979), *Extranjeros en la guerra civil española: los peruanos*, Lima: Industrial Gráfica.

Bayer, O. (1975), *Los anarquistas expropiadores. Simón Radowitzky y otros ensayos*, Buenos Aires: Galerna.

Boragina, J. (2015), *Las Brigadas Internacionales: nuevas perspectivas en la historia de la Guerra Civil y del exilio*, Tarragona: Universitat Rovira i Virgili.

Boragina, J. and E. R. Somaro. (2016), *Voluntarios judeoargentinos en la Guerra civil española*, Buenos Aires: Idisher Cultur Farband, Federación de Entidades Culturales Judías en la Argentina.

Deutscher, I. (1968), *The non-Jewish Jew and Other Essays*. Oxford: Oxford University Press.

Díaz, J. (2016), "El anarquismo en el movimiento obrero judío de Buenos Aires, 1905–1909." *Archivos, Year IV*, 8: 119–40.

Doorslaer, R. V. (1993), "Portrait d'une identité communiste juive : Les Juifs de Belgique dans la guerre civile espagnole," *Pardes*, 17:148.

Dujovne Ortiz, A. (2015), *La más agraciada*, Buenos Aires: Emecé.

Escales, V. (2020), *Arroja la bomba! Salvadora Medina Onrubia y el feminismo anarco*, Buenos Aires: Marea.

Gabbay, C. (2022), "Iterología de Micaela Feldman/Etchebehere tras la guerra civil española: entre el insilio melancólico y el exilio de imaginación cosmopolita," in C. Nickel and D. Santos Sánchez (eds.), *Women in Exile: Female Literary Networks of the 1939 Republican Exile*, Special Volume in *Journal of Spanish Cultural Studies* 23 (1), 51–70.

Gabbay, C. (2020a), "El onceavo mandamiento: memoria del fuego en la literatura judía y feminista de la guerra civil española," in E. Kahan, A. Raber, and W. Wechsler (eds.), *Hacer Patria. Estudios sobre la vida judía en Argentina*, 31–67, Buenos Aires: Teseo.

Gabbay, C. (2020b), "(Jewish) Women's Narratives of *Caring* and Medical Practices during the Spanish Civil War," in Miriam Offer (ed.), *Nashim: A Journal of Jewish Women's Studies and Gender Issues, 36, Jewish Women Medical Practitioners in Europe Before, During and After the Holocaust*, 205–33, Bloomington: Indiana University Press.

Ibáñez Sperber, R. (2006), "Judíos en las Brigadas Internacionales. Algunas consideraciones generales," *Historia Actual Online*, 9. Available online: https://www.researchgate.net/publication/40905795_Judios_en_las_Brigadas_Internacionales_Algunas_consideraciones_generales (Accessed September 5, 2020).

Katz, P. (1946), *Geklibene Shriftn*, Buenos Aires: ICUF, V.

Katz, P. (1980), *Páginas Selectas*, Buenos Aires: ICUF.

Kirschenbaum, L.A. (2015), "International Communists and the Memory of the Spanish Civil War, 1939-1953," in *International Communism and the Spanish Civil War: Solidarity and Suspicion*, 181-236, Cambridge: Cambridge University Press.

Llevadot, L. (2001), "La confesión, género literario. La escritura y la vida," *Aurora, Papeles del Seminario María Zambrano*, 3: 60-7. Available online: https://www.academia.edu/4953897/La_confesi%C3%B3n_g%C3%A9nero_literario_La_escritura_y_la_vida (Accessed November 2, 2020).

Marti, A. (2011), *Simón Radowitzky. Del atentado a Falcón a la Guerra Civil Española*, La Plata: De la Campana.

Montseny, F. (1956), "Ideas y Figuras: Simón Radowitzky," in A. Souchy (ed.), *Una vida y un ideal*, 83-4, Mexico D.F.: Grupo de Amigos de Simón Radowitzky.

Ortiz, J. (2015), "La epopeya de los guerrilleros españoles en Francia," in J. S.Cervelló, and Sebastián Blanco (eds.), *Las Brigadas Internacionales: Nuevas perspectivas en la historia de la Guerra Civil y del exilio*, 327-43, Tarragona: Universitat Rovira i Virgili.

Radowitzky, S. (2004/2005). "Documento: Catorce cartas inéditas de Simón Radowitzky a Salvadora Medina Onrubia," *Política de la Memoria*, 5: 142-7.

Rueda Laffond, C. (2019), "Judíos, comunistas e interbrigadistas: intersecciones y ambivalencias en los años treinta desde un enfoque transnacional," *Revista Brasileira de Historia*, 39 (82): 241-63.

Sánchez Cuervo, A. (2011), "Destierro y Exilio: categorías del pensar de María Zambrano," in A. Sánchez Cuervo and F. Hermedia de Blas (eds.), *Pensamiento exiliado español. El legado filosófico de 39 y su dimensión iberoamericana*, 268-322, Madrid: CSIC.

Sánchez Cuervo, A. (2014), "Fuera de lugar, en otro tiempo. El exilio como figura política," in A. Aguirre, A.Sánchez Cuervo, L. Roniger (eds.), *Tres Estudios sobre el exilio*, 107-94, Benemérita Universidad Autónoma de Puebla: EDAF.

Sánchez Vásquez, A. (1997), *Fin del exilio y exilio sin fin. Del exilo en México. Recuerdos y reflexiones*, México DF: Grijalbo.

Senkman, L. and A. Milgram (eds.). (2020), *Cultura, Ideología y Fascismo. Sociedad Civil Iberoamericana y Holocausto*, Madrid/Frankfurt: Iberoamericana Vervuert, 787-809.

Tarcus, H. (2004/2005), "Simón Radowitzky y Salvadora Medina Onrubia: Anarquismo y teosofía," *Políticas de la Memoria*, 5: 138-41.

Traverso, E. (2006), "Judaïsme allemand et cosmopolitisme," *Matériaux pour l'histoire de notre temps*, 4 (84): 5-11.

Traverso, E. (2014), *El final de la modernidad judía: historia de un giro conservador*, Buenos Aires: Fondo de Cultura Económica.

Violi, P. (1987), "La intimidad de la ausencia: formas de la estructura epistolar," *Revista de Occidente*, 68: 94-7.

Zambrano, M. (1995), *La Confesión: Género literario*, Madrid: Siruela.

Zambrano, M. ([1979] 2004), *Los bienaventurados*, Madrid: Siruela.

4

Max Aub, the Exile Who Returns to the Diaspora[1]

Mauricio Pilatowsky Braverman

The same intolerance that threw you out of Cologne . . . For the same cause, for the same reasons. Have you ever heard this cry? "We shall not allow our blood to mix with an impure one!" Doesn't it ring a bell?[2]

(Max Aub, *San Juan*)

Introduction

This chapter approaches a writer who, in his work, left a vivid testimony of his own experience. Max Aub, a Spanish Republican exile who took asylum in Mexico, was also the heir to another heartbreaking experience: he was an assimilated Jew. Based on one of his most relevant texts about exile—*San Juan*—we shall reflect on the issue of the Spanish Republican exile and also on Aub's own personal experience dealing with it. The reading of this play, in which he seeks to reproduce the distressing experience of those exiles who navigated from port to port in the hope of finding refuge, transmits to us what thousands of exiles lived in those years and what Aub himself experienced. The disconcerting matter about this tragedy is that the characters are not Spanish Republicans but, rather, Jews fleeing Nazism. The reason for this choice is enigmatic. One might expect an exiled Spanish Republican writer, who talks about his own experience, to recreate the situation of his compatriots fleeing Francoism and not that of the Jews. To approach this problem it is necessary to understand what exile meant for Aub and his way of expressing this significance in this emblematic work.

In order to understand the deep significance of this tragedy and the author's reason for addressing the issue of exile based on the Jewish experience and not on the Spanish one, we shall reflect on what it meant to be a diasporic Jew as a way to differentiate it from the experience of sheer political exile. First, we shall expose, in a schematic

---

[1] This chapter has been translated from Spanish by Claudia Larios Padilla.
[2] The original says: "La misma intolerancia que os echó de Colonia . . . Por el mismo motivo, por las mismas razones. ¿No ha oído nunca este grito?: '¡No consentiremos que nuestra sangre se mezcle con otra impura!' ¿No le suena?"

way, how we understand the Jewish diaspora and what the text represents in this millenary tradition. Continuing with this reflection, we shall review Aub's positions concerning the central themes of politics, society, and culture. In this sense, it should be remembered that he was a multifaceted writer: in addition to novels, plays, and poems, throughout his life, he wrote articles for many newspapers, including the most renowned ones. Before analyzing *San Juan*, we shall stop at these journalistic pieces to determine what the author thought about nationalism, religious beliefs, and sectarian appropriations of literature. For the purpose of illustrating this condition—which we identify as diasporic—we shall stop at Aub's reflection on two authors with whom he identified: Franz Kafka and Heinrich Heine. In these two great writers, he saw his own desire reflected: to make literature an instrument of criticism and a source of hope. In 1964, on the occasion of its publication in Spain, Aub wrote: "*San Juan* still represents the idea that I have of my time's literature; it does not and cannot go without being a chronicle and a denunciation" (Aub 1998: 225–6).[3] His literary analyses of these two writers explain the denunciation he has in mind when he retrospectively refers to this play while in exile during the Spanish Civil War. After exposing all the elements that make it possible to differentiate exile and diaspora and that help us comprehend how Aub understood his role as a writer, we shall go on to analyze his work *San Juan* to determine why this great Spanish writer chose as traveling companions the stateless Jews, whose fate had nothing to do with the Spanish Civil War.

Spanish Republican Exile and Jewish Diaspora

The terms *exile* and *diaspora* refer to different phenomena, although not entirely disconnected. The first one alludes to the condition of a person or a collective that is expelled from their place of residence and cannot return to it because of external reasons. The second one refers to the dispersion of a community or its members in different places who, despite their spread, do not lose the link with their origin.

There are countless experiences of exiles throughout history and each of them responds to very particular circumstances. In this reflection, we shall focus on what has been defined as the Spanish Republican exile, which originated from the coup led by Francisco Franco in 1936. The military uprising led to a three-year war that ended with the establishment of a dictatorship and the expulsion of many Republicans. Mexico provided refuge for thousands of these exiles, among whom was Max Aub, who arrived in 1942.

The term *diaspora* also refers to different collective experiences. In this chapter, we shall focus on what is known as the Jewish diaspora.[4] During the first century, the

---

[3] "*San Juan* representa todavía la idea que tengo de la literatura de mi tiempo; no pasa ni puede pasar de ser crónica y denuncia."
[4] In the history of the Jewish people two exiles should be specially recalled: the one that is known as Babylonian exile in the late sixth century BCE, and the Roman exile in the first century CE, which lasted until the creation of the current State of Israel. The term *diaspora* generally refers to the latter.

Romans quelled the Jewish rebellion in Palestine, destroyed the Second Temple, and expelled the Jews, beginning what the Hebrew tradition knows as *galut*:

> The Jews gave an expiatory explanation for their segregation and suffering, relating them to their unique position as the chosen people. As a result of this new interpretation, they shifted the centers of authority: from the political-religious structures (of their life as a nation in their State before exile) to the study of the scriptures and the adaptation of the written laws (in order to rule a nation that lived in exile). (Pilatowsky 2008: 59)

This adaptation to life in exile has specific characteristics and elements and has had—and still has—many interesting ways of expressing itself. Now we shall describe some of these elements, as they are related (generally) to Aub's conception of his own life and experiences and (specifically) to his play *San Juan*.

Elements of the Jewish Diaspora Reflected in Aub's Work

The policies implemented by Western governments in the late eighteenth and early nineteenth centuries under the directive of achieving equality for all citizens dismantled the areas where the Jews were confined and sought to assimilate them into society. However, they did not focus on changing the prevailing measures of exclusion in Christian society. This supposed emancipation did not achieve its objective and, rather, generated a rejection that resorted to a biological imaginary. The concept of *race* replaced that of *faith* and modern antisemitism took the place of medieval anti-Judaism.

The transition from medieval anti-Judaism to modern antisemitism did not allow religious conversion to achieve true integration. The discrimination against converts and their descendants continued. The reason the Nazis murdered Christians, agnostics, and atheists was that their grandparents had been Jews: according to racial laws this condition—Judaism—was transmitted by blood. In the case of Jews who had renounced their faith and who sought to assimilate into Christian society, there was an ambivalent relationship with respect to Judaism as they sought to erase its traces and, at the same time, recognized that they were not fully accepted. Aub's parents were in this situation, as they tried to assimilate completely, but failed.

Another aspect that characterized Jewish diaspora since the Enlightenment was the rise of Orthodox Judaism. The change in religious practices that it fostered with the aim of facing massive conversion to Christianity focused on the radicalization of differentiating elements such as clothing. Access to unauthorized press and literature was restricted by the religious authorities, and there was a prohibition of social exchanges with the Christian majority as well. Along the same lines, marriage with non-Jews was condemned and the norms for conversion to Judaism were hardened. The ascription to a community where its members' lives were regulated—as the Orthodox communities did and still do—implied exclusion of those who were not willing to participate. Aub considered this demand a form of exclusion as reprehensible as any other.

Another solution found by the Jewish collective to the paradoxical situation posed by the breakdown of their traditional ways was the adoption of nationalism. There were different expressions of this nationalism; the one that finally prevailed was the one that identified the land of the current State of Israel as the place for the concentration of the Jewish diaspora.

The resignification of the text is one of the most important elements of the Jewish diaspora. George Steiner describes the condition of the diasporic people:

> On the other hand, assuredly, writing has been the indestructible guarantor, the "underwriter," of the identity of the Jew: across the frontiers of his harrying, across the centuries, across the languages of which he has been a forced borrower and frequent master. Like a snail, his antennae towards menace, the Jew has carried the house of the text on his back. What other domicile has been allowed him? (Steiner 1985: 7–8)

We can find examples of diasporic Jews—who, as Steiner describes them, carry their house of text on their back—in all forms of knowledge, in the different expressions of art, and in the diversity of political reflections.

What Steiner argues is that in the diasporic experience the relationship with the text acquired very particular characteristics among which prevailed "the mystique of fidelity to the written word, the reverence bestowed on its expositors and transmitters" (Steiner 1985: 17). According to this author—who also assumed his citizenship within this territory—in the transition to modernity contents were secularized, but the devotion to the truth was not lost, nor was the admiration for beauty or the demand for justice:

> It is these which have made so many Jewish men and, more recently, women most native to modern intelligence. It is these that have generated the provocative pre-eminence of the Jew in modernity, be it humanistic or scientific. The "bookish" genius of Marx and of Freud, of Wittgenstein and of Lévi-Strauss, is a secular deployment of the long schooling in abstract, speculative commentary and clerkship in the exegetic legacy. (Steiner 1985)

Many of these figures abandoned the Jewish religion or even declared themselves atheists, critical of all forms of exclusive communitarianism. They distanced themselves from Jewish centers and did not identify with Zionism; in search of inclusive universality, they clung to the text with a devotion that did not admit concessions. In this territory, we can perfectly locate Max Aub, who dedicated his life to writing, where he always embraced truth, beauty, and justice as his highest values.

Max Aub's Biographical Note

Max Aub was born in Paris on June 2, 1903. His father, Frederick William Aub Marx, came from Bavaria and his mother, Susana Mohenwitz, was born in France, but her family was of Saxon origin. Both his parents had Jewish origins, but they had already separated from religion and raised Max in agnosticism. During the first years of his life, "he faced for the first time the bitter xenophobic insults of *sales juifs!* which he would never forget" (Meyer 2007: 11). His family moved to Spain in 1914 for his father's business. From a young age, Aub learned German and French, and very soon also Spanish.

In 1920 he finished high school, a significant period for him since when asked about his nationality, he always replied: "one is from where one studies high school" (Meyer 2007: 233).[5] This statement can be understood as a recognition of the determining factor that his adolescent experience was, but it is also a questioning of what the great nationalistic ideals mean. For Aub, it is only a circumstantial element that determines his identification as a Spaniard.

He joined the Partido Socialista Obrero Español (PSOE, Spanish Socialist Workers' Party) in 1928; throughout his life, he considered himself a socialist and identified with democratic Marxism. From 1936 to 1937 he was sent to France as cultural attaché of the Spanish Embassy. After the coup of 1936 he had to leave Spain and was interned in various concentration camps and prisons in France and Algeria until 1942 when he got his release and was welcomed by the Mexican government; the play *San Juan* refers to this moment in his life. Throughout his life, he visited many countries, where he was invited to give courses and lectures; we shall highlight only two of them that are related to our subject: he traveled to Israel in 1966 and to Spain in 1969 and 1972. He died in Mexico City, shortly after his last trip to Spain, on July 22, 1972.

Max Aub's Position toward Exclusive Identifications

Any attempt to ascribe to Aub a religious, national, or cultural tradition ends up reproducing the complexity and even inappropriateness of this task. To begin with, his name is included in the list of Spanish Republican exiles that arrived in Mexico; however, when reading his reflections on this experience, this identification becomes questionable.[6] The Mexican imaginary also includes him, since, in 1956, he received citizenship; however, this ascription is also questioned by him. Some of the scholars who address his personality identify him as Jewish because of his ancestry, but, at the same time, point out that he did not receive any religious education and that he

---

[5] "Se es de donde se hace el bachillerato."
[6] "It is undeniable that many exiles lived in exile as a sacrifice for the Republic, hoping that one day it could yield results in republican restoration. A few, like María Zambrano or Max Aub, however, thought that with exile, a way of understanding the State was closed and another opened, one that had nothing to do with the past" (Mate 2019). Translation is mine.

remained on the margins of the community life and did not identify himself with Zionism. Aub himself, in his diaries, alludes to what it meant to have been left out of identity classifications and how writing gave him the strength to face this situation:

> What harm has it not done to me, in our closed world, not belonging anywhere! Being named as I am named, with a first and last name that can be from one country or another [...] In these hours of closed nationalism, being born in Paris and being Spanish, having a Spanish father born in Germany, a Parisian mother but also of German origin and with a Slavic last name, and speaking with that French accent that tears my Spanish apart, what harm has it not done to me! The agnosticism of my parents—freethinkers—in a Catholic country like Spain, or their Jewish ancestry in an anti-Semitic country like France, what annoyances, what humiliations has it not caused me! What a shame! I have drawn some of my strength to fight against so much ignominy. (Meyer 2007: 19)[7]

In this passage, it can be seen how this condition of not belonging anywhere pushed him to exclusion and even caused him harm. The only place where he found refuge was the text.

Later on, we shall return to Aub's relationship with writing and how, for him, it represented a place of identification; but first, and in order to understand what he describes as the damage of not belonging anywhere, we shall observe his considerations on his identification with the Jewish, the Spanish, and the Mexican. Regarding his relationship with Judaism, Aub makes the following reflection after returning from a trip to Israel in 1966:

> I thought I was somewhat Jewish, not because of the blood (which, poor thing, what does it know about that?), but because of my ancestors' religion—my parents did not have it—and I came here with the idea of resenting something, I don't know what, of facing myself. And there was nothing. I have nothing to do with these people more than with others, as I have nothing to do with the Germans, or the Poles, or the Japanese, or the Argentinians. My ties are with the Mexicans, the Spaniards, the French and, perhaps a little, with the English. Perhaps more with the Spaniards, but maybe only with those of my time. I am not Jewish at all.

---

[7] "¡Qué daño no me ha hecho, en nuestro mundo cerrado, no ser de ninguna parte! El llamarme como me llamo, con nombre y apellido que lo mismo pueden ser de un país que de otro. [...] En estas horas de nacionalismo cerrado, el haber nacido en París y ser español, tener padre español nacido en Alemania, madre parisina, pero de origen también alemán y de apellido eslavo, y hablar con ese acento francés que desgarra mi castellano ¡qué daño no me ha hecho! El agnosticismo de mis padres—librepensadores—, en un país católico como España, o su prosapia judía en un país antisemita como Francia ¡qué disgustos, qué humillaciones no me ha acarreado! ¡Qué vergüenza! Algo de mi fuerza—de mis fuerzas—, he sacado para luchar contra la ignominia."

I am sorry, but I cannot cry, they are strangers to me, as much or more than the Norwegians or the Turks. (Meyer 2007: 29)[8]

This consideration clears any doubt: he did not feel any particular closeness to the Israelis, neither based on the religion of his ancestors, nor from a definition of biological nature, nor in relation to the national element. What is interesting to highlight here is his recognition of a concern that required clarification, since he comments that he believed he was somewhat Jewish. The confession of a need to examine his emotional identifications with respect to the Jewish element, as expressed in his account, refers to the existence of something that was present in him and that he identified as Jewish and of what he could finally get rid of after the trip. It is difficult to decipher what that something meant. What Aub wrote in other texts leads us to suppose that what aroused that feeling was the antisemitism he suffered throughout his life.

Regarding nationalism, a mention should be made in relation to a conference he gave in December 1963 in the Sociedad de Cultura Española, "De la literatura de nuestros días y de la española en particular" (On Contemporary Literature and on Spanish Literature in Particular) (1964: 262-72), where he clearly spoke out against it. In it, he questioned any national appropriation of literature based on the language in which it was written:

> Perhaps tomorrow, for the sake of common markets, languages will again depend on themselves and not on geography—that is, on nationalism. There will be no reason to speak of Belgian or Swiss literature if in fact there is no longer, economically, with their borders, Belgium or Switzerland. And the English will be what is spoken in English, and the Spanish what is spoken in Spanish. It is my long-term hope against nationalism, a cancer that still gnaws—day and night— our world. (Meyer 2007: 735-44)[9]

To reinforce this statement, another of Aub's remarks regarding Spanish nationalism can be read:

---

[8] "Creí tener algo de judío, no por la sangre (que, pobrecita, ¿qué sabe de eso?), sino por la religión de mis antepasados—mis padres no la tuvieron—, y vine aquí con la idea de que iba a resentir algo, no sé qué, que me *iba* a enfrentar conmigo mismo. Y no hubo nada. No tengo que ver con estas gentes que no sea lo mismo que con los demás, como nada tengo que ver con los alemanes, ni con los polacos, ni con los japoneses, ni con los argentinos. Mis ligazones son con los mexicanos, los españoles, los franceses y, algo tal vez, con los ingleses. Tal vez más con los españoles, pero sólo quizá con los de mi tiempo. No tengo nada de judío. Lo siento, pero no puedo llorar, me son extraños, tanto o más que los noruegos o los turcos."

[9] "Tal vez mañana, por mor de los mercados comunes, los idiomas dependerán otra vez de sí y no de la geografía—es decir, del nacionalismo—. No habrá razón de hablar de literatura belga o suiza si de hecho dejan de ser, económicamente, con fronteras, Bélgica o Suiza. Y lo inglés será lo hablado en inglés; y lo español será lo hablado en español. Es mi esperanza, para dentro de mucho tiempo, en contra del nacionalismo, cáncer que roe—de día y de noche—, todavía nuestro mundo."

We Spaniards are extraordinary because a Genoese Jew discovered America, because a German king founded the empire, because thanks to an English general we resisted Napoleon, because with the help of multicolored communists and anarchists of all kinds during three years we fought other Spaniards, helped by uniformed Germans and Italians. (Meyer 2007: 849)[10]

From these words, we can conclude that Aub did not conceive of himself as a Spanish writer in the nationalistic sense of this term. Although he recognized that his language of expression was Spanish, he rejected being considered a Hispanic author.

Aub's criticism of all nationalism did not exclude the Mexican one: "the truth is that we are a handful of people with no place in the world. In Mexico, despite being Mexican, they do not consider us as such. Here we can only live in silence" (Meyer 2007).[11] Also, in the article "La cultura en México" (The Culture in Mexico) (1963), he stated: "Since the beginning (Death to the *gachupines*!), nor recognizing Spain [*sic*]. Neither Franco nor, tomorrow, whoever. The Malinche, unforgettable. Absurd at first glance. But a rationalist who wants to love Mexico must give up many things. This is the only way to preserve oneself" (Meyer 2007: 716).[12] Aub was neither Spanish, nor Jewish, nor Mexican; he was, rather, a citizen of the world who adopted a language different from his native one and used it to describe, in his writings, a culture filled with pieces of many others which he considered part of his own.

Max Aub and the Text as Territory of Permanent Residence

Aub, unlike many of the Spanish Republican exiles who arrived in Mexico, did not see this episode of his life as something that reinforced his religious or national identifications. In his writings, we find rather a critical distancing from them. The aspect of his life nurtured by this experience was his conviction that writing can be used as a tool to fight injustice and build a better world.

In a piece written in 1962 and entitled *Homenaje a los que nos han seguido* (Homage to Those Who Have Followed Us) (*Revista de la Universidad de México*, 1962), Aub presents a reflection on the link between exile and writing. What can be read there are

---

[10] "Los españoles somos extraordinarios porque un judío genovés descubrió América, porque un rey alemán fundó su imperio, porque gracias a un general inglés resistimos a Napoleón, porque con la ayuda de comunistas multicolores y anarquistas de todas clases combatimos durante tres años a otros españoles ayudados por uniformados alemanes e italianos."

[11] "La verdad es que somos un puñado de gente sin sitio en el mundo. En México, a pesar de ser mexicanos, no nos consideran como tales. Aquí no podemos vivir más que mudos."

[12] "Desde el principio (¡Mueran los gachupines!), no reconocer a España. Ni a Franco ni, el día de mañana, a quien sea. La Malinche, inolvidable. Absurdo a primera vista. Pero un racionalista que quiere amar a México debe renunciar a muchas cosas. Sólo así se salva uno." In Mexico, the term *gachupín* (plural: *gachupines*) is used to pejoratively refer to the Spaniards. Malinche is, in Mexican imaginary, the woman who helped Hernán Cortés as a translator; she was also, allegedly, his mistress.

the considerations of a man in his seventies who chooses to understand his life, and particularly his exile, from a writer's perspective:

> It is difficult to talk about the homeland when one gets old far away from it because, what is it like, even knowing how it is? There are no other images than those brought by the encouragement—or the discouragement—of others' words. They recount and they do not end. Without great variations, optimistic and non-optimistic ones can only agree that the only visible thing of the old seed of freedom that, in its day—by the force of things—we incarnate are students and writers. Too much honor for those of us who only know how to write. (Meyer 2007: 656-7)[13]

Aub considered himself a member of a group that he identified as "a writers' fraternity." While in exile he learned to appreciate this fraternity and the people he considered its members, he thought of the writers of yesteryear as his masters and guides, and the ones to come were valuable for him because they represented a hope for the present and the future of literature, which was the path Aub saw to escape as established and exclusive identifications, including that imposed on him by Franco's dictatorship:

> Even if we do not want to, we are all one. From others we come to others. We are always children of the best. If you scratch my bark, you will find the sap of Cervantes, Quevedo, Galdós, and even the humors—good or bad—of Ortega, and those of Tolstoy and Martin du Gard. (And in the worst poet those of Bécquer, Rubén, Juan Ramón, without considering Gil Vicente, Garcilaso, Lope, Quevedo or Jorge Manrique.)
>
> They wanted to rip us out of Spain, without success. There, more alive than ever, Antonio Machado, Federico García Lorca, Miguel Hernández and the living that I name, in the blood of the new ones. (Meyer 2007: 657)[14]

This account gives us examples of the members of that writers' fraternity which Aub considered so important. Also, in Aub's work, it is possible to find literary analyses that allow us to understand more clearly the value he placed on writing. We shall address just two very illustrative examples of his analyses: the literature of Franz Kafka (1883-1924) and that of Heinrich Heine (1797-1856).

---

[13] "Es difícil hablar de su patria cuando uno se hace viejo lejos de ella, porque ¿cómo es, aun sabiendo cómo está? No hay más imágenes que las traídas por el aliento—o el desaliento—, de las palabras ajenas. Cuentan y no acaban. Sin grandes variaciones optimistas y los que no lo son coinciden en que lo único visible de la vieja semilla de la libertad que, en su día—por la fuerza de las cosas—, encarnamos, son estudiantes y escritores. Demasiada honra para los que sólo sabemos escribir."

[14] "Aunque no queramos, todos somos unos. De otros venimos a otros. Siempre somos hijos de los mejores. Si rascáis mi corteza hallaréis la savia de Cervantes, de Quevedo, de Galdós, y aun los humores—buenos y malos—de Ortega, y los de Tolstoi y los de Martín du Gard. (Y en los del peor poeta, los de Bécquer, Rubén, Juan Ramón por no traer a cuenta y cuento de Gil Vicente, a Garcilaso, a Lope, a Quevedo o a Jorge Manrique). Quisieron arrancarnos de cuajo de España, sin lograrlo. Allí más vivos que nunca, Antonio Machado, Federico García Lorca, Miguel Hernández y los vivos que nombro, en la sangre de los nuevos."

Kafka

Aub's reflections on Kafka's life and work are centered on two aspects with which he identifies: his distancing of nationalist and religious affiliations and the emancipatory function of writing. In 1948, he wrote a sequence of three articles in which he presented, in a very synthetic way, his analysis of the author's literature. In "El proceso de Franz Kafka" (Franz Kafka's Process, *Últimas noticias*, March 9, 1948), he comments on the staging of a theater adaptation of *The Process*. After addressing the adaptation, he goes on to analyze the psychology of the writer: "Kafka spent his painful life accusing himself of the 'crime of being born'. *The Process* is nothing more than this trial. His hero ignores the reason for the persecution to which he is subjected by beings that are both real and ghostly" (Meyer 2007: 290).[15] Aub interprets the novel as the expression of the feeling that accompanied the author throughout his life. The representation of an absurdity where a judicial process does not require the concrete specification of the crime alludes to Kafka's personal condition but acquires its universal literary value when he describes the way in which society operates: "Judges have been the subject of bloody ridicule since the administration is the administration, with its bureaucracy and its mountains of files. But Kafka's bitter irony has gone further: he has completely dehumanized them" (Meyer 2007: 291).[16]

In the second article of this series, "Drama de nuestro tiempo" (Drama of Our Time, *Últimas noticias*, March 10, 1948), he continues with his reflection on *The Process*, and among other things he affirms that: "Kafka always fled from himself, even from his own body, from health to illness. Life was for him 'a perpetual deviation that does not even allow one knowing it is deviating'" (Meyer 2007: 292).[17] There is a clear allusion to the writer's tuberculosis, but Aub's description goes beyond that. He talks about Kafka's position on life in general: "only the author's work and life make the trance clear: his hero's punishment is due, above all, to his loneliness" (Meyer 2007).[18]

In the last article of the series, *El sacrificio de Abraham* (Abraham's Sacrifice, *Últimas noticias*, March 12, 1948), Aub resorts to Kafka's diary to explain the link between the author and his work:

> "I assumed["]—writes Kafka—["]my time's denial . . . I have no right to fight it but, in a certain way, I represent it." Crucified between Christianity and Judaism he only glimpses the possibility of saving himself by "creating himself." "It was

---

[15] "Kafka pasó su dolorosa vida acusándose del 'delito de haber nacido'. *El proceso* no es otra cosa que este juicio. Su héroe ignora el porqué de la persecución de la cual es objeto por seres a la vez reales y fantasmagóricos."
[16] "Los jueces han sido motivo de burlas sangrientas desde que la administración es la administración, con su burocracia y sus montañas de expedientes. Pero la amarguísima ironía de Kafka ha ido más lejos: los ha deshumanizado por completo."
[17] "Kafka huyó siempre de sí mismo, aun de su propio cuerpo, de la salud a la enfermedad. La vida fue para él 'una perpetua desviación que no permite siquiera saber que se desvía.'"
[18] "Sólo la obra, y la vida del autor, deja el trance claro: el castigo de su héroe se debe, ante todo, a su soledad."

not laziness, ill will, or clumsiness that led me to fail in everything: family life, friendship, marriage, profession, literature, but the absence of soil, of air, of law." (Meyer 2007: 293)[19]

Aub interprets Kafka's work as the paradoxical expression of the messianic feeling of diasporic Judaism where, without soil, air, and law, writing becomes the last resort to dream of a better world. In that sense he quotes the Czech writer: "'Writing is praying'—he even said 'God does not want me to write'" (Meyer 2007: 294).[20] This is how we can understand Kafka's determination to represent his time's negative aspect, despite feeling like a failure, since, according to Aub: "he still harbored a messianic hope, the same one abandoned, in the negative sense and that will end up drowning them, by the existentialists greatly influenced by him" (Meyer 2007: 293).[21]

Heine

Heine was an author with whom Aub identified in a particular sense. In an article published in 1956, *Notas acerca de Enrique Heine: Homenaje a Enrique Heine* (Notes about Heinrich Heine: Homage to Heinrich Heine, *Novedades*, May 6, 1956), Aub recovers some notes he had taken at a conference that he gave that same year, along with María Douglas, on February 17 at an event commemorating the poet's centenary. In a few lines he affirms that: "the greatness of Heine, like that of all important writers, lies on his power of rebellion. He rebelled against his times' society, against his country, against the one that sheltered him, against God" (Meyer 2007: 550).[22] In Heine, Aub saw an author who managed to touch his readers regardless of borders, languages, or beliefs, precisely because he did not feel attached to any of these. "Heine was always a foreigner because he never felt his feet step on solid ground. He always had the sensation of being in the air. Perhaps that is why his poetry is so winged, so out of nowhere, so universal, so well understood by everyone" (Meyer 2007: 546).[23]

Heine was born in Germany, into a Jewish family. He converted to Christianity in order to survive in a very inhospitable environment for the Jews. Aub emphasizes

---

[19] "'Asumí[']—escribe Kafka—[']la negación de mi tiempo . . . no tengo derecho a combatirlo, pero, en cierta manera, lo represento.' Crucificado entre el cristianismo y el judaísmo sólo vislumbró la posibilidad de salvarse 'creándose'. 'No fueron la pereza, ni la mala voluntad, ni la torpeza las que me llevaron a fracasar, en toda cosa: vida de familia, amistad, matrimonio, profesión, literatura, pero sí la ausencia de suelo, de aire, de ley.'"
[20] "'Escribir es rezar'—llegó a decir 'Dios no quiere que escriba.'"
[21] "Abrigaba todavía una esperanza mesiánica, en la misma que han abandonado, en el plan negativo, que acabará por ahogarlos, los existencialistas, en quien tanto ha influido."
[22] "La grandeza de Heine, como la de todos los escritores que cuentan, depende de su potencia de rebeldía. Se rebeló contra la sociedad de su tiempo, contra su país, contra el que lo albergó, contra Dios."
[23] "Heine fue siempre extranjero porque nunca sintió que sus pies pisaran tierra firme. Siempre tuvo la sensación de estar en el aire. Tal vez por eso su poesía es tan alada, tan de ninguna parte, tan universal, tan bien comprendida por todos."

this motivation when he states that: "he wanted to be a Protestant and married in the Catholic Church. Surely he wanted to 'alternate', to blend together with indifferent people, perhaps to live unnoticed as was the dark and deep desire of so many Israelites" (Meyer 2007).[24] According to Aub, Heine's conversion did not have a religious inspiration and it did not mean an approach to God in any of his expressions: "It is not surprising that Heine never took well-established religions seriously; he demonstrated it with his conversion to Protestantism, with his Catholic marriage without a new baptism. He died as he lived, skeptical, despite those who want to suppose that his *Hebrew melodies* represent a return to his family's religion" (Meyer 2007: 546–7). [25]

In the opinion of Aub, Heine exemplifies the condition of the Jews who sought, unsuccessfully, to break away from their heritage, but without really wanting to assimilate into Christian society. In another article ("Heine," *Excelsior*, July 8, 1956) Aub rejects the attempts to Judaize Heine by identifying his claims for social justice as a characteristic of the Jewish tradition present in him. He states:

> "War against injustice, reigning stupidity and evil," he wrote to Inmermann, at the beginning of his literary life. A background of this magnitude is enough to take on the rest of humanity, even without being Jew.
>
> Social justice, as promotion of the literary, may be Hebrew leaven, although, if it were, it would be necessary to recognize that the push is not its, but that of its persecutions. Heine writes to Moser, before leaving the country, that the reason he was leaving was "less the desire to wander the world, than the martyrdom of my personal situation—for example, Jewishness is not going away, no matter how much I wash myself." (Meyer 2007: 565)[26]

Aub identifies with Heine for many reasons: for his posture toward religion, his questioning of nationalism, his fight against injustices, and, above all, his quest to find in writing the art that allows people to continue longing for coexistence exempt from exclusions or exiles.

---

[24] "Quiso ser protestante y se casó por la Iglesia católica. Seguramente quería 'alternar', confundirse con gente indiferente, tal vez vivir inadvertido como fue el oscuro y profundo deseo de tantos israelitas."

[25] "No es de extrañar que Heine no tomara nunca en serio las religiones bien ordenadas; lo demostró con su conversión al protestantismo, con su matrimonio católico sin otro nuevo bautismo. Murió como vivió, escéptico, a pesar de los que quieren suponer que sus *Melodías hebreas* representan una vuelta a la religión familiar."

[26] "'Guerra a la injusticia, a la estupidez reinante y al mal', escribía a Inmermann, al principio de su vida literaria. Un bagaje de esta envergadura es suficiente para echarse encima al resto de la humanidad, aun no siendo judío. La justicia social, como fomento de lo literario, tal vez sea levadura hebrea, aunque, si así fuera, habría que reconocer que el empuje no es suyo, sino de sus perseguidores. Heine escribe a Moser, antes de expatriarse, que lo que le echaban eran 'menos las ganas de vagar por el mundo que el martirio de mi situación personal–por ejemplo, lo judío que no se me quita por mucho que me lave.'"

San Juan

Based on the analysis done to this point, a hypothesis can be ventured regarding Aub's motives to write *San Juan*, a tragedy where he attempts to talk about his exile as a Spanish Republican by referring to the experience of the Jewish exiles fleeing Nazism. We can affirm that the play *San Juan* reflects the diasporic experience more than the political exile. Throughout this text, we have highlighted Aub's distancing from identity elements that were important for other Spanish Republican exiles, such as religion, nation, language, or political ideologies. With his writing, he managed to recreate the situation of the Jews, who no longer had a place to return to, and who could only hope for a better world, one where limitations in the national borders did not end up exterminating them.

We can thus answer the question with which we opened this text: why are *San Juan*'s characters Jews and not Spanish Republicans? As we mentioned at the beginning, this tragedy, written in 1943, short after Aub arrived in Mexico, is set on a ship where a group of Jews travels, while fleeing the Nazis, searching for a place of refuge. This fiction must be read as the literary elaboration of a personal experience. Aub himself commented on the matter:

> As for what prompted me to write this tragedy—in addition to considering it to some extent representative of one of the phases of our times' drama—was simply the reading of the event briefly recounted in a newspaper. I had the set before me in the hold of "Sidi Aicha," the ship in which the Vichy France deported me to the Sahara. (Aub 1998: 245)[27]

Although this work is part of the author's writings on the vicissitudes of the Spanish Civil War, we find in it a situation that could be understood as alien to this historical event, for the central character's exile is not related to Franco's coup. The only way to understand why the author decided to express his personal exile with a fiction where the characters were Jews is by understanding that he identified himself with them, and not with the Spanish Republicans. In this sense, it is important to note that the Spanish war is mentioned in the play only in an incidental way. In the first act we read:

> GUEDEL: Is there any news?
> RABBI: Nothing. Nothing. The Captain has not returned.
> ABRAHAM: Send fifty dollars' worth of telegrams! Fifty dollars' worth of herring would be better!
> GUEDEL: What does the radio say?
> RABBI: The Spanish republicans have started an offensive by the Ebro.
> (Aub 1998: 139)[28]

---

[27] "En cuanto a lo que me motivó a escribir esta tragedia—a más de considerarla hasta cierto punto representativa de una de las fases del drama de nuestro tiempo—, fue sencillamente la lectura del suceso escuetamente contado en un periódico. El decorado lo tuve ante mí en la bodega del 'Sidi Aicha', barco en el cual los franceses de Vichy me deportaron al Sahara."

[28] "GUEDEL: ¿Hay noticias? RABINO: Nada. Nada. El Capitán no ha vuelto. ABRAHÁM: ¡Ponga usted cincuenta dólares de telegramas! ¡Más valdrían cincuenta dólares de arenques! GUEDEL: ¿Qué dice la radio? RABINO: Los republicanos españoles han empezado una ofensiva por el Ebro."

The allusion to this historical event, which the author put in the words of a rabbi, is not in line with the story and, also, has no follow-up in it. The plot focuses, rather, on the tragic condition of the Jewish exiles. Aub recognized that the tragedy is inspired by the experience of his own exile and asylum search, so we can say that he felt closer to these Jews than to his Spanish compatriots, although without ceasing to refer to this aspect of his identity.

Aub's identification with the Jewish condition is also reflected in another dialogue in the play when one of the characters rebukes a young communist with the following words: "Stop right now. You are not here as a communist, but because of your sad ancestry. You will say: 'what does that have to do with it?' You are blind! Are you not here? No! You live in a fantasy world. Do you know what you are? Some disgusting idealists" (Aub 1998: 136).[29] In this passage, we see how the author makes a clear difference between those who were exiled for their political ideas and positions and the Jews, who were persecuted only for being Jews. It does not cease to surprise that in his literary expression he highlights the Jewish condition over political factors, as he himself was exiled for being a Republican.

Unlike Spanish Republican exiles, not all the Jews fleeing Nazism had participated in politics; many had not fought in a war, nor were all persecuted for their ideas or actions, but for their condition. And for the same reason—their condition—they were rejected in most countries where they asked for refuge. In his play *San Juan*, Aub reproduces that feeling of powerlessness and injustice. One of the characters comments:

> BERNHEIM: What a danger we represent to humanity! Huh? What a danger to America! What a danger to England! What a danger to Turkey! Six accountants, one-hundred-forty merchants, fifty-three lawyers, two rabbis, twenty farmers, one-hundred odd shop assistants, three stage directors, six journalists, two-hundred old men and women who are totally wiped out, thirty-five children . . . ! Is Brazil not big enough? Is there no room in Palestine anymore? What a danger are these fugitives of the Nazis! (Aub 1998: 147)[30]

This quote sums up everything that has been said so far about the Jewish condition. Here can be seen how characters with such different professions come together because of their stateless situation and how their fate is not defined. There is a banker, representing the Jewish bourgeoisie, a communist militant, representing the proletarian

---

[29] "Para la burra. No estás aquí por comunista, sino por tu triste ascendencia. Dirás: '¿qué tiene que ver?' ¡Oh, ciego! ¿No estás aquí? ¡No! Vives en las nubes. ¿Sabéis lo que sois? Unos asquerosos idealistas."

[30] "BERNHEIM: ¡Qué peligro representamos para la humanidad! ¿Eh? ¡Qué peligro para América! ¡Qué peligro para Inglaterra! ¡Qué peligro para Turquía! ¡Seis contables, ciento cuarenta comerciantes, cincuenta y tres abogados, dos rabinos, veinte agricultores, ciento y pico dependientes de comercio, tres directores de escena, seis periodistas, doscientos viejos y viejas que ya no pueden con su alma, treinta y cinco niños . . . ! ¿Es que el Brasil no es bastante grande? ¿Ya no cabe nadie en Palestina? ¡Qué peligro estos huidos de los nazis!"

sector and the social fighters, a rabbi, representing the religious element; Palestine is also mentioned, a reference to the aspirations of Jewish nationalism. Hopelessness unifies the passengers of the *San Juan*, as expressed by one of them:

> CARLOS: What you want are children, of course, children. You are in the age. For what? So that they flee, like us, from town to town, from hour to year, and that not only the right hand is ashamed of the left one, but the right of the right. Are you not enough? You want more and more. As long as I live, no. (Aub 1998)[31]

Nevertheless, a character who is not present on this ship, where despair is prevalent, is the writer. As we were able to identify in his analyses of Kafka and Heine—two diasporic Jews—there is always a possibility of hope, even in the most extreme conditions. In this sense, the tragedy *San Juan* is a work, on the one hand, where the extreme condition of the Jews persecuted by the Nazis is represented and, on the other, where Aub places a possibility of hope, for it denounces the evil and seeks to fight against it.

Conclusions

Max Aub was a writer whose talent allowed him to express himself in all literary genres: novels, plays, poems, and essays. His commitment to justice represented an incorruptible search for truth; this is what he identified as the mission of the writer. Throughout his life, he distanced himself from nationalistic claims over languages and from any religious expression.

The historical and personal circumstances that he experienced made him a Spanish Republican who, along with thousands of his comrades, ended up settling in Mexico, where he lived most of his life. What was unique about his experience, what distinguished him from most Spanish writers and intellectuals who suffered exile, was the factor of his Jewish diasporic condition. This is how it can be explained why in his work *San Juan*, written during the Spanish Civil War and where he sought to transmit his experiences of this historic event, he reproduced the situation of a handful of Jews fleeing Nazism, which was not related to what happened in the Iberian country.

In his way of understanding the Jewish condition as a radical expression of exile, Aub, using Steiner's expression, understood himself as "a snail, his antennae towards menace" (1985: 7–8). With that safeconduct he went from a circumstantial exile to the diasporic condition, where he could finally obtain universal citizenship, the one granted only to the guardians of the text.

---

[31] "CARLOS. Lo que quieres son hijos, claro, hijos. Estás en la edad. ¿Para qué? Para que vayan huyendo, como nosotros, de pueblo en pueblo, de hora en año, y que no solamente se avergüence la mano derecha de la izquierda, sino la derecha de la derecha. ¿No te basta contigo? Quieres más, más . . . Mientras yo viva, no."

References

Aub, M. (1964), "De la literatura de nuestros días y de la española en particular," *Cuadernos Americanos*, 23 (3): 262–72.

Aub, M. (1998), *San Juan*, ed. M. Aznar Soler, Madrid: Pretextos.

Mate, R. (2019), "Un exilio poco republicano," *El Periódico*, 7 May. Available online: https://www.elperiodico.com/es/opinion/20190507/articulo-opinion-reyes-mate-un-exilio-poco-republicano-guerra-civil-7442895 (accessed January 10, 2021).

Meyer, E. (2007), *Los tiempos mexicanos de Max Aub. Legado periodístico (1943–1972)*, Valencia: FCE.

Pilatowsky, M. (2008), *La autoridad del exilio: una aproximación al pensamiento de Cohen, Kafka, Rosenzweig y Buber*, México: UNAM.

Steiner, G. (1985), "Our Homeland, the Text," *Salmagundi*, 66: 4–25.

5

The Holy War on Fascism

Deborah A. Green

As a Yiddish translator, I have studied Yiddish correspondence and memoirs for decades, particularly those written by Jewish volunteers in the International Brigades. As a result, I developed a broad understanding of the internationalist spirit, the different motivations, as well as the underlying circumstances, that inspired Jewish participation in the Spanish Civil War. Historical research also enriched my work on this topic (Diamant 1967; Zaagsma 2017). The translations contained herein serve to further enhance the history of the Jewish volunteers by providing the imaginaries within which internationalists produced their personal narratives.

The letters reveal the values these Jewish volunteers believed in and fought for and allow a glimpse into their "imaginaries." Sygmunt Stein, whom I reference herein, argues that some of these letters were the product of the Comintern propaganda machine; that they intentionally distort or manipulate the Jewish imaginary, thus creating a misunderstanding of the history of the Jewish volunteers in the Spanish Civil War.

Some of these letters may have been faked but based on my translations of letters and memoirs of Jews who fought in the Spanish Civil War as well as my translations of other Yiddish letters and memoirs that predated the Spanish War, I do not believe that such alleged manipulation created a false narrative for the Jewish internationals. They did not go to Spain because they believed the propaganda; the propaganda merely reinforced that which they already believed: fascism must be destroyed.

Translation Notes

A word-for-word translation of the Yiddish letters contained in this chapter would be incomprehensible to the non-Yiddish-speaking reader because their true meaning can only be understood within the cultural context, i.e., pre-1939 Europe. The text is therefore translated to make the concepts understandable to the modern reader because "[w]hen in doubt, translators are well advised to tilt to the target audience and its expectations, not to the source text" (Lefevere 1992: 19).

All translations contained herein are my own.

The letters included in this chapter are confessional writings coming from the writers' hearts; as they say in Yiddish, they add the "raisin" to the scholarly research. Where known, I have included the "where" and "when" these letters were written, but occasionally, even the writer's name is unknown. I have included information about these people wherever possible, but I believe what they said was more important than who they were. And what they all said was that they were in Spain to fight fascism because they understood what fascism would mean to them as Jews.[1]

Why Spain?

The 1492 Edict of Expulsion banished Jews from Spain unless they converted to Catholicism. Converts suspected of heresy were tortured, then burned at the stake. Despite the ill-treatment of their ancestors, one-fourth of the 40,000 International Brigade volunteers who came to Spain's aid were Jewish (Sugarman 2016). Gerben Zaagsma's book, *Jewish Volunteers, the International Brigades and the Spanish Civil War* (2017), focuses on French, pre–Second World War leftist Jewish newspapers. He writes that the Jewish volunteers came to Spain to prove that they were not cowards: "Representation on Jewish volunteers in *Naye Prese* until December 1937 were characterized by an emphasis on Jewish heroism and by suggestions, both implicit and explicit, of how it disproved stereotypes and accusations of Jewish cowardice" (78). But I found little emphasis on that issue in the referenced letters; the emphasis was always on the need to eradicate fascism and antisemitism.

To encourage Jews fighting in Spain and the Jewish masses throughout the world who supported them, Yiddish and International Brigade newspapers often printed their correspondence. Some of those letters were beautifully expressed in prose and metaphor which gives rise to the following question: was the language used that of a simple worker or were they the words of a communist propaganda department? Sygmunt Stein, a disillusioned Soviet propagandist, believed the latter (Stein 1961: 81). But the real issue is: why did these Jewish volunteers want to fight for Spain? The translated documents and letters allow these people to speak for themselves.[2]

The Naftali Botwin Company

The Naftali Botwin Company, the first Jewish company to be led by a Jewish commander in centuries, issued a collective manifesto to Jews around the world in July 1938. The following prescient excerpt unequivocally answers the question as to why Jews fought in Spain on behalf of the Spanish Republic:

---

[1] For more such letters, visit the translator's website at https://jewsfightingfascism.com/.
[2] For reasons of space, the full excerpts are unable to be included in this chapter. For those interested, fuller excerpts and a link to the original Yiddish may be found at the translator's website, op. cit.

> The battle of the Spanish people has a particular meaning for the Jewish masses. *The Jewish people know that if fascism wins in Europe it will mean our complete enslavement* [emphasis added]; the political, material, and spiritual ruin of hundreds of thousands of lives, the bondage and destruction of millions, physical eradication. Germany and Austria's treatment of their Jews is a menacing warning for all Jews. The truth was obvious to the Jewish folk-masses on the first day of the Spanish people's struggle. (Diamant 1967: 530)

Gina Medem, a communist and a reporter for the American *Morgn Dzshurnal*, the Parisian *Naye Prese*, the Kharkov *Shtern*, and other Soviet Yiddish newspapers (Diamant 1967: 303), was one of the most striking Jewish figures of her time. She appeared on every front, in every hospital, anywhere a Jewish volunteer was to be found. She supported these men tirelessly, held long conversations with them, encouraged them, and popularized their struggles in her reportage. Her articles about Jewish militiamen provided insight into the volunteers' motivation. She quoted her own pamphlet, *Los Judíos—Luchadores de la libertad* (Medem 1937), which she then translated into Yiddish, including a forward by Luigi Gallo, commissioner inspector of the International Brigades, describing the role of Jewish volunteers and why they were in Spain:

> What possessed young Jewish working men, vigorous young girls, middle-aged and elderly Jews to leave their homes in Hungary, Palestine, Poland, Bukovina and Besarabia, and travel to the heart of the Spanish Civil War?
>
> The Italian anti-fascist, Luigi Gallo, General Inspector of all International Brigades, provided a brief explanation in his forward to my pamphlet, *Los Judíos—Luchadores de la Libertad* [Jewish Freedom Fighters in Spain], (Madrid, October 1937). He described his encounter with a Jewish volunteer:
>
> "I remember as if it were yesterday, an intense, black-haired young man entered my office. It was during the early days when Jewish volunteers were first arriving at the International Brigade base in Albacete. He was good-looking, charming, and determined. He had organized a group of 15 Jewish volunteers from within the International Brigades and led them with pride through the streets of Albacete and was their spokesman.
>
> He wanted to organize Jews into an independent military unit within the International Brigades: 'We want to show the entire world what we Jews are capable of. The fascists accuse us of being cowards and parasites. We want to show the world we can fight like heroes.'
>
> I said I agreed with his feelings and political motivation. The young comrade left me, tears of joy streaming down his face, grateful for the opportunity to avenge the fascists' ugly defamation of his people.
>
> The young comrade and his 15 young men from Paris were ordered to the Madrid front, I arrived a week later. I wanted to see him again, but he had fallen while defending University City during the first days of battle. He died a hero and showed the world Jewish heroism." (Medem 1939: 7)

The man Gallo spoke of was Albert Neramivokh (identified by Zaagsma as Russian-born "Albert Nakhumi Weitz") (Zaagsma 2017: 41):

> Albert Nakhumi Weitz's anguished request answers the question initially posed: what prompted Jews of every social class and age to go to Spain? They were motivated by the opportunity to fight in a separate, Jewish military unit. I learned later that even a larger number of Jews would have joined had such a Jewish unit been created sooner. They wanted the Nazis to know whom they were fighting.
>
> These Jewish fighters represent our people, our new leadership. They do not have titles or university degrees, but they are the vanguard of the first armed opposition to fascism in history, their hatred intent on destroying international fascism in Spain. Every anti-fascist returning from Spain will find solace in the time they spent defending and fighting for the Spanish soil that cost so much blood. (Medem 1939: 7)

Ephraim Wuzek, an original member and quartermaster of the Naftali Botwin Company, describes Jewish pride when the company was formed:

> December 12, 1937 was a miserable day on the Tardienta front. The sky was filled with clouds and a cold wind was blowing. We were huddled in the command post when the telephone rang. Commander Gutman lifted the receiver and tersely responded: "Good! At your command!" Putting down the telephone, he informed us that in a few moments Comrade Mietek, the Communist Party's representative, and Comrade Gershon Dua-Bogen would be arriving. They would formally notify us of the Dombrowski Brigade's decision to convert our generic Second Company into a Jewish unit to be called the Naftali Botwin Company.
>
> The night was freezing, but the news electrified us . . . Crowded, crammed, pushing against one another—Jews, Poles, Spaniards—we all stood hunched over one another and listened as Comrade Dua-Bogen described the struggle and aims to which the members of the new Botwin Company had obligated themselves.
>
> The "Order of the Day" was read in the darkness of the trenches, establishing the Botwin Company. It explained the need for creating a Jewish military unit in Spain to prove to the world that Jews would pick up guns and sacrifice their lives for freedom, as would any other nation. It read in part:
>
> *"To honor the important role of the Jewish Brigaders in the Dombrowski Brigade and to honor the memory of the Jewish fighters who fell fighting for freedom, we confirm the establishment of the Second Company of the heroic Polish Palafox Battalion as a Jewish company* [emphasis added] *bearing the name of Naftali Botwin . . ."*
>
> Lying in the trenches for hours, covered only by our greatcoats, Marcin Shimanski and I spoke of Botwin and of our new unit, the Botwin Company. We weren't the only ones. The trenches buzzed with excitement all night; Jewish Volunteers were telling their non-Jewish comrades of Naftali Botwin's bravery, the

young Jewish communist bootmaker who sacrificed his life in the struggle for a better tomorrow. (Wuzek 1964: 11–13)

Wuzek claimed he knew the Botwin Company commander, Karol Gutman, well. Describing the last night of Gutman's life, Wuzek wrote: "The Extremadura campaign was not Commander Gutman's first battle on Spanish soil but it would be his last. What were his thoughts? Was he thinking of the honor bestowed upon him to lead a Jewish unit into battle against fascism, the sworn enemy of his people?" (Wuzek 1964: 11–13). Obviously, no one knows Gutman's last thoughts, but it is striking that Wuzek considered the Jewish aspect, not the political one, of greater concern to Gutman.

In describing a harrowing escape from a fascist patrol and separation from his unit, Wuzek recalls:

> With bullets flying over my head, I ran back toward Lerida. After running for 500 meters and still hearing gunfire, I stopped for a moment and noticed Lekhter not too far off in the distance. We were thrilled not to have fallen into fascist hands but were worried about Commissar Reger and for the guys who stayed on the truck. We also regretted that the food and clothing we were bringing to the battalion had been captured by the fascists.
>
> Disheartened, we returned to Lerida. Lekhter and I mourned the Commissar, but found both him and our battalion in Alpacat the next day. The Commissar, thinking Lekhter and I were both dead, had also been in mourning for us. Overjoyed at our deliverance, we all chanted the *goyml* [*Baruch ata Adonai, Eloheinu melech ha-olam, ha-gomel l'chayavim tovot she-g'malani kol tov* (Blessed are You, Lord our God, ruler of the world, who rewards the undeserving with goodness, and who has rewarded me with goodness)]. (Wuzek 1964: 39)

It's notable that these three "communists" were chanting a prayer thanking God for allowing them to escape a near-death situation. Wuzek again referred to Jewish religious observance when he described the Botwins' participation in the Ebro River offensive:

> It was late at night on July 25, 1938, when our Company commander summoned the section leaders and issued the final orders—when and where the Botwin Company would cross the Ebro River and what we were to do once we crossed over.
>
> The night was calm as we slowly edged closer to the river's edge. The water flowed quietly, not a rustle was heard. We contemplated our oblivious enemy, sound asleep, unaware that in a few hours we would give him the honor of a *maftir*. (Wuzek 1964: 49)

Wuzek's reference to the *maftir* required considerable knowledge of Judaism. He had to know that Tisha b'Av is a day of mourning for the destruction of both the First and Second Jerusalem Temples. Religious Jews believe that on Tisha b'Av, separated by several centuries, both the First and Second Jerusalem Temples were destroyed. It is part of Jewish folklore that if something evil is to befall the Jews, it will usually occur on Tisha b'Av (the ninth day of the month of Av on the Jewish lunar calendar).

To commemorate the destruction of the Temple, the *maftir* prayer, the third and final section of the Torah portion, is recited on that day. As it is considered an honor to be called up to the altar to read the Torah, Wuzek is using the term "give him the honor of a *maftir*," ironically, as that particular Bible verse starts with: "I will make an end of them—declares the LORD: / No grapes left on the vine, / No figs on the fig tree, / The leaves all withered; Whatever I have given them is gone" (Jeremiah 8:13–9:23). The Republicans were therefore giving the fascists the "honor" of chanting a prayer for their own destruction. Although many Jewish communists knew their religion, Wuzek would also have had to know that Tisha b'Av fell on August 6, 1938, that year; not a date that an ardent communist would necessarily keep track of on a battlefield.

Disillusionment

Sygmunt Stein, also a member of the Botwin Company, described his feelings about Judaism and communism in his memoir:

> I traveled through the cities and towns of beautiful Jewish Galicia [Poland, not Spain], and brought the wonderful fairytales of Jewish life rising on the wings of Soviet power into Jewish homes. The love that I carried in my heart for Jewish culture, for *Yiddishkayt* [Jewishness, especially in its concrete manifestations (Beinfeld 2013: 341)], for Jews, was tightly interwoven with my firm belief in the historical role of the Soviets.
>
> Eastern Galicia was deeply ingrained with *Yiddishkayt*, as it struggled with poverty and persecution. The love with which the Jewish masses surrounded their culture, was brutally oppressed by material need and the political atmosphere in Poland. (Stein 1961: 12)

While Stein traveled through Poland, the antisemitic and fascist Endek political party that succeeded Piłsudski's regime was passing antisemitic laws almost daily: sanctioning pogroms, reviving talk of expelling Jews to Madagascar, and adopting Germany's racist policies (Lestschinsky 1951: 23–104).

Stein believed the emergence of Birobidzhan, designated as a Jewish homeland in 1928, with Yiddish as its official language, would be a potential haven for Jews in response to the Endek-inspired surge of antisemitism. In 1928, Birobidzhan, located on the Trans-Siberian Railway, near the China–Russia border, was further proof to Stein of "the Jewish Spring under the friendly sun of Marx-Engels-Lenin-Stalin." He did not consider those words a mere phrase; "they were as blood and flesh, just as the words *modeh ani* [*Modeh ani l'fanecha melech chai v'kayam shehechezarta bi nishmati b'chemla raba emunatecha* (I thank You, living and eternal King, for having mercifully restored my soul to me; Your faithfulness is great)] are the first words of the morning prayer spoken by a religious Jew while still in bed, were to a religious Jew" (Stein 1961: 13).

But Stein would later say of communism: "How was it possible for me to do things that so sharply contradicted with my own character, but made me unable to see that very contradiction, that antithesis between Communism and humanity, until so much later? Communism was not only a black blindfold, it was also a liquid that poisoned the blood and every individual cell" (Stein 1961: 14). Stein was not the only Jew to become disillusioned with communism, particularly after Stalin and Hitler entered the Nazi–Soviet Non-Aggression Pact of 1939. Many Jews in Europe and the United States disavowed their Communist Party membership, disillusioned and disheartened. Some Jewish communists had rationalized the show-trials occurring in Moscow during the Spanish Civil War but finally, opposition to antisemitism outweighed loyalty to communism (Schatz 1991: 102).

Stein's descriptions of his experiences as a Jewish volunteer in Spain make it clear that his commitment to Judaism was clearly on his mind. He cynically disparaged the Soviet Union's aid to Spain when a Russian gun he was examining fell apart in his hands. Stein wrote:

> Afraid of being accused of sabotage I decided not to risk puttering with the rifle any longer. The gun was an example of the type of assistance being provided by the Socialist Fatherland to aid the struggling Spanish Revolution.
>
> Warsawski [. . .] was thinking his own thoughts. He called out to me: "It's amazing. Here we are, two Jews standing on Spanish soil and guarding a Jewish company fighting against Spanish reactionaries. I'm wondering if, after 450 years, this isn't a spiritual Jewish revenge on our former tormentors?"
>
> He was right. I had also felt something like a mystical shudder go through me. Four hundred and fifty years ago Spanish reactionaries banished the Jews who had lived here for more than a thousand years. Now, so many years later, we were back to settle accounts. (Stein 1961: 227)

Stein was not the only Jewish international who would comment on the Jewish return to Spain to fight fascism (Bogen 1938; Shneiderman 1938: 36, 39, 74, 75, 80).

Letters

Both the Jewish press and the Communist Party wanted to encourage Jewish volunteers and the Jews that supported them. Reporters and writers therefore made certain that the volunteers' stories were told. David Diamant, in addition to being a volunteer, was also the secretary of the Jewish-Spanish Aid Committee in Paris during the Spanish Civil War. He considered the Jewish presence in that war a precursor to Jewish resistance during the Second World War. In writing of the Jewish volunteers, Y. Lerman, in his forward to David Diamant's memoir, wrote:

The participation of Jewish fighters in the International Brigades was important to our people. *A wave of anti-Jewish persecution accompanied the growth of fascism in Europe during the 1930s and antisemitism became a focal point of Hitler's program* [emphasis added]. The Nazis used antisemitic propaganda to prepare the people to accept the coming genocide of the Jewish people with indifference.

Antisemitic propaganda was spread in countries led by reactionary leaders, such as Poland and Romania. Even in countries such as France, Belgium, and England, fascist groups pushed their antisemitic agendas. Jews were presented as parasites, degenerates, and cowards to the rest of the population and these arguments were accepted by the population's more backward citizens. It was therefore politically important that Jewish anti-fascists fought on Spanish battlefields—it was the best counter-argument to antisemitic hatred. (Diamant 1967: 48–9)

Letter from Emmanuel Mink, a Botwin Company Commander

Mink was a Polish carpenter and an active communist. Arrested several times because of his revolutionary activities and harassed by the police, he emigrated to Belgium where he continued his activities. Mink was in Spain to participate in Barcelona's Popular Olympiad when the Spanish Civil War erupted. He immediately joined the International Brigades. Seriously wounded in Jarama, Mink spent seven months in hospital. He was then assigned to the Officer's Training School and then to Casas-Ibáñez, where he instructed Jewish volunteers who were being sent to reinforce the Botwin Company.

Mink was ordered to lead the Botwin Company himself in April 1938, during its toughest campaigns on the Ebro front. He was once more seriously wounded. Interned in the d'Argelès concentration camp in southern France after the Republican defeat in 1939, he escaped and joined the French Resistance in 1941. He was caught and deported to Auschwitz (Wuzek 1964: 83–4) where he was active in the Birkenau resistance movement. After surviving the camp and returning to Poland, he emigrated to Israel because of the resurgence of Polish antisemitism in 1968 (Zaagsma 2017: 125). While leading the Botwins, he wrote the following letter to his friends in Poland:

July 7, 1938, Eastern Front

Dearest Friends!

I just received a heartfelt letter from Comrade Edzhe. I was happy to learn that you are all still alive. Unfortunately, we hear so little about the Tomaszow comrades that I was beginning to have doubts. At the same time I received Edzhe's letter, I received greetings from our comrades in the Tomaszow group.

The arrests are continuing but that only proves that our members are active. I understand that our brothers who are suffering in the fascist prisons are receiving both material and spiritual assistance from you.

איך בין שטאָלץ און גליקלעך צו זיין קאָמענדאַנט
פֿון דער באָטוויןˇקאָמפּאַניע

מזרחˇפֿראָנט, דעם 1938.7.7

מײַנע חבֿרים!

איך האָב נאָר וואָס דערהאַלטן אַ האַרציקן בריוו פֿון חברטע עדושע־
ליענענדיק, האָב איך געהאַט די אָנגענעמע איבערראַשונג זיך צו דער־
וויסן, אַז איר לעבט נאָך. לײַדער הערט מען אין שפּאַניע אַזוי ווייניק
ווען מאַמאַשאָוער חבֿרים, אַז איך האָב ווען דעם שוין אָנגעהויבן צו
צווייפֿלען. דאקעגן האָב איך כּסדר געהאַט גרוסן פֿון אונדזערע חבֿרים
אין מאַמאַשאָוו גופֿא. די ערשטע הערן דאָרט נישט אויף, עס איז אַ באַ־
וויז דערויפֿער, אַז אונדזערע חבֿרים זענען אַקטיוו. איך נעם אָן, אַז אינ־
דערע ברידער, וואָס שמאַכטן אין די פֿאַשיסטישע תּפֿיסות, באַקומע
פֿון אײַך די ברידערלע מאַטעריעלע און מאָראלישע הילף.

איך דערוויס זיך אויך, אַז איר האָט אונטערגענומען אַ סאָלידאַרי־
טעטסאַקציע לטובֿת די מאַמאַשאָוער פֿרײַוויליקע אין שפּאניע. דאָס איז
זייער גוט.

ליבע לאַנדסלײַט! מיר דערנענטערן זיך צום דריטן יאָרטאָג פֿון
אויסבראָך פֿון שפּאַנישן קריג. עס קומען מיר אין זכרון יענע היסטאַרישע
טעג פֿון 18ˇטן און 19ˇטן יולי 1936, ווען כ'האָב צום ערשטן מאָל אין
מײַן לעבן מיט אַ ביקס אין האַנט נאַכגעפּאָלגט די פֿאַשיסטן אויף די
באַרימטע ראַמבלאַס פֿון באַרצעלאָנע. אין מײַן מוח זענען דא בליצשנעל
פֿאַרבײַגעלאָפֿן סצענעס פֿון אומדזערע יונגעˇיאָרן אין מאַמאַשאָוו. אין
ישטוב פֿון מײַן טאַטן, דעם שמיט, האָט שטענדיק געהערשט נויט. צו 13
יאָר האָב איך שוין געמוזט האָרעווען און שלעפֿן שווערע ברעטער אויפֿן
קאָפּ. פֿאַראינלענט אַלס ייד, אַלס אָנהענגער פֿון פֿרײַהײט, אַלס רעוואָ־
לוציאַנערער אַרבעטער, דורכמאכנדיק פֿיל יאָרן פֿון תּפֿיסה און עמיגרא־
ציע, האָט זיך אין מיר אָנגעזאמלט האַס און שנאה צו אונדזערע פֿיינט,
ווי אויסנוצער, אַנטיסעמיטן און פֿאַשיסטן. די דאָזיקע סיבה פֿירט מיך
שוין צוויי יאָר צײַט אײַבער אַלע שפּאַנישע פֿראָנטן. אין הײַליקן קריג קענען
באַרבאַרוסן, פֿאַר פֿרײַהײט און גליקלעכער צוקונפֿט פֿאַרן ייִדישן פֿאָלק
און אלע אנדערע פֿעלקער.

איצט בין איך שטאָלץ און גליקלעך צו זיין קאָמענדאַנט פֿון דער
באָטווין־קאָמפּאַניע, אָנצופֿירן מיטן הערלעכן קאַמף פֿון די העלדישע

426

ייִדישע, פּוילישע און שפּאַנישע סאָלדאַטן, וואָס שלאָגן זיך אַזוי מוטיק
פֿאַר אונדזער שותּפֿותדיקער זאַך. איך בין איבערצײַגט, אַז אונדזער
אײַנהײם וועט אויך אין דער צוקונפֿט פֿאַרזעצן אירע רומפֿולע טראַדי־
ציעס, וועלכע עס האָט דער ערשטער געשאַפֿן דער אומפאַרגעסלעכער
קאָמענדאַנט פֿון אונדזער קאָמפּאַניע, דער מוטמערחאַפֿטער ייִדישער רע־
וואָלוציאָנער — קאַרל שוואַרץ גוטמאַן.

גריסט אין מײַן נאָמען אונדזערע מאַמאַשאַוער פֿרײַנד, פֿאַרזיכערט
זײ, אַז מיר וועלן אַלץ טאָן, כּדי וואָס שנעלער צו דערגרייכן דעם זיג.
און איר, פֿון אײַער זײַט, פֿאַרשטאַרקט די סאָלידאַריטעט, וואָס איז אַזוי
נייטיק אין די איצטיקע באדינגונגען.

אין דעם געענטסטן בריוו וועל איך אײַך צושיקן די אדרעסן פֿון
די מאַמאַשאָוער לאַנדסלײַט אין שפּאַניע, וועלכע קעמפֿן אין אונדזער
בריגאַדע. שרײַבט אָן און דערצײַלט וואָס פֿאַר אַ נייעס באַקומט איר פֿון
אונדזער שטאָט.

מיט הײסע חברישע קאָמפּס־גרוסן.

אײַער עמנואל מינק

קאָמענדאַנט פֿון דער באָטווין־קאָמפּאַניע

Figures 5.1 and 5.2 Original letter by Emmanuel Mink included in David Diamant 1967, 426.

I was also glad to learn that you have undertaken solidarity activities on behalf of the Tomaszow volunteers in Spain.

Dearest compatriots! It will soon be three years since the Spanish war began. I remind myself of those historic days, July 18th and 19th, when I pursued the fascists for the first time on the famous Ramblas in Barcelona with a gun in my hand. I had flashes of our younger days in Tomaszow.

My father was the sexton of our synagogue and we grew up poor. I was already working at thirteen, carrying wooden boards on my head. Persecuted as a Jew, as a supporter of freedom, as a revolutionary worker, I spent many years in prison until I emigrated. I developed a deep hatred toward our enemies, the exploiters, antisemites, and fascists. It was for those reasons that I have traipsed all over the Spanish front these past two years. *I was in pursuit of the holy war against barbarism and in pursuit of freedom and a happy future for the Jewish people and for all other people* [emphasis added].

I am proud and fortunate to be the Botwin Company commander and to lead the magnificent struggle of the heroic Jewish, Polish, and Spanish soldiers that fight so bravely for our shared goal. I am convinced that our unity will continue and will maintain the traditions that were put into place by our exemplary first commander, the Jewish revolutionary, Karol Gutman.

Send my regards to our Tomaszow friends, assure them we will do everything in our power to achieve victory. On your part, strengthen the solidarity that is so necessary under these conditions. With sincere, comradely, victorious regards.

Yours, Emmanuel Mink, Commander of the Botwin Company. (Diamant 1967: 426)

Letter from Helena B., a Botwin Company Nurse

After first completing certain medical courses, several women whose men were volunteers were permitted to enter Spain. They were assigned to various hospitals, medical units, and pharmacies. Jewish women (and some men) were assigned mainly to the International Brigade medical units where from the beginning, they organized health services that included numerous hospitals, clinics, convalescent homes, and orphanages for the children of fallen soldiers. Helena B. was a nurse assigned to the Botwin Company—she may have been Helena Brzostoska, identified as a nurse by Martin Sugarman (2016). She described an instance when her hospital unit was moved because of the approaching enemy. The serious patients were left behind until the new hospital unit could be prepared for them. The following is an excerpt of her story:

> Working conditions in a division hospital are difficult. We try to set up as close as possible to our unit's encampment to spare the injured painful transport to our facilities, but we don't always find appropriate housing. Often, we set up near

stables and warehouses in small, uncomfortable little buildings. Frequently, there is no running water or electricity and we must work around those conditions.

Everyone in our hospital was concerned about the wounded. Had something happened to them *en route*? They were our most serious cases, but we had no choice but to leave them behind so we could prepare to receive them here. Lacking space, we set up the hospital pharmacy in a different building, a distance away from us. We frequently found ourselves waiting for unavailable, life-saving medications to be delivered.

Finally, after a tension-filled wait, we heard a motor and our patients arrived. While transferring them into the hospital, the wind was so strong it blew off their blankets and forced the doors open, slamming them into the walls. Although we were functioning in complete darkness, our patients suffered no harm because several orderlies lit our way with candles. Within the hour, our patients were comfortable and we started the usual night's work. In semi-darkness I heard a weak voice calling, "Nurse . . . ." Dropping everything, I rushed over. A compress, a bottle for urine, a change of position, and the patient was once again calm. I tiptoed away. Someone else was calling me.

The night passed and when relieved in the morning, I threw a loving last glance at my comrades and thought to myself, how good it is, that I, a Jewish schoolgirl from Lodz, can relieve the suffering of my freedom fighting brothers, at least a little.

I remember a certain patient with a wonderful attitude. His name was Khefetz, from Palestine.[3] He lost his vision in battle but insisted that he was proud to have sacrificed his eyes in the battle against fascism.

We were evacuated at the end of September. There were 25 to 30 nurses, some of whom I already knew, stationed in Segarra where a large hotel had been converted to a hospital. I worked with two nurses, Dora[4] and Adela.[5] Both were from Palestine. Adela was not the only member of her family in Spain, her sister's husband had already died here.

One night we learned Barcelona had fallen. We were ordered to evacuate to the French border. It was a horrible night—the head nurse, Manya or Henye, told us to get some sleep and wait for further orders. We were awakened at 1:00 A.M. and

---

[3] Pinkhas Khefetz was born in Jerusalem in 1912. By 1926 he was active in the illegal Palestine Communist movement and spent several years in Palestine prisons. He joined the Botwin Company in early 1938 and while fighting in Lerida, was shot in the eye. Although immediately blinded, he did not lose consciousness and had the presence of mind to pass his hand grenades to his friends, telling them: "Take the grenades—you may be able to use them." He died in the Soviet Union during the Second World War (Wuzek 1964: 95–6).

[4] Dora Levin aka Birnbach was born in Lemberg/L'viv in 1912 or in Sokolov, Poland in 1911. She moved to Palestine in 1933 and returned to Poland after the Spanish Civil War. She moved back to Israel in 1968 when a new wave of antisemitism arose in Poland. While in Spain she worked as an operating room nurse (Sugarman 2016).

[5] Adela Stever/Weintraub, aka Adela Botviniska, was born in Podwoloczyska, a small town in Poland near Tarnopol. She and her family suffered through pogroms and she became an ardent Zionist, moving to Palestine in 1926, where she trained as a nurse. After the war she returned to Palestine where she died in 1969 (Sugarman 2016).

told to pack underwear for the patients; we were going to prepare a new medical unit and we foreigners were asked which of us wanted to work there. We had spent days digging trenches with pickaxes to keep our patients safe here and we were sorry to leave, but we agreed to go.

That morning we were transported to a castle, where Dora, two Spanish girls and I put together a new medical unit. The next day the head doctor arrived in a chauffeur-driven vehicle and swiftly drove us two kilometers to La Jonquera, where patients were waiting for us. A battle between the Republicans and the fascists began shortly after we arrived. Some International Brigades leaders approached us about volunteering for the Madrid front. We agreed to go and left with a group of civilian refugees, mainly women and children. (Diamant 1967: 288–91)

Some letters sent to the Jewish volunteers by their family members found their way into general and International Brigade newspapers.

A Letter from Moniek Borenshtein's Mother

Moniek Borenshtein, a revolutionary from Minsk-Mosevietsk, upon seeing fascist tanks advancing, crawled out of his trench and attacked them with hand grenades. He destroyed the tanks and stopped the advance (Wuzek 1964: 35). (Another hero unafraid to fend off a fascist tank single-handed, but afraid to tell his mother where he was going.) Borenshtein's story is similar to that of Antoni Coll Prohens, who stopped four German tanks using the same tactics on the Madrid front (Shneiderman 1938: 152).

The letter from Moniek Borenshtein's mother was typical—she believed in her son's communist goals but asked God to help him accomplish them. Once she learned where Moniek was, she wrote to him, sprinkling a little guilt:

My darling son!

Thank you for letting me know the truth although my tired heart told me you were no longer in Paris. Better the bitter truth than lies.

Dearest Moniesh! You know how difficult it was for me to let you leave; how much I hoped to meet you abroad, particularly as my health grows worse every day and it becomes even more difficult to make ends meet.

Even so, I forgive you, my dearest. I am not angry and I do not reproach you. I understand that you had no choice but to go to Spain. You did what your conscience dictated. I know you love us and your decision rests heavily on your soul.

I send you my blessings and I beg God to take good care and protect you. I also pray for your comrades: Poles, Jews, Russians, Frenchmen, Spaniards, all of you who share one goal. They also have mothers and families waiting for them with fear in their hearts.

Your friends visit me and say they envy you. I believe they are being truthful but I doubt they understand a mother's heart. They ask if I need anything and go out of their way to help me. I often wonder why they think I'm such a lucky woman. Is it because you are on the Spanish front or is it because your younger brother, Romek, is now in *Kartuz-Bereza* [an infamous Polish prison], and has been there for the last few weeks, something of which you are probably not aware.

I look at your friends but all I see are you and Romek. Although I cry, it gladdens my heart that your friends remember you both. I also see the tears in the eyes of these communists . . . . I know you are all unified in achieving your single goal, or, as you would say, your one idea. Let God help you, perhaps it will be a better world.

Dearest son! I can write no more. I send you warm kisses and heartfelt regards to your comrades. Write often. Every day without news from you is torture for me.

Until we meet again, your loving mother. (Wuzek 1964: 35–6)

Sygmunt Stein, the disenchanted communist and propagandist previously mentioned, believed the aforementioned letters and the one following, allegedly written by Shlomo Yaffe, were in fact written by the Soviet propaganda machine on the Albacete base (Stein 1961: 80–1):

Haifa, April 28

Dear Friends,

The news of my brother's death was very painful to me. Everyone knows such things happen on the front, but as you know, our Yitzkhok wasn't given enough time to be the best he could be. He learned quickly and soon became one of the finest soldiers. It made no difference. We must sacrifice in our fight against the enemy. I am happy that several villages were returned to the Spanish people and the fascists were once more beaten back during the battle in which my brother fell. Something was accomplished so my brother's blood was not shed in vain.

When my father heard the news he said nothing, but the pain he felt was written on his face. Yitzkhok was his favorite son. After several hours passed in silence, he turned to me and said: "Shlomo, you will go and take your brother's place, they need you there! The war is not over and no one may stand on the sidelines!"

Yes, dear friends, I will be arriving soon and will try to get assigned to your battalion, and if possible, the same Company in which my brother served.

Stay well and please pass on a strong Red-Front greeting to all the comrades and particularly to those who were Yitzkhok's friends.

Shlomo (Diamant 1967: 465)

Stein's belief that these letters were nothing more than propaganda was based on an encounter with several young Palestinians. Although the two Jaffa brothers were already dead by the time Stein arrived in Spain, a letter allegedly written by their father was circulating that read: "I am proud that my two sons were on the battle fields of the Spanish Revolution. God gave me one more son who is with me in Palestine. I am sending him to Spain to avenge the death of his two brothers and for all antifascists who have fallen" (Stein 1961: 81).

The Palestinian Jews told Stein they knew the fallen boys' father very well. He was a religious Jew from the Middle East, who was not only despondent that his sons were killed but devastated that they had sacrificed their lives over a secular matter. According to Stein, the only truthful thing contained in that father's alleged letter was that a third brother had also come to Spain (Stein 1961). Stein believed that the only explanation for these similar letters from parents who lived in different regions, was that the letters were created in the Albacete editorial office. As additional evidence that these letters were fabricated, according to Stein, many came from parents who were both "proud" and "lucky" to have received notice that their sons had been killed in action. The Polish newspaper *Dombrowszcak* printed most of these letters, many ending with the words: "My son died *za lashon ee vashon vollaszc*," Polish for the Dombrowski slogan, "for your freedom and ours."

Stein may have been right; many letters may have been drafted by the propaganda department, but it is difficult to believe that the letters mentioned in S. L. Shneiderman's reportage were written for propaganda purposes. Shneiderman wrote for the Yiddish press about Spain. Because he traveled so extensively throughout the country, many letters were forwarded to him by editors and friends of people seeking information about family members. Unfortunately, Shneiderman did not identify the writers of the following excerpts:

> "The best have fallen," are the words heard everywhere. Desperate mothers from all over the world write letters to their sons. Written in every language, they are no longer opened—they are sent to the dead-letter box, a designated cupboard located in the International Brigades' central post office. They are drenched in tears, their content almost identical:
> "Where is my husband?"
> "Where is my son?"
> "Where is my brother?"
> "Please, just tell me the truth, hide nothing", these letters beg. (Shneiderman 1938: 85)

Shneiderman never found anyone who was being sought in these letters (Shneiderman 1938: 86).

Conclusion

An answer to a question may be inferred from the existence or non-existence of other facts (Richardson 1928: 68). The bravery of the Jews who went to Spain may be inferred from the same facts applicable to all the other volunteers—they *volunteered* to go; they didn't have to go. There was no reason for these Jews to be there except one—they wanted to be there. By going to Spain, they risked a loss of citizenship, friends, family, and death. Yet still, they went.

Zaagsma's contention that they came because they were ordered to do so by the Communist Party is not supported by the evidence (2017: 42). Nothing other than supposition supports the claim that they were ordered to go (Zaagsma 2017: 21). As stated earlier, 25 percent of the volunteers in the International Brigades were Jewish; therefore 75 percent were not. However, the percentage of Jews in Spain was overwhelming based on their representation within the population at large.

Forty-five percent of the Poles in Spain were Jewish yet Jews comprised only 10 percent of the Polish population; 38 percent of the American volunteers were Jewish but comprised only four percent of the USA population; 15 percent of the French volunteers were Jewish but only 0.5 percent of the population; 15 percent of the British volunteers were Jewish but only 0.5 percent of the population; 10 percent of Argentinian volunteers were Jewish but only 1.6 percent of the population (Sugarman 2016).

It may therefore be inferred that if communists were being ordered to go to Spain, a far greater percentage of them would have been Gentile, based on their representation within the population.

Zaagsma also alleges that "there is no direct evidence that indicates why the Brigade staff agreed to the formation of a Jewish military unit in December 1937" (Zaagsma 2017: 43), but the "Order of the Day" issued by the International Brigade leadership on December 12, 1937, as reported in the *Botvin* newspaper is clear; it was "to honor the important role of the Jewish Brigaders in the Dombrowski Brigade and to honor the memory of the Jewish fighters who fell fighting for freedom" (Zaagsma 2017: 45). The reasons for Jewish ubiquity in the International Brigades are explained in the Jewish volunteers' own words in their Yiddish letters and in reportage: they wanted to defeat fascism and find a haven for themselves and their families.

Shneiderman, by asking high-ranking Spanish officials whether Jews would be welcomed in Spain, was trying to find a home to which Jews could escape (1938: 68, 69, 76); Stein was concerned about the increase of antisemitism in the Soviet Union (1961: 14, 35, 36, 62, 214, 238); Wuzek wanted the world to acknowledge Jewish, not communist bravery (1964: 11–15, 39, 49); and Medem explained that Jews wanted a Jewish unit to fight Nazis to be created (1939: 8). These examples are just a few; many more exist.[6]

As the Botwin Company said in the final words of its manifesto to the Jewish community: "Long live the Jewish people's unified fight against right-wing reaction, fascism, and antisemitism!" (Diamant 1967: 535).

---

[6] For further cases see https://jewsfightingfascism.com/.

References

Beinfeld, S. and H.Bochner (eds.). (2013), *Comprehensive Yiddish-English Dictionary*, Bloomington: Indiana University Press.
Bogen, G. (1938), "Der Geburt fun der Botvin Companie," *Der Hamer*, July.
Diamant, D. (1967), *Yidn in Shpanishn Krig, 1936–1939*, Warsaw and Paris: Yiddish Bukh.
Farrell, Richard T. (1995), *Richardson on Evidence*, 11th ed., Brooklyn Law School.
Lefevere, A. (1992), *Translating Literature: Practice and Theory in a Comparative Literature Context*, New York: The Modern Language Association of America.
Lestschinsky, J. (1951), *Erev Khurbn: Fun Yiddishn Lebn in Poyln, 1935–1937*, Buenos Aires: Tsentral-Farband fun Poyleshe Yidn in Argentina.
Medem, Gina. (1937). *Los Judíos—-Luchadores de la Libertad.*
Medem, Gina. (1939), "Di Rol fun Yiddishe Kemfer in di Internatzionale Brigadn in Shpanye," *Neileben*, March.
Schatz, J. (1991), *The Generation: The Rise and Fall of the Jewish Communists of Poland*, Berkeley: University of California Press.
Shneiderman, S. L. (1938), *Krig in Shpanyen, Hinterland, I*, Warsaw: Yiddishe Universal Bibliotek.
Stein, S. (1961), *Der Birger-Krig in Shpanye: Zikhroynes Fun a Militzianer*, Paris: A. Schipper.
Sugarman, M. (2016), *Jews in the Spanish Civil War*, Available online: https://www.jewishvirtuallibrary.org/jews-who-served-in-the-international-brigade-in-the-spanish-civil-war (accessed December 18, 2020).
Wuzek, E. (1964), *Zikhroynes Fun a Botvinist*, Warsaw: Yiddish Bukh.
Zaagsma, G. (2017), *Jewish Volunteers, the International Brigades and the Spanish Civil War*, London: Bloomsbury Academic.

Online Resources:

Kaddish for the Fallen, https://jewsfightingfascism.com/ *Jews in the Spanish Civil War*, Available online: https://www.jewishvirtuallibrary.org/jews-who-served-in-the-international-brigade-in-the-spanish-civil-war#intro (accessed January 9, 2021).
Sistema d'Informació Digital sobre las Brigades Internacionals, University of Barcelona, Available online: http://sidbrint.ub.edu/ca (accessed January 10, 2021).
The Volunteer. Founded by the Veterans of the Abraham Lincoln Brigade, Available online: https://albavolunteer.org/2010/11/dora-levin-1911-2010/ (accessed January 10, 2021).

Part Two

Textualities of Memory and Postmemory in Contemporary Literature and Thought

6

Jewish Argentine Perspectives and Intellectual Mission around the Spanish Civil War

The Cases of Alberto Gerchunoff and Enrique Espinoza

Melina Di Miro

The Spanish Civil War, as well as the preceding tensions during the "black biennium" of the Second Spanish Republic, had important repercussions on the Argentine literary and intellectual scenes in the 1930s and 1940s. At that time, Argentine Jewish writers expressed their position in this regard in poems, travel diaries, essays, and fictional prologues. In Argentine society, confirming or publicly rejecting support for Spanish Republican ideals provided ideological-intellectual identifications in an increasingly polarized political climate between liberalism and conservatism. The position of Jewish Argentines toward the Spanish situation must be understood in relation to this historical context as well as in relation to what the advance of authoritarian regimes, internationally and locally, could imply specifically for Jews (Rein 2014).

If the collapse of liberalism manifested itself in Europe with growing support for Nazism, fascism, and the right-wing Spanish parties—in a scenario further complicated by Stalinism in the Soviet Union—in Argentina the liberal republic faced the advance of what Loris Zanatta (1996) has called "the Catholic nation." Woven from conservative redefinitions of Argentine national identity in the 1930s, the appearance of the image of "the Catholic nation" was forged by factions supporting conservative, anti-liberal, anti-democratic, and anti-communist ideologies. In this way, during the so-called "Infamous Decade" (1930–43) a new right-wing Catholic and antisemitic nationalism was affirmed. Newspapers and groups such as *La nueva república* and *Criterio*, whose discursive construction of the country's internal enemies would crystallize the thesis of the universal Jewish plot (Lvovich 2003), had generated support for the coup d'état of 1930 led by General José Félix Uriburu. Likewise, these nationalist groups would be the radical critical wing of his successor, General Agustín Justo.

In this context, support or rejection of the Spanish Republican side was a local password for one's own location in a political-intellectual field in Argentina. Against this historical backdrop, a handful of publications by Jewish Argentine authors published between 1934 and 1944 established a literary imaginary for the political conflict in Spain. Among them, it is possible to identify two specific sets of texts. The first is a group of poems in which pro-Spanish Republican images are evoked. Such is the case in poems by César Tiempo (Israel Zeitlin), Bernado Kordon, and Rubén Sinay (Gabbay 2020). A second set of texts of mixed literary genres highlights the intersection between the juncture around the Spanish Civil War and Jewish Argentine perspectives, giving rise to a political-cultural criticism in relation to the Spanish conflicts as well as producing singular representations regarding the mission of Jewish Argentine writers.

The primary focus of this chapter is to analyze a set of works written in these coordinates by two Jewish Argentine authors: Alberto Gerchunoff (1883-1950) and Enrique Espinoza, the pseudonym of Samuel Glusberg (1898-1987). Gerchunoff's texts are: the fictional prologue "Advertencia pertinente," which is part of his novel *El Hombre Importante* (1934), the lecture "El libro y el espíritu" (1937), and the essay "Noche de Pascua de 1940" (1944). I also discuss Espinoza's writings that form a part of the book, *Chicos de España (1935)* (1938), the travel diary "Notas de viaje" (1935), and the essays "Por qué los judíos deben ayudar al pueblo español," "Un discurso de León Felipe,"[1] and "Significación histórica del *Mono Azul*."

In this chapter then, from a text-centered, comparative approach, I analyze critical representations of Spanish political and cultural events by Gerchunoff and Espinoza, as well as their heterogeneous conceptions about the mission of the Jewish Argentine writers in relation to the Spanish conflict and the advance of conservative politics in Argentina. On the one hand, this analysis will reveal the ways in which Gerchunoff and Espinoza approached the tensions between the Spanish Republic and the complex alliance of its opponents. On the other hand, this chapter will demonstrate how Gerchunoff and Espinoza's views on the Spanish conflicts—ultimately representing their fears about the advance of conservative nationalisms in Europe and Argentina—related to the authors' self-representations (Gramuglio 2013; Said 1994) and their broader understandings of the mission of the Jewish Argentine writer. I argue that these authors redefined the meaning of "Jewishness" through these self-representations, against a backdrop of national debates and power struggles in Europe and the Southern Cone.

Two main premises structure the analysis undertaken in this chapter. Firstly, I embrace a broad definition of literary discourse that includes not only traditional fictional genres but also the travel diary and the formal essay insofar as they appeal to a polysemic and metaphorical use of language and its poetic function. The essay, the travel diary, and the fictional prologue showcase an indivisible relationship between the referential, the expressive, and the poetic functions of discourse (Alburquerque García 2006; Aullón de Haro 2005; Genette 2001: 154). I will observe how these genres allowed Espinoza and Gerchunoff to address the Argentine and Spanish sociopolitical realities of the 1930s in literary discourse, while at the same time positioning themselves as Jewish Argentine authors within their intellectual milieus.

---

[1] Felipe Camino García de la Rosa (1884-1968), known as León Felipe, was a Spanish Republican poet who went into exile to Mexico in 1938.

Secondly, I explore a conception of Jewish literature that, moving beyond oversimplified thematic or essentialist criteria, approaches the concept of Jewish literature in relation to three parameters: 1. a literary interpretation of reality employing complex themes rooted in the Jewish tradition, with the implicit or explicit presence of the question of "Jewish identity" (Sosnowski 1987), 2. the relation to recognizably Jewish texts and literary traditions (Aizenberg 2001), and 3. the discursive configuration of the image of the author in relation to ethnic markers of Jewishness, regardless of biological descent.

Alberto Gerchunoff and His Republican and Messianic Ideal against Conservative Nationalism

By the 1930s, Gerchunoff was a recognized writer in Argentina, so much so that he was nominated to join the Academia Argentina de Letras (AAL),[2] an honor that he would later reject. His authorial image was linked to *Los gauchos judíos* (1910), a book about Jewish immigrants in the Argentine countryside. In addition, in his essays on Miguel de Cervantes Saavedra's literature and journalistic writings, he intervened in political-cultural debates on national and international levels to defend his liberal, Republican convictions (Szurmuk 2018).

The political conflict in Spain was a focal point in public declarations of his political beliefs, exemplified by his act of signing the letter of collective support for the Spanish Republican government published by the literary magazine, *Sur*, on July 30, 1936. In addition, in prologues, essays, and lectures, he referred critically to counter-Republican advances, as early as 1934, as the Spanish Confederation of Autonomous Rights (CEDA) gained organizational momentum. The fictional prologue "Advertencia pertinente" and the essays "El libro y el espíritu" and "Noche de Pascua de 1940" contain these ideas.

In 1934, Gerchunoff published "Advertencia pertinente" (A Pertinent Warning) as a prologue to his novel *El Hombre Importante* (The Important Man). This prologue takes the shape of a fictional epistolary response addressed to the "secretary of the Caracatambo Academy of Letters and History" by "the author of *The Important Man*." The identification between Gerchunoff and the enunciator of this prologue is evident. However, there is also a subtle distance between the factual author and the authorial alter ego as the recipient of the letter is an invented character. Such a mode of distancing allowed Gerchunoff to more freely and ironically articulate his opinions about the political and intellectual figures mentioned or alluded to in the text. The secretary of Caractambo Academy asks to know why the membership of "the author of *The Important Man*" in this academic society was refused. To answer this question, Gerchunoff's alter ego weaves an "essay on academic societies," throughout which

---

[2] The creation of the AAL, by Félix Uriburu, was a manifestation of the corporatist nationalist and Catholic nationalist currents (Glozman 2013).

Figure 6.1 Alberto Gerchunoff, unknown photographer. Courtesy of Jorge F. Payró.

he criticizes conservative nationalism and builds an authorial self-configuration that bases its mission on resisting it (Gerchunoff 1934: 44).

This "essay on academic societies" unfolds the history of an emergent, conservative "academic spirit," with examples and descriptions of its multiple manifestations. It is a homogenizing, normativizing, and exclusive "spirit" that sterilizes all creative potential and eliminates ethnic, cultural, class, ideological, and subjective differences in both art and politics that do not conform to sanctioned norms. Indeed, in "Advertencia pertinente," the academic spirit is shown as the constitutive impulse not only of academic societies but also of anti-democratic governments and factions. By establishing a parallel between the advance of conservative nationalism and elitism in the academy, he links the rejection of the fictional author by the "Caracatambo Academy" to authoritarianism, and above all, he highlights the intrinsically retrograde nature of this type of institution.

To demonstrate this comparison, Gerchunoff's alter ego traces the history of academic societies, foregrounding the case in Germany, in which Wilhelm Hohenzollern "Academicized the German spirit" and set out to found an academy (1934: 33). Hitler's antisemitism is considered a continuation of this academic process. In another paradigmatic case, through digressions, dichotomies, and comparisons, Gerchunoff launches a political critique of the right-wing Spanish Catholic factions in his discussion of the Real Academia Española (RAE).

Affirming that, during the reign of Alfonso XIII, the RAE was dedicated to discussing banalities and insulting brilliant writers, Gerchunoff's alter ego refers to the lovers of the overthrown Spanish monarch, portraying the king as superfluous and as disconnected from reality as the RAE. He caricatures the figure of Alfonso XIII by making a "sensual encyclopedia" of the monarch's life (1934: 26) and showing him as "un rey de naipe" (a playing card king)—that is, a king who does not know how to rule. For Gerchunoff's alter ego, the true exemplar of this negative academic spirit is Miguel

Primo de Rivera, whom he associates with Benito Mussolini (1934: 29) and, indirectly, with the authoritarian Mexican president Porfirio Díaz (1934: 25).

In line with these insights, Gerchunoff's alter ego identifies a dichotomy between two principal forces determining the fate of Spanish national identity: an agonizing, monarchical Spain, alien to the public square and symbolized by the figure of Primo de Rivera; and a creative, quixotic, germinal Spain, linked to the people and represented by Manuel Azaña.³ In Azaña, the narrator identifies one of the "rebuilders of Spain, of the pluralist Spain, [. . .] womb of the America" (1934: 29). Gerchunoff had already raised this opposition of the two Spains, contrasting the figures of Fernando el Católico and Felipe II (as standard-bearers of segregationism), with Cervantes and Don Quixote (symbols of freedom) (Gerchunoff 1922).

In "Advertencia pertinente," Gerchunoff's alter ego sees that the members of the RAE "embody the monarchical spirit of that agonizing period" (Gerchunoff 1922: 28) under the influence of Alfonso XIII and Primo de Rivera. However, upon further consideration, the narrator also decides that under Azaña's leadership, the RAE subsequently remained a conservative academy. For this reason, and with clear political connotations, the author criticizes the entrance into the RAE of Pío Baroja, Ramón Peréz de Ayala, and Gregorio Marañón, the latter two being founders of Agrupación al Servicio de la República (Grouping in Favor of the Republic). To implement this critique, which has a double meaning, Gerchunoff's alter ego establishes a comparison between the academic societies and what he calls "the community of Origen."

As he explains, Origen of Alexandria defied Roman nationalism but was a flawed icon because of his excessive pursuit of perfection. This led Origen to engage in the inhumane act of self-castration, and with that act, to support the very thing that he rejected. That is the reason why, for Gerchunoff, they who strive for exclusionary norms and for absolute purity in any field are considered members of a metaphorical, monolithic community tied to Origen's legacy. The physical body and the "community of Origen," on the one hand, become a metaphor for the disciplining of the academic societies and for the social body that cuts off its own members (ethnic, social, political) "out of the rule." On the other hand, the attitude of Origen of Alexandria symbolizes that of the intellectuals who, for the sake of maintaining their "unpolluted virtue," end up defending an enemy. Thus, when Gerchunoff's alter ego asks Azorín, Baroja, Pérez de Ayala, and Marañón not to associate with "Origen's friendship" (Gerchunoff 1922: 35) during the height of the influence of the CEDA, it can be understood to reflect a demand for more decisive support for democratic currents on their part.

Maintaining consistency in his critique, Gerchunoff identifies the mission of the intellectual as the defense of an "anti-academic" spirit in the cultural and sociopolitical sphere and a rejection of the homogenizing forces of an authoritarian spirit present in the right-wing Spanish factions and the governments of Hitler, Mussolini, and, indirectly, Uriburu in Argentina. In this way, he proclaims the essential duty of writers to defend this "anti-academic spirit" as a *sine qua non* condition for the birth of new

---

[3] Manuel Azaña Díaz (1880–1940) was president of the Council of Ministers during the First Biennium of the Second Spanish Republic (1931–3) and president of the Second Republic (1936–9).

works and societies based on the principles of freedom and inclusion with respect to linguistic, ethnic, cultural, and religious difference. What is significant about this perspective is the presence of elements of Jewish tradition and Christian tradition combined and resignified to project a particular messianism as a social utopia.

Indeed, Gerchunoff identifies this "anti-academic force," on the one hand, with the Holy Spirit, which he redefines here as the "flame of creation" that cuts through the regulations of the institutions. According to Gerchunoff's proclamation, writers must be the "messengers of the Holy Spirit" and announce "the daily coming of the Messiah" (Gerchunoff 1922: 18). On the other hand, he also compares this critical spirit to the "soul of King David" in the form of a panegyric to a liberal Argentina that once openly received new immigrants, in contrast to the restrictions initiated during the 1930s.[4] Moreover, Gerchunoff equates "Jewishness" to a historical manifestation of the anti-academic spirit (and, therefore, of the "Holy Spirit") by virtue of what would be an idiosyncratic affirmation of the right to difference and freedom in the face of the status quo and persecution.

When the author, referring to the situation in the Third Reich, refers to the Jews, he underlines their "rebellious, unassimilable character" in a positive light: "The Jews [. . .] persecuted as a race and religion because they are a persistence of Christ as well as a difference, or because they are the ferment of originality, [. . .], deny the imperviousness of any stratification" (1934: 35).[5] Therefore, in the face of anti-democratic movements, the recurring negative stereotype of the unassimilable character of the Jews is transformed into a valuable trait. Furthermore, in the face of Catholic nationalism gaining support in Spain and Argentina, Gerchunoff dismantles the archetype of the deicidal Jew, postulating, on the contrary, that they are actually a "persistence of Christ."

The idea that the Jews were the true proponents of the message of Jesus, as well as the syncretism between Jewish and Christian messianisms underlying this notion, had been developing in Gerchunoff's writing since at least *El cristianismo precristiano* (The Pre-Christian Christianism).[6] In this book, he based this idea on the fact that, due to their historical exclusion, the Jews would still expect an earthly kingdom of justice. Likewise, Gerchunoff argues in *El cristianismo precristiano* that Christianity had universalized the message of redemption embedded in Hebraic wisdom. He equates Jewish messianism with Christian messianism to the extent that both advocate for human redemption. In fact, Gerchunoff affirms that "Catholicism is an organized Judaism" (Gerchunoff 1924: 31) due to the similarity of the "prophetic word" between

---

[4] The ideal of an ethnically homogeneous nation in Argentina, free of communism, was the basis for limiting immigration policy, which affected the entry of Jewish and Spanish refugees.
[5] "Los judíos [. . .] perseguidos como raza y como credo, porque son una persistencia de Cristo y una diferenciación, o sea un fermento de originalidad, [. . .], descoinciden con la impermeabilidad de lo estratificable."
[6] See also "El hombre de las manos luminosas" (The Man of Luminous Hands) (1925) and "Una entrevista con el doctor Mefistófeles" (An Interview with Doctor Mephistopheles) (1925). There, Jewish and Christian messianisms are diffusely equated with the socialist goal of an egalitarian society while denouncing that the West (including fascism) had not realized true Christianity.

the Old and New Testament (Gerchunoff 1924: 10). According to this interpretation, Jewish and Christian messianisms thus carried a social doctrine: to fight for a world of equity, tolerance, and freedom. These messianic ideas reappear in "Advertencia pertinente," alongside Gerchunoff's belief about the moral duties of the writer:

> This work of the Holy Spirit encloses an important lesson for these times [. . .] of Stalin, the mighty barbarian who hates the non-Communist thinker; of Hitler, the barbarian [. . .] who hates all those who embody with their unwavering word the unconquerable decency of humanity. For these reasons, because the writer is the *shofar*, the ram's horn from which the Holy Spirit is sounded and sings, I have refused the honor to appear in the list of corresponding members of the Caracatambo Academy. That is, I have earlier renounced, in my own country, an identical distinction. (1934: 19)[7]

By resigning from the academic societies, Gerchunoff's alter ego assumes his responsibility as an author. Through this act, he defines the writer's responsibility by invoking the conjunction between Jewish and Christian traditions as a symbol of freedom and brotherhood to which writers themselves must commit. The *shofar* appears as a ritual instrument of Judaism mentioned in Exodus 19:16, in the theophany of Sinai, a horn that would announce the Year of Jubilee and the "proclamation of freedom in all the earth" (Leviticus 25:9–10). However, here, the Christian Holy Spirit vibrates through the *shofar*. Therefore, a message of union is encrypted in this metaphor promoting a singular messianism, which reconciles Judaism and Christianity, as a social doctrine. In other words, while academic societies and conservative national movements authoritatively arbitrate on "purity in the language" in the "social body," here, using nothing less than a Hebraism, the mission of the writer is defined as the defense of human decency over linguistic-cultural, religious, and political divisions, in pursuit of free and inclusive societies.

It is in the name of such a mission that Gerchunoff's alter ego, assuming himself to be a Jewish Argentine writer, warns of the struggle between two forces brewing in Spain as well as the crisis of the liberal republic in Argentina. He objects to Nazism and fascism and affirms the embodiment of Jewish difference as a way of defending human decency. In this sense, as a Jewish Argentine author, the "duty of the writer" is carried out in "Advertencia pertinente" through his refusal to integrate into conservative government institutions. As such, he affirms the possibility of a multicultural Argentine nation. Furthermore, he is able to challenge Spanish writers to lend their support to the popular process of the Republic by denouncing the advance of totalitarian currents

---

[7] "Este procedimiento del Espíritu Santo encierra una grave lección en estos tiempos [. . .], de Stalin, el bárbaro grande que odia al pensador no comunista; de Hitler, el bárbaro [. . .] que odia a los que encarnan con su verbo indómito el inabatible decoro de la humanidad. Por estos motivos, porque el escritor es el *shofar*, el cuerno de macho cabrío en que suena y canta el Espíritu Santo, rehusé el honor de figurar en la lista de los miembros correspondientes de la Academia de Caracatambo. Es que antes había renunciado, en mi propio país, a idéntica distinción."

understood as manifestations of the academic spirit. In the Americas, this warning is made particularly relevant to ethnic minorities, whom he suggests have the most to lose in a society organized under such principles.

In the years following the publication of "Advertencia pertinente," Gerchunoff once again spoke out on the Spanish political conflict. Further dedicating himself to a defense of values associated with his particular messianism as a social utopia, he continued to fight against the "academic spirit." In this way, the lecture "El libro y el espíritu"[8] begins with the following denunciation:

> General Franco [. . .] decreed purification of public libraries [. . .]. Commissions of wise men of the Falange will be in charge [. . .] of preparing the lists of the works "not convenient to read," as the censors of the Middle Ages qualified them [. . .]. Such screening of culture through an official and dogmatic sieve is not new in the Spain that General Franco intends to bring back from the depths of time.[9] (1937: 369)

Reappearing in this lecture is the idea of two Spains in conflict with each other, represented, on the one hand, as embodying a spirit of tolerance, freedom, and creation, and on the other, as a despotic, censorial force—in short, academic. In this sense, Franco's Spain is a dire return to the time of the Inquisition, and in his ironic phrase, "wise men of the Falange," we can read Gerchunoff's lament of the "atavistic" return of medieval censorship. Gerchunoff offers, then, the famous scene from Cervantes in which the priest and the barber decide to "cure" Don Quixote and which serves as a literary symbol of that ancestral struggle between two forces. Furthermore, Gerchunoff elevates this scene as a metaphor for a psychological period of return to despotism taking place throughout all of Europe, with the regimes of Hitler, Mussolini, and Stalin.

A few years later in 1944, Gerchunoff once again presents his conception of the Jews as "the persistence of Christ" as authentic believers in a utopian social messianism in "Noche de Pascua de 1940." He further explains that Christian peoples could finally understand the reason for the hatred of the Jew (that is, as heralds of a just world) in the context of the advance of totalitarianism in Europe, since, like them, they were now repressed and yearning for freedom and equality. In this text, moreover, Gerchunoff not only contrasts a messianism based on the equation between Jewish and Christian prophetism with conservative nationalism once again. He also transforms both the biblical narrative of captivity in Egypt and historic anti-Jewish persecutions

---

[8] Lecture given at the festival of the fortieth anniversary of Biblioteca Obrera Juan B. Justo and published in *La vanguardia* in 1937.
[9] "El general Franco [. . .] dispuso en un decreto la depuración de las bibliotecas públicas [. . .]. Comisiones de sabios de la Falange tendrán a su cargo [. . .] preparar las listas de las obras "non cumplideras de leer," como las calificaban los censores de la Edad Media [. . .]. Tal cernimiento de la cultura a través de un tamiz oficial y dogmático, no es nuevo en la España que el general Franco se propone extraer del fondo del tiempo."

into metaphors for the subjugation of Spanish, French, and Belgians by authoritarian governments (Gerchunoff 1944: 91).

In "Noche de Pascua de 1940," Spain is presented as a nation submissive to a "lacklustre oppressor," in a clear reference to Franco, who handed over the Spanish to a foreign enemy (Gerchunoff 1944: 91). Ironically, that opacity connoted that this dictator was a spectral projection of Hitler, his shadow. In earlier works, Gerchunoff had already developed this vision of Franco as the ambassador of Nazism. For example, in "Franco nos aconseja" (1941), he warns that the triumph of the Axis implies a legitimation of Franco's imperialist interests over the Latin American republics.

Before concluding this section, it is essential to clarify that the criticism of the counter-Republican camp did not mean that Gerchunoff fully identified with the Republicans. In fact, he observes that the Republicans themselves were a heterogeneous conglomerate group that made even the triumph of the Republic a difficult pursuit (Gerchunoff [1940] 1979). Rather, Gerchunoff interpreted the Spanish Civil War as the struggle between the two Spains that he describes, synecdoches, in turn, of the battle between liberalism and authoritarianism on a global scale. This is why, in 1936, Gerchunoff objected to Baroja's failure to understand the fundamental stakes of the political contest, when Baroja indiscriminately criticized the Popular Front and the reactionaries. This is an intellectual attitude that Gerchunoff describes as a "trembling gesture" (1936: 5). In other words, Gerchunoff warns Baroja that no intellectual gesture was left out of the war and that, therefore, to return to the terminology of "Advertencia pertinente," by pretending to embody (as Origen) an immaculate virtue, he ended up crediting the triumph of traditionalist nationalism.

Espinoza's Point of View: Jews, *Criollos*,[10] and Spanish People in the Face of a Common Enemy

By the mid-1930s, Enrique Espinoza was a multifaceted figure: editor, critic, cultural agent, essayist, and fiction writer. In his literary journals, he promoted Latin American intellectual networks and progressive political conceptions (Ferreti and Fuentes 2015). His storybooks, *La levita gris* (1924) and *Ruth y Noemí* (1934), portrayed Jewish life in Buenos Aires. Espinoza did not lack contacts in the Argentine intellectual milieu. However, his inclination toward socialism, and later, Trotskyism, his ideal of North and South American cultural union, and even his own Jewish self-adscription would lead him to confrontation with different groups in the Buenos Aires scene, from both the liberal and conservative sides (Tarcus 2001). In 1935, Espinoza worried about the increasingly retrograde political-cultural climate in Argentina, and he left for Chile where he married Catalina Talesnik, with whom he traveled to Spain that same year. After different trips, Espinoza finally settled in Chile until 1973. When he published

---

[10] *Criollos* refers in this chapter to those born in Latin America who have a Spanish origin in their ancestry.

Chicos de España (1935) his authorial image remained linked to the Buenos Aires scene. Although Espinoza was concerned with Latin American affairs, I consider here, first of all, how his Jewish Argentine perspective is reflected in his literary works.

During the aforementioned trip to Spain in 1935, Espinoza wrote a series of notes that record his journeys through a country gripped by tensions just prior to the outbreak of the Spanish Civil War. Part of these writings appear in *Columna* magazine in 1937. However, they were not published in their entirety until 1938, under the subtitle "Notas de viaje" in *Chicos de España (1935)*. This book also included three essays written after 1936, under the subtitle "¿Y Ahora?" Both "Notas de viaje" and these other essays present, not just an overview of Spanish society and politics, but also an interpretation of Spanish sociopolitical relations from a particular Jewish Argentine— and Jewish Latin American—perspective. As I will demonstrate, such an interpretation has points in comparison with Gerchunoff's ideas. However, Espinoza's point of view was influenced by left-wing thinking that will mark a fundamental difference between the two authors in their respective representations of the Spanish conflict and of the mission of the Jewish intellectual in relation to it.

"Notas de viaje" is organized into nine chapters, related to each of the cities visited. Although Espinoza assures in the prologue that, in 1935, he never imagined there would be a civil war, his observations reveal the latent conflicts that would soon lead to armed confrontation. In addition, in this diary, Espinoza provides condensed versions of arguments regarding his thesis on the obligation of the Jews to support the Republican cause, which will appear in his later essays.

In "Notas de viaje," the traveler's gaze reveals political and socioeconomic conflicts in the details and contrasts he observes in the urban and rural landscapes. In this way,

Figure 6.2 Samuel Glusberg and his wife Catalina Talesnik in the gardens of Hampton Court Castle, London. Courtesy of Centro de Documentación e Investigación de la Cultura de Izquierdas (CeDInCI), Buenos Aires.

Espinoza registers the yellow insignia of the railway staff as a sequel to the repression of the Asturian Revolution (Tarcus 2001: 23). He draws attention to graffiti expressing ideological battles, such as "Vivas a Largo Caballero y Mueras a Lerroux" and the anagram "FAI" (Federación Anarquista Ibérica) on the wall of a church (Tarcus 2001: 33-4). He reads social inequality on billboards about the caravans of peasants who bear fruits to pay the rent (Tarcus 2001: 33). Similarly, Espinoza highlights the contrasts between wealth and poverty in cities. For example, in Córdoba, he notices the incongruity between a "luxurious café" and the starving boys in the street (Tarcus 2001: 59). Poor children trying to earn a living by helping the tourist appear repeatedly in Espinoza's travelogue. They are, in fact, the inspiration for the title of the book.

In the diary, these observations reiterate the idea of the existence of two Spains through different symbols. For example, a sick woman who screams on the train, consoled by a soldier and a friar, represents, for Espinoza, the Spain that he rejects. That is, he portrays a Spain dominated by ecclesiastical and military power, as opposed to the "Spain of our heart" (Tarcus 2001: 25). In Ronda, the gaze of the traveler opposes the "old Spain," expressed in the vision of ghostly nuns and the exploitation of the smallholder farmers, to "the young Spain," embodied in the workers who do not look favorably toward the side where the monarchists live (Tarcus 2001: 34). Similarly, Espinoza establishes an opposition between aristocratic Madrilenians who shout the iconic "¡Arriba España!" as "the subjects of Mussolini and Hitler" to the Spanish people who seek to build the workers' republic (Tarcus 2001: 82).[11]

In this sense, Espinoza's conception of the existence of two Spains has points of contact with that which I have pointed out in Gerchunoff. In fact, both Jewish Argentine authors rejected a Spanish nation identified with military power, the monastic worldview, and the monarchical ideology. However, while for Gerchunoff the central conflict is between authoritarianism and liberalism, for Espinoza the touchstone is the opposition between "owners and workers." In other words, the fundamental battle that had to take place, according to Espinoza, was between capitalism and socialism. The contrast between "the two mosques" of Córdoba—the historic mosque-cathedral and a brewery called "the mosque"—clearly suggested that conflicts between capital and labor power had replaced the old battles over religion (Tarcus 2001: 66).

The traveler does not observe this conflict outwardly, but he takes sides in it with the choice of the places visited, the scenes portrayed and the personalities contacted. For example, rather than listening to José Ortega y Gasset at Congreso del Libro, he prefers to buy *Discurso a los trabajadores* (A Speech for the Workers) by Largo Caballero (Tarcus 2001: 73) and to meet with León Felipe. In this sense, there are a series of associations in "Notas de viaje" of the Spanish situation, on the one hand, with Argentina (and Latin America) and, on the other hand, with Jewishness, whose implications function as arguments of such taking position in favor of the Republican.

---

[11] The division into two Spains allows us to understand this hispanophilia in an author like Espinoza who had campaigned against the cultural dependence of Latin America on Spain, although such hispanophilia may also have a connection with the revaluation of the "motherland" in the face of the Spanish conflict by various Hispanic-American progressive intellectuals (Binns 2014).

In effect, in Espinoza's detailed mapping of Spanish physical and cultural landscapes saturated with political imagery and symbolism, his perspective as a Jewish Argentine served as a lens through which he could understand the sociohistorical reality of Spain. Furthermore, these portraits of Spanish life also produce sociopolitical meanings in reference to Argentina, Latin America, and Jewishness itself.

In this way, comparisons between Argentine and Spanish landscapes reveal not only the similarities between urban settings but, above all, what Espinoza considers to be their shared fundamental problem: political-economic organization. Thus, for example, the Gran Via of Granada, an avenue whose splendor clashes with the dirty streets of the rest of the city, reminds him of Callao Street (Tarcus 2001: 38). Seville gives him the impression of being in Buenos Aires, firstly, because of the anti-fascist graffiti on the factory walls, and secondly, because of the similarity between the wide avenues that Primo de Rivera (in Spain) and Félix Uriburu (in Argentina) had built to glorify their leadership in their respective cities (Tarcus 2001: 50). This mode of comparison suggested that the advance of modernity in both Spain and Argentina was a mere facade due to a dual problem: governments continued to distance themselves from working-class people and the people did not have access to ownership of the land.

Espinoza extends this diagnosis through an analysis of what he views as the problem with private property in all of Latin America. Indeed, the influence of Marxism on Espinoza's beliefs about Spanish and Latin American social issues is apparent in his comments following conversations with Andalusian peasants: "The evil of Spain is the same of Latin America. The land does not belong to those who work it. The landowners also make up the government" (Tarcus 2001: 24).[12] In this sense, for the author, the Mexico of Lázaro Cárdenas is the point of comparison that illuminates the common path that the Americas and Spain should follow. He creates a parallel between the revolutionary slogan of Dolores Ibárruri in Spain and Zapatista proclamations in Mexico (Tarcus 2001: 81).

Now, Espinoza also associates the Jewish references in "Notas de viaje" with this political-economic dimension that he brings to the fore with respect to the conflictive Spanish scene. In effect, Espinoza establishes the nexus between the "Jewish condition" and the "Worker condition" beginning in Chapter 1. In this chapter, he describes a crowd of poorly dressed Spaniards waiting to enter La Linea from Gibraltar, which reminds him of the ghettos of the Middle Ages (Tarcus 2001: 19). There is a clear identification between "Spanish working people" and "Jews" in this association between the medieval ghettos and the Gibraltar scene. Likewise, Espinoza postulates again the mentioned parallel when a bookseller mistakenly says "Barrio Obrero" (working-class neighborhood) instead of "Barrio Hebreo" (Jewish neighborhood). Espinoza comments in the face of such a "lapse" that, "It is the same" (Tarcus 2001: 35). In this fashion, by equating "Jew" and "worker," Espinoza's support for the Spanish Republic is linked to a question of loyalty to his own ethnic origin.

---

[12] "El mal de España es el mismo de América. La tierra no pertenece a los que trabajan. Los terratenientes forman, asimismo, el gobierno."

Jewish references also appear in this text in relation to the Spanish Jewish past. In fact, as Mesa Gancedo (2012) has shown, the choice of the order of the traveler's itinerary is guided by the traces of the old Jewish quarters. It is also by virtue of a singular interpretation of the Spanish Jewish past that Espinoza positions himself in favor of the "workers' republic." Indeed, like Gerchunoff, Espinoza rescues the legendary Spain of three cultures as an ideal space of tolerance and the basis of an intrinsic bond between Spain and the Jews, whether of Sephardic or Ashkenazi origins (Di Miro 2018). "A history of centuries weighs on us, oh, in our hearts" (1938: 56),[13] Espinoza writes upon arriving in Córdoba, and he establishes a genealogy between the Hispano-Hebrew poets and Heinrich Heine as proof of such a bond. Espinoza also argues that such harmonious sociability had been possible, exclusively, thanks to an understanding between Jews and the Spanish people, since, on the contrary, the powerful looked at Jews suspiciously (1938: 64). In short, in "Notas de viaje," Espinoza associates "Jewishness" with a proletarian condition and with the old bond with Sepharad. Such a conception of "Jewishness" foregrounds Espinoza's Jewish self-identification as a tacit reason for his positionality in relation to the political-economic dichotomies that he highlights in the cases both of Spain and Argentina.

As I have anticipated, the ideas of the existence of two Spains, the intrinsic Jewish hispanophilia, the identification between Jews and workers, and the confluence of political-economic problems between Spain and Latin America suggested fragmentarily in "Notas de viaje" will be developed in Espinoza's later essays. He does this with the aim of both explaining the Spanish Civil War and arguing why Jews, especially Latin American Jews, should support the Republican position. In these essays, Espinoza takes up the idea of the two Spains, and he conceives of the war as a conflict between "Money, the Church, and Diplomacy" (1938: 133) and the "true" Spanish people. That is, this conflict is ultimately a class war between the humble and working-class sectors and the wealthiest sectors of society defended by the "ecclesiastical-military caste."

According to Espinoza's biased and anachronistic interpretation grounded in a materialist view of history these same forces—working people and powerful groups—would have clashed in two other historical events: the expulsion of Jews from Spain and the Spanish American wars of independence. For Espinoza, *criollos* and Jews would have fought to defend a society in which they had no privileges. Likewise, from the perspective of this author, such forces were also those that were currently in dispute on the international scene. Hitler, Mussolini, Franco, as well as their Latin American sympathizers, would only be defending, above all, an economically hierarchical society within their respective countries. Consequently, Espinoza argued that Jews and "*criollos* de abajo"[14]—both identified by him as the workforce—should support the Republicans to stop this common enemy, if they did not want to suffer the same fate as the German Jews (1938: 106). Espinoza identifies a connection between the shared experience of "Jews," "Spanish people," and "Argentine and Latin American people"

---

[13] "Una historia de siglos nos pesa, ay, en el corazón."
[14] That is to say, "*criollos* who come from humble origin."

to such an extent that he associates the defense of Madrid against the rebel troops (supported by the Nazis) with the "*criolla*" resistance during the British invasions of the River Plate (1938: 121). Furthermore, he equates the Argentine poem *Martín Fierro* by José Hernández with Miguel Hernández' poetry (1938: 123).

In addition, Espinoza appealed again to the argument of the "timeless connection" (*adhesión intemporal*) (1938: 100) of the Jews to Spain. In the context of these essays, the description of the nature of such a "connection" implied a rejection of the conception of the Spanish Civil War as a "holy war" (Pattin 2019). Indeed, for Espinoza, this timeless connection was not based on a conception of an Iberian origin of Jewishness. On the contrary, as he explained, such a Jewish hispanophilia, based on the historical coexistence in Spain of the three cultures, proved that neither "ethnic" nor "racial" ties, nor religious identity could explain alliances or antagonisms between peoples and nations. Espinoza ironically brings in another example to eliminate any doubts: the understanding between "Germans" and "Latinos"[15] to massacre from heaven a Catholic village of Biscay, "in the shadow of the Pope" (Pattin 2019: 101). In this way, Espinoza denied the authenticity of the religious motivations that were wielded by the nationalists to legitimize their cause, and once again, he foregrounded his belief that it was a conflict of "the richest against the poorest" (Pattin 2019: 107).

In summary, Espinoza postulated that as a Jewish Argentine and Jewish Latin American intellectual, his dual Jewish and *criollo* identities imposed on him the duty to defend the Republican position because Jews and Argentine and Latin American people had been historically attacked in the name of the same interests embodied in nationalist ideologies. In this sense, León Felipe is seen as a role model of intellectual engagement, since Espinoza identifies in Felipe's work conjunction between Jewish tradition and resistance against the powerful.

Indeed, Espinoza, on the one hand, interprets León Felipe's work as the actualization of a universal message of justice proclaimed, at least, since the prophet Isaiah (Pattin 2019: 115). On the other hand, Espinoza compares the censorship suffered by the Spanish author in Panama for supporting the Republicans with the destruction of Diego Rivera's mural at Rockefeller Center (Pattin 2019: 114). Spanish tradition and Jewish tradition would come together in León Felipe's word as a proclamation of justice. In this sense, in this essay, there are echoes of Gerchunoff in the reinterpretation of Jewish messianism in defense of freedom and justice as the key to the duty of all intellectuals, and above all, of intellectuals of Jewish origin. But also in Espinoza's text, the evocation of the destruction of Rivera's work made clear, once again, not only Espinoza's socioeconomic interpretation of that justice but also that the intellectual's duty was to spread the message of the workers' struggle, just as he did, for example, by broadcasting the iconic Republican magazine, *El mono azul*, in Chile and Argentina.

---

[15] Author's allusion to the intervention of the German Legion Condor in the Spanish Civil War.

Final Remarks

Both Espinoza and Gerchunoff conceived of the Spanish Civil War as a struggle between two forces that manifested more broadly throughout the rest of Europe, Argentina, and Latin America. Both authors wrote in favor of the Republican position with the conviction that the defeat of the Spanish Republic also implied a threat to Jewish emancipation. As I have detailed, however, the "two Spains," according to Gerchunoff, respectively embodied conservative nationalism and democratic liberalism in relation to "the academic spirit" and the "anti-academic spirit." Instead, for Espinoza, the imagery of the two Spains was a clash, ultimately, of social classes. These two interpretations are linked to the way in which each of the authors conceived of the mission of the Jewish Argentine writer and constructed their authorial self-representations.

In this sense, both Espinoza and Gerchunoff attributed differing interpretations of the Spanish conflict with redefinitions of "Jewishness." For Gerchunoff, the Jews could not be indifferent to the advance of the Spanish right, which he considered above all undemocratic, because Jews would have historically embodied freedom, equality, and tolerance. For Espinoza, Jewishness was synonymous with the "working-class condition." Jews could not be indifferent to the attack on the Spanish Republic as this was understood by him as the "Republic of workers." The contrasting conceptions about Jewishness articulated by these authors foreground the values that each author saw as threatened during the offensive against the Second Republic.

The essay, the travel diary, and the fictional prologue—presented here—were suitable literary genres to express those webs of ideas. Through these genres, both Espinoza and Gerchunoff were able to interweave the referential, expressive, and poetic discursive functions of language to provide an account of the commonalities between Argentine and Spanish sociopolitical movements of the 1930s. But also, through these genres, they invented images of Jewishness. And, in this sense, Gerchunoff's image of Jewishness would have a greater prevalence in future representations of Jewishness in Jewish Argentine literature.

References

Aizenberg, E. (2001), "How a Samovar Helped Me Theorize Latin American Jewish Writing," *Shofar*, 19 (3): 3–40.

Alburquerque García, L. (2006), "Los libros de viajes como género literario," in M. Lucena and J. Pimentel (eds.), *Diez estudios sobre literatura de viajes*, 67–87, Madrid: CSIC.

Aullón de Haro, P. (2005), "El género ensayo, los géneros ensayísticos y el sistema de géneros," in V. Cervera, B. Hernández and M. Adsuar (eds.), *El ensayo como género literario*, 13–24, Murcia: Universidad de Murcia.

Binns, N. (2014), "Intelectuales de Hispanoamérica y la Guerra civil española," *Guaraguao*, 18 (46): 9–36.

Di Miro, M. (2018), "Alberto Gerchunoff y la venganza de Shylock," *Hispamérica*, 140: 109-15.
Espinoza, E. (1938), *Chicos de España (1935)*, Buenos Aires: Perseo.
Ferreti, P. and Fuentes, L. (2015), "Los proyectos culturales de Samuel Glusberg. Aportes a la historia de la edición independiente en la primera mitad del siglo XX," *Andamios*, 12 (29): 183-206.
Gabbay, C. (2020), "Una cuestión de espacio: promesas de liberación y utopía en la poesía yidis e hispana de la guerra civil española," in P. Molina Taracena (ed.), *La poesía de la guerra civil española: una perspectiva comparatista*, 153-78, Bern: Peter Lang.
Genette, G. (2001), *Umbrales*, México: Siglo Veintiuno.
Gerchunoff, A. (1922), *La jofaina maravillosa*, Buenos Aires: Babel.
Gerchunoff, A (1924), *El Cristianismo Precristiano*, Buenos Aires: Hebraica.
Gerchunoff, A. (1925), *La asamblea de la bohardilla*, Buenos Aires: Gleizer.
Gerchunoff, A. (1934), *El Hombre Importante*, Montevideo: Sociedad Amigos del libro.
Gerchunoff, A. (1936), "Agenda," *Flecha*, II (16): 5.
Gerchunoff, A. (1937), "El libro y el espíritu," *Repertorio americano*, XIX (24): 369-72.
Gerchunoff, A. (1941), "Franco nos aconseja," *Repertorio americano*, XXII (24): 376.
Gerchunoff, A. (1944), "Noche de pascua de 1940," *Judaica*, XI (128-129): 88-91.
Gerchunoff, A. ([1940] 1979), "Manuel Azaña," in Vernáculas (ed.), *Figuras de Nuestro Tiempo*, 151-8, Buenos Aires: Vernáculas.
Glozman, M. (2013), "Corporativismo, política intelectual y regulación lingüística: la creación de la Academia Argentina de Letras," *Lenguaje*, II (41): 455-78.
Gramuglio, M T. (2013), *Nacionalismo y cosmopolitismo en la Literatura Argentina*, Rosario: Editorial Municipal de Rosario.
Lvovich, D. (2003), *Nacionalismo y antisemitismo en la Argentina*, Buenos Aires: Vergara.
Mesa Gancedo, D. (2012), "Notas de viaje de un judío errante. Chicos de España, de Enrique Espinoza," in C. de M. Valcárcel and A. García Morales (eds.), *Viajeros, diplomáticos y exiliados: Escritores hispanoamericanos en España (1914-1939)*, Vol. 2, 369-92, Bern: Peter Lang.
Pattin, S. (2019), "Guerra española, guerra santa: apuntes a partir de una controversia conceptual en Argentina (1936-1937)," *Historia Contemporánea*, 60: 619-46.
Rein, R. (2014), "A Trans-National Struggle with National and Ethnic Goals: Jewish-Argentines and Solidarity with the Republicans during the Spanish Civil War," *Journal of Iberian and Latin American Research*, 20 (2): 171-82.
Said, E. (1994), *Representations of the Intellectual*, New York: Pantheon.
Sosnowski, S. (1987), *La orilla inminente*, Buenos Aires: Legasa.
Szurmuk, M. (2018), *La vocación desmesurada: una biografía de Alberto Gerchunoff*, Buenos Aires: Sudamericana.
Tarcus, H. (2001), *Mariátegui en la Argentina o las políticas culturales de Samuel Glusberg*, Buenos Aires: El cielo por asalto.
Zanatta, L. (1996), *Del estado liberal a la nación católica. Iglesia y Ejército en los orígenes el peronismo, 1930-1943*, Buenos Aires: UNQUI.

7

"The World Exists and We Are Part of It"
The Inzikh's Poetic Response to the Spanish Civil War

Golda van der Meer

"Di velt iz do un mir zeynen a teyl fun ir"[1] (The world exists and we are part of it) (*Inzikh*, January 1920: 2; Harshav 2007: 774). With this statement, the avant-garde Yiddish poetic movement in New York, called the Inzikh,[2] declared that the poetry in their journal would be written by socially conscious poets writing about worldly issues "oyf vifl zi shpigelt zikh op in unz, oyf vifl rirt unz on" (as it is mirrored in us, as it touches us) (Harshav 2007). In this vein, this chapter will address the reception of the Spanish Civil War by the Inzikh poets as well as the war's impact on the *Inzikh* journal. The aim is to explore questions regarding the Inzikh poets and their relationship with the Spanish Civil War by discussing their interest in international affairs along with the effects the war had on their poetical innovations.

Although the Spanish Civil War was a civil conflict fought in Spain from 1936 to 1939, Yiddish writers from around the world supported the fight of the Republicans, loyal to the left-popular front, against the fascist Francoist dictatorship. In exploring this matter, some of the questions addressed in this chapter are: how did these European Jewish writers, exiled in New York, relate to the Spanish Civil War? To what extent did the Spanish Civil War influence their poetic rhythms? How did they go from representing the noises and rhythms of the streets of New York to representing the sounds and rhythms of the bombs in the Spanish fields? These questions will be explored by studying publications found in the *Inzikh* journal. The Inzikh's interest in international affairs, such as the Spanish Civil War, was an interest shared with other Yiddish poets of the interwar period, and it also extended to the ways in which the war affected their poetical work. This chapter will firstly present a brief overview of the Yiddish literary movements of the early twentieth century in New York, in order

---

[1] The original Yiddish version is transcribed using the transcriptional system favored by the Institute for Jewish Research (YIVO).
[2] The name Inzikh was first written in two words, *In zikh*, when it first appeared in their published poetic anthology of 1919 but was then contracted into one word, Inzikh, when published in their journal in 1920. Inzikh would then become the name of their movement and their contributors would be known as the Inzikhists (Introspectivists).

to provide some context of the literary scene at the time. Then I will discuss the poems of two Inzikh poets, Jacob Glatstein and Aaron Glanz-Leyeles, founders of the Inzikh movement, who engaged with the theme of the Spanish Civil War in an attempt to explore the questions mentioned earlier.

Yiddish Literary Movements of the Early Twentieth Century in New York

Jewish immigrants who arrived in New York in the period from the end of the nineteenth century to the beginning of the twentieth century created new literary movements in Yiddish, dealing with themes that ranged from labor and protest to the modernist and the avant-garde. The poetry and prose of Yiddish writers of the 1880s were published primarily in periodicals devoted to ideological persuasion. Such poetry and prose were written mainly by poets who considered themselves apostles of political liberation or by workers in sweatshops who fought for the dignity of speech (Howe 1989: 418). This movement, which came to be called the Sweatshop Poets, the most recognized of them being Morris Rosenfeld, was set apart from both world literature and the flowering of Yiddish fiction that had begun in Eastern Europe. In these early years, Yiddish literature was "unsophisticated in technique but stormy-voiced, expressing the feelings of the workers and addressing the rising disgruntlement of the Jewish masses as they tried to cope with poverty" (Howe 1989).

In 1907, opposing the Sweatshop Poets' movement, a new movement called Di Yunge emerged. What soon made Di Yunge a revolutionary force within Yiddish literature was that they rejected political commitment and denied any obligation to speak for national ideals. Di Yunge poets never felt at home in the United States or used the English language. These young poets turned instead to European literature and, above all, to ideas of aesthetic autonomy and symbolist refinement. Most of them were poor immigrant workers: Mani Leib was a shoemaker, Zisha Landau was a house painter, and H. Leivick hung advertising posters in the street (Howe 1989: 431). At the time, independent poetry magazines were being formed to free Yiddish writing from commercial pressures and the demands of the editors of larger newspapers. Di Yunge did not write about the growing metropolis of New York, nor did they write about the exploitation of Jewish life happening before their eyes. They dreamed of being pure poets and saw themselves as distant cousins of great European poets, such as A. Pushkin and R. M. Rilke. In short, they were considered Esthetes, their creed being art for art's sake (Howe 1989).

Women poets were part of these new literary trends. Still, they were hardly recognized in the Yiddish literary world until Korman compiled a volume of Yiddish poems by women, entitled *Yidishe dikhterins: antologye* (Yiddish Women Poets: Anthology)[3] in 1928, regrouping an impressive array of 70 women who had been

---

[3] Korman's anthology was made in response to the male dominated Bassin's *Antologye: finf hundert yor yidishe poezye* (Anthology: Five Hundred Years of Yiddish Poetry). Hellerstein states how

writing poetry in Yiddish for over five centuries. Although Yiddish women poets have not been strictly associated with one poetic movement some did come to represent the credos of a particular movement in question. This can be seen in the Inzikh movement where Leyeles[4] played a major role to make Yiddish avant-garde poetry written by women more visible. A pertinent example is that the first issue of the *Inzikh* journal in January 1920 opens with two poems by Celia Dropkin followed right after the Inzikh manifesto. Other women poets such as Razel Zykhlinsky, Anna Margolin, Malka Heifetz Tussman, Rokhl Korn, and Debora Vogel, among others, also published in the *Inzikh* journal; the latter became one of the major woman poets to be published in the *Inzikh* journal in the 1930s. Coincidently, Vogel published a poem in reference to the Spanish Civil War the same year as Leyeles's poem "Shpanishe balade," but Vogel's poem was published in another journal. The poem in question is titled "Kalter ruzsh,"[5] (Cold Rouge) published in *Der nayer morgn. Lemberger togblat* in 1939.

Breaking away from the Yiddish literary tradition and the Yiddish poetic movements formerly mentioned, the Inzikh movement, founded in the 1920s, marks an important turning point. Through their work, the Yiddish language underwent a great transformation with the aim of creating a new poetic language by innovating their poetic style. For many of the Inzikh writers, being part of an avant-garde group allowed them to be faithful to the Yiddish language while reaching toward a broader and more universal goal. Their objective was to be recognized as forming part of the canons of universal literature as poets who wrote in the Yiddish language.

The Inzikh poets constructed cosmopolitan imaginaries through their poetry. Demonstrating this cosmopolitan urge, Leyeles wrote an essay published in the *Inzikh* issue of March 1937, titled "Yidishe literatur un di velt" (Yiddish Literature and the World). For Leyeles "yidish a velt-shprakh loyt ir farshpreytkeyt un—afile bulgarish oder katalonish kukt dreyster, mit mer zelbstvirde, der droysndiker velt in di oygn arayn" (Yiddish is a world-language in its scope, and yet even Bulgarian and Catalan looks more courageously, with more dignity straight into the eyes of the external world) (*Inzikh*, March 1937: 93; Harshav 2007: 800). Leyeles's reference to the Catalan[6] language in this statement, a language persecuted during the Spanish Civil War and forbidden in Spain during Franco's dictatorship, reflects the knowledge this poet had of the Spanish conflict. Two other pertinent examples of the Inzikh poets' awareness of the Spanish conflict are the poems "Shpanishe balade" (Spanish Ballad), written by

---

Korman's alternate intention in making the anthology was "to establish the place of women poets in the tradition of Yiddish writing" (261).

[4] In October 1915, Leyeles wrote an article in the New York newspaper *Di fraye arbeter shtime* (The Free Worker's Voice) titled "Kultur un di froy" (Culture and Woman) where he "complained of the monotony and redundancy of recent poetry and philosophical writings, which he blamed on the absence of 'Woman' from the creative scene" (Hellerstein 2014: 30).

[5] In the poem, Vogel narrates how "on a wall on Boulevard Saint-Michel / hangs a blue sign commemorating / all the anarchists of Spain: / Spain is in danger of isolation. / (Oh, the land of castanets and tangolita / is now the beloved of dictators)" (English translation is mine).

[6] In 1913, Yiddish philologist Ber Borokhov wrote about the Catalan language, among other minority languages, and their fight for prevalence as examples that could serve the Yiddish language. See a further comparison of the two languages (Catalan and Yiddish) in Nath (1998: 51–61).

Leyeles and published in 1939 in the special fiftieth edition of the *Inzikh* journal, and "Shtile Shpanie" (Silent Spain) by Glatstein published in the *Inzikh* journal in 1938. These two poems will be discussed in this chapter. Leyeles and Glatstein were dissident poets who saw their own struggles mirrored in those carried out in other world arenas, such as the Spanish front. By writing about worldly issues, Leyeles and Glatstein were at the same time fleeing their Jewish traditions by embracing a poetic language that reflected the complexities, associations, and perceptions of the modern man.

Introducing the Inzikh Movement

The Inzikh poets (also known as Introspectivists) displayed their condition as exiles by way of modernizing the Yiddish language through form and rhythm and equating it to any modern language of that time.[7] The *Inzikh* journal, a monthly poetic journal written in Yiddish, was founded in 1920 in New York by three young Yiddish poets: Aaron Glanz-Leyeles (1889–1966), Jacob Glatstein (1896–1971), and Nokhem Borekh Minkov (1893–1958). Its aim was to propose new Yiddish avant-garde poetry along with reviews and translations of world literature into Yiddish in its aspiration to become a cosmopolitan journal. In the mid-1930s, due to the rise of fascism in Europe, it became increasingly difficult for Jewish immigrants to return to their countries of origin. This, in turn, shaped the evolution of the creative output in the *Inzikh* journal. In the 1920s, the *Inzikh* journal primarily published avant-garde poetry, poetic theory, and literary criticism. In the 1930s, its focus began to shift from poems that were initially inspired by Walt Whitman to more international affairs, such as the Spanish Civil War.

The *Inzikh* journal was modeled after the Anglo-American "little magazine,"[8] a term used by the *Encyclopædia Britannica* for journals devoted to "serious literary writings, usually avant-garde and non-commercial." The influences for their art came from all around the world. As Harshav states,

> the Yiddish Introspectivists absorbed the ideas on art that were developed in recent Modernist movements. In their arguments one can find traces of Italian and Russian Futurism, German and Yiddish Expressionism, English Imagism and Vorticism, as well as ideas raised by Nietzsche, Croce, Freud, and T. S. Eliot. (Harshav 1990: 176)

---

[7] Glatstein wrote a parody titled, "Ven dzhoys volt geshribn yidish: a parode" (If Joyce Had Written in Yiddish: A Parody) (*Inzikh*, July 1928: 68–70) where he simulates Joyce's writing in *Finnegans Wake*. In doing so Glatstein also adapted Joyce's associative technique of fusion terms in his later poems (Hadda 1980: 57).

[8] By the 1910s the phenomenon of the "little magazine" influenced Yiddish poetic movements to print their artistic credos and poetic works, reacting to the constraints and commercial purposes of the press. Jewish poets created "little magazines" of Yiddish poetry as a form of resistance to linguistic assimilation to the new country. This act of resisting to linguistic assimilation was a small but significant literary revolution. For the Introspectivists, the *Inzikh* journal became a reflection of their condition of exile, where amongst poems, poetry criticism, translations of world literature into Yiddish and linguistic reflections, the magazine editors also contributed with their own reflections of the demise of Yiddish in the new country, and the political situation of their times.

The *Inzikh* journal was a monthly periodical, but it was not published consistently. The period of publication can be divided into two phases: from 1920 to 1930 and from 1934 to 1940. There are various reasons the journal was published intermittently, financial reasons being the most predominant. Through the years, the journal switched its preference from a cosmopolitan magazine, publishing translations from international literature from Europe, Asia, and Anglo-America, to focus more on critical essays on issues pertaining to the Yiddish language and political affairs. The second phase of publication (1934–40) was a more mature period during which Inzikh was already established as a movement. It was then that many poets joined the journal. It is also during this time that the journal changed its tone into a more political one, demonstrating concern over the global political events of the time, as exemplified by articles published in the journal on a variety of topics that ranged from Maxim Gorki to the Spanish Civil War.

The aim of the founders in creating this new Yiddish poetic movement was to further the development of Yiddish literature, by applying avant-garde techniques in their poetical style. At the same time, the Inzikh poets' aim was to add the Yiddish voice to the international modernist movement in order to demonstrate that the Yiddish language was more than just part of their cultural heritage: the Inzikh poets believed that the Yiddish language should be considered part of a linguistic and cultural world heritage. Yiddish ceases to be a language of immigrants and is now proclaimed a language of universal letters, a language of the world. The Introspectivists disassociated themselves from their ethnic condition, avoiding Jewish themes or traditional or folk literature. What connected them to Jewishness was the Yiddish language, which became no longer just an identity but a political element. Not only did the articles in the journal become more politically inclined but also its poetry was changing. It was so that the Introspectivists managed to turn political activism into poetical activism.

The Introspectivists engaged further with this activism in their journal in the mid-1930s, in response to the rise of fascism in Europe, when it became increasingly difficult for Jewish immigrants to return to their countries of origin. These difficulties stirred up a political debate and opened a new creative output in their journal. The Inzikh poets were not the only Yiddish poets who turned their attention to the Spanish Civil War, however. Some of the most renowned Yiddish poets who wrote about the Spanish Civil War were Peretz Markish (1895–1952), Yacob Glantz (1902–82), and Aaron Kurtz (1891–1964). According to Cynthia Gabbay, Kurtz, as well as Glantz, had the absolute conviction that the fight against fascism was also carried out in the media and in the world of literature: "they fought against the war using pen and paper echoing those who fought on the republican battlefield" (2020: 165).[9] None of these Yiddish poets that wrote about the Spanish Civil War had been to Spain, thus "the Spanish soil [is] described from a distance" (Glaser 2020: 146). These poets reflected in their poems a broader struggle. Jewish poetics became international, as "the Spanish Civil

---

[9] "combatieron desde la letra y el papel haciendo eco de quienes luchaban en el campo de batalla republicano" (English translation is mine).

War evoked the sympathies of Left-identified Yiddish writers and readers spanning multiple continents" (Glaser 2020: 141). While many Jews volunteered to go fight on the Spanish front against fascism, these Yiddish poets "fought in a literary front" (Glaser 2020).

The Inzikh poets' interest in the Spanish Civil War was reflected in several editorials in their journal, such as "Oyfn Shpanishn front" (On the Spanish Front) written by Leyeles and published in the *Inzikh* issue of June 1937, and "Khurbn Shpanie" (The Destruction of Spain) written by Zekhariah Shuster in the *Inzikh* issue of March 1939. The Introspectivists' preoccupation with worldly issues did not only change their editorial line but also the themes of their poems. The interest of my study relies on the poetical representation of the Spanish Civil War published in the *Inzikh* journal. Such representation can be found in poems written by Glatstein and Leyeles.

Glatstein and "Shtile Shpanie" (Silent Spain)

Glatstein, one of the founders of the Inzikh movement, would become a central figure on the strength of his poetic talent. As Leyeles wrote, even those critics who opposed the *Inzikh* movement as a whole often made an exception for Glatstein's poetry. "He possessed a unique feel for language, erudition in both Yiddish and world literature, and an emotional honesty that demanded acknowledgement" (Ponichtera 2012: 52). Glatstein was born in Lublin, Poland, in 1896 and immigrated to New York in 1914 due to the rise of antisemitism in Lublin. In 1918 he studied law at New York University where he met Minkov, who reignited his interest in Yiddish literature. He worked briefly as a journalist in the Yiddish press until 1919, the year he participated in the founding of the *Inzikh* journal. Despite Glatstein's efforts to bring Yiddish poetry into the mainstream of modern literature, he became best known for his post-Holocaust poems and not for his achievement of creating a new Yiddish poetic style.

Glatstein saw the poet as a proletariat of the word as he describes in his poem, "Mir, di Wortproletarier" (We the Wordproletariat): "nakht. In di tunklste erter finklen verter. / s'geyen op gantse shifn mit bagrifn. / un du, bapantsert mit shvaygn un klugzayn, / viklst op vort fun meyn" (Night. In the darkest places sparkle traces / Of words. Loaded ships with ideo-glyphs / Sail away. And you, armored in silence and wisdom, / Unwrap word from sense) (Glatstein 1937: 40; Harshav and Harshav 2007: 275). The concept of silence[10] is brought up again in Glatstein's poem about the Spanish Civil War titled "Shtile Shpanie" (Silent Spain):

In joyful hearts,
Spain sings with mournful rifles.
Bombs plant plants in ruins,
which don't grow green,

---

[10] For a study on the concept of silence in Jewish literature see Neher (1980) and Steiner (1977).

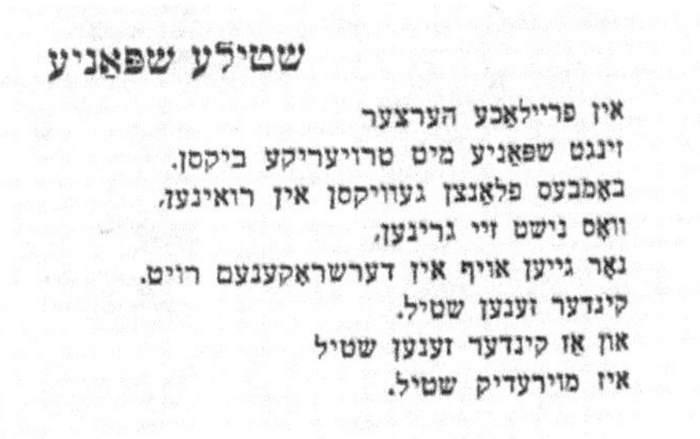

שטילע שפּאַניע

אין פֿריילאַכע הערצער
זינגט שפּאַניע מיט טרויעריקע ביקסן.
באָמבעס פֿלאַנצן געוויקסן אין רואינען,
וואָס נישט זיי גרינען,
נאָר גייען אויף אין דערשראָקענעם רויט.
קינדער זענען שטיל.
און אַז קינדער זענען שטיל
איז מוירעדיק שטיל.

Figure 7.1 Glatstein's poem "Shtile Shpanie" (*Inzikh* June 1938: 145). YIVO's Archive.

but rise in fearful red.
Children are silent,
and when children are silent,
it's dreadfully silent.[11]

Glatstein's short poem was published in the *Inzikh* issue of June 1938. On an interesting note, this poem cannot be found in any of Glatstein's published books of poems, and as a result, there is no English translation of the poem. It is the only poem written by Glatstein that refers to the Spanish Civil War. It is therefore uncertain why Glatstein decided to dedicate a short poem to the Spanish political situation. It is likely that he was influenced by other Yiddish poets who wrote about the Spanish Civil War during the 1930s. These were poets such as Peretz Markish, Esther Shumiatcher, Aaron Kurtz, and Jacob Glantz, the two former ones having published in the *Inzikh* journal. Markish published, among other works, a poem titled "Spain" in the *Naye Folkstaytung* in 1936. Kurtz published a book titled *No pasaran: Lider, balades un poemes fun Shpanishn folk in zayn kamf kegn fashizm* (No Pasaran: Songs, Ballads, and Poems of the Spanish People in Its Struggle against Fascism) in 1938 in New York. It is not until the Holocaust years that Glatstein's poetry assumes a more reflective and combative tone with poems such as "A gute nakht, velt" (Good Night, World) published in 1938.

A closer reading of Glatstein's poem "Shtile Shpanie" (Silent Spain), reveals that the term *silent* contrasts with the terms such as *song* and *ballad* used by other Yiddish poets in their anti-war, social, and political poetry written during the 1930s. Much of that poetry was adapted to marching songs that called for action, whereas Glatstein's poem focuses its attention on the silence caused by the Civil War. The concept of silence is not only present in the title but dominates the entire poem. The songs sung by the riffles and bombs silence the children, and, as a result, according to the poet, the whole of Spain is silenced. In this poem, the riffles and the bombs, loud noises followed by the complete absence of any noise, are a telltale sign of death and destruction. But this absence of noise is also an important factor as a consequence of living under an oppressive state. In opposition to that stillness, the poet rises to give voice to those who have been quieted by the riffles and the bombs by creating his own reality. Glatstein shapes his own reality

---

[11] The English translation is mine.

of the Spanish Civil War from afar, describing that since the whole of Spain is silent, the Yiddish poets must narrate their perceived reality by using their poetical language. After all, "in what ultimately is a quintessential modernist gesture, Glatstein commits himself to being a language artist above all" (Zaritt 2015: 187). Adam Fales observes how Spanish authors like Valle-Inclán,[12] with his work *Divinas Palabras* (Divine Words), and Luis Martín-Santos, with his novel *Tiempo de Silencio* (Time of Silence),

> experiment with ways of representing how people perceive reality. In each case, language—specifically the sound of language—shapes reality, though with different effects [. . .]. For each author, the approaches to aspects of sound show how these experiments in perception change the lived reality as well. If reality sounds different, it may be different too. (2018: n/p)[13]

Glatstein's poem, consisting of eight verses, is written in free verse, except for the three last verses where he intentionally repeats the word "*shtil*" (silent). A key element of the Inzikh aesthetic program was the use of free verse, an innovation in Yiddish literature. The Introspectivists saw free verse as "best suited to the individuality of the rhythm and of the poem as a whole" (Harshav 2007: 777). Their interest in the individuality of the poet extended to a concern for the individuality of the poem—their aim was that the poem would be able to develop freely, without the constraints of tradition. These revolutionary writers were constructing a new path through their poetic language. Their responsibility was not to worship the ashes of a burdensome past but to keep the fire of poetic expression alive. Poems then become the weapons to combat fascism on the literary front. The poet, or according to Glatstein, a word proletariat, "armored in silence and wisdom, / Unwrap[s] word from sense." With "Shtile Shpanie" (Silent Spain), Glatstein presents his poetic credo "wherein authentic artistic expression originated in the silence of the woods" (Schwarz 2005: 112) and where the poem presents Glatstein's "poetics as independent of any ulterior motive save the artistic refinement of poetic musicality, the sounds and rhythms of word" (Schwarz 2005: 113).[14]

Glatstein's poem on the Spanish Civil War, besides presenting the Inzikh movement's interest in international affairs, became a preface to what would later become his most renowned poems of the Holocaust. As Glaser and Weintraub eloquently put it "history would prove the Spanish Civil War to be a dress rehearsal for a struggle against fascism and Nazism" (2005: 315). This poem was to be the epitome of a movement lured by universal themes to challenge the Jewish world to go back to its origins. Harshav establishes how, although in Glatstein's early poetry there is no denial of a

---

[12] Ramón María del Valle-Inclán (1866–1936) was an early modernist, member of the Spanish Generation of 1898, who bitterly satirized the Spanish society of his time. Glatstein refers to Valle-Inclán in his novel *Ven Yash iz geforn* (Homeward Bound), when Yash, the narrator, "is reminded of a Spanish book (he) once read—the allusion is to *Autumn and Winter Sonatas* by Ramon del Valle-Inclán" (Wisse 2010: xix).
[13] The English translation is mine.
[14] In the book *Yankev Glatshteyn* (1980), Hadda establishes how Glatstein, for instance, not only did not follow the Introspectivists' norms but moved beyond them through the years.

sort of Jewishness, it is somewhat irrelevant to the themes of the poems. That relation with Jewishness is represented in a reflection of the European world experienced in the chaos of the noisy metropolis of New York (Harshav 1990: 189). Overall, the true Jewishness is illustrated in the use of the Yiddish language, as Harshav explains how "the direct, coarse, juicy, rich, spoken language, with its diminutives, allusions, stylistic clashes, and ironic twists, is as Jewish as Yiddish lyrical poetry ever was before, even though thematically it is a cosmopolitan poem" (Harshav 1990: 189–90).

The Inzikh movement "sought to create a 'consciously modernist poetics' attuned to how modern 'man' internalizes the political/historical moment" (Garrett 1998: 207). The Spanish Civil War was one of the most significant moments in twentieth-century European history and in representing that moment, these "consciously modernist poetics" adopted a range of forms, from defying silence in Glatstein's poetry to creating new rhythms in Leyeles's poem.

Leyeles and the "Shpanishe Balade" (Spanish Ballad)

Leyeles, born in 1889 in Wloclawek, Poland, played a particularly influential role in the early years of the Inzikh movement. He studied philosophy at the University of London (1905–8) and, after immigrating to New York in 1909, he studied literature at Columbia University (1910–13). He was also politically active: in London, he became part of the Socialist-Territorialist Party. This party, also known as the Jewish Territorialist Organization, which was institutionalized in 1905, had as its main objective to find an alternative territory to that in Israel, preferred by the Zionist movement, for the creation of a Jewish homeland. The organization adopted what became known as Jewish territorialism, also referred to as Jewish statism. Despite the fact that Leyeles turned to avant-garde poetic expression in his more mature years, his political activism was a latent drive throughout his years as a poet. This can also be seen in his translations into Yiddish of works that range from E. A. Poe to L. Trotsky. As mentioned earlier in the chapter, Leyeles's interest in the Spanish Civil War was expressed in such editorials as "Oyfn Shpanishn front" (On the Spanish Front), published in the *Inzikh* issue of June 1937. Leyeles also composed a poem on the Spanish Civil War titled "Shpanishe balade" (Spanish Ballad) published in the *Inzikh* issue of March 1939.

Firstly, it should be noted that it is no coincidence that Leyeles uses a child as the main character for his poem, "Pepito iz shoyn gantse, shoyn gantse fir yor alt" (Pepito Is Already a Four-Year-Old Young Man) (*Inzikh*, March 1939: 20; Kramer 1989: 151).[15] According to Glaser, "for many people observing Spain from afar, the

---

[15] Leyeles's poem "Spanish Ballad" was published in the English version in the anthology *A Century of Yiddish Poetry*, edited and translated by Aaron Kramer in 1989. Considering his approach toward translations, Kramer observes that "rather than misrepresent the predominant form of Yiddish poetry (traditional rhymed stanzas), thus catering to the current bias against rhyme and pattern with the convenient rationale that they are impossible to replicate well, I have insisted on matching

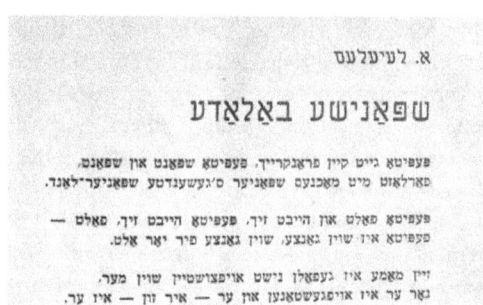

Figure 7.2 A fragment of Leyeles's poem "*Shpanishe balade*" (*Inzikh*, March 1939: 20). YIVO's Archive.

most moving stories from Spain involved children" (2020: 161). The use of children is also present in Glatstein's poem mentioned earlier: "kinder zenen shtil. / un az kinder zenen shtil / iz moyredik stil" (Children are silent. / And when children are silent / is dreadfully silent). One interpretation of this preoccupation with the fate of children may be that children are portrayed as the key element of a country's future voice.[16] The use of children in Yiddish poetry about the war can also be found in poems by Aaron Kurtz ("Shpanish viglikh" [Spanish Lullaby], 1938) and Dora Teitelboim ("Milkhome viglikh" [War Lullaby], 1944) (for both poems see Glaser and Weintraub 2005: 318, 330).

In the poem, Leyeles narrates the journey of a Spanish boy named Pepito into exile: "Pepito geyt keyn frankreykh, Pepito shpant un shpant, / farlozt mit makhnes shpanier s'geshendte shpanier-land" (Pepito comes a-marching, Pepito heads for France; he flees, with hosts of Spaniards, the shattered Spanish lands) (*Inzikh*, March 1939: 20; Kramer 1989: 151). The name of the main character of the poem, Pepito, is a diminutive of Pepe that derives from José, a traditional Spanish name. The use of this diminutive throughout the poem reminds the reader repeatedly that the character of the poem is a child and evokes a sense of endearment with the character. The natural flow of language seen in the poem mirrors the rhyme in couplets (seventeen in total) which emulate the rhythm of Pepito's arduous and long

---

the form of a poem because form is an intrinsic part of what is being said, and it is the translator's duty to transmit the total experience offered by a poem" (Kramer 1989: 22). Thus, Kramer matches the form in Leyeles's original Yiddish version into his English version where the rhythm of the poem becomes an intrinsic part of its interpretation.

[16] It is no coincidence that upon arriving in the United States, Leyeles, one of the chief ideologues of the Inzikh movement, worked on building Yiddish schools around the United States. Leyeles also collaborated with the Workmen's Circle, which is to this day a center for teaching Yiddish language and culture in New York. Leyeles's involvement in schools and teaching demonstrates his ideas about how education bears the seeds that will bring to fruition the democratic values of the future through children.

stride, the "shpant un shpant" (comes a-marching)¹⁷ or the rhythm of the falling bombs "asakh, asakh, asakh" (hundreds upon hundreds). This rhythm in couplets is a free interpretation of Leyeles's understanding of a traditional ballad. This was something common in Leyeles's poetry, as he adapted and re-created in Yiddish classic poetic forms from European, American, and Chinese poetry. According to Harshav, "there was a tendency to enrich the gamut of poetic rhythms through mastering difficult strophic forms, both as found in the European tradition, and as originally constructed by the poet" (2007: 46). Leyeles does present some commonalities with the structure of a ballad, where Pepito is presented as the main character already in the first line and where he uses memorable lines as the chorus, such as "Pepito geyt keyn frankreykh" (Pepito heads for France) repeated as an ongoing march toward exile. Repetition throughout the poem also emphasizes Pepito's marching and stumbling during his stride toward France and reminds the reader several times that Pepito is a child: "Pepito iz shoyn gantse, shoyn gantse fir yor alt" (Pepito is already a four-year-old young man). The use of dialogue is also adopted by Leyeles to portray the inner thoughts of Pepito while at the same time he pictures the horrors and calamities of war,

> When asked where he is heading, he promptly says "To France";
> Pepito's heard and answered that question more than once.
>
> "To France, from whose wide heavens no bursts of fire fall
> without the slightest warning, to catch you in the skull.
>
> "Where up to now the hateful have had no time to kill
> old people, mothers, children—to strike them down at will."
>
> That's what his mother told him as Barcelona bled;
> but she could not awaken when those around her fled.
>
> (Kramer 1989: 151–2)

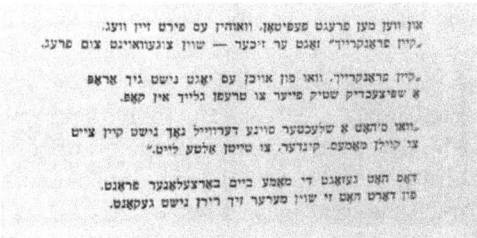

Figure 7.3 A fragment of Leyeles's poem "*Shpanishe balade*" (*Inzikh*, March 1939: 20). YIVO's Archive.

---

¹⁷ The English translations used of the poem in this chapter are from Kramer (1989: 151–2).

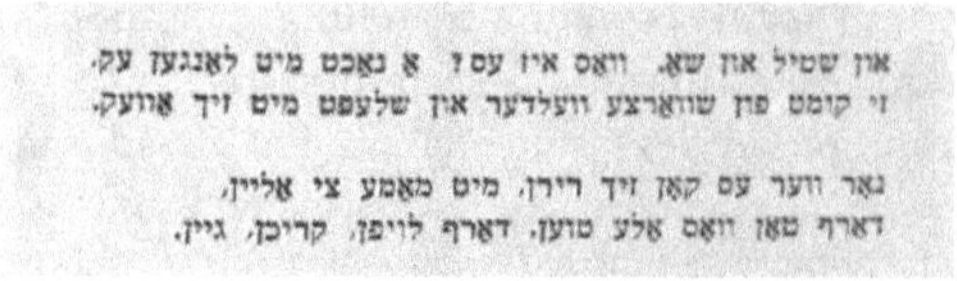

138 Jewish Imaginaries of the Spanish Civil War

אוּן שטיל און שאַ. װאָס איז עס? אַ נאַכט מיט לאַנגען עק,
זי קומט פֿון שװאַרצע װעלדער און שלעפּט מיט זיך אַװעק.

נאָר װער עס קאָן זיך רירן, מיט מאַמע צי אַלײן,
דאַרף מאָן װאָס אַלע טוען, דאַרף לױפֿן, קריכן, גײן.

Figure 7.4 A fragment of Leyeles's poem *"Shpanishe balade"* (*Inzikh*, March 1939: 20). YIVO's Archive.

Leyeles narrates the journey of Pepito into exile, which is also the journey of the reader that accompanies him through his struggles and burdens, to the point of suggesting the reader go on this journey as well, as seen in the following verses,

> Quiet and still: what is it? A long-tailed Night who'll crawl
> from pitch-black woods and drag off her trophies one and all.
> But those who *can* keep moving, with mother or alone,
> must do what all are doing, must run, must stagger on.
>
> (Kramer 1989: 151)

Leyeles use of the pronoun *ver es* (*he who*, translated by Kramer as "those") in the couplet shown here is followed by the instruction of what "those" *darfn tuen* (must do). It is the only time in the poem that Leyeles uses the pronoun *ver es* (those) instead of *er* (he, referring to Pepito) as if to involve the reader in Pepito's exile. It is here that the poet instructs the reader indirectly to "*loyfn, krikhn, geyn*" (run, crawl, go). Leyeles argued that a poem had to be dynamic, that a poem is a means for dialogue. Hence, in many of Leyeles's poems, as in the series *In Sobvey* (In the Subway), his experience as an immigrant may be perceived as a form of dialogue between the narrator and the city of New York. The title of the poem "In Sobvey" which is written in English with Hebrew letters, is also an example of the exilic experience where the new language intrudes on the mother tongue. The new rhythms of the new technologies in the city, such as the subway, fascinated the Yiddish poets. It was a time of technological change, and that change was also incorporated into the themes and rhythms of the poem.[18] The Inzikh poets viewed rhythm adapted to its contemporary life. With the changing times, the need arose for them to create "a new art and new and different rhythms" (Harshav 2007: 778). Rhythm was the inner essence of a poem, the soul, that bound together the "poetry of feeling" and the "poetry of thought."

Leyeles's own experience of exile is also portrayed in "Shpanishe balade" (Spanish Ballad), this time through the eyes of a child who is forced into exile under the rise of fascism in Europe. During and after the Spanish Civil War, over 500,000 people were exiled from Spain, most of them crossing the border to France, as narrated in Leyeles's

---

[18] An example can be found in Leyeles's poem "In Sobvey III": "Kumt tsu der stantsie / a toyter tsug. / durkhgeshhtokhene oygn. / tseblutikte msyler. / in di toyte lecher— / goldene mintsn ,/ blitsike sharfn, / vos di hant hot gevorfn / in der sobvey-ban / oyf dem untererdishn van-van-vanzin" (To the station comes / A dead train. / Pierced eyes. / Bloody mouths. / In dead holes— / Golden coins, / Flashing blades, / Dropped by a hand / In a subway train / In the underground / mad-mad-madness) (Harshav 2007: 103).

poem. Leyeles had experienced exile himself when he immigrated to New York in 1909. More than two million Jews were exiled to the United States from the 1890s to the 1920s due to the rise of antisemitism in Europe. By emphasizing the concept of the Spanish exile in the poem, Leyeles also projects exile as the continuum of the Jewish heritage.

The allusions to Spain as a reference for exile can be found not only in Leyeles's "Shpanishe balade" (Spanish Ballad) but also in a poem he wrote about Yehuda Halevi.[19] The Yiddish poet Rajzel Zychlinsky, a poet who contributed to the *Inzikh* journal, also wrote about the relation with Spain and exile in her poem "Vegn vos hot gezungen der letster yidisher dikhter af shpanisher erd?" (About What Did the Last Jewish Poet on Spanish Soil Sing?) written in 1939. In the English translation, titled "Ibn Dagan of Andalusia," Zychlinsky writes how,

> All the Jews were driven out of Castille
> and Aragon.
> About what did he sing then,
> Ibn Dagan?
> Here history is silent.[20]

The silence of history that Zychlinsky foregrounds in the poem will be transformed into verse by the Yiddish poets of modern times, as seen in Glatstein's poem "Shtile Shpanie" (Silent Spain) discussed in the previous section. The uses of the word silent by both poets are different in their original Yiddish. In "Shtile Shpanie" (Silent Spain), Glatstein uses the Yiddish word *shtil* (silent), an adjective, as if to describe from afar an event, while Zychlinsky, in her poem, uses the Yiddish word *shvaygn* (to keep silent), a verb, as if to call for action to reverse the condition of silence. The Yiddish word *shvayg* may carry a more political connotation as well because of its association with Peretz's renowned novel *Bontshe shvayg* (Bontshe the Silent). Peretz's novel, published in 1894, narrates the story of Bontshe, a man who never speaks up for himself. Bontshe came to represent the oppressed, those kept in perpetual silence under the governing society's cruelty. According to Glaser, "Yiddish poets around the world hastened to depict Spain as the epicenter of current and past pain" (2020: 140). The focus on Spain triggered reminisces of the Inquisition and at the same time was a prelude to the fight against fascism prior to the Second World War (2020).

---

[19] The poem "Yehuda Halevi" by Leyeles was published in 1918 in his poetry collection *Labirint* (Labyrinth). While most of the poems deal with universal and not specifically Jewish themes, his last poem "Yehuda Halevi" is the only exception. This poem tells the story of the yearning of a Sephardic troubadour for his ideally projected Zion and his death at the gates of Jerusalem when he was about to realize his dream. It narrates, in short, the impossibility of a return. In the twelfth century, the Hebrew-Spanish poet Yehuda Halevi established a personal and poetic model for the concept of return based not only on the pilgrimage but also on settlement in the Holy Land (Ezrahi 2000: 27). The possibility of a return to the Holy Land would be truncated, as Leyeles tells us in the seventh section of the poem, when a Bedouin murders Halevi.

[20] "Men hot fartribn di yidn / fun Kastilye un Aragon; / vegn vos hot demolt gezungen / Ibn Danan? / do shvaygt di geshichte." Translation into English by Barnet Zumoff, Aaron Kramer, and Marek Kanter (1997: 54–5).

Concluding Thoughts

In an editorial in the *Inzikh* journal published in June 1937, Leyeles, regarding the suffering of the Basques at the hands of the fascists in Spain, laments "Azoy, libe mentshheyt, kuk oyf di baskn. Dos iz dayn shpigl haynttsutog" (So, beloved humankind, look at the Basques. This is your mirror nowadays) (*Inzikh*, June 1937: 191; Glaser 2020: 161). From Glatstein's poem discussed in this chapter and from Leyeles's statement quoted here, it follows that "Leyeles and Glatstein identified modern Yiddish culture with political progressiveness, and modern poetry with revolutionary change" (Wisse 1997: 138). By presenting these poems by Glatstein and Leyeles about the Spanish Civil War published in the *Inzikh* journal the intention was to shed some light on the interest of the movement in international affairs, and specifically on the Spanish Civil War, as a contemporary tragedy of universal concern. Although the *Inzikh* journal focused its main aims on publishing avant-garde Yiddish poetry and securing innovations for the Yiddish language, as, for them, the modernization of Yiddish was the only possible way for the language to persist in exile and take its rightful place in the American literary world, these poems about the Spanish Civil War "managed to place national collective memory in service to a current struggle against fascism" (Glaser 2020: 150). The poems discussed in this chapter foreground the aesthetic theories of the movement, where universal themes along with their poetic innovations in the Yiddish language reinforce what these poets proclaimed in their manifesto: they were to "present life [. . .] as it is mirrored in ourselves" because "the world exists and we are part of it" (Harshav 2007: 774–5).

References

Ezrahi, S. DeKoven. (2000), *Booking Passage. Exile and Homecoming in the Modern Jewish Imagination*, Berkeley and Los Angeles: University of California Press.

Fales, A. (2018), "Palabras silenciosas: Lenguaje, sonido, y pensamiento en Valle-Inclán y Martín-Santos," *Bricolage: The Journal of Comparative Literature at Fordham University*, New York. Available online:http://bricolage-fordham.squarespace.com/select-works/2018/2/15/palabras-silenciosas-lenguaje-sonido-y-pensamiento-en-valle-inclan-y-martin-santos (accessed December 15, 2020).

Gabbay, C. (2020), "Una cuestión de espacio: promesas de liberación y utopía en la poesía yidis e hispana de la guerra civil española," in P. Molina Taracena (ed.), *Poesía de la guerra civil española: una perspectiva comparatista*, 153–78, Bern: Peter Lang.

Garrett, L. (1998), "The Self as Marrano in Jacob Glatstein's Autobiographical Novels," *Prooftexts*, 18 (3): 207–23.

Glaser, A. (2020), "NO PASARÁN: Jewish Collective Memory in the Spanish Civil War," in *Songs in Dark Times: Yiddish Poetry of Struggle from Scottsboro to Palestine*, 139–73, Cambridge: Harvard University Press.

Glaser, A. and D. Weintraub. (2005), *Proletpen: America's Rebel Yiddish Poets*, Wisconsin: The University of Wisconsin Press.

Glatstein, J. (1937), "*Shtile shpanie*," (Silent Spain), Inzikh, June issue: 145, New York.
Hadda, J. R. (1980), *Yankev Glatshteyn*, Boston: Twayne Publishers.
Harshav, B. (1990), *The meaning of Yiddish*, Stanford: Stanford University Press.
Harshav, B. and B. Harshav. (2007), *American Yiddish Poetry: A Bilingual Anthology*, Berkeley: University of California Press.
Hellerstein, K. (2014), *A Question of Tradition: Women Poets in Yiddish, 1586–1987*, Stanford: Stanford University Press.
Howe, I. (1989), *World of Our Fathers. The Journey of the East European Jews to America and the Life they Found and Made*, New York: Schocken Books.
"*Introspektivizm*," (Introspectivist manifesto). (1920), *Inzikh* January issue: 2–10, New York.
Inzikh, various editors. January 1920–February 1930; April 1934–December 1940, New York.
Kramer, A. (ed. and trans.). (1989), *A Century of Yiddish Poetry*, New York: Cornwall Books.
Leyeles, A. (1937a), "*Yidishe literatur un di velt*" [Yiddish literature and the World], Inzikh, March issue: 93–6, New York.
Leyeles, A. (1937b), "*Oyfn Shpanishn Front*," [On the Spanish Front], *Inzikh* June issue: 191, New York.
Leyeles, A. (1939), "*Shpanishe balade*," [Spanish Ballad], *Inzikh* March issue: 20–1, New York.
Nath, H. (1998), "The First International Conference of the Catalan Language in Barcelona (1906): A Spiritual Precursor to Czernowitz (1908)?" in D.-B. Kerler (ed.), *The Politics of Yiddish*, 51–61, Walnut Creek, CA: Altamira Press.
Neher, A. (1980), *Exile of the Word: From the Silence of the Bible to the Silence of Auschwitz*, trans. David Maisel, Lincoln: University of Nebraska Press.
Ponichtera, S. (2012), "Yiddish and the Avant-Garde in American Jewish Poetry," PhD diss., Graduate School of Arts and Sciences, Columbia University.
Schwarz, J. (2005), *Imagining Lives: Autobiographical Fiction of Yiddish Writers*, Wisconsin: University of Wisconsin Press.
Steiner, G. (1977), *Language and Silence: Essays on Language, Literature and the Inhuman*, New York: Atheneum.
Wisse, R. (1997), "Language as fate: Reflections on Jewish literature in America," in E. Mendelsohn (ed.), *Studies in Contemporary Jewry XII. Literary Strategies: Jewish Texts and Contexts*, Vol. 12, 129–46, USA: OUP.
Wisse, R. (2010), *The Glatstein Chronicles*, New Haven and London: Yale University Press.
Zaritt, S. (2015), "'The World Awaits Your Yiddish Word': Jacob Glatstein and the Problem of World Literature," *Studies in American Jewish Literature* (1981–), 34 (2): 175–203.
Zychlinsy, R. (1997), *God Hid His Face*, trans. B. Zumoff, A. Kramer and M. Kanter, California: Word & Quill Press.

8

A Better Earth

Spain's Land and Inquisition in Jewish Canadian Spanish Civil War Literature

Emily Robins Sharpe

But this time it will be a better earth ... It better be.
(Ted Allan, *This Time a Better Earth*)

A territory of the heart. A country of the imagination.
(Mordecai Richler, *Joshua Then and Now*)

"Everything, everything that you have found favorable in my songs and my poetry is inspired by this soil," Montreal musician and writer Leonard Cohen stated when he accepted his 2011 Prince of Asturias Award for Literature ([2011] 2018: 269). In his speech, he credited Spain for his creative success, citing the writer Federico García Lorca and his own first guitar teacher as personal inspirations. Among his works of fiction, poetry, and music, Cohen repeatedly wrote about Spanish locations and individuals and translated multiple García Lorca poems. Here, Cohen's emphasis on Spain's people along with its "soil" alludes to an integral aspect of much Jewish Canadian literature about the Spanish Civil War: a fixation on Canada and Spain's earth. In this chapter, I argue for this literary trope as a key facet of Jewish Canadian literature about the Spanish Civil War: one technique among many that authors employed to articulate a literary vision of a patriotic Canadian identity that both includes Jewish people and reifies transnational commitments.[1]

Despite low rates of immigration between Spain and Canada and a language barrier, the Spanish Civil War quickly became a vital cause for many Canadians. In addition to motivating 1,700 Canadians to volunteer—illegally, as the Foreign Enlistment

---

[1] Related techniques include the authorial adoption of gentile pseudonyms and narrative voices, the emphasis on Jewish Canadian whiteness through an explicit contrast with African and African American characters, the depiction of feminist spaces and sympathetic Holocaust victims, and the adaptation of García Lorca's poetry into Canadian contexts.

Act prohibited serving in another country's army—the war inspired an outpouring of cultural production and remains one of the most extensively documented world-historical events in Canadian literature.[2]

Canadians who traveled to Spain left behind a country in social crisis. The Great Depression hit Canada hard, with massive unemployment and poverty. Anti-Indigenous racism, xenophobia, and antisemitism flourished.[3] With Franco's coup, Canada's government pledged non-intervention in Spain. Experiences of poverty, unemployment, and marginalization politicized many, and they connected the rise of Canadian white ethnonationalism to the spread of European fascism. Spain's war was an opportunity to stop both.

Canadians who traveled to Spain also left behind a country in the midst of an identity crisis—a newly independent dominion whose inhabitants still remained British subjects. Canadian volunteers in Spain were the first to fight in a war independently of British rule. Those within the International Brigades formed a Canadian division in 1937: the Mackenzie-Papineau Battalion was named for William Lyon Mackenzie and Louis-Joseph Papineau, the Anglophone and Francophone leaders of the 1837-8 rebellions against British rule. These patriotic bona fides are especially notable given that most Canadian volunteers had immigrated to Canada within the decade before they traveled to Spain, and between thirty-eight and fifty-two of the volunteers were Jewish (Momryk n.d.: 5; Petrou 2008: 22–3). The volunteers' affiliation with Mackenzie and Papineau suggests their pride in Canada's history of anticolonialism, even as it obscures the anti-British rebels'—and many of the volunteers' own—participation in settler colonialism.

The name of the Mackenzie-Papineau Battalion reflects how Canada's identity crisis was treated in literature: the developing canon of Canadian literature of the early twentieth century frequently concerns the meaning of Canadianness, beyond an identity predicated on rejection—not British, not French, not American—or on bifurcation—half-British, half-French. These literary constructions of Canadian identity by white settler authors obscure Canada's Indigenous populations, and they only rarely incorporate non-British or non-French immigrants. The literary fixation on Canadian identity is also an integral part of a blossoming subgenre: in the midst of the era's antisemitism, the 1930s and 1940s are also marked by the growth of Jewish Canadian literature. Furthermore, many of the most widely renowned Jewish Canadian authors from this period write about the Spanish Civil War: "Canada's Anglo-Jewish authors and poets of the twentieth century played a formative role in the creation of a tradition of Canadian literature and are some of the country's leading writers" (Margolis 2016: 438). In depicting the war for an Anglophone Canadian audience, these authors—primarily Ashkenazi immigrants or their children—incorporate the

---

[2] The Canada and the Spanish Civil War Project, which I co-direct with Bart Vautour, has assembled a bibliography of Canadian cultural production about the war currently totaling 390 pages; available online at www.spanishcivilwar.ca.

[3] For more on the exclusion of Jewish immigrants from Canada and of Jewish Canadians from Canadian life, see Walker (2012).

ambient social tensions over Canadian identity, Jewish immigration, and the French-British divide.[4] They write their own communities into mainstream white Canadian society while warning of the dangers of domestic and foreign fascism and Nazism. They construct Canadian identity as an inclusive, transnationally minded ethos of global participation and local pride. Later in the century and into the early twenty-first century, Jewish Canadian authors including Matt Cohen, Leonard Cohen, Mordecai Richler, Miriam Waddington, Irving Layton, Sonja Ruth Greckol, and Seymour Mayne reflect on the Spanish Civil War and its lost promise both locally and globally.

In configuring Canadian identity, Canadian literature of the early twentieth century often emphasizes the country's landscape. The claims to geographic rootedness of this patriotic literature are a fiction, at once foundational to many white settler authors' assertions of Canadian identity and yet unavailable to individuals actually indigenous to the land. Jewish Canadian authors of this time period take up this trope of Canada's majestic landscapes and fill those landscapes with white ethnic immigrants and outsiders—assuming new roots in the newly independent country. If, as Mordecai Richler's character Simcha Kravitz memorably quips in the 1959 novel *The Apprenticeship of Duddy Kravitz*, "A man without land is nobody" ([1959] 1989: 49)—a remark that prompts Simcha's grandson Duddy to dedicate his life to acquiring his "promised land" in Canada—then to be a landowner is to be Canadian. And to be Canadian is to be acknowledged within normative, colonial whiteness—even as Richler's broader oeuvre criticizes these attempts to mimic gentile social norms and underscores the emptiness of the signifier "Canadian."[5]

The assertion of newly planted but strong Canadian roots is pervasive in Jewish Canadian literature. And, in fiction and poetry about the Spanish Civil War, this fascination with the land fulfills a dual purpose: not only do Jewish Canadian authors participate in a Canadian literary trope of identifying with the land but, in describing Spain's land for a Canadian readership, authors make Spain visible, knowable, and therefore sympathetic. The unexpected resemblances between Canada's landscape and Spain's suggest the countries' shared struggles and values: their entwined futures. Jewish Canadian authors write about Spain to an audience that often doubted Jewish claims to Canadian belonging. These writings instead connect the Spanish earth to the Canadian landscape, demonstrating a cosmopolitan concern for Spain's citizens and environment and articulating the ethical dimension of international anti-fascism as vital components of Canadian identity.

Jewish Canadian authors' fixation on Spain's earth suggests something else: a reclamation of land that might once have been theirs. While Jewish Canadian depictions of Canadian landscapes at times embrace a white settler mentality and erase Indigenous peoples, Jewish Canadian depictions of Spanish landscapes implicitly recall the land's earlier inhabitants—Spanish Jews and Muslims.[6] Writing about Spanish land

---

[4] Francophone Canada only minimally supported the Spanish Republic (Dionne n.d.).
[5] See Singer (2010).
[6] Of the complex context within Spain, Linhard argues, "writers and witnesses narrate instances of Jewish life in Spain's turbulent twentieth century by invoking the remote past" (2014: 4).

further compels Jewish Canadian authors to recall earlier unrest on Spain's earth: the murders, forced conversions, Inquisition, and expulsion of Jews and Muslims. Franco's attack becomes an extension and a reinvention of Spain's centuries-old violent animosity toward Jewish and Muslim Spaniards—and a harbinger of the Holocaust and the destruction threatening all of Europe. In analyzing Spanish literature, Tabea Alexa Linhard argues, these "are not comparable, much less interchangeable, events ... This process [of connecting them] is problematic (because events, individuals, and institutions are taken out of context) but also necessary (because it allows authors to articulate coherent narratives about the past)" (2014: 189). In the Canadian context, I contend that these literary depictions offer a possible, if problematic, Jewish Canadian origin story. If Jewish Canadians write about Canada's land to demonstrate their growing familiarity with it—to put down new roots—they write about Spain's land as a way of claiming potential ancestral ties, in what Cynthia Gabbay refers to as an "imaginary reunion between Spain and Sepharad" ("Conclusion," this volume). In describing Spain's landscapes, Jewish Canadian writers underscore their own possible roots in Spain, while simultaneously claiming their place within Canadian society: a compounded experience of exile, outsiderness, and loyalty.

In this essay, I look at descriptions of Canadian and Spanish land in Jewish Canadian writings from the Spanish Civil War's midst to the present day. Early authors connect Spain's cause to both Canada's future and Jewish history; contemporary writers' nostalgia for the cause is conjoined with a conviction that to remember Spain's Civil War is to memorialize a longer history of Spanish antisemitism. First, I examine Jewish Canadian writers' invocations of Spain's earth; then, I turn to their allusions to the Spanish Inquisition and the Holocaust. Together, these sections demonstrate the ineffable cosmopolitanism of Jewish Canadian literature: authors connect Spain and Canada's lands to Jewish ancestral histories of exile, and international support for Spain's Republic to Canadian identity.

The Spanish Earth

Jewish Canadian authors often focus on Spain's landscapes in order to emphasize the stakes of Spain's cause. Spain's land figures in their fiction and poetry in diverse ways. In Philadelphia-born Montreal author Charles Yale Harrison's satirical novel *Meet Me on the Barricades* (1938), for instance, the protagonist's unwillingness to endanger himself in Spain is symptomatic of his larger failures of political conviction and transnational sympathy. His dream of Spain's land is imaginary, just as his idea of Spanish Civil War participation is romanticized, fantastical, and false. Ted Allan's novel *This Time a Better Earth* (1939), on the other hand, is a fictionalized version of its author's own time in Spain, imbued with intimate depictions of Spain's landscapes. Born Alan Herman, Allan adopted a gentile pseudonym to help his journalism career when he infiltrated and reported on a fascist organization. He covered the war as a journalist for the Canadian leftist press and became the political commissar of Canadian doctor Norman Bethune's mobile blood transfusion service. His novel narrates the experiences of a young Canadian Mackenzie-Papineau soldier named Bob. Bob falls in love with a German photographer, Lisa, who is killed while photographing the conflict's front lines. He ultimately chooses to return to the battlefields with his comrades. Even as the fascist triumph became more and more inevitable, Allan's fictionalized retelling ends on an optimistic note of resilience and transnational solidarity.

This Time a Better Earth is loosely based on Allan's own relationship with the Jewish German photographer Gerda Taro (born Gerta Pohorylle), widely acknowledged as the first female photographer killed while covering a war, and the romantic and professional partner of Robert Capa (born Andre Friedmann). While working together in Spain, they collectively signed their photos "Robert Capa." Before publishing *This Time a Better Earth* Allan also published short stories: "A Gun Is Watered" (1938) describes the alternating drudgery and terror of the trenches, while "Lisa: A Story" (1938) presents an early iteration of the scene in which the female protagonist dies. In all of these fictional texts, Allan takes care to describe Spain's landscapes as his characters travel to different cities, towns, battlefields, and field hospitals.

This Time a Better Earth also owes much to the established tropes of war romance novels, as Bob and Lisa's profound wartime love is both heightened and compromised by violence. The lovers' separation and Lisa's death could be read as an individuated example of Spain's large-scale tragedy. The novel also inserts Jewish heroics into this trope, as Allan describes an epic love story about two gentile characters who are fictionalized versions of real-life Jewish people (Sharpe 2020: 34–41). What's more, these heroics take place on the Spanish earth—the "better earth" of the novel's title— which acts as a locus for characters to focus their compassion, rather than toward any individual or community.

The novel's epigraph is a quotation from Ecclesiastes 1:4: "One generation passeth away, and another generation cometh: but the earth abideth forever." This biblical reminder of the earth's endurance also hints that the Spanish earth's previous and future inhabitants are vital presences within the novel. However, foreign volunteer characters articulate their dedication to the Republic in terms of the country's earth, not its occupants. This biblical quotation reappears in the novel's text when the two protagonists discuss their ethical responsibility to anti-fascism. In response to Bob quoting this passage, Lisa replies, "But this time it will be a better earth . . . It better be" (Allan [1939] 2015: 122). Lisa's conviction is not realized within the novel, and the optimistic conclusion belies what readers would already have known about the actual war's end.

While Lisa's death precludes the possibility of her contribution to a future generation, it also spurs Bob's anti-fascism. He returns to the battlefront where his comrade Milton, an American volunteer and the novel's only Jewish primary character, is finally recognized for his bravery and ability, and the novel concludes with his promise to share his wartime life with Bob: "We'll all share the same dug-out . . . and I'll teach you how to shoot a gun good" (Allan [1939] 2015: 162). Arm in arm, they walk toward their trench. This homosocial, North American wartime context of living on the Spanish earth and learning masculine skills highlights these characters' isolation from the war's actual stakes. Without Lisa—or any Spanish characters, for that matter—the Spanish cause's importance seems to fade as the characters take delight in male camaraderie and marksmanship. The Spanish earth, in the form of a trench, is their temporary home, but the better earth of the novel's title remains elusive.

Both the distanced safety of Charles Yale Harrison's novel and the personal pastoral of Ted Allan's novel are echoed in Montreal author A.M. Klein's Spanish Civil War poem "Of Castles in Spain" (1938). Klein was a central figure in Jewish Canadian literature who incorporated both Canadian and Yiddish traditions into his poetry and fiction: "the first non-Anglo, non-francophone ethnic voice to gain an important foothold in the Canadian canon" (Ravvin 2012: 185). Where Allan's novel concludes with hope for the possibility of a better Spain and a "better earth," Klein's three-part poem imagines many of Spain's stereotypical sights—a bullfight, aristocrats drinking sherry in a plaza, a priest—into a withering denunciation of the country's potential postwar monarchist classism. The poem's title explicitly invokes a longstanding monarchical history and then, through its three sections, depict different aspects of Spain's current and future reality.

The first section, "To One Gone to the Wars," is dedicated to "S.H.A.," Klein's friend and volunteer Samuel H. Abramson, and expresses the speaker's shame over not joining in the cause they both believe in. Instead, because he must "from the barracks watch the barricade," the speaker offers Abramson a "meek sacrifice, unvaliant gift, / My non-liturgic prayer" for his success (Klein [1938] 1990: 473, lines 18–19). Throughout this section, Klein demarcates the differences between the dangers of the front and the comforts of the academic's life: while Abramson struggles in a "street-fight" the speaker "in an armchair—weigh[s] and measure[s] Marx" (1990, lines 11, 12). The luxuries of leftist Canadian life rest on the dangerous sacrifices of Republican Spain.

The subsequent two sections are both set only in Spain, but implicitly connected to Canada through this first section's linkage. In "Toreador," the speaker addresses the bullfighter and envisions his violent success over the bull as a Spanish Republican triumph. In "Sonnet without Music," Klein most explicitly addresses Spain's land through an imagined future fascist Spain. In this vision, Spanish aristocrats drink sherry and enjoy the return of their previously collectivized land; priests gorge themselves while briefly remembering the many who died in the war; underneath the plaza where they all sit, the murdered Republican peasants lie, "feeding with the earthworm" (1990: 474, line 42). Klein's unrhyming, free verse sonnet concludes by addressing a single aristocrat, "Don Pelph," with the promise of a future class uprising, as the peasants will again unite against the monarchy, aristocracy, and church and "heil you to the fascist realm of death!" (1990, line 46). Written even before the war's tragic end and the Second World War's outbreak, this conclusion promises a future class revolution while underscoring the connections between classism, monarchy, fascism, and Nazism. Klein's use of the term "heil"—the Nazi salute that Franco and his followers adopted—makes explicit the Nazi support for the Spanish insurgency, while also connecting Spain's conflict to the spread of Nazism across Europe. The monarchy, aristocracy, and Catholic Church's support for Franco were well known; however, here, Klein reframes these centuries-old institutions as earlier instantiations of contemporary, ongoing oppression—oppression based, in part, on land ownership.

Decades after the war's conclusion, poet Irving Layton published a set of three poems about Spain's ongoing conflicts over historical memory. Read alongside Klein's earlier poem, these poems form a timeline of Spain's evolving violence and discrimination, framed in terms of the impact on the natural world. "On Spanish Soil" (1964) is only obliquely about the Spanish Civil War. The poem's first stanza begins, "On Spanish soil how everything comes clear" (Layton 1964b: 44), enumerating the ways in which the natural world showcases both pain and life. A twisted tree produces leaves, a tail-less lizard eats a fly, and extinct stars still appear to shine overhead: Spain's land only appears dormant. The middle stanza casts the speaker as the dormant one, a figure aged and fixated on ghosts, whose mind is like a "decayed villa" (Layton 1964b)—another image drawn from Spain's landscapes. In the concluding stanza, the speaker promises that the land, too, will awaken: the natural world's ability to persevere becomes a "censure" of the speaker's own inactivity, as they vow to be won over "from defiance and black hate" (Layton 1964b). The suffering of Spain's earth becomes a personal challenge to live and advocate.

The following poem, "El Caudillo," contrasts the silence around Francoism amongst the Spanish people with the pervasiveness of his physical markers across the country. The speaker explains, "in every village and town / there are at least / one *Avenida* and one *Calle* / named for him / —yet nobody speaks his name!" (Layton 1964a: 45). The profusion of streets named for Franco serves as a constant reminder of his repressive rule so that speaking of him becomes superfluous. Yet, the speaker adds, the Civil Guards in their bull-like hats terrifyingly reinforce Franco's rule, acting as an extension—like the street signs—of his power. While in "On Spanish Soil" Spain's natural world continues to live through death, in "El Caudillo" Spain's manmade structures, streets, and institutions are not only unnatural impositions on the land but also extensions of Franco's fascist domination.

Layton's final poem "El Gusano" draws together motifs from "On Spanish Soil" and "El Caudillo" through the speaker's encounter with a worm. The poem begins with the speaker sweating in Alicante's midday heat while watching workers split rocks to build a road. In the midst of pitying these overheated laborers, the speaker notices a worm, notable for its "rich, feudal colour" that looks like "the Spanish soil" and for the fact that it seems to know its way around the town (Layton 1964c: 46). The speaker goes on to praise worms for their democratic approach to eating the dead: oblivious to income, profession, ancestry, and class, they "will dine with impartial relish / On one who splits stones or sells fish / Or, if it comes to that, a prince / Or a generalissimo" (Layton 1964c: 47). The laborers who first elicited the speaker's sympathy and the dictator currently ruling the country will all come to the same end. Worms' egalitarianism remains, in the midst of Francoist repression of all political opposition, "the sole underground," a pun that recalls the horrifying violence to which *conversos, moriscos, marranos*, and later Spanish Republicans were subjected (Layton 1964c).

As the worm crawls away, the speaker imagines its future travels to Andalusia, Castile, and Aragon, and hopes that it will remind those across the country of democracy. Even as Spain currently remains "plundered, sold-out, and lovely / . . . traduced, dismembered" (Layton 1964c), the worm represents the potential for another way of life in the country, one more natural, democratic, and honest. Together, Layton's poems represent fascism as unnatural, suggesting that a return to democracy is not only possible but aligns with the natural world's own wishes and tendencies. The flora and fauna of Spain become reminders of individual potential for rebirth and renewal.

Where Layton and Klein's poetry underscores Spain's longstanding, ongoing cruelty, Miriam Dworkin Waddington's career-spanning engagement with Spain's conflict evinces not only the danger and violence but also the community and potential of the Spanish earth. Although she would become a writer, critic, and social worker, even as a university student in Toronto she wrote about Spain's land and community. Later, decades after the war's conclusion, she continued to grapple with the international community's failure to intervene.

Waddington's earliest published poem imagines a small community bidding each other and their beloved country farewell before each goes into solitary exile. "The Exiles: Spain" (1936) emphasizes the joy these individuals take in their communal camaraderie and loyalty. However, their fear of what may happen after exile—to themselves and their homeland—is reflected in the landscape around them. While these individuals, when together, remain defiantly brave and affectionate, the nature that surrounds them is personified and frightening. The poem's speaker repeatedly implores, "Come my friends, let us dance" (Waddington [1936] 2014: 2, lines 1, 5), and describes the shore where "the cold sun sets with a distant grief; / . . . the black waves fret at the naked reef" (Waddington [1936] 2014, lines 2–3) as well as the "ruins / Of all we fought and bravely failed" (Waddington [1936] 2014, lines 5–6). Through pathetic fallacy—the sun's sorrow, the water's anxiety, the reef's vulnerability, the (literal or metaphorical) ruins—Waddington suggests the feelings that underpin the speaker's request for a final dance. The poem concludes tentatively, without confirmation of whether the friends have gathered, and with the speaker's finally stated uncertainty about "whether we [will] know this sun once more— / And whether we [will] live through these evil days" (Waddington [1936] 2014, lines 9–10).

Another poem about the war published just a year later imagines how Spain's different regions might also offer safety and comfort. In "Spanish Lovers Seek Respite" (1937) Waddington's speaker implores their lover to spend a night together away from the inescapable violence. In Waddington's imagined Spanish landscape, the fields are "hot and heavy" (Waddington [1937] 2014: 4, line 5) but the mountains provide "peace, dry wind, / And sky clean and dark" (2014, lines 19–20). As with "The Exiles: Spain," the poem never clarifies whether the speaker's request is fulfilled. Yet, Spain's landscape provides both shelter and temporary peace, allowing the speaker to articulate a symbiotic relationship with the natural world: the lovers fight for Spain, and in turn, Spain's land cares for them, enabling their continued loyalty.

Waddington's later poems return to Spain's war, but mostly from a geographical distance—a distance she critiques and attempts to overcome. In "Dog Days" (1945) the speaker describes a sense of looming peril even from Canada's relative safety. In "Icons" (1962) the speaker recounts a romantic encounter with a Spanish factory worker whose body bears the scars of war. "The Nineteen Thirties Are Over" (1970) articulates a sense of nostalgia for younger revolutionary days as the speaker reflects "I am not really /

the middle-aged professor / but someone from / Winnipeg whose bones ache / with the broken revolutions / of Europe" (Waddington [1970] 2014: 500, lines 42-7). "The Woman in the Hall" (1992) describes a personification of global trauma, a lonely woman living isolated and alone in "a nebulous city" (Waddington [1992] 2014: 768, line 5) who is also "Guernica / and Madrid she is Moscow / besieged and Dieppe / betrayed, she is all the / sombre-eyed girls in Goya's / drawings forever mourning" (Waddington [1992] 2014, lines 21-6). By enumerating the woman's volatile characteristics and locations, this poem links the Spanish Civil War, the Second World War, and the Holocaust to global poverty and Spanish colonization, insisting on them as one long conflict rather than discrete events. In so doing, Waddington's poem exemplifies what Cynthia Gabbay has termed the "epistemic event" of the Spanish Civil War and the Holocaust ("Introduction," this volume). The nameless woman's geographical imprecision allows Waddington to collapse the physical and chronological distance between the reader and these events: the woman's "nebulous city" is their city; the destruction of Guernica, Madrid, Moscow, and Dieppe is theirs too. "The Woman in the Hall" becomes a plea for transnational sympathy and activism, a reminder of individual responsibility. As Waddington concludes, the woman "at last awakens in you / your broken promises your / ancient righteousness" (Waddington [1992] 2014: 770, lines 83-5; see Sharpe 2020: 108-14).

Spain's Inquisitions

If during the midcentury Jewish Canadian writers write about Spain's struggles to connect the cause to Canada, later Jewish Canadian authors further reflect on the Spanish conflict's place within a longer history of antisemitism. For Waddington, Spain's violent history of colonization and its 1930s Civil War are inextricable from the Holocaust. For others, the Civil War and Holocaust represent a continuation of the anti-Jewish and anti-Muslim violence of the Spanish Inquisition.

Matt Cohen's novel *The Spanish Doctor* (1984) and his short stories "The Sins of Tomas Benares" and "Sentimental Meetings" (1983) are all connected to Spain's land across a vast chronological spread. *The Spanish Doctor* is set between the late fourteenth and early fifteenth centuries and depicts the experiences of a *marrano* Jewish doctor forced to flee Spain, finally settling in Kyiv. Cohen's short stories are concerned with another Jewish doctor: the titular Tomas Benares, who emigrated to Toronto fleeing Franco, and whose grandson returns to Spain to retrace the origins of a family scattered by the Spanish Civil War and the Holocaust. These three stories of Cohen's represent a fictionalized study of centuries of Spanish antisemitism (Greenstein 1989: 191), a genealogy of Jewish characters rooted in—yet excluded from—Spain. Cohen suggests the ongoing and unbreakable connection between Canadian Jewry and Spain—and by extension, their rootedness in both countries.[7]

---

[7] In "Outside Spain" Cohen wrote, "The destruction of Spanish Jewry—through the Inquisition and the expulsion—was to be the most tragic event in Jewish history until the Second World War" (1994: 185).

"The Sins of Tomas Benares" focuses on Tomas's life in Toronto, a life marred by death and loss as well as the memories of his pre–Civil War beginnings in Spain. Tomas traces his family roots back to pre-Inquisition Toledo, then to Kyiv, then a return to Spain before he fled Franco to Toronto. Spain is "the cradle of his ancestors," but Toronto is where he has meticulously cared for his house and its garden for nearly fifty years (Cohen 1985b: 81). Even in his nineties, Tomas takes pride in this garden, insisting on tending it himself as his gardener watches. His garden flourishes, evidence of Tomas's own commitment to Canada.

Tomas's grandson revisits the family's ancestral home in "Sentimental Meetings." With Tomas's introductions, Joseph flies to France to meet a distant relative. Hanna shares with Joseph the documents and photos of their history, explaining how "[f]irst Franco and then Hitler" destroyed the family (Cohen 1985a: 117). Together, Joseph and Hanna travel to Toledo to visit the synagogue (which had been converted into a church during the Inquisition). The building has been restored to its Jewish usage in order to attract tourists but is closed to visitors as a German film crew makes a documentary about Spain's modern-day religious freedom. Joseph and Hanna are incensed that the film crew occupies a sacred space while they are excluded—a space that they both claim as their own. When the director complains about the difficulty of finding a rabbi in Toledo (and bemoans German suffering during the Second World War), Hanna retorts, "You should have been here six hundred years ago. There were dozens of Rabbis then" (Cohen 1985a: 124). Hanna and Joseph spend their time in Toledo grieving its Jewish and Muslim antecedents—their personal past—while the director and his crew are more interested in "put[ting] the past behind us" (Cohen 1985a: 124). Yet, the story suggests, traumatic histories and hopeful futures can coexist. It is, strangely, the director who articulates Joseph's Toledo birthright at the story's conclusion: "Welcome home" (Cohen 1985a: 130). This belated acknowledgment of Jewish Canadian entitlement to Spanish roots articulates the family history that has been silenced by the country's policies and social norms.[8]

Where Cohen's writings offer individual narratives of the Spanish Inquisition and Civil War's lasting repercussions, Seymour Mayne's Spain poems examine the Civil War's ongoing reverberations, as the earth "sleeps again, / wounded," as he puts it in "Madrid Evening" (1995: 210; 2003). His 1977 poem "Parrots, Generals" emphasizes the impact of Spain's so-called *pacto del olvido*, or pact of forgetting. The social pact inhibiting political and public discussions of the war has slowly thawed in the years since Franco's death. In "Parrots, Generals," two years after Franco's death, Mayne imagines this widespread silence emanating from the earth itself, "imperceptibly / ris[ing] from the land" (1977b: 98). Spain's inhabitants are physically damaged by their country's divisive and violent history with "scar tissue / on their tongues" and, in Mayne's representation, also culpable: "A generation salts / this earth still" (1977b: 98). In the following poem of his collection *Diasporas*, "Castile," Mayne even more forcefully indicts Spain's antisemitic history and poisoned land. The speaker addresses

---

[8] Greenstein reads this moment ironically, "as if meetings and reconciliations are possible after Europe's treatment of its Jews" (1989. 192).

Canadian blood transfusion doctor and Spanish Civil War volunteer Norman Bethune, asking if it was "for this" landscape and "Castilian hauteur / that turns away from its soil" that he saved Republican lives (Mayne 1977a: 99). Castile's land—its "soiled earth bleeding darkly"—is formed of the Republican dead as well as "the Jews, ancestors of mine, / who paid in flesh and bone / over and over again" (Mayne 1977a: 98). In Mayne's construction, Spain itself is built on murder—the country is made of the bodies of the murdered—so that its claim to Catholic piety is undercut by its violent religious "mani[a]" (Mayne 1977a). Together, Mayne's poems participate in a Spanish and transnational loosening of the *pacto del olvido*, contending that even those who carry previous generations' trauma must also reckon with their country's antisemitic, repressive history or else continue to participate in poisoning their land.

The metaphor of fascism and silence poisoning Spain's land is expanded in Montreal author Mordecai Richler's writings. Richler returned to the Spanish Civil War throughout his writing, most notably in his earliest novel *The Acrobats* (1954) and his later novel *Joshua Then and Now* (1980).[9] His attention to the war's problematic, nostalgic significance for Jewish Canadian men as a marker of gentile masculinity overlaps with a broader concern with how Spain's land and people were impacted by war and fascism. In Richler's fiction, Spain is a catalyzing location for North American Jewish self-reckoning, always within the conjoined contexts of medieval and twentieth-century Spanish violence. The country likewise provides the space for other marginalized, foreign characters—particularly women and queer characters—to reflect. This clarity is mostly only available to North American characters, however, as Spanish characters play secondary roles. Still, Richler's novels do not represent Spain as merely a location for North American Jews to find themselves; instead, these characters' growing understanding of Spain's violent history becomes their route into a clearer perception of their own evolving relationship to Judaism and patriotism.

The Acrobats is set in mid-century Valencia, a Francoist wasteland where locals and tourists try to obliterate their memories of suffering caused by antisemitism, homophobia, sexual abuse, and violent trauma, while the Fallas festival celebrates the burning of the parade floats. The narrative takes place in crowded, decaying, intimate spaces—bedrooms, restaurants, bars, brothels, and squares (including the Plaza del Caudillo), all overshadowed by the constant presence of the Guardia Civil. The city's buildings are "faded orange and sometimes sickly grey," covered in "chalk slogans and obscenities . . . along the damp peeling walls" (Richler [1954] 2002: 27); it smells of "[t]he stink of stale drainage and decaying fish" (Richler [1954] 2002: 27). While the narrator recalls the city's ancient history, often of Catholic domination—Roman soldiers, Seneca, El Cid—this history is overlaid with more recent events: "German shells belching news of the modern world" (Richler [1954] 2002: 48).

Richler's representation of history's layered impact on the city leads to an uneasy sense of un-rootedness, a sense that is especially acute for Jewish characters, who do

---

[9] See also Richler's travelogue, *Images of Spain* (1977). Kramer notes that Richler's unpublished memoir was titled "Back to Ibiza" (2008: 74–6).

not feel at home in Spain or North America. Nowhere is welcoming—not even the newly established state of Israel, despite one character's claim that it is "Our land! A place where a Jew can go if he's in trouble and be sure to find friends" (Richler [1954] 2002: 115). Characters long to escape Valencia but suffer traumatic flashbacks to Munich, New York, Montreal, and "the Warsaw ghetto where those who were not burnt now walked the cold desert land, tugging at their beards, mourning murdered sons and murdered daughters, wondering if it was truly hot in the promised land" (Richler [1954] 2002: 13). No land is promised, the novel suggests: the excitement of the Spanish Republic's potential degenerates into the daily realities of Francoism, and the possibilities of New World pluralism devolve into assimilation and discrimination.

Richler's later novel, *Joshua Then and Now*, is a narrative of another character's reckoning with the lost potential of Spain, the uneven tolerance for the Jewish people of Canada, the pitfalls of nostalgia, and the difficulties of making a home. The titular character is a writer whose life encompasses the tensions between his working-class Jewish Montreal childhood and his adult professional achievement, his emotional connection to Spain and his familial ties to Canada, and his political convictions and cynicisms. The novel is also humorous and satirical: it valorizes the values of the Spanish Civil War while critiquing the war's nostalgic place of honor within a particular Montreal Jewish construction of masculinity.

Spain's land and war form some of Joshua's earliest memories, always at a remove: he cuts out photos of the war from *Life Magazine* for his scrapbook, listens to the news on the radio, and reads about it in books. After a short stint in Ibiza, he makes the Spanish Civil War his career, following the paths of the Republican armies and interviewing veterans to write a book. In Spain in the early 1950s, Joshua's experiences are overlaid with his knowledge of Spanish Civil War history, so that he sees not the land itself, but the attacks, evacuations, and massacres that once took place. On a research trip to Córdoba and Madrid, Joshua explicitly connects the Spanish Civil War to the Spanish Inquisition. In Córdoba, Joshua recounts the history of the Jewish philosopher and doctor Maimonides, forced to flee his hometown by the "Moors" which saved his life: "a mob descended on the Juderia of Cordoba shortly after Ash Wednesday 1391, and reduced the quarter where Maimonides had been born to ashes" (Richler 1980: 190). As Joshua wanders through the Jewish quarter, his usually linear narratives of Spanish history devolve and fragment as his own feelings and reactions intrude. In Madrid, he finds his "Jewishness obtrude[s]": "Some four hundred years ago, during the Inquisition, they used to burn Jews here, right here, for sport. / *Auto de fe*" (Richler 1980: 191).

After visualizing Spain's history of Jewish oppression, Joshua encounters Spanish antisemitism firsthand. Returning to Ibiza, his new friends are both fascinated and repulsed by Joshua's Jewishness, and he finds himself uneasy around the town's lone *marrano* Jew (decades later, he will find out that this man was refused entry to "his promised land" because Israeli officials deemed him Catholic, even as his fellow Spaniards classified—stigmatized—him as Jewish [Richler 1980: 395]). Finally, Joshua concludes, "Damn. Making Ibiza his base, he had come to Spain to look at battlefields, talk to survivors, learn what he could about the Spanish Civil War. Instead, he was discovering that he was Jewish. Something anybody could have told him" (Richler 1980: 221). Spain is simultaneously a location and a lens, allowing Joshua to see himself more clearly when he is outside of his family and social context.

Years later, Joshua concludes that for him and for many of his fellow Montreal Jewish friends, all too young to have volunteered, Spain's Civil War represents not only the last great cause but also a lost opportunity to prove their own masculinity and bravery. As a result, the country itself has become, for them, an idealized, venerated space, "a territory of the heart. A country of the imagination" (Richler 1980: 233). It is only upon returning to Spain that he also realizes, "Not only Spain had changed in twenty-five years, but so have I" (Richler 1980: 381). Again, Spain provides a clarifying, distancing lens through which Joshua can view himself. At the novel's conclusion, Joshua is more rooted in Canada than ever—in his family's vegetable garden surrounded by his family. Yet, this rootedness could only come about through his travels around Spain, his acknowledgment of Spain and Canada's antisemitic histories, and his deconstruction of Jewish identity.

Conclusion: Better Earths

In drawing connections between Spanish and Canadian landscapes, and between Spain's land and its longstanding history of antisemitic violence, Jewish Canadian authors construct an inclusive vision of Canadian patriotism that obliges a duty of transnational care. Sonja Ruth Greckol's poetry refracts this essential critique of Spain's history onto Canada's, as she interrogates Canada's violent colonial history alongside Spain's and analyzes Jewish Canadian land claims and identity. In the Preface to *No Line in Time* (2018), Greckol notes that her own family was able to settle on Albertan land after fleeing Eastern Europe because of "the brutal 'clearing' of Indigenous communities by starvation, disease, warfare, treachery, the burgeoning bureaucracy of Treaty 6" (2018c: 11). She connects the Spanish "Reconquista" to her family: her ancestors were expelled from their homes, only able to settle in Canada because Indigenous people had likewise been expelled from theirs.

Greckol also repeatedly alludes to the strands connecting the Spanish Civil War to the Spanish Inquisition, crafting a new idiom and grammar in which to recount this multilingual, transnational, transhistorical narrative. In the poem "La Convi•v•encia" she describes the clothing worn by the Muslim soldiers who supported Aragon against Castile in 1285 and its influence on later uniforms: "sumptuous threads from Aragon to Franco's Moroccan guard and ceremonial still in fez and *burnouse*" (Greckol 2018a: 51). The poem's title refers to the medieval Iberian coexistence of Jews, Muslims, and Christians, yet, fractured by dots, the supposed peace is preemptively shattered. In "Palimpsest" she notes how the celebratory atmosphere of Madrid's Puerta del Sol belies its onetime location as "the square where Franco's torture chambers fuelled treachery" (Greckol 2018b: 97), while the poet writes, "poeming a homunculus in the wake of Hitler's ghost binding time" (Greckol 2018b: 111). *No Line in Time* reconstructs Spain and Canada's pasts with poetic narratives of their Jewish and Muslim and Indigenous histories. Read alongside nearly ninety years' worth of Jewish Canadian literature about the Spanish Civil War and Spanish and Canadian land, antisemitism, and identity, Greckol's poetry vitally expands our understanding of the Spanish Civil War's origins, effects, and resonances. Jewish Canadian Spanish Civil War literature calls for new languages, histories, and interpretations of land and belonging.

References

Allan, T. (1938a), "A Gun is Watered," *Monthly Literary Supplement of New Masses*, 26 (3, 11 January): 25–8.
Allan, T. (1938b), "Lisa: A Story," *Harper's*, 177 (2, July): 187–93.
Allan, T. ([1939] 2015), *This Time a Better Earth*, ed. B. Vautour, Ottawa: University of Ottawa Press.
Cohen, L. ([2011] 2018), "Acceptance Address for the Prince of Asturias Award," in R. Faggen and A. Pleshoyano (eds.), *The Flame: Poems, Notebooks, Lyrics, Drawings*, 267–9, New York: Farrar, Straus and Giroux.
Cohen, M. (1985a), "Sentimental Meetings," in *Life on this Planet and Other Stories*, 114–30, New York: Beaufort Books.
Cohen, M. (1985b), "The Sins of Tomas Benares," in *Life on this Planet and Other Stories*, 76–102, New York: Beaufort Books.
Cohen, M. (1994), "Outside Spain," *Canadian Literature*, 142–143 (Autumn–Winter): 183–7.
Dionne, B. (n.d.), "Bibliographie en français sur le Canada, la guerre civile en Espagne et l'engagement des communistes et du bataillon Mackenzie-Papineau," in *Canada and the Spanish Civil War: Canadian Cultural History about the Spanish Civil War*. Available online: spanishcivilwar.ca/content/bibliography/francophone-sources (accessed June 30, 2018).
Greckol, S.R. (2018a), "La Convi•v•encia," in *No Line in Time*, 37–55, Toronto: Tightrope Books.
Greckol, S.R. (2018b), "Palimpsest," in *No Line in Time*, 93–112, Toronto: Tightrope Books.
Greckol, S.R. (2018c), "Preface," in *No Line in Time*, 11–12, Toronto: Tightrope Books.
Greenstein, M. (1989), *Third Solitudes: Tradition and Discontinuity in Jewish-Canadian Literature*, Montreal and Kingston: McGill-Queen's University Press.
Klein, A.M. ([1938] 1990), "Of Castles in Spain," in Z. Pollock (ed.), *Complete Poems*, 473–4, Toronto: University of Toronto Press.
Kramer, R. (2008), *Mordecai Richler: Leaving St Urbain*, Montreal and Kingston: McGill-Queen's University Press.
Layton, I. (1964a), "El Caudillo," *The Tamarack Review*, 30 (Winter): 45.
Layton, I. (1964b), "On Spanish Soil," *The Tamarack Review*, 30 (Winter): 44.
Layton, I. (1964c), "El Gusano," *The Tamarack Review*, 30 (Winter): 46–7.
Linhard, T.A. (2014), *Jewish Spain: A Mediterranean Memory*, Stanford: Stanford University Press.
Margolis, R. (2016), "Across the Border: Canadian Jewish Writing," in H. Wirth-Nesher (ed.), *The Cambridge History of Jewish American Literature*, 432–46, Cambridge: Cambridge University Press.

Mayne, S. (1977a), "Castile," in *Diasporas*, 99, Oakville: Mosaic.
Mayne, S. (1977b), "Parrots, Generals," in *Diasporas*, 98, Oakville: Mosaic.
Mayne, S. (1995), "Madrid Evening," in N. Vulpe and M. Albari (eds.), *Sealed in Struggle: Canadian Poetry and the Spanish Civil War*, 210, La Laguna: Centre for Canadian Studies.
Mayne, S. (2003), *Dragon Trees. Friday Circle Chapbooks: Series I*, Ottawa: University of Ottawa Creative Writing Program.
Momryk, M. (n.d.), "'Canadian Jewish Boys in Spain': Jewish Volunteers from Canada in the Spanish Civil War, 1936-1939," 29 typescript pages.
Petrou, M. (2008), *Renegades: Canadians in the Spanish Civil War*, Vancouver: University of British Columbia Press.
Ravvin, N. (2012), "The War and Before in Canadian Literary Life," in L.R. Klein (ed.), *Nazi Germany, Canadian Responses: Confronting Antisemitism in the Shadow of War*, 183-217, Montreal and Kingston: McGill-Queen's University Press.
Richler, M. ([1954] 2002), *The Acrobats*, Toronto: New Canadian Library.
Richler, M. ([1959] 1989), *The Apprenticeship of Duddy Kravitz*, Toronto: New Canadian Library.
Richler, M. (1977), *Images of Spain*, photo. P. Christopher, Toronto: McClelland and Stewart.
Richler, M. (1980), *Joshua Then and Now*, New York: Alfred A. Knopf.
Sharpe, E.R. (2020), *Mosaic Fictions: Writing Identity in the Spanish Civil War*, Toronto: University of Toronto Press.
Singer, M.B. (2010), "'Is Richler Canadian Content?': Jewishness, Race, and Diaspora," *Canadian Literature*, 207 (Winter): 11-24.
Waddington, M. ([1936] 2014), "The Exiles: Spain," in R. Panofsky (ed.), *The Collected Poems of Miriam Waddington*, 2, Ottawa: University of Ottawa Press.
Waddington, M. ([1937] 2014), "Spanish Lovers Seek Respite," in R. Panofsky (ed.), *The Collected Poems of Miriam Waddington*, 4, Ottawa: University of Ottawa Press.
Waddington, M. ([1945] 2014), "Dog Days," in R. Panofsky (ed.), *The Collected Poems of Miriam Waddington*, 81, Ottawa: University of Ottawa Press.
Waddington, M. ([1962] 2014), "Icons," in R. Panofsky (ed.), *The Collected Poems of Miriam Waddington*, 435-8, Ottawa: University of Ottawa Press.
Waddington, M. ([1992] 2014), "The Woman in the Hall," in R. Panofsky (ed.), *The Collected Poems of Miriam Waddington*, 768-70, Ottawa: University of Ottawa Press.
Waddington, M. ([1970] 2014), "The Nineteen Thirties Are Over," in R. Panofsky (ed.), *The Collected Poems of Miriam Waddington*, 499-500, Ottawa: University of Ottawa Press.
Walker, J. (2012), "Claiming Equality for Canadian Jewry: The Struggle for Inclusion, 1930-1945," in L.R. Klein (ed.), *Nazi Germany, Canadian Responses: Confronting Antisemitism in the Shadow of War*, 218-62, Montreal and Kingston: McGill-Queen's University Press.

9

A Novel That Never Was

Ruth Rewald's *Vier Spanische Jungen*

Tabea Alexa Linhard

The story is so good, it is almost formulaic: it begins when hostile troops seize a small town. Eventually, four steadfast and bright boys, knowing that they and their loved ones are in danger, manage to escape. Not far from their home, friendly soldiers are fighting the invaders. When the boys, aged 12–14, encounter a group of combatants, the children first assume that they happened upon the enemy, and they do not reveal their identity. The soldiers, who actually are on their side, also initially believe that the boys may not be trusted. Yet the misunderstanding is soon solved, and the friendly soldiers pledge to take care of the youngsters, promising that once the boys are of age, they will be welcomed into their army. The children are elated to be part of this "good fight," and victory seems to be just a matter of time.

This story could easily take place in a variety of contexts, both actual and imagined, and in periods ranging from a remote past to an envisioned future. After all, literature for children and young adults from across the world is filled with tales about youths who make better decisions than their elders, and who take on roles (wizards, detectives, resistance fighters with a penchant for overthrowing totalitarian regimes, etc.) for which they are too young, but smart enough and, for sure, more than brave enough. These also are stories that, for the most part, tend to end well. Even though hardship and loss are an important part of such narratives, in the end, the young heroes succeed in their multiple quests. Their enemies, no matter how powerful, end up defeated. Yet this begs the question of what happens when a happy ending, or at least a sense of closure, has become so unthinkable that the book telling this story becomes obsolete. This is what happened with Ruth Rewald's novel *Vier Spanische Jungen* (Four Spanish Boys), but this is only part of its story.

The aforementioned narration is not only a good one, it also is based on actual events. Journalist Alfred Kantorowicz (1899–1979), who served as an officer with the Tschapaiew Battalion of the International Brigades (the Battalion belonged to the Dabrowski/Dombrowski Brigade, Brigade XIII) recorded it in their newspaper, *Tschapaiew – Das Batallion der 21 Nationen*. Rewald's spouse, Hans Schaul, who (just like Kantorowicz) was a Jewish volunteer in the same battalion, even photographed

Figure 9.1 The original cover of Rewald's *Vier Spanische Jungen* (Köln: Pahl Rügenstein Verlag, 1987). Cover design by Reinhard Alff. Courtesy of Dirk Krüger.

the four boys. Their picture appears on the cover of the 1987 edition of the book that Rewald wrote, yet did not live to see published.

It is thanks to the work of Germanist Dirk Krüger, who is responsible for the most comprehensive research on Ruth Rewald and for the 1987 edition of *Vier Spanische Jungen*, that today it is possible to include Rewald as an author in a volume on Jewish imaginaries of the Spanish Civil War. Rewald's book also is (to my knowledge) one of only two children's novels written in German by a Jewish author about the Spanish Civil War.[1]

The aforementioned four Spanish boys indeed escaped Peñarroya (in the province of Cordova) after the Nationalists had captured the town. Knowing that the Nationalists would sooner or later harm them, and also hoping to join their fathers who were fighting with the Republicans, the boys crossed the lines and eventually happened upon the German-speaking volunteers of the Tschapaiew Battalion. Kantorowicz, Schaul, and others felt that the boys' story needed to be shared with young audiences across the world, and so Schaul contacted Rewald, who had already written three novels for young readers.[2] She agreed, and so she got to spend four months at the Ernst Thälmann

---

[1] The other novel is Hermann Kesten's *Die Kinder von Gernika* (1939). Kesten's life and work demand an analysis of their own. Differently from Rewald, Kesten was able to leave occupied Europe and find asylum in the United States. Unlike Rewald, he also did not exclusively write for young audiences. For more information, see Bell (1992).

[2] As Mathilde Leveque points out, a number of exiled authors, among them Rewald's friend Lisa Tetzner, were already engaged in an anti-fascist struggle and writing for young audiences about this topic.

Orphanage outside Madrid, getting to know the children of the Spanish Civil War (Krüger 1987: 181, 1990: 228–36).

Rewald delivered: she produced a manuscript, but never saw it in print. The book's ending may be one of the factors that explain this, as Krüger suggests in the postscript of the posthumous edition of the novel, yet it is not the only one. Rewald was murdered at Auschwitz in 1942 and the manuscript for *Vier Spanische Jungen* was lost for almost fifty years; its (to this date) only edition became a reality in 1987. It is difficult to avoid reading the novel without dwelling on what happened after its publication, including the victory of the Nationalists, the author's deportation and death (one more among millions), the novel's disappearance, and its eventual resurfacing in the late years of the Cold War. *Vier Spanische Jungen* is invariably connected to the author's fate, yet this is not the sole factor that makes the novel an example of Jewish writing from the Spanish Civil War. Rather, the novel provides a window into what fighting fascism in Spain meant for exiled Jewish writers, among them Rewald. Her book captures a particular moment when an event involving children in war-torn Spain becomes an opportunity to tell a story that is as much about the war in Spain as it is about fostering empathy between Spanish children and children everywhere, children who now could be a part of a proactive struggle against fascism. Rewald told the children she met at the Ernst Thälmann orphanage that, as they would know, "children can awaken adults," referring to the ways in which children in France and elsewhere could convince their elders to support the Spanish Republic (Krüger 1987: 183).[3]

Even though there are no references to Jewishness (or to antisemitism) in the novel, it still is a prime example of what a "search for poetic justice" (Gabbay, this volume) could mean for a Jewish author. By the time Rewald completed the book, its ending had become outdated, and a long archival journey followed for the unpublished manuscript. Reading *Vier Spanische Jungen* invariably takes us back to a moment that, with Rewald's death, was frozen in time; this act also transforms, even if just in a small way, the memory of the intersections between Jewish history and the history of the Spanish Civil War. Three separate, yet related factors make it possible to place Rewald's novel on what Dan Miron has called a "map of modern Jewish writing no matter how fuzzily drawn" (2008: 18). First, her death and the subsequent disappearance of the novel for almost five decades situate the book within a Jewish imaginary of the Spanish Civil War. Second, this story about four Spanish boys also is a story about Jewish participation in the International Brigades. To be more specific, Kantorowicz's, Schaul's, and Rewald's relationship with the Brigades make the telling of this story possible. *Vier Spanische Jungen* documents what fighting in the Brigades meant for Jewish volunteers who, like Kantorowicz or Schaul, had joined from their exile in France. Third, the fact that Rewald writes a German book in France about Spain implies a particular linguistic crossroads. *Vier Spanische Jungen* is built on multiple and ongoing translations, and sometimes even mistranslations, bearing witness to "the complex communicative and translatorial actions performed in everyday life during

---

[3] "Kinder können auch Erwachsene wachrütteln." Unless otherwise noted, all translations are my own.

the war" (Kölbl, Orlova, and Wolf 2020: 9). Rewald wrote *about* and *for* children, which also means that her books are regularly pigeonholed as genre fiction and consequently overlooked in literary histories and in studies of the International Brigades. Studying a work like *Vier Spanische Jungen* in relation to other texts, for adults, children, and everybody in between, attempts to remedy this omission.

Rewald's Fate, Her Novel's Fate

Rewald was born to a Jewish secular family in 1906. By the time she was forced to flee to France in 1933, she had already published two books, *Rudi und sein Radio* (Rudi and His Radio) (1931) and *Müllerstraße—Jungens von heute* (Müller Street—Today's Boys) (1932). Her sole book with a female protagonist *Achtung Renate* (Careful, Renate) never made it to print. The other two books appeared with the Stuttgart-based publisher D. Gundert and may have done so right in time, as in 1933 the editor informed Rewald that they would no longer be able to support her work (Krüger 1988: 111). Rewald settled in Paris, and Schaul, now barred from practicing law in Germany, followed shortly afterward. Life in exile was not easy, yet Rewald managed to support herself by writing commercial copy and with occasional teaching gigs.[4] She also completed two more novels: *Janko. Der Junge aus Mexiko* (Janko: The Boy from Mexico) (1934) and *Tsao und Jing Ling—Kinderleben in China* (Tsao and Jing Ling—Children's Lives in China) (1937).[5] As Rewald's titles already indicate, her protagonists usually were boys, sometimes living in faraway places. Had she lived to see her daughter Anja grow up, she may have produced many other books with female protagonists, and yet that never happened: Anja did not live to see her eighth birthday.

When Anja was born in May of 1937, her father already was fighting with the International Brigades in Spain. Rewald joined him there for four months in order to do the research for *Vier Spanische Jungen*. At Rewald's return to Paris, the tides of the war in Spain had turned. In October 1938 the International Brigades departed from Spain, a month later the Republicans suffered a brutal defeat in the Ebro region, Barcelona fell in January of 1939, and on April 1 of that year, the Nationalists claimed victory. Rewald's by then completed manuscript, writes Krüger, no longer corresponded to the realities of war (1987: 117).

Yet the Nazi invasion of France sealed the fate of the text even more. Rewald and Anja fled; they first made it to Saint Nazaire and then found refuge in Les Roisiers-sur-Loire in Pays de la Loire (western France). But even the kindness of the locals could not help a Jewish woman in occupied France. Rewald was arrested in July of 1942. Schaul, now a veteran of the International Brigades, was a prisoner of war in a camp in Djelfa,

---

[4] Robert Cohen provides a semi-fictional account Rewald's life in his novel *Das Exil der frechen Frauen* (2009).
[5] Rewald's friend and fellow author Lisa Tetzner, by then living in exile in Switzerland, helped her publish this novel in installments in the Swiss periodical *Der öffentliche Dienst*, where it appeared between May and July of 1937. The book's most recent edition is from 2021.

Figure 9.2 Ruth Rewald and her daughter Anja in 1937, reproduced in *Vier Spanische Jungen* (Köln: Pahl Rügenstein Verlag, 1987). Courtesy of Dirk Krüger.

Algeria. There he received his wife's last letter before she disappeared, a cyphered message telling him that she was about to be deported to the east (Krüger 1987: 173).[6] Rewald still assures her husband that he will hear from her and that her only worry is being separated from her daughter. At this point, Anja appears to be protected, as a neighbor promised to take care of her until the child's teacher, Mme. Renaud, would become her legal guardian. Anja, however, was not safe: she was deported and killed two years later. Today, in a French village by the Loire, an elementary school is named in Anja's memory.[7]

Only Schaul, Rewald's husband and Anja's father, survived and it would take almost four decades for him to learn that the manuscript for *Vier Spanische Jungen* outlasted the war (Krüger 1987: 170). At the time of Rewald's arrest and deportation, the Gestapo confiscated her belongings (including letters and the unpublished manuscript of *Vier Spanische Jungen*). After the Allied victory, the box containing Rewald's writing ended up in Moscow; the documents eventually were transferred back to the GDR in the 1960s. The Germanist Silvia Schlenstedt located it and informed Schaul about its existence (Krüger 1987: 171). While the novel finally saw its first edition in 1987, it remains a largely unknown, if not forgotten text.

Now, the claim that Rewald's fate makes this book an example of Jewish writing could be considered to be based on "fixed conceptions of Jewishness," an assessment contrary to a more contemporary notion of "multiple cultural meanings and the

---

[6] In her message Rewald wrote that she was going to work on the harvest (Ich fahre zur Erntearbeit), either near Schaul's place of birth in the Prussian Province of Posen (today Poznan in Poland) or near where the Doctor is; the "Doctor" would be Stalin (Krüger 1987: 173). With this, Rewald communicates to her husband that she is about to be taken to a camp in the east.

[7] Ecole Primaire Anja Schaul, www.education.gouv.fr/annuaire/49-maine-et-loire/gennes-val-de-loire/etab/ecole-primaire-anja-schaul.html.

complex place Jewish history holds for any discussion of diaspora" (Morris 2010: 770). And it is worth noting that while the novel clearly is about the destructive force of fascism, it contains no reference to Jewishness. Neither does Rewald's 1934 *Janko. Der Junge aus Mexiko*. Janko, the "boy from Mexico" is stateless and he ends up in a small German town at the beginning of the text. While the situation that led to his statelessness is the sparring between Mexico and the United States, young Janko (not unlike the protagonists of *Vier Spanische Jungen*) rises to the occasion and faces his fate with more responsibility and grace than most grown-ups ever would. Rewald never left Europe, yet by inventing a displaced Mexican protagonist she creates a scenario that makes it possible for her to explain to her young readers what it means to be stateless and alone in the world. Janko's displacement reflects Jewish fates in this historical moment, and the fact that Jewish culture, as Morris points out, is habitually described as an "aesthetics and politics of homelessness" also comes to mind (2010: 764). To paraphrase Deborah Dwork and Jan van Pelt, fleeing has not written refugees out of the story (of the Holocaust) but has simply taken the story elsewhere, and also everywhere (2009: xiii). From this "elsewhere" Rewald wrote a book about four steadfast boys and their desire to fight fascism in Spain. While it is true that the novel's ending had become a counterfactual by the time she finished it, the book could only appear posthumously because the author never had the chance to either rethink the ending or try out different publishers. The Nazi genocide had made that impossible.

"There is simply no such thing as one modern Jewish literature" writes Miron (2008: 32). Instead, he argues that there are "multiple Jewish literatures and a rich plethora of Jewish literary works written in non-Jewish languages and belonging within their respective non-Jewish literary milieus" (2008). Even though references to Jews or Jewishness (or to antisemitism) are lacking in Rewald's texts, her books are "formed and informed by Jewish experience—no matter of what nature and whether it was directly or indirectly articulated" (2008). This means that a book like *Vier Spanische Jungen* would also "belong, together with the literatures clearly defined as Jewish, within a large and fluid complex that evades simple definitions and demarcations. We can compare this complex to a galaxy: though parts of it constantly move away from each other, they also form one spatial configuration" (2008). Another one of these moving parts is the participation of Jewish volunteers in the International Brigades.

The International Brigades

Josie McLellan describes Schaul as a "typical case" of a German-Jewish volunteer, specifically, "a communist-voting lawyer in the Weimar republic, he lost his job in 1933, and was forced to emigrate to France. Schaul's politicization was accelerated by first-hand experience of police brutality at antifascist demonstrations and contact with the communist movement, and when the war broke out in Spain, he immediately decided to go" (2004: 18). She then adds that "Membership of the International Brigades was a chance for Germans to fight fascism legally and legitimately" (2004: 18). Yet the question of whether Schaul (and Kantorowicz and, of course, Rewald) also saw this struggle as a specifically Jewish one is trickier. As mentioned earlier, Schaul and Kantorowicz belonged to the Tschapaiew Battalion, a multinational group, sometimes also called the "Battalion of the 21 Nations." Unlike the Botwin Company, which also operated within the above-mentioned Polish Dombrowsky Brigade, the Tschapaiew Battalion was not exclusively formed of Jewish volunteers, even though many of its members (like Schaul and Kantorowicz) were Jewish. It is worth noting that for veterans of the Botwin Company like Albert Prago, the war in Spain represented a fight in which Jewish volunteers were resisting fascism, Hitler, and the Nazis (Zaagsma 2017: 2). Gerben Zaagsma points out, however, that Prago wrote his testimony years after the war, and his comments reveal that

> the Holocaust has fundamentally shaped the way in which the participation of Jewish volunteers in the International Brigades has come to be seen. Against the background of post-Holocaust debates about wartime Jewish responses and behavior, their participation is inscribed in a larger Jewish resistance narrative that aims to counter the myth of Jewish passivity in the face of Nazi onslaught. (2017: 3)

In *Vier Spanische Jungen* the struggle against fascism is not depicted as a specifically Jewish resistance to fascism, but unlike Prago's testimony, the book was written before the post-Holocaust debates that Zaagsma addresses took place.

The International Brigades appear rather late in *Vier Spanische Jungen*. The bulk of the novel takes place in Peñarroya, giving Rewald a chance to depict the hardships of daily life in rural Spain and the lived realities under the repression of the Nationalists. Rewald thereby connects the anecdote that was the genesis of the book (four boys escaping from a village occupied by the Nationalists) to a much longer and more complex history of systematic oppression and inequality.

Rewald also brings up some of the short-lived changes and reforms that the coming of the Second Republic brought with it. The site where these changes are most visible is the local schoolhouse. Not only are the depictions of these changes historically accurate, but education also was very important for Rewald. She often wrote about educators, especially those committed to supporting children's autonomy and creativity. In *Janko. Der Junge aus Mexiko*, for example, the main character's strongest ally is his teacher, and Janko himself ends up becoming an educator by the novel's end. The relationship that the children of Peñarroya have with their teacher Luis and with everything he embodies does not last long: once the Nationalists take over the town, they swiftly execute the teacher—a rather accurate depiction of what was a common occurrence in the period.

As expected, the narrator has words of praise for the International Brigades. Unlike most democratic governments that left the Spanish Republic to its fate, individuals (workers, peasants, and other "friends of the people") supported the war efforts financially.[8] But there were others, in the thousands, who gave even more than that: their lives.

---

[8] "Volksfreunde."

They came from all countries. Workers, peasants, and anti-fascists from all classes and parties, they came from America, France, England, Scandinavia, from Cuba, China and Japan, in order to fight fascism together with their Spanish brothers. And German, Italian and Hungarian anti-fascists came, anti-fascists who had already gotten to know the prisons and penal camps of the fascist rulers, who had barely escaped them. All of them, so different in shape, skin color and language, they were all one in their enthusiasm for the Spanish struggle for freedom and their hatred of fascism. (1987: 119)[9]

Rewald highlights the idea that the Brigades are a crucial part of a unified fight against fascism. In this context Rewald also appeals directly to her audience by mentioning the children who were engaged in the struggle by helping to raise funds "at school and at home" in order to sustain the "good fight": "Children raised money at school and at home. Field hospitals, rehabilitation centers, orphanages were created" (1987: 119).[10] Coincidentally, before the Nationalists take over Peñarroya, and during the teacher's brief tenure at the local school, the children do just that. They not only organize the schoolhouse much better than any of their adult counterparts ever had, but also ensure that funds are available to support the people of Peñarroya and the soldiers fighting the Nationalists. The message that comes across in the text is that even the most vulnerable can be a part of a broader, if not global struggle against fascism. This is also how the book illustrates what being part of the International Brigades could mean for German Jews who were living in exile, among them Hans Schaul.

Yet something else is at stake here, as Hannah Arendt makes evident in a brief reference to the International Brigades in *The Origins of Totalitarianism*. In a quickly changing Europe, a series of ruptures (the end of empire, the puzzling situation of minorities and the stateless, and the clashes between ideologies that would confront one another once civil war breaks out in Spain) were altering forms of citizenship and belonging. Arendt reads the participation of volunteers in the International Brigades as part of these ruptures, which, Arendt writes, alarmed European democracies:

Not only were people expelled from country and citizenship, but more and more persons of all countries, including the Western democracies, volunteered to fight in civil wars abroad (something which up to then only a few idealists or adventurers had done) even if this meant cutting themselves off from their

---

[9] "Sie kamen aus allen Ländern. Arbeiter, Bauern und Antifaschisten aller Schichten und Parteien, sie kamen aus Amerika, Frankreich, England, Skandinavien, aus Cuba, China und Japan, um mit ihren Spanischen Brüdern gegen den Faschismus zu kämpfen. Und es kamen deutsche, italienische und ungarische Antifaschisten, die in ihrer Heimat schon die Gefängnisse und grausamen Straflager der faschistischen Machthaber kennengelernt hatten oder ihnen knapp entronnen waren. Sie alle, so verschieden in Gestalt, Hautfarbe und Sprache, waren eins in ihrer Begeisterung für den Spanischem Freiheitskampf und in ihrem Hass gegen den Faschismus."

[10] "Kinder sammelten in den Schulen und daheim. Lazarette, Erholungsheime, Kinderheime wurden geschaffen."

national communities. This was the lesson of the Spanish Civil War and one of the reasons why the governments were so frightened by the International Brigades. Matters would not have been quite so bad if this had meant that people no longer clung so closely to their nationality and were ready eventually to be assimilated into another national community. But this was not the case. (Arendt 1966: 282)

Arendt identifies an inherent contradiction: she bases her argument on the fact that the different battalions were structured around national origin (such as the Abraham Lincoln Brigade or the Garibaldi Brigade), or, at least, in relation to a common language (1966: 282–3; Kölbl et al. 2020: 9). This situation was particularly complex for Jewish volunteers, who often were multilingual and who may have become stateless by the time the war in Spain broke out. Yet, as Arendt shows, while the enemies that the volunteers met in battle were the Nationalists (and the supporting troops from Morocco), they also embodied other adversaries.

Arendt's reference to the International Brigades is about the ways in which citizenship and belonging were evolving in Europe, and about a contradiction: breaking a connection with a government, and yet remaining attached to a nationality. Referring again to the volunteers of the International Brigades, Arendt describes this contradiction in the following terms: "Even though they had renounced their citizenship, no longer had any connection or loyalty to their country of origin, and did not identify their nationality with a visible, fully recognizable government they retained a strong attachment to their nationality" (1966: 283).

Of course, these attachments become more complex for Jewish volunteers who had not exactly renounced their citizenship: the government had taken it away. Rewald's book, while written by a German-born Jewish woman living in France who got to spend four months in Spain is not, at least not specifically, about any of these nations, but about a larger, transnational, and transhistorical fight against fascism. Fascism, of course, has a specific history that Rewald does not ignore, but in her novel fascism also becomes an all-encompassing term for oppression and repression. The text includes references to Germany and Italy, and Rewald writes that the Nationalists received support from these "fascist states" (1987: 58, 108). Moreover, Rewald also connects the virulent force of fascism in the early twentieth century to a *longue durée* of precarity that results from oppression and inequality. Even in the most rural areas, everybody understands who the fascists are: "Fascist was the feudal lord who for centuries has owned the land, where hundreds of peasants could have managed on their own for centuries" (1987: 84).[11]

When Arendt writes about the ways in which volunteering for the International Brigades often meant remaining committed to fighting for a nationality, she recognizes a contradiction. In Rewald's novel, this contradiction can be found not in a loyalty (or lack thereof) to a country of origin, but to a language. What matters then for the last book that Rewald completed before her death is not only that she wrote it against all

---

[11] "Faschist, das war der Schlossherr, dem seit Jahrhunderten Landesstrecken gehörten, auf denen Hunderte von Bäuern ihre kleinen Wirtschaft hätten betreiben könnten."

odds and against the times, but also that writing about all of this in German made it possible for her to reclaim a language as hers. Victor Klemperer (who, unlike Rewald, survived the Nazi genocide) has famously written about the grip that the Nazis had on the German language; numerous Jewish exiled writers who (also unlike Rewald) were able to escape from occupied Europe continued writing in German and also establishing publishing houses and newspapers. Even though Rewald could not participate in these later endeavors from a safe place of exile (Lisa Tetzner in Switzerland, Thomas Mann in the United States, or Anna Seghers in Mexico come to mind) her book should still be considered part of that same effort.

I have mentioned earlier that *Vier Spanische Jungen* provides a window into a specific moment in history, a moment before the victory of the Nationalists and before the Nazi genocide. Rewald's linguistic choices in the novel reveal the very contradictions and tensions of the period, which also are part of the soundscape of the International Brigades of the Spanish Civil War.

Language

The novel is written in German, but the four Spanish boys and all other characters (except for the members of the Tchapaiew Battalion) are supposed to be expressing themselves in Spanish. This would make *Vier Spanische Jungen* a novel that is, to use Rebecca Walkowitz's term, "born translated." Walkowitz writes about novels (all of them written decades after Rewald's death) for which translation "is not secondary or incidental," but rather a condition of their production. Like John Coetzee's *The Childhood of Jesus*, a text that Walkowitz analyses, *Vier Spanische Jungen* "pretends to take place in Spanish" (2015: 4). *Vier Spanische Jungen*, however, does not appear in multiple languages, it does not circulate across national literatures and publishing markets, and so it does not "start as world literature" (2015). And while *Vier Spanische Jungen* precedes most of the texts that Walkowitz discusses, her description of these still fits Rewald's book: "These works are *written for translation*, in the hope of being translated, but they are often also *written as translations*, pretending to take place in a language other than the one in which they have, in fact, been composed" (2015). Beyond the fact that Rewald indeed hoped that the novel would be published and subsequently translated into several languages, traces of translation are everywhere in the novel, ranging from Germanized and otherwise creative spellings of names and toponyms to the creation of certain hybrid words, such as the nouns *Responsablo* and *Responsablen*, that do not exist in any language (1987: 53).[12] Here, Rewald has taken a Spanish noun, *responsables*, and given it a German grammatical declination in order to refer to the group of children who become active once the education reforms of the Second Republic are a reality in Peñarroya. Specifically, the *Responsablen* are the

---

[12] These would include, among others, the spelling of "Josepha," the "Calle Andalusia," the "Plaza d'Espana" among others.

children that work with the teacher Luis in order to make the local school a better and fairer place that would (in today's terms) promote equity. Needless to say, our four heroes, the *Vier Spanische Jungen*, belong to that group. Rewald also immediately translates the word she just coined, by adding that *Responsablo* means *Verantwortliche* (1987: 53). Other Spanish words that appear in the text (*Rubio* [*Blonder*]; *Garbanzos* [*die murmelgroßen Spanischen Erbsen*]) are also followed by translation. Others, like the construction "*Viva die antifaschistische Jugendfront*" are left as is (1987: 94).[13] Even though Rewald's book was envisioned for audiences who probably did not know Spanish, the work's linguistic texture reflects the contradictions of the period. In this sense, a book published two years after Rewald completed *Vier Spanische Jungen* comes to mind: Ernest Hemingway's *For Whom the Bell Tolls*. To be clear, my goal here is not to look for analogies between these two texts, and much less to suggest that Hemingway's strategic mistranslations have a Jewish character. As a reminder, a relationship with translation places *Vier Spanische Jungen* on the "fuzzily drawn" map of Jewish writing (Miron 2008), but only because this relationship is intrinsically related to the other elements that make it possible to situate the novel on that map. Hemingway's novel is relevant here because the author uses a particular stylistic strategy: namely, "the incorporation into English of the structures and idioms of another language, in this case Spanish" (Londsdale 2015: 2). If "Hemingway's literal translations, his puns, and his use of false cognates point towards mistranslation as a theme, towards a sense of the danger that language will fail him in attempting to capture the civil war and that comprehension will founder," in *Vier Spanische Jungen* the creative spellings and the hybrid constructions that do not fully make sense in German or in Spanish are a constitutive part of the meanings that the novel conveys (Londsdale 2015: 12). The relationship with translation (and, perhaps, its limits) reveals that the novel not only tells a story about four boys in the Spanish Civil War, a story that could be considered to be exemplary and inspirational to youths across the world. This also is a story that reflects a unique and short-lived moment, when displacement, multiple languages, and even optimism intersected, ultimately leading to a manuscript doomed to be a type of utopia and also an anachronism.

An alternative reading of the novel's relationship with translation and mistranslation would be that it simply was not possible to use the services of a more linguistically proficient editor who could have remedied the inconsistencies in the novel. Arguably, that could have been done when the novel was finally published in 1987. However, that type of editing would have erased much of the novel's texture.

The relationship with translation becomes even more apparent once, toward the end of the novel, the boys encounter the members of the Tschapaiew Battalion, one of the most linguistically diverse groups within the International Brigades.[14] Given

---

[13] "The marble-sized Spanish peas"; "Long live the anti-fascist youth front."
[14] It had 389 members; the majority were German (seventy-nine), closely followed by Polish (sixty-seven), fifty-nine were Spanish, forty-one Austrian, twenty Swiss, twenty Palestinian, and the remaining, in the teens or below, ranging from fourteen Dutch soldiers to just one Brazilian (Kantorowicz 1948).

that the majority hailed from German-speaking countries, German ended up being the strongest, but certainly not the sole, language spoken among the members of the battalion.

When the youngsters happen upon the soldiers of the Tschapaiew Battalion a number of misunderstandings (linguistic and otherwise) ensue. Before seeing the soldiers, the boys notice cannons, and so they assume that they remain trapped in enemy territory. This is reinforced once they see men who are "half-naked and tanned," which immediately leads them to conclude that the men must be "moors, for sure moors" referring to the Moroccan soldiers who fought with the Nationalists during the Civil War (Rewald 1987: 150).[15] Indeed, earlier in the text a number of racially marked stereotypes about the Moroccan soldiers (common in the discourse of the period on both sides of the war) appear mentioned (Rewald 1987: 22, 87). It therefore hardly is surprising that when the four boys first encounter the soldiers (who are resting between battles, their skins tanned and covered in the red clay earth of the trenches) they are terrified. The misunderstanding that then ensues appears in Kantorowicz's description of the event and in Rewald's narration of it (Kantorowicz 1948: 154).

In Rewald's longer and more elaborate account the demeanor of the children and of the grown-ups is more solemn than in Kantorowicz's version. She also uses this opportunity to portray the different origins of the German-speaking soldiers: their inflections reveal that they hail from Austria, Bavaria, and Berlin (Rewald 1987: 155, 156). Given that Rewald was a refugee who had been living and working in France (as a teacher and writer) for five years, it hardly is surprising that she was particularly attuned to the subtleties of language and speech. The soldiers are chatting and joking around, but their banter is interrupted when they see the frightened boys. The children (who still think that they are facing the enemy) can only think of saying one thing: a greeting that would make the soldiers identify them as supporters of the Nationalists: "Arriba España" (Rewald 1987: 155). Then, just like in Kantorowicz's account, one of the "half-naked and tanned" soldiers clears his voice before saying "Nix Arriba." Here Rewald points out a linguistic muddle: "The Spanish boys did not understand this Spanish-German language mishmash and they still looked frightened" (1987: 155).[16] At that point, the same soldier screams out only one word, "Antifascistas!" pounding on his chest at the same time. To this Jerónimo, one of the boys, responds "We are anti-fascists, too!" The child here uses a German grammatical structure: "*somos también antifascistas*" in lieu of "*también somos antifascistas*."

With the multilingual soundscape of the International Brigades still in her ears, Rewald crafted a narrative aiming to explain to young audiences what fighting fascism in Spain means.[17] *Vier Spanische Jungen* displays interactions between several languages, but none of these are "Jewish language" like Yiddish or Ladino. However,

---

[15] "Halbnackt und rotbraun"; "Moros, bestimmt Moros."
[16] "Die spanischen Jungen verstanden dieses spanisch-deutsche Sprachgemisch nicht und schauten noch genauso angstvoll drein."
[17] For an in-depth analysis of that soundscape and an explanation of attempts that were made to remedy such "language mishmash," see Naya Ortega and Prades Artigas (2020).

as Morris writes, "to the claim that Jewish literature contributes to transnationalism, multilingualism, hybridity, and the klezmerical, let me add that Jewish subjectivity and Jewish text are always subject to translation" (2021: 76). The multiple translations and encounters that defined Jewish fates in the twentieth century materialize in the book's intrinsic and also intimate relationship with a linguistic crossroads.

Children's Literature

I have argued that the interaction between three factors (the author's fate and the novel's fate, the role of the International Brigades, and the importance of language and translation) situate the novel on Miron's "fuzzily drawn" map of modern Jewish writing, but have not discussed thus far the fact that *Vier Spanische Jungen* is a book written for young readers.

Just a brief reference in the documents that Rewald and Schaul left behind suggests that she actually was interested in writing a book for adults—so just *a novel* and not a novel with any kind of qualifiers that may diminish its value in literary history and shared memory (Krüger 1987: 181). Indeed, the fact that the two men (Rewald's own husband and Kantorowicz) insisted that she should write a children's book demands a longer and more intimate exploration of Rewald's biography, and of the gendered nature of literature written for children. Had Rewald not been murdered, she may very well have had the chance to write all kinds of books: with female protagonists, for adults, about everybody, and for everybody.

When Rewald first arrived at the Ernst Thälmann Orphanage she was impressed with what she called the children's "spirit of camaraderie" (Krüger 1990: 232).[18] Moreover, her novels can be collectively seen as, Krüger suggests, "a song of praise for children's spirit of camaraderie" (1987: 186).[19] Rewald's novels may take place in faraway locations, but no matter how distant (from Germany) the settings of her books may be, no matter how "exotic" her protagonists are, their bonhomie and their sense of solidarity make it possible for young readers to establish a meaningful, empathetic, and emotional connection with them.

Vier Spanische Jungen is more than a forgotten text: it represents a crucial moment in Spanish Civil War literature, Jewish literature, children's literature, and also world literature. Children's literature is a rather "unruly subject," difficult to delimit and define, and this chapter's remaining pages would not suffice to fully engage with that debate (Gubar 2011: 209). For the present purposes, it is useful to again bring up Miron's "fuzzily drawn" map of modern Jewish writing: because the map of children's literature, this "reservoir for the collective memory of national, regional, or ethnic groups" is just as "fuzzily drawn" (O'Sullivan 2011: 190). Marah Gubar uses the same term Miron does—fuzzy—when she addresses the difficulty of defining this body of writing:

---

[18] "Kameradschaftsgeist."
[19] "Hohelied kindlichen Kameradschaftgeistes."

The fact that something is very difficult to define—even "impossible to define exactly"—does not mean that it does not exist or cannot be talked about. In such cases we simply have to accept that the concept under consideration is complex and capacious; it may also be unstable (its meaning shifts over time and across different cultures) and fuzzy at the edges (its boundaries are not fixed and exact). (2011: 212)

Vier Spanische Jungen indeed is a book about children and for children, and its pedagogical, if not ideological, aims are rather transparent. The boys, especially Jerónimo, aka "Rubio" can also be mischievous at times. Readers are introduced to him as a trickster who just stole some items from the local barbershop in order to "dress up" as a Chinese man and so play a prank on the people of the town (Rewald 1987: 15). While the "four Spanish boys" are as good at playing pranks as most heroes of children's literature (from Pippi Longstocking to the Weasley twins) tend to be, the boys' behavior, more than anything, is commendable. Rewald's book has characters that are relatable and compelling, and yet the author never loses sight of the book's anti-fascist message. As she told the children at the orphanage outside Madrid, it is never too late to awaken political awareness of otherwise complacent adults, and children (or at least certain children) seem to be well suited for that task (Krüger 1987: 183). We will never know whether the novel could have accomplished all this in 1938 (or during the difficult years that followed), and yet it is important to take this novel seriously as a source of knowledge and meaning about the moment it was produced.

Children's literature provides young readers the vocabularies they need to read the world into which they venture; overtly or latently reflecting dominant social and cultural norms, it passes down information, beliefs, and customs, and it is the branch of literature read and shared by the greatest number of members of most communities. As a sanctioned location of intergenerational communication about group belonging, children's literature is a reservoir for the collective memory of national, regional, or ethnic groups. (O'Sullivan 2011: 190)

The Nazi genocide disappeared Rewald and almost all of her traces, and yet the unexpected survival of *Vier Spanische Jungen* is a form of "poetic justice." Mostly forgotten and very easy to overlook in the longer histories of the Spanish Civil War, the Holocaust, and their respective aftermaths, the moment of optimism and hope for a good outcome that appears at the novel's end remains there, frozen in time, and yet undeniably present.

References

Arendt, H. (1966), *The Origins of Totalitarianism*, New York: Harcourt, Barce & World Inc.
Bell, R. (1992), "Of Terror, Guilt and Legacy. Hermann Kesten's Family Novel 'Die Kinder von Gernika,'" in Luís Costa (ed.), *German and International Perspectives on the Spanish Civil War. The Aesthetics of Partisanship*, 79–95, Columbia, S.C.: Camden House.
Cohen, R. (2009), *Das Exil der frechen Frauen*, Berlin: Rotbuch Verlag.

Dwork, D. and J. Van Pelt (2009), *Flight from the Reich: Refugee Jews, 1933-1946*, New York: W. W. Norton & Company.
Gubar, M. (2011), "On Not Defining Children's Literature," *PMLA* 126 (1): 209–16.
Kantorowicz, A. (1948), *Das Bataillon der 21 Nationen*, Rudolstadt: Greifenverlag.
Klemperer, V. (1949), *LTi; Notizbuch eines philologen*, Berlin: Aufbau Verlag.
Kölbl, J., I. Orlova and M. Wolf (2020), *¿Pasarán? Kommunikation im Spanischen Bürgerkrieg. Interacting in the Spanish Civil War*, Hamburg and Vienna: New Academic Press.
Krüger, D. (1987), "Nachwort," in R. Rewald, *Vier Spanische Jungen*, Köln: Röderberg.
Krüger, D. (1988), "Vergessen und verbrannt," *Zeitschrift für Literaturwissenschaft und Linguistik*, 18 (70): 111–19.
Krüger, D. (1990) *Die deutsch-jüdische Kinder – und Jugendbuchautorin Ruth Rewald und die Kinder – und Jugendliteratur im Exil*, Frankfurt: Dipa.
Leveque, M. (2010), *Vier spanische Jungen de Ruth Rewald : l'unique roman allemand pour la jeunesse sur la guerre d'Espagne*, Revue du G.I.E.N., Groupe interdisciplinaire d'études nizaniennes (GIEN), 61–73.
Lonsdale, L. (2015), "The Perils and Possibilities of Mistranslation: Equivocation and Barbarism in *For Whom the Bell Tolls*," *Readings*, 1: 1–14.
McLelllan, J. (2004), *AntiFascism and Memory in East Germany: Remembering the International Brigades 1945–1989*, Oxford: Clarendon Press.
Miron D. (2008), "From Continuity to Contiguity: Thoughts on the Theory of Jewish Literature, Jewish Literatures and Cultures," in Y. Z. Eliav and A. Norich (eds.), *Context and Intertext*, 9–36, Providence: Brown Judaic Studies.
Morris, L. (2010), "Placing and Displacing Jewish Studies: Notes on the Future of a Field," *PMLA*, 125 (3): 764–73.
Naya-Ortega, R. and L. Prades-Artigas. (2020), "Una nueva torre de Babel. El aprendizaje de lenguas en las Brigadas Internacionales," in J. Kölbl, I. Orlova and M. Wolf (eds.), *¿Pasarán? Kommunikation im Spanischen Bürgerkrieg. Interacting in the Spanish Civil War*, 49–66, Hamburg and Vienna: New Academic Press.
O'Sullivan, E. (2011), "Comparative Children's Literature," *PMLA* 126 (1): 189–96.
Rewald, R. (1987), *Vier Spanische Jungen*, Köln: Pahl Rugenstein Verlag.
Rewald, R. (2002). *Janko. Der Junge aus Mexiko*, Berlin: Arco Verlag, 2007.
Rewald, R. (2021), *Tsao und Jing-Ling: Kinderleben in China*, Berlin: Arco Verlag.
Vietor-Engländer, D. (2009), "What's in a Name? What is Jewishness? New Definitions for Two Generations: Elsa Bernstein, Anna Gmeyner, Ruth Rewald and Others," in M. H. Gelber, J. Hessing, and R. Jütte (eds.), *Integration und Ausgrenzung*, 467–82, Berlin: De Gruyter.
Walkowitz, R. (2015), *Born Translated. The Contemporary Novel in an Age of World Literature*, New York: Columbia University Press.
Zaagsma, G. (2017), *Jewish Volunteers, the International Brigades and the Spanish Civil War*, New York: Bloomsbury Academic.

10

Using the Kabbalah to Make Sense of the Spanish Civil War

Angelina Muñiz-Huberman's *War of the Unicorn* (1983)

E. Helena Houvenaghel

War and Exile

Angelina Muñiz-Huberman[1] was born in France (Hyères) at the outbreak of the Spanish Civil War (1936), after her Spanish Jewish parents fled their country of origin, Spain. Three years later, the fascist regime of the dictator Francisco Franco (1939–75) was established. Muñiz-Huberman's parents set off to safer places in the Americas. They first headed for Cuba, and later went to Mexico, the country where the family settled down. Hence, Angelina Muñiz-Huberman was born as a child of war and exile.

War and exile became two central themes in her ample oeuvre. In Muñiz-Huberman's early works of the 1970s and 1980s, her approach to these topics was rather veiled but in her later work, she dealt with the Spanish Civil War in a more direct way. In her collection of historical and philosophical essays *The Century of Disenchantment* (*El siglo del desencanto*, 2002), written at the turn of the century, Muñiz-Huberman described the Spanish Civil War and the Shoah as "the two descents into hell of the twentieth century" (Muñiz-Huberman 2002: 26–7). In the same essay collection, she further expressed the Spanish Civil War as "destruction of utopia and hope," "total death," "dispersion of the people," "what could never again return to be," and "the irreversible." In the face of these "descents into hell" (Muñiz-Huberman 2002), and the chaos they caused, Muñiz-Huberman put an emphasis on the poet's mission to

---

[1] Angelina Muñiz-Huberman was elected in January 2021 as a new member of the Mexican Academy of Language. Her oeuvre spans over forty-five works and has won numerous prizes and awards, such as the Prize Magda Donato (1972), the Prize Xavier Villaurrutia (1985), the Prize Sor Juana Inés de la Cruz (1993), the Medal of Jerusalem (2003), the Woman of Valor Award (2003), the Prize of the National University (2003), and the most important award in Mexican Literature: the National Prize of Arts and Literature (2018).

"desperately seek harmony in the disorder and violence" of the twentieth century (Muñiz-Huberman 2002: 26).

In her early literary work, especially in her first trilogy (*Morada interior* [1972]; *Tierra adentro* [1977]; *La guerra del unicornio* [1983]), Muñiz-Huberman adopted what Payne calls "oblique approaches" (Payne 1997: 43) to the theme of war and exile. I agree with Payne that back then, the author held a clear distance from these topics by situating conflict and banishment in vague, distant, or imaginary times and places, or by interpreting them in a secretive, spiritual, or philosophical way. Payne (1997: 431) suggests that Muñiz-Huberman chooses these approaches to the topics of war and exile "because being young and still greatly affected by the environment in which she was brought up, she felt too close to the experience to treat it directly."[2] Still, I argue that this indirect approach is not inspired by the closeness of the events nor by the author's youth. I make the case that this indirect, mystic, and philosophical approach is Muñiz-Huberman's way to make sense of war and exile. The combination of fiction, on the one hand, and philosophy, ethics, and mysticism, on the other, is a fundamental part of Muñiz-Huberman's hybrid writing by which she gives meaning to armed conflict and expulsion.

The first part of the trilogy is *Morada interior* (*Inner Abode*, 1972). It offers a spiritual exploration of the concept of exile. The title is a reference to the vision of the sixteenth-century Spanish mystic Santa Teresa of Ávila, a descendant of converted Jews, who saw the human soul as exiled to earth from its union with God. The soul, according to the mystic's vision, can undertake a journey to unite itself with God. The soul is represented as a castle with seven mansions (dwelling places, or "moradas"). These places stand for the seven stages of the journey toward the union with God. This vision inspired Teresa's work *The Interior Castle* or *The Mansions* (*Las moradas*, 1577), a guide for spiritual development, to which Angelina Muñiz-Huberman gave a central role in the first part of the trilogy, *Morada interior* (Houvenaghel 2021c).

The second part of the trilogy, *Tierra adentro* (*Inland*, 1977) offers a historical approach to the concept of exile via the emblematic case of Jewish persecutions and banishments. *Inland* superimposes two layers of Jewish history: the expulsion of the Sephardic Jewish community from Spain in the fifteenth and sixteenth centuries, on the one hand, and the expulsion of the Jewish community from Europe in the twentieth century, on the other. It tells the story of a young Jew who is persecuted and expulsed from his home country and makes the journey, in a period of armed conflict, to Jerusalem, where he is intending to start a new life with his young bride. This journey is depicted in a context that resembles the Spanish Inquisition and the religious wars of the sixteenth century. At the same time, the work can be read as an allegory of the Jewish people's persecution by the Nazis during the Second World War and as an evocation of their escape routes to a safe country (Houvenaghel 2021b). By combining these different layers of Jewish exile, situated in distant times and places, *Inland* reflects on the repetitive character of the exclusion of minorities throughout history and foregrounds the importance of a safe haven for the persecuted and exiled.

---

[2] Payne's interpretation is based on Angelina Muñiz-Huberman's testimony in *La Jornada Semanal* (1993).

The third part of the trilogy, *The War of the Unicorn* (1983),[3] finally comprises, in my view, a spiritual approach to the Spanish Civil War that aims at giving this conflict a meaning. The work represents the stages of a battle between good and evil knights which is an allegorical representation of the conflict between Republicans and Nationalists in the Spanish Civil War. At the same time, the battle can be understood as the allegorical depiction of an inner, spiritual struggle, in line with the thought of the ecstatic thirteenth-century kabbalist Abraham Abulafia. According to Abulafia's teaching, "good and evil forces within the human psyche are continually at war with one another" (Idel 1988) and conflict is a necessary step on the mystical path.

I propose that these are the ways in which Muñiz-Huberman represents and reflects on war and exile in her first trilogy. In part one of the trilogy, she considers the spiritual exile of the soul and its journey toward mystical union; in part two, the author intertwines the repetitive exiles of the Jewish people and the corresponding journeys toward a safe place in the land of promise; and in part three, she foregrounds the inner battle between good and evil as a necessary step toward inner harmony. Still, the order of the trilogy's parts is misleading. Angelina Muñiz-Huberman (Salazar and Rodríguez Plaza 1993: 168) explains that *The War of the Unicorn*, which ended up being the third part of the trilogy, was intended to be its opening novel. It is because of difficulties getting her early work published that *WU* appeared after and not before *Inner Abode* and *Inland*. This clarification gives a different and significant insight into how Angelina Muñiz's thoughts on war and exile developed and turns the *WU* into its cornerstone. By means of this novel on the Spanish Civil War, the author first tried to "pull out the thorn of war" (Jofresa Marqués 1999: 22) before interpreting exile in the two next parts of the trilogy.

Hybridity

Coming back to Muñiz-Huberman's trilogy of war and exile, besides this thematic leitmotiv of war and exile, the formal characteristic of generic hybridity runs as a continuous thread through the trilogy.[4] Muñiz-Huberman combines argumentative prose (biography, historical essay, philosophical dialogue) and narrative prose (both autobiographical and fictional) in these three works. More generally, "the dissipation of the limits between literary genres is one of the most constant features of Muñiz-Huberman's writing from 1972 throughout her most recent work" (Houvenaghel 2020b: 12). Her "border-crossing attitude" toward generic rules creates a "liberating and transgressive sense of movement" (Houvenaghel 2015: 98) and a multilayered meaning in her writing (Houvenaghel and Carrillo 2021).

---

[3] Henceforth abbreviated as: *WU*. All citations are made from the 2011 edition of *WU*.
[4] This hybridity has not been fully explored in any of the three parts of the trilogy of war and exile. It has especially been understudied in the third part of Muñiz-Huberman's trilogy, *WU*. Some scholars have briefly suggested that *WU* combines a narrative and a "philosophical" or "essayistic" layer (Patán 1984 cited by Gambarte 1992; Cánovas 2012).

In *The War of the Unicorn*, the combination of narrative and argumentative genres makes it possible, first, to create movement between a fantastic setting, the Spain of the 1930s, and the wandering existence of the thirteenth-century Jewish kabbalist Abulafia, and, second, to give a spiritual meaning to the conflict between Nationalists and Republicans in the Spanish Civil War.

The narrative layer of *The War of the Unicorn* comprises a fantastic story of rival knights which is a historical allegory of the Spanish Civil War. The work situates the armed conflict in a timeless setting in the kingdom of Alamo and opens when the good knights depose their king. The king goes into exile and the good knights initiate new laws and regulations. The story's opening can thus be connected with the end of the monarchy in Spain, the exile of the Spanish king, and the Republican reforms. In the narrative, the unrest caused by the reforms leads to the uprising of the Knights of Sable, associated with the black eagle. The Knights of Sable, who represent evil and aim at gaining control of the country for themselves, confront the Knights of Gules, who are associated with justice and honor. The references to Franco's military revolt, on the one hand, and to the Republican Army, on the other, are clear. The representation of the different stages of the rival knights' battle and the eventual victory of the Knights of Sable corresponds, respectively, to the course of the Spanish Civil War and to the Nationalist victory.

The argumentative layer of the book foregrounds the Kabbalah and combines biographical fiction, on the one hand, and the philosophical dialogue (a dramatized way of representing philosophical ideas), on the other. This layer foregrounds the life of the kabbalist Abulafia and dedicates special attention to his thought on good and evil. Abulafia's teaching leads the reader to a second interpretation of the book's narrative layer. On a deeper level that goes beyond the historical allegory of the Spanish Civil War, the story offers an allegory of ideas. The story's plot exemplifies the thought of the kabbalist Abraham Abulafia on the interdependence of good and evil.

Scholars have generally interpreted the story of the rival knights told in *The War of the Unicorn* as a historical allegory of the Spanish Civil War and hereby focused on the story's intertextual relations with medieval French and Spanish chivalry novels.[5] Still, neither the argumentative layer concerning the life and thought of the Jewish kabbalist Abulafia nor its function as an intertext to the narrative layer has been analyzed by the critics. Hence, I zoom in on the text's combination of genres and connect this hybridity with the way Muñiz-Huberman gives meaning to the Spanish Civil War.

The Argumentative Layer: Biography and Philosophical Dialogue

Fictional biography is a hybrid genre in which the boundaries between fiction and nonfiction are fluid. It offers a creative account of a historical person's life. In *The War*

---

[5] This allegorical meaning of the novel has been analyzed by several critics (Patán 1984; Gambarte 1992; McInnis 2001; Pérez Aparicio 2014) and has been confirmed by Angelina Muñiz-Huberman (Jofresa Marqués 1999: 21).

of the Unicorn, this historical person is the thirteenth-century Spanish Jewish kabbalist Abraham Abulafia, who is converted into the personage "Abraham of Talamanca." Both the fictitious personage and the historical figure will play a role in future writings by Muñiz-Huberman, such as *Huerto cerrado, huerto sellado* (1985) (*Enclosed Garden*, 1988) and *Las raíces y las ramas* ([1993] 2015) (*The Roots and the Branches*). Angelina Muñiz-Huberman thus seems to be fascinated by Abulafia, "one of the most enigmatic and intriguing [. . .] figures in the history of Jewish mysticism" whose "messianic self-conception and colorful life story" stand out (Sagerman 2011: vii). The information on his life that we have at our disposition is mainly based on the detailed way in which Abulafia documented his own life experiences. Given Abulafia's "fecund imagination," it is not easy, in his self-construal, to disentangle "fantasy [. . .] from facticity" (Wolfson 2011: 68). On this basis, the creative account of the kabbalist's life in *WU* lays, in between fact and fiction, the foundations for understanding the circumstances in which his thinking was conceived.

The biography evokes Abraham Abulafia's extraordinary life via the memories and thoughts of the fictional personage Abraham of Talamanca. Interesting in the text's biographical approach to Abulafia's life and works is the temporal and spatial framework. Even though the narration follows a chronological order (by starting with Abraham Abulafia's youth and studies under the guidance of his father, continuing with Abulafia's travels to the east, his return and period of intense studying, teaching, and wandering, and ending with his mystical revelations), it does not include any dates. The text does not include the year of his birth (1239 or 1240), nor the year of his death (sometime after 1291). Other important dates that are missing are his father's death (1260), Abulafia's journey to the east and subsequent return (1260), and Abulafia's first mystical experiences (1270) (Sagerman 2011: 1–3; Wolfson 2011: 68–9).

The names of the important places in the story of Abulafia's wandering life are also not mentioned, except for references to mythical and religious places, such as the legendary river Sambatyon that Abulafia sought in his 1260 journey, or the Holy Land. When referring to other places, such as Abulafia's birthplace in Spain, his period in Greece, his return to Spain, his first mystical revelations in Catalonia, and his later resettlement in Sicily, the text uses invented names such as "Talamanca" or uses metaphorical descriptions such as "Tierra de Aloma," "tierras de Rocalta," "tierras de montaña y tierras marinas," and "tierras de Catalá" (*WU*: 22–34).

The vague spatiotemporal framework makes the biography fit in the book's fantastic setting of rival knights and does not hinder the allegorical reading related to the Spanish Civil War. But more importantly, this vague spatiotemporal framework enables the text to put the emphasis on Abulafia's inner life and thoughts, on his continuous wandering, the symbol of his spiritual quest. The quest to find and understand "the name of all things and the name of God" (*WU*: 27)[6] is the first point that the book mentions about "Abraham of Talamanca." The text hereby refers in simplified terms to Abulafia's spiritual unraveling of the two Divine Names, the "name of the seventy-two letters" and the Tetragrammaton (Idel 1988: 22).

---

[6] This and all further translations of *The War of the Unicorn* are mine.

The biography is selective and highlights certain aspects of the historical Abulafia's life while silencing others. It does not mention, for example, Abulafia's journey to Rome with the intention to convert Pope Nicholas III to Judaism in 1280. Furthermore, the biography does not include Abulafia's messianic self-conception although it does allude to his period and success as a prophet. Rather than Abulafia's messianic self-construal and plan to convert the pope, it is his continuous wandering, the complexity of his readings, and the arduous mission to decipher the name of God and to understand the creation that identify Abulafia in this biography. The text does refer in length to the complex texts that Abulafia studied intensely in the framework of his quest, especially *The Guide of the Perplexed* by Maimonides, and the anonymous *Sefer Yetsirá* (*Book of Creation*) that explains the creation of the world and of humanity as based on Hebrew letter combinations. Finally, the biography dedicates special attention to Abulafia's insight into the relationship between good and evil. This line of Abulafia's thought will be used in the narration of *The War of the Unicorn* to give an ethical meaning to the violence and destruction caused by the Spanish Civil War. Hence, the fictional personage and the historical figure are similar but not identical. The personage's role in *WU* is supportive, secondary to the book's search for a way to make sense of the Spanish Civil War.

One particular component of Abulafia's teaching will be brought to the attention of the reader by means of another literary genre, the philosophical dialogue, which forms the spiritual pivot of the book. The book reaches a climax in the meeting between the knight-protagonist of the fantastic narration and the Jewish kabbalist "Abraham of Talamanca," the personage based on the historical figure of Abulafia. This meeting is announced and then several times delayed for different reasons. The postponement contributes to giving importance to both the encounter and the question that is dealt with in their dialogue. The question that preoccupies the knight-protagonist and leads him toward the Jewish kabbalist is double: "Why does evil exist?" and "Is a world without evil possible?"

By means of this question, the book foregrounds a fundamental point of kabbalah: "The formulation of the powers of evil as an independent enemy of the divine, and the description of human life as being conducted in a dualistic universe in which evil and good are in constant struggle, is the contribution of the kabbalah to the Jewish worldview" (Dan 2007: 51).

The dialogue is the framework used to communicate the heart of Abulafia's teaching, namely, the way in which good and evil are closely related. Abulafia proposes that evil serves the good and, moreover, is necessary for the good (Sagerman 2011: 191). For Abulafia, good and evil are intertwined as they mutually arise from the other: "the polarities between good and evil" are "ephemeral at their root" (Sagerman 2011: 191). From this perspective, as good and evil share the same roots, "flux governs polarities" between good and evil, "dichotomies are fugacious," and "good and evil often interpenetrate" (Sagerman 2011: 191).

At the beginning of this philosophical dialogue, a scene is set in which the personage of the good knight and the personage of Abulafia sit down together and raise the topic of good and evil. In their introductory conversation, the borders between good and evil are already presented as blurred:

The light of the way is the first question. God himself had to separate the light from the darkness and also had to grope around in the dark until he could disentangle the creation. He had to divide the world and he forgot to wipe out the traces of the division. That is why we, every day, move from good to evil, every day we retrace the line and every day we make mistakes and we don't know on what side we are. Black and white. The equilibrium is unstable. (*WU*: 57–8)[7]

The personage of the knight proposes to ask the question that is troubling him not directly but by means of a fable. The Jewish kabbalist agrees and elaborates on the didactic effect of the fable. The fable told by the good knight is protagonized by animals, as the genre requires, and expresses the central ethical question about the possibility to eliminate evil. This is how the story goes:

> What if the lion, as the king of the animals, thinks that the establishment of an equilibrium and justice under his reign, goodness and freedom, could eliminate evil and make the hyena and the panther forget who they are and, by denying their self, turn to the good, and this is how the lamb and the wolf will lay side by side [. . .]. What if the lion thinks that restoring goodness in his kingdom means that goodness will reign, because each and every one of the living creatures will be good accordingly. (*WU*: 59–60)[8]

The Jewish Rabbi answers with questions:

> Did you forget that life is a cycle that follows the rhythm of opposites? Did you forget that God did good on the one side and evil on the reverse side? Did you forget that black and white are inseparable? Did you forget that moral and divine law need their denial as an instrument of affirmation? Don't you understand that life without death would not be life? (*WU*: 60)[9]

The personage Abraham of Talamanca thus explains what the historical Abraham Abulafia sustained: that evil exists because it serves the good, that "to expect God to produce the good without the evil upon which it depends is to demand a logical

---

[7] "La luz del camino es la primera pregunta. Dios mismo tuvo que separar la luz de las tinieblas y también anduvo a tientas hasta desenmarañar la creación. Tuvo que dividir el mundo y se olvidó de borrar la división. Por eso nosotros, cada día, pasamos del bien al mal, cada día volvemos a trazar la línea y cada día nos equivocamos y no sabemos en qué lado estamos. Blanco y negro. El equilibrio es inestable" (*WU*: 57–8).

[8] "Si el león, como rey de los animales, piensa que al establecer equilibrio y justicia bajo su bandera, bondad y libertad, podrá borrar el mal y que la hiena y la pantera olvidarán su proceder y se negarán a sí mismas para caer en el bien, y luego el cordero y el lobo se amarán [. . .]. Si piensa el león que restituir el bien es que gobierne el bien, porque todas y cada una de las criaturas vivas serán buenas en consecuencia" (*WU*: 59–60).

[9] "Olvidaste que la vida es ciclo y ritmo de opuestos? ¿Olvidaste que Dios hizo el bien y en su reverso el mal? ¿Olvidaste que blanco y negro son inseparables? ¿Olvidaste que moral y ley divina necesitan su negación para afirmarse? ¿No comprendes que la vida sin la muerte no sería vida?" (*WU*: 60).

and ontological impossibility" (Horwitz 2016: 240). Without evil, good would be unrecognizable and unattainable. Hence, for Abulafia, it is central to unite, within the self, the opposites (Sagerman 2011: 179), thus reaching a state "in which evil and good are contained together as one, and not one in which evil and good are separated" (Wolfson 2011: 88).

Dynamics between the Narrative and Argumentative Layer

The narrative layer of *The War of the Unicorn*, a story of two troops of rival knights and their fight in a fantastic setting, allegorically evokes the Spanish Civil War. Besides this historical intertext and the literary intertext of medieval chivalry novels, the thought of the Jewish kabbalist Abulafia serves as another, mystical religious, intertext to the narrative layer. Allusions to Abulafia's doctrine, according to which the evil serves the good and good cannot exist without evil, are intertwined in the rival knights' story told in *WU* while giving meaning to this armed conflict.

The opposition of black and white, present in the philosophical dialogue, is often used in the story to represent the interpenetration of good and evil. It runs as a thread through the narration, and is present in the battle between the white knights and the black nights (with their black capes and black souls), in the image of the traitor on his black horse, in the figure of the white dame whose heart belongs to the protagonist-knight, and, finally, in the magical appearance of the completely white unicorn that will turn black if the black knights win the battle.

Still, the most continuous example of the union between good and evil is the intelligent black-and-white dog that is the faithful and inseparable companion of one of the story's main characters. The dog thus becomes ubiquitous. This omnipresent dog is exactly half white and half black (*WU*: 36), he is "blanquinegro," "black and white, depending on the side you are looking at" (*WU*: 42). He is close to both the black traitor and to the snow-white unicorn and embodies Abulafia's agonic union of good and evil.

The story's ending highlights the importance of kabbalist thought in two ways. First, the insight into the inevitable connection between good and evil enables the black traitor to win the battle. The black traitor affirms that not the fighting has been the decisive factor in the battle but his understanding of the intertwined nature of good and evil. He has used this knowledge to his benefit: by stealing the Beaker of the Unicorn, he has brought the black knights to victory. Therefore, he drew on the knowledge that evil is originated in the good (*WU*: 121). His words clearly refer to Abulafia's doctrine according to which evil and good have the same roots and are contained together as one. In this way, the black traitor claims, the division between good and evil comes to an end, all is one and is completely black. The black traitor describes this victory as "total destruction and death," a situation wherein "no return to life is possible," and that is "reigned by complete darkness" (*WU*: 121). Hence, the fantastic narration seems to lead to the final triumph of the black knights.

Simultaneously, the same insight into the intertwined nature of good and evil is valuable for the interpretation of the volume's ending. In line with Abulafia's thoughts, the reader realizes that this cannot be the end, for total darkness cannot exist and will inevitably lead to the good. This insight brings the reader to the true end of the fantastic story: the certainty that the good arises from evil and that there is always good that will fight evil. The reader remembers the words spoken by the Jewish kabbalist in one of the dialogues: "For each poison, a counter-poison exists. For each sickness, its cure. For the black, the white. For evil, the good" (*WU*: 139). The final image in the book evokes the path to harmony that "reintegrates hope in the darkness of suffering" (*WU*: 123) and explains that and how it can be achieved. In this image, the white lady brings the necessary sacrifice. She leaves her knight behind to dedicate herself to the unicorn. The lady and the unicorn form a black-and-white harmony, because, as the reader infers, the unicorn has become black as a consequence of the victory of the black knights. Their black-and-white harmony is reinforced by the black-and-white dog that is already on his way to join them, his black-and-white fur serving as a promise that good will arise from evil.

Conclusions

I started this study by referring to Muñiz-Huberman's evocation of the Spanish Civil War in *The Century of Disenchantment* (*El siglo del desencanto*). In this essay collection written at the turn of the century, Muñiz-Huberman describes the Spanish Civil War and the oppression of the Spanish Republican ideals as "destruction of utopia and hope," "total death," "what could never again return to be," "the irreversible," and "descent into hell". Let us now, after having read *The War of the Unicorn* (1983), take a second look at these words. The reader of *WU* recognizes them. Exactly the same words are pronounced by the black traitor in the last pages of the book when the victory of evil seems to be irreversible and the darkness complete. Still, in the light of Abulafia's thought, the reader of *WU* also knows that the black traitor is mistaken. Therefore, *WU* does not end by giving the black traitor the last word. The book goes beyond evil by giving it a purpose: it is only from evil that the good can arise.

By means of a story on rival knights in a fantastic setting, Muñiz-Huberman tried, in the late 1970s and early 1980s, to "pull out the thorn of war." She drew on kabbalist thinking to give meaning to the pain and destruction of the Spanish Civil War given that "the face that objects and beings show on the surface is but the minimum manifestation of their hidden essence" (Muñiz-Huberman 2013: 26). This corresponds to the mission that she, more than two decades later, would describe, in *The Century of Disenchantment*, as today's poets' ethical task: to "desperately seek harmony in the disorder and violence of the twentieth century" (Muñiz-Huberman 2002: 26). Hence, for Muñiz-Huberman, the literary expression of the Spanish Civil War requires "the deciphering" of this conflict's significance and "deeper meaning" as a necessary step toward harmony.

For this purpose, Muñiz-Huberman combined fiction and Jewish mysticism. The volume's connection between a fantastic story, a fictional biography of a Jewish kabbalist, and a philosophical dialogue concerning kabbalist thought made it possible to find the conflict's deeper meaning. More concretely, it is the interconnection between evil and good in Abulafia's kabbalist thought that enabled the author to make sense of the Spanish Civil War. Indeed, in the introduction of her *Sephardic Anthology* (1989), Huberman emphasizes the importance of ethics in Jewish thought: "Ethics are inseparable from the Jewish people. It is their contribution to the human values, as aesthetics are the contribution on the part of the Greek people" (1989: 19). *The War of the Unicorn* thus brought about a merge between the poet's task in the face of the twentieth century's "disorder and violence," on the one hand, and the inheritance of Jewish ethics, on the other.

Muñiz-Huberman's quest for deeper meaning by combining fiction and mysticism makes a case against the Platonic rejection of fiction as the construction of mere aesthetically enjoyable inventions.[10] In her essay "Castles of Reason and Dreams of Innocence" (2002a: 109–26), included in *The Century of Disenchantment*, Muñiz-Huberman explains how the generically hybrid combination of fiction and philosophy can be understood as a work of unification (Houvenaghel 2020). She puts this combination of fictional and philosophical genres in the light of Iris Murdoch's study on Plato's separation of literature and philosophy (1978, *Why Plato Banished the Artists*). Muñiz-Huberman foregrounds how philosophers, such as María Zambrano, together with novelists, storytellers, poets, and playwrights, have not shied away from combining philosophy and fiction, in spite of Plato's rejection of them. These writers have thus combined the impact of poetic imagery, fictional plot, and dramatic conflict with philosophical thought. Her own work *The War of the Unicorn* belongs to the same category as it recuperates this lost unity by combining mysticism and fiction. Generic hybridity, a key feature of *WU* and of Muñiz-Huberman's oeuvre as a whole (Houvenaghel 2020), is thus inspired by the author's view that the reunification of fiction and knowledge is an important step toward finding and revealing the deeper meaning of historical manifestations of evil.

The study's focus on the thought of the Kabbalah opens a window not only to understand the way the writer makes sense of the Spanish Civil War but also to shed a light on the writer's view of armed conflict and exclusion throughout history. Previous studies have shown that in her collection of essays *The Century of Disenchantment*, Muñiz-Huberman views evil (war, destruction, exclusion, torture, slavery, genocide, dictatorship, repression) as "a repetitive and constantly recurring issue across all historical periods" (Serlet and Houvenaghel 2015: 68). Her concept of the cyclic and never-ending return of war and exile can possibly be better understood in the light of

---

[10] Plato refers to poetry in different dialogues: the *Ion*, the *Republic*, the *Gorgias*, and the *Phaedrus*. He objects to poetry on various grounds: education (*Republic* II), philosophy (*Republic* X), and ethics (*Republic* X). Plato considers poetry not educational because heroes of epic poetry foster vices in young people, not philosophical because it does not provide true knowledge, and not ethical because it promotes undesirable passions above the rational principle.

Abulafia's teaching according to which the good is inextricably entangled with the evil, and the evil is rooted in the good.

For Abulafia, "good and evil forces [...] are continually at war with one another" (Idel 1988) and conflict is a necessary step toward inner harmony. This view corresponds to the kabbalistic view that the dualism of good/evil is present at the origins of all things and that "everything was emanated and created within the framework of divine attempts to rid itself from the dualism and bring about, for the first time, divine perfection and unity" (Dan 2007: 77).

> The creation of Adam was an attempt to overcome dualism: Adam was created as a dual entity, including within him the elements of good and evil. If Adam had obeyed God, good would have triumphed over evil and the cosmic and divine dualism would have been abolished. However, when Adam transgressed, the opposite happened: [. . .] the evil powers were strengthened. God then chose a people, the people of Israel, to carry on the struggle to dispose of evil. They were almost successful when they assembled near Mount Sinai to accept the Torah. Then they transgressed when they worshipped the golden calf, [. . .] and so on, throughout history. (Dan 2007: 77–8)

Accordingly, in Muñiz-Huberman's view of history, the manifestations of evil and the manifestations of good constantly interact and alternate, forming, together, an ever-returning cycle. Hence, Muñiz-Huberman "pulls out the thorn of war" by drawing on the wisdom of the Kabbalah to give the Spanish Civil War a place and a meaning within the cycle of good and evil.

References

Cánovas, R. (2012), "Habitando el Sefarad: los escritos de Angelina Muñiz Huberman," *Taller de letras*, 50: 27–35.
Dan, J. (2007), *Kabbalah. A Very Short Introduction*, Oxford: Oxford University Press.
Gambarte, E. M. (1992), "Angelina Muñiz Huberman: escritora hispanomexicana," *Cuadernos de investigación filológica*, 18 (1–2): 65–83.
Horwitz, D. M. (2016), "The Problem of Evil in Kabbalah," in D.M. Horwitz (ed.), *A Kabbalah and Jewish Mysticism Reader*, 240–54, Nebraska, University of Nebraska Press.
Houvenaghel, E. H. (2015), "Cruzando fronteras: espacio e identidad en el ensayo de Angelina Muñiz," in E. H. Houvenaghel (ed.), *Escribir en Nepantla: la prosa sin fronteras de Angelina Muñiz, hija del exilio republicano. Monográfico. Anales de Literatura Hispanoamericana*, Vol. 44, 87–99.
Houvenaghel, E. H. (2020), "La hibridez genérica en el espejo: Angelina Muñiz-Huberman y María Zambrano," *Cuadernos del Hipogrifo. Revista de Literatura Hispanoamericana y comparada*, 13: 12–24.
Houvenaghel, E. H. (2021a), "Los pueblos sefardí y askenazi. Tierras dejadas atrás en *Tierra adentro* (1977) de Angelina Muñiz Huberman," *Connotas*, 23: 7–20.

Houvenaghel, E. H. (2021b), "Hacia el centro de una refugiada española en Francia: María Casarès y Santa Teresa de Ávila," in A. Amo Sánchez, M. Carrilo and M. Galéra (eds.), *La Retirada. Mémoires culturelles et artistiques de l'exil républicain en France. Carnet de Recherches Hypothèses*, Avignon: Editions Universitaires d'Avignon, (hal-03563135)
Houvenaghel, E. H. and M. Carrillo. (2021), "Presentación: Angelina Muñiz-Huberman: una voz inconformista," in E. H. Houvenaghel and M. Carrillo (eds.), *Angelina Muñiz-Huberman: una voz inconformista, Dossier. INTI Revista de literatura hispánica 1*, 93–4.
Idel, M. (1988), *The Mystical Experience in Abraham Abulafia*, New York: State University of New York Press.
Jofresa Marqués, S. (1999), "Estudio introductorio. La herencia de un exilio," in A. Muñiz-Huberman (ed.), *El canto del peregrino*, 6–56, Sevilla: Biblioteca del Exilio.
McInnes, J. (2001), "Arthurian Material in Angelina Muñiz-Huberman's *La Guerra del unicornio*," *Hispanic Journal*, 22 (1): 217–25.
Muñiz-Huberman, A. (1972), *Morada interior*, México: Joaquín Mortiz.
Muñiz-Huberman, A. (1977), *Tierra adentro*, México: Joaquín Mortiz.
Muñiz-Huberman, A. (1985), *Huerto cerrado, huerto sellado*, Mexico: City Oasis.
Muñiz-Huberman, A. (1988), *Enclosed Garden*, trans. Lois Parkinson Zamora. Pittsburgh: Latin American Literary Review Press.
Muñiz-Huberman, A. (2002), *El siglo del desencanto*, Mexico: Fondo de Cultura Económica.
Muñiz-Huberman, A. (2011), *La guerra del unicornio*, México: Editorial Grupo Destiempos.
Muñiz-Huberman, A. (2013), *Las vueltas a la noria*, México: UNAM/Equilibrista.
Muñiz-Huberman, A. ([1993] 2015), *Las raíces y las ramas. Fuentes y derivaciones de la Cábala hispanohebrea*, México: Fondo de Cultura Económica.
Patán, F. (1984), "Angelina Muñiz: la guerra del unicornio," *Sábado*, 21: IV.
Payne, J. (1997), "Writing and Reconciling Exile: the Novels of Angelina Muñiz Huberman," *Bulletin of Hispanic Studies*, 74 (4): 431–59.
Pérez Aparicio, N. (2014), "La representación de la batalla del Ebro y la lucha entre el bien y el mal: *La guerra del unicornio* de Angelina Muñiz Huberman," in B. Greco (ed.), *Sobrenatural, fantástico y metarreal: la perspectiva de América Latina*, 169–80, Madrid: Biblioteca Nueva.
Sagerman, R. (2011), *The Serpent Kills Or the Serpent Gives Life: The Kabbalist Abraham Abulafia*, Leiden: Brill.
Salazar, S. and J. Rodríguez Plaza. (1993), "Conversaciones con Angelina Muñiz-Huberman," in A. Marquet (ed.), *Tema y variaciones de literatura*, 2, México: Universidad Autónoma de México, Acapotzalco, División de Ciencias Sociales y Humanidades.
Serlet, F. and E.H. Houvenaghel. (2015), "El personaje femenino y la libertad temporal en tres novelas históricas de Angelina Muñiz: Morada interior (1972), El Mercader de Tudela (1995) y La Burladora de Toledo (2008)," *Anales de Literatura Hispanoamericana*, 44: 59–72.
Wolfson, E. R. (2011), "Abraham ben Samuel Abulafia and the prophetic Kabbalah," in E.R. Wolfson (ed.), *Jewish mysticism and Kabbalah*, 68–90, New York: New York University Press.

11

A Jewish-Spanish Outlook on the Civil War

La canción de Ruth by Marifé Santiago Bolaños

Rose Duroux

"Dad—I said—, what is Sepharad?"
"Your mother—he answered me."
(Marifé Santiago Bolaños[1])

To the Brigadists
From a balcony of the condemned Barcelona, I witnessed the farewell to the International Volunteers: tears, kisses and flowers. My mother told me this story again and again and I transmitted it to my sons.[2]

Can Jewish literature be accurately defined? This is a question as nagging as it is thorny. The category of Jewish literature includes writers from different countries writing in different languages and perspectives, each of them doing so in their unique voices. Therefore, Jewish literature is transnational. In this chapter, we will shed light on the philo-Sephardic contemporary fictional narrative in Spain. The question is: can a literary work such as *La canción de Ruth* be categorized as Jewish literature despite the non-Jewish origin of its author, Santiago Bolaños?[3]

---

[1] The translator of all the quotations is the author of these lines.
[2] Rose Duroux's first name was given to one of the characters in the novel presented in the following article because the novelist, Marifé Santiago Bolaños, was inspired by her trajectory as a child of the Spanish Civil War. The author's gratitude goes to Erika Collins, daughter of the Brigadist Emil Edel, a Viennese doctor, and Anny Edel, also a volunteer, for reviewing this chapter.
[3] The question arises as well for many other works, such as *Sefarad* by A. Muñoz Molina or *The Scent of Lemon Leaves* by C. Sánchez (2013). T. N. Beckwith (2020) examines the stereotypes about Jews in a wide range of Spanish historical novels; many of them recount stories set in medieval Jewish quarters during key times in Jewish history (1492, 1942, or 1992).

Sephardism and Spain: Ways and Voices in Question

Gradually from the end of the nineteenth century to the present day, despite various obstacles, a cultural philo-Sephardism has taken shape in Spain (Bendahan 2014). Among the Spanish pioneers are the novelists Benito Pérez Galdós, Carmen de Burgos, and Concha Espina and the intellectual Ángel Pulido. The trend was accentuated at the end of the First World War with the fall of the Central Empires[4] and the arrival in Spain of Mediterranean, German, and Austro-Hungarian Jewish citizens (among them many renowned Jewish families, like Nordau, Aub, Bleiberg, etc.). Some descendants of this migratory wave, such as writers Max Aub or Máximo Josef Kahn, for example, were involved in the Spanish Civil War and followed the long paths of the exile of the Spanish Republicans in Latin America.

In the 1930s, with the rise of Nazism, German and other Central European Jews found a haven in Spain. When the Spanish Civil War broke out in 1936, anti-fascist volunteers came to support the young Republic; in the International Brigades, about one-fifth of them were Jews. Some of these "Interbrigadists" would later nourish their memorialist or fictional work with the memories of this fundamental war, like, for example, César Covo, Hanns-Erich Kaminski, Upton Sinclair, Stephen Spender, Efraïm Wuzek, and the singular "Capitana," Micaela Feldman de Etchebéhère, author of *Ma guerre d'Espagne à moi* (Gabbay 2020).

In spite of Franco's dictatorship, a cultural philo-Sephardism continued to develop. For the fifth centenary of the Expulsion of the Jews, the King of Spain declared that "Sepharad is no longer a Nostalgia but a Home."[5] In 2006, finally, the Sepharad-Israel Center opened its doors in Madrid. It was in this climate that the reference work of this contribution came into existence: *La canción de Ruth* (The Song of Ruth), a novel published in 2010 by Marifé Santiago Bolaños. It is highly significant that the storyteller (a female narrator) bears the emblematic first name of Nostalgia.[6] *La canción de Ruth* echoes the Book of Ruth, but this will be only revealed in the last chapter of the novel.

Clearly, the contours of "Jewish literature" are difficult to draw neatly as they are blurred by history, geography, politics, and even poetics. For her part, the Spanish writer of Sephardic origin, Esther Bendahan (2014: 30), stresses that doubts inevitably arise, such as whether or not to take into account those who, without being Jews, want to include themselves. On the other hand, even if they are Jews and even if they have at one time had a production linked to this identity, they may prefer to exclude themselves for various reasons (both personal and political). In search of an open definition, Bendahan

---

[4] Central Empires, also "Central Powers": a coalition composed of Germany, Austria-Hungary, the Ottoman Empire, and Bulgaria, and opposed to the "Allied Powers."
[5] "Sefarad no es ya una nostalgia sino un hogar"; www.casareal.es/GL/actividades/Paginas/actividades _discursos_detalle.aspx?data=4131 (accessed on November 20, 2020).
[6] Greek etymology: *algos*, "pain," and *nostos*, "homecoming."

adds: "even if it is in various languages other than Hebrew, for works written by *Jews or non-Jews* [emphasis added] on Jewish subjects, one must speak of 'Judaic.'"[7]

Should researchers wishing to tighten the focus on literature related to the Sephardic diaspora target only the works of writers whose "Jewishness is proven"? Isn't it equally relevant to consider the production of Spanish writers of non-Jewish origins whose writing is inhabited by Sepharad (understood as Sephardic Spain)? At first sight, nothing prevents us from thinking that they have their place in an inclusive Jewish library, certainly a *sui generis* place.

The Spanish writer Antonio Muñoz Molina brings grist to my mill with his novel *Sefarad* (2001). It is a work about persecution and exile which intertwines fiction and autobiography, and whose heroes are Primo Levi, Milena Jesenská, Evgenia Ginzburg, and many other Jewish figures. The novel *Sefarad* has received numerous literary prizes, including the Jerusalem Prize, which Jorge Semprún also received. However, Muñoz Molina (2003) affirms loud and clear that it is not necessary to be Jewish to portray the horrors of the Shoah, nor resident of a communist country to denounce totalitarian barbarism: "What kind of nonsense is this! [. . .] The heart of literature is to put yourself in the place of who you are not, to be capable of empathy."[8]

Before going any further, we should go deeper into the notion of philo-Sephardism. This word, although in common use, does not appear in the dictionary of the Royal Spanish Academy (nor in many other dictionaries); it therefore deserves all the more our attention. Let us first recall that philo-Sephardism and philo-Semitism do not go hand in hand. For example, the Spanish writer Ernesto Giménez Caballero, a notorious antisemite, used to flaunt philo-Sephardism. It is true that this term has uncertain contours: it can cover "questions of identity and political issues, collective imaginations and pragmatic considerations" (Rozenberg 2006: 152). It seems that today, in Spain, the literary treatment of the Sephardic theme aims to crystalize the representation of a plural Spain. This is the case of *La canción de Ruth* which relies on the Sephardic to better question the identity of Spain.

Definitely, the deep substratum of the novel is the great amputation that the mass exodus of Jews and Republicans has meant for Spain, centuries later. The fiction indeed combines, in time and space, the paths of two major dispersions, that of the "Sephardim" of Hispania Judaica and that of the "Exiliados" of España Republicana.

Plotline of the Novel

Following a poetic incipit consisting of a nostalgic lullaby with Sephardic accents, the author propels the readers into the Spanish Civil War with the assassination of a "maquis" (clandestine resistant), and his unlikely burial in a village of Extremadura

---

[7] "Yo añadiría que aunque sea en diversas lenguas fuera del hebreo, para las obras escritas por judíos o no judíos sobre temas judíos, debe hablarse de 'Judaica.'"
[8] "Qu'est-ce que c'est que ces sornettes ! [. . .] Le cœur de la littérature, c'est de se mettre à la place de celui qu'on n'est pas, être capable d'empathie."

under Franco's control. The widow and her youngest daughter, Catalina, move to Madrid; the eldest daughter, Basilisa, had been evacuated before to Russia with a colony of Spanish children. What awaits them, in Madrid, is the misery of the defeated, and for the girl, rape. In 1944, young Imre and his parents, Sephardim survivors from Budapest and Istanbul, also arrive in Madrid. The two families, the Republican and the Sephardic, carry a deep wound. The families merge when Imre and Catalina get married; their daughter, Nostalgia, is the narrator of our story. Although its narrative embraces the violence of the twentieth century with its wars, exoduses, and infamies, the novel is not just a simple historical novel. In fact, the essence of *La canción de Ruth* lies in its melody, as it is the Sephardic song and the lament of the Civil War that gives rhythms and unites the exploded trajectories.

Genealogical Tree of Nostalgia's Family

La canción de Ruth encompasses four generations of women who draw an upward social curve: a peasant woman, a linen maid, a schoolteacher, an architect. Usually, the action is told through the eyes of a woman.
Paternal ancestors

Grandpa: Budapest/Tel Aviv
Grandma: Istanbul/Tel Aviv
Father: Imre—Budapest in the 1930s/Madrid

Maternal ancestors and collaterals

Great-grandfather: Extremadura
Great-grandmother: Extremadura
Grandpa: c. 1908 Extremadura/1937 murdered
Grandma: c. 1910 Extremadura/Madrid
Mother: Catalina*—c. 1933 Madrid
Aunt: Basilisa*—c. 1927 Madrid/Moscow
Cousin: Vasilissa—Moscow in the 1960s

*Both sisters have a Jewish husband.

A Litanic Prose

The opening noun of the title of the novel, "Song," naturally invites musical decoding. Indeed, entire segments obey the principle of repetition of the "*modern verse.*" The almost systematic use of the anaphora—i.e., the resumption of the same element at the beginning of several sentences—gives many chapters the appearance of litanies. They are undoubtedly prayers in the face of the horrors of History. Moreover, one of the chapters is called "Orisons": "May fate protect those who have lost their lovers, brothers, and parents in the ignominy of the mass graves [. . .] May we not go mad, may we not go mad" ("Quinto tratado: Oraciones": 116–17). Unifying the whole book is a simple lullaby, a song fictitiously correlated with the biblical Ruth, the gleaner, the healer. It is a melody of 32 free verses ("X": 26–7) through which melancholy floats: "Today you can't sleep, / today you can't sleep." Its stanzas punctuate the story, denoting a need for reidentification in the turning points of life (58, 74). For all these reasons we take the risk of applying to *La canción de Ruth* an oxymoron and defining it as a "novel-poem."

In general, the delicious "nanas" (lullabies) whispered in the child's ear carry the mother's dreams and complaints. But in the novel, contrary to custom, on the one hand, it is the father who sings the lullaby, sowing in the cradle of Nostalgia the Jewish seed. On the other hand, it is not in Judeo-Spanish that Imre lulls his daughter but in modern Spanish because he arrived in Spain as a child. However, when he remembers the horrifying days of raids on Jews in Budapest, Imre finds the tender lullaby that his grandmother sang, embracing him (154): "Durme, durme, amor: / Agora es Sefarad; durme" (Sleep, sleep, my love: / Now it's Sepharad; sleep). The terms "durme" and "agora" belong to the ancient Spanish used by the Sephardim in their wandering. Only this exiled language brings him the "tenderness from other times, which is alive, and therefore full of comfort," just as Juan Gelman suggested elsewhere (2012: 815).[9]

It should be emphasized that "Durme, durme, amor: / Agora es Sefarad" is the only example of the Sephardic lexicon in *La canción de Ruth*. These words from the past cross Imre's mind like a flashback, unchanged, at the time of his separation from his parents who left Madrid for Tel Aviv. In fact, throughout the novel, the Sephardic imprint does not reside in the lexicon but in the way of kneading it, namely, by appealing to what is the *sine qua non* of transmission: musical reiteration. What Santiago Bolaños also communicates through this double use of sung poetry (ancient and modern) is that this constantly reincarnated orality perpetuates roots beyond space and time.

On balance, the whole dough of writing is kneaded with the Jewish leaven. Nevertheless, does this essential fermentation bring the work into "Jewish literature"? The objective here is to provide some elements that would allow us to move forward on this path.

Emblematic Locations of the Massacres: Extremadura 1936/ Budapest 1944

Santiago Bolaños locates the inaugural assassination of her story in a village in Extremadura where historically, the cycle of violence began: the killings in Extremadura (notably the massacre orchestrated by Franco's officer Yagüe, called the "Butcher of Badajoz") set an example and served as a general warning. The massacre

---

[9] "Una ternura de otros tiempos que está viva y, por eso, llena de consuelo."

was such that it is sometimes called—rightly or wrongly—"Holocaust," among others, by Paul Preston (2012). About three-quarters of the "irregular" deaths of the Spanish Civil War occurred between July and December 1936, as a result of the military occupation operations which took place mainly during the first weeks of the conflict. The assassination resides within the time frame that inaugurates and haunts the novel.

Extremadura, characterized by the *latifundia* system, soon fell into the hands of the Francoists. The peasants, who had benefited from the agrarian law passed by the Spanish Republic, often paid for it with their lives: shot against cemetery walls (as in the novel) or thrown into an uncertain grave. Very symbolically, a fatal gunshot marks the action's kick-off point and its obsessive clacking resounds throughout the story.

In parallel, Santiago Bolaños examines the Holocaust through the filter of killings along the Danube. As we know, the history of the Sephardic family begins in Budapest. And here too, the choice of the place is not fortuitous. Hungary, like Franco's Spain, was an ally of Nazi Germany. Following the German occupation in March 1944, the Arrow Cross Party, which came to power in October 1944, massively deported Jews (one in ten victims of the Holocaust was said to be of Hungarian origin). In Budapest, pro-Nazi militias shot thousands of Jews and threw them barefoot into the Danube; a recent memorial, "Shoes on the Danube Bank," recalls this massacre. The history of the murdered Jews "on the banks of the beautiful Danube" (Santiago Bolaños 2010: 117) runs through the novel and is crowned by this prayer: "May the Danube not overflow with pain" (Santiago Bolaños 2010).[10] Research is still underway to try to identify the victims and divers at this time probe river, just as the Spaniards search for their missing ones by probing the ditches.

Metonymic Narrative Choices: The Part for the Whole

The assassination of a peasant from Extremadura is in itself a symbol of the violence unleashed by the military coup of July 18, 1936. Through a bereaved family, Santiago Bolaños exemplifies the drama of Spain and, by extension, of all humanity—"porque quien llora eres tú . . . es todos los seres humanos" (because it is you who weeps . . . it is all humans) (Santiago Bolaños 2010: 37).

The murdered grandfather haunts four generations, whether remembered as son (*hijo*), husband (*marido*), father (*padre*), or grandfather (*abuelo*), but the war is very often seen through the stunned eyes of a child (*niño*). Children's war traumas can be considered an essential reading key (Duroux and Keren 2013). This is personified in the novel by the exodus to France and the evacuation to Russia of two little girls, Rose and Basilisa, intersecting on February 4, 1939, in the snow-covered Pyrenees, in the middle of an "ocean of desperation" (Duroux and Keren 2013: 65).

---

[10] "La historia de los judíos asesinados a la orilla del bello Danubio"; "Que no se desborde el Danubio de dolor."

Figure 11.1 Rose Duroux as a refugee child from the SCW in Orléans (France), and wearing a pullover donated by the Quakers, April 26, 1940. Courtesy of Rose Duroux.

La canción de Ruth illustrates the trajectory of the approximately 3,000 Spanish children evacuated to Russia through the wanderings of the little Basilisa who goes from a Republican colony in Valencia to a Moscow colony. The Soviets made it a point of honor to offer Spanish children a precious commodity: education, and the "Niños de Russia" led a rather privileged life from 1937 to 1940. However, the Second World War shook this advantageous position. Like millions of Soviets trying to escape the bombs and the occupation, they were dragged into a terrible exodus to the east. All hope of quick repatriation had vanished. Basilisa is even sent to a work camp close to the one where Marina Tsvetaeva was detained[11]—the Russian poet with a tragic fate whose repeated invocation sheds a singular light on the novel. In addition to this, the letters sent to the family fell into the dungeons of Franco's censorship (Sierra Blas 2009). Therefore, the evacuation considered by the Spanish government as an aid often resulted in a gap that was impossible to fill, and for Basilisa, it became existential angst.

Archaeology of Trauma: Stories in the Feminine

La canción de Ruth is based on brutal events. One of the most obvious signs of the prevalence of trauma in the novel is the *repression*, in other words, the defense mechanism for maintaining an event out of one's consciousness. The other constitutive

---

[11] Both Basilisa and Marina experience the gulag in Tatarstan (119): *"se llevaron a Basilisa a un campo de concentración cerca de donde Marina Tsvietaieva se había quitado la vida"* ("they took Basilisa to a concentration camp near where Marina Tsvetaeva had taken her life" [suicide in Yelabuga, 1941]). See also Santiago Bolaños (2020).

element is, conversely, the rehashing: the resurfacing of repressed memories, these ghosts who return to haunt the family. The author crosses the traumas of several generations and several branches of the family, a family of "*perdedores*," both peninsular and diasporic *losers*: "Your grandparents from Extremadura, in that Spain of losers; your Hungarian grandparents in that Europe of losers" (Sierra Blas 2009: 145).[12] The traumas are all the more deeply rooted in the psyche as they are unnamed (Sierra Blas 2009: 200): "perhaps, we have not lived, but others have experienced them instead of you and for you. And there they are."[13]

The novel essentially shows a line of women who are caught between personal strategies of flight or resistance. Great-grandmother and grandmother become mute following the assassination of the grandfather by Franco's police. The family sinks into silence: never explain, never complain, never cry. Everything is only "dry pain" (Sierra Blas 2009: 35), swallowed tears. This narrative leitmotiv states and denounces the immobility induced by the survival instinct which pushes the characters to keep their secret unsaid, for fear that verbalization could lead to new trauma. Naturally, in the long run, repressed memories affect identity. As for the mother, Catalina, she will keep silent for decades about the gang rape she was subjected to at fifteen years of age; she is well aware of her pathology and familiar with Freudian theoretical concepts: "I've read a lot about victim syndrome; but, you know, the written words, in my case, have been useless" (Sierra Blas 2009: 101). It was not until the day of her husband's funeral that Catalina confided to her daughter the secret that had undermined her life. In the process of self-exclusion and self-annihilation of victims, Marifé Santiago Bolaños sees a double victory for the aggressors: "Words disappear, destinies are emptied, feelings become sick [. . .] pure evil is unforgettable: it is another one of their triumphs" (2013: 40).[14]

Reverse Peregrinations

Each generation is subject to breaks in normality that divide time into a before and an after. Among the upheavals caused by the Spanish Civil War were the evacuations of children mentioned earlier. For Basilisa and her little sister Catalina, parting was a real amputation:

> I should have told her something about the knot in her throat that almost choked a little girl when these people told her that they were taking her sister away [. . .], because her life ended when they put her in a car and the two sisters said

---

[12] "Tus abuelos de Extremadura, en esa España de perdedores; tus abuelos húngaros en esa Europa de perdedores."
[13] "Quizás, no hemos vivido, pero los han vivido otros por ti y para ti. Y ahí están."
[14] "Se van las palabras, se vacían los destinos, enferman los sentimientos [. . .] el mal puro es inolvidable: es otro de sus triunfos."

goodbye forever. And they forbade her to cry. And she learned this. (Santiago Bolaños 2010: 164)[15]

As a counterpoint, another child, Imre, is forced to flee with his Sephardic parents from his home city of Budapest, which fell to the Nazis and whose beautiful Danube now carries corpses. They reach Madrid, thanks to Ángel Sanz Briz, at the time secretary of the Spanish Legation. This Spanish ambassador recounted how he was able to save Jews in Budapest in 1942: authorized to provide papers for about 200 Jews, he managed to considerably increase this quota (Carcedo 2005). Some of them would cross Spain and embark in Portugal for America. For Imre and his parents, it was Madrid, where they received help from an equally historical figure, the Jewish banker Ignacio Bauer.

Nostalgia (fourth generation, therefore), daughter of Imre, seeks to contextualize the welcome received in Madrid by her family from Budapest. She explains how, by sorting out scattered clues on her own, she was able to reconstruct the conditions in which her family settled (Carcedo 2005: 131–2): "What I know of those first years, of that arrival in Sepharad, I learned on my own, without anyone in my family having made the slightest effort to tell me about it."[16]

Narrative Levels

As can be seen in the last extract, historical and narrative perspectives intersect. The fictional and the factual overlap. This is true everywhere else. The following excerpt confirms it:

> Between 1939 and 1945, some thirty-five thousand European Jews save their lives by crossing Spain. In 1944, my father's family, for example; he is a child who has learned to think in Turkish and Hungarian, but who feels, laughs and cries in the language in which his dreams speak, the language he hears when he arrives in Madrid and everyone speaks as it was spoken in the lap of his grandmothers and in the living room of his abandoned house [the language of caresses]. (Carcedo 2005: 31)[17]

---

[15] "Tendría que haberle dicho algo del nudo en la garganta que casi ahoga a una niña pequeña cuando le dijeron que se llevaban a su hermana [. . .]. Porque la vida se le acabó cuando la metieron en un coche y se despidieron para siempre y le prohibieron que llorara. / Y ella se lo aprendió."

[16] "Lo que sé de aquellos primeros años, de aquella llegada a Sefarad, lo he ido aprendiendo sola, sin que nadie en mi familia haya hecho el mínimo esfuerzo por contármelo."

[17] "Entre 1939 y 1945, unos treinta y cinco mil judíos europeos salvaron su vida cruzando España. En 1944, la familia de mi padre, por ejemplo; él es un niño que ha aprendido el pensamiento en turco y en húngaro, pero que siente, ríe y llora en la lengua en la que hablan sus sueños; la lengua que escucha cuando llega a Madrid y todos hablan como se hablaba en el regazo de las abuelas y en la sala de estar de su casa abandonada [la lengua de las caricias]."

"Imre" becomes "Enrique." There is another Imre underlying this character: Imre Kertész, "the survivor," the Hungarian writer who received the Nobel Prize for Literature in 2002 "for writing that upholds the fragile experience of the individual against the barbaric arbitrariness of history."[18]

All the narrative paths of *La canción de Ruth* have to do with the notion of original belonging. This is why genealogy is put to use with all its generations and lifelines that go from León and its Maragatería to the Golden Horn, from the Danube to the Moskva River. The challenge for the reader of this complex novel is first to decipher the mechanisms of character identification and to clarify the various levels of narrative. Names are seldom revealed from the start; one must discern kinship between the characters, who sometimes say "I," sometimes "he" or "she," in different places or at different times. Little by little the reader distinguishes the different voices thanks to the specificity of places, times, and tones, and also thanks to the continual resurgence of specific nightmares born of traumatic experiences prematurely buried.

Above all the other voices, the voice of the representative of the last generation, the narrator's voice, rises: an orchestrator's voice. Indeed, Nostalgia supplies the narrative framework which includes the narrations of the secondary relaters (sometimes in the typographical form of long parentheses, e.g., pages 39–42). In the end, the pieces of the puzzle fit together and the relationship between the factual and the fictional becomes clearer.

Know Where We Come From

It is clear that, in *La canción de Ruth*, memory retrieval happens through women. Nostalgia, in constant search of knowledge, looks back to try to discover the history of previous generations and what has remained unsaid concerning the past. She engages in this process with the aim of capturing a "historical continuity." She feels that it is by knowing her mother's past, which is locked in the silencing of a taboo trauma, that she will be able to free herself and reposition herself in the present to build her future: "And I grew up accepting that the family is a dark shadow full of questions that no one answers, before whose silhouette you must always rise up so that it does not crush you" (Santiago Bolaños 2010: 13).[19] Those secrets instill in her the feeling of groping along blind paths ("caminos cegados").

From the opening of the novel, there is the Spanish Civil War and the *ignominy* in the primary sense of the word (*unnamed*) signified by the absence of funeral rituals for the defeated whose names will not be inscribed in the public space or in the historical memory of the community. The great-grandmother of Extremadura had to beg on her knees to have a burial for her son, this son whose eyes she couldn't close. Clearly, in this

---

[18] www.nobelprize.org/prizes/literature/2002/ (accessed November 26, 2020).
[19] "Y yo crecí aceptando que la familia es una sombra oscura llena de preguntas que nadie responde, ante cuya silueta hay que erguirse siempre para que no te aplaste."

sequence, the author condemns the scandal of the innumerable and unspeakable "mass graves" of Franco's regime, which in the twenty-first century still await the exhumation of the thousands of graveless victims. It should be noted that at the time she wrote *La canción de Ruth*, Marifé Santiago Bolaños was head of the Education and Culture Department under President Rodríguez Zapatero, whose government was very active on issues of historic memory. This is shown in the 52/2007 law, popularly known as the Law of Historical Memory, in favor of those who suffered persecution during the Civil War and the dictatorship.[20]

As for the grandmother and mother, ostracized in a village under the rule of the victors, they eventually flee to the capital, breaking the peasant memory chain. This happened in 1944, the same year that Imre and his parents arrived in Madrid fleeing from the Nazis. Once again, the fiction ties destinies into a symbolic space-time.

Interpretation of Motifs

Building on mere traces of the past, the Spanish narrator, Nostalgia, tries to fill in the silences. In order to organize the resurgence of memory, she looks for all sorts of revealing objects. The first objects are the photos, those very tangible snapshots of the past, which her cousin Vasilissa showed her during her trip to Moscow. Significantly, their grandmother is referred to as "grandmother sepia" in the story. In addition, despite everything else, there are small legacies whose passing from hand to hand establishes a continuity of memory and by the same token, an identity. In particular, a scarf paradigm crosses the novel: scarves ("*pañuelos*") of farewells and returns, tied around the neck, offered, inherited, exchanged. These scarves connect generations and siblings and metaphorize a non-disappearance, a survival. For example, the colorful scarf of Istanbul's grandmother revives the connection with Sepharad.

Other tangible motifs, often minuscule, allow us to grasp the path of a thought, a lineage, a hope: the Turkish sweetness ("un dulzor"), the white pebble charged since antiquity with thoughts of hope, like the white stone that the Turkish grandmother deposits at the first frontier, or the menorah she takes with her. The gifts brought back from Israel by Imre, father of Nostalgia, are part of this symbolism: "I brought you this old *Zohar* that belonged to my father. He gives Mother a beautiful handkerchief with some embroidered peacocks:—It was my mother's; the only thing she kept from her adolescence in Turkey" (Santiago Bolaños 2010: 135).[21]

Finally, cemeteries are also an Ariadne's thread in the maze of *La canción de Ruth*: the executions wall of the village of Extremadura where the grandfather was murdered and the Novodevichy cemetery in Moscow where aunt Basilisa is buried. Nostalgia, an architect by trade, after having declared throughout the narrative that she wanted

---

[20] www.boe.es/eli/es/l/2007/12/26/52/con (accessed December 6, 2020).
[21] "Te he traído este viejo *Zohar* que era de mi padre. A mamá le regala un precioso pañuelo con unos pavos reales bordados:—Era de mi madre; lo único que conservaba de su adolescencia en Turquía."

to build "houses where people would be happy," agrees to construct "a star-shaped cemetery" (Santiago Bolaños 2010: 49) in the city of León, where she went with the *Zohar* or *Book of Splendour*.

As we know, the "star" is polysemic. It is very present in the interpolated tales of *La canción de Ruth* where it illuminates children's foreheads as a promise of the future. Following the example of Georges Didi Huberman (2009: 133), let us call "fireflies" the small resurgences of hope that slowly seem to distill resilient thinking.

The readers' complicity is essential to interpreting the myriad of symbols offered across the novel. It is up to them to detect and explore the numerous mythical and biblical homologies and correspondences in the novel thereby unveiling the hermeneutic keys. Each sign of recognition, by the value it carries and by its ritualistic function, participates in the intergenerational chain and transmission of memory.

A Book about Books: An Intertextual Strategy

The dialogue with the reader is often driven by biblical and esoteric intertextuality. In particular, the first chapters of Genesis; the poetic books of the Old Testament, such as the Song of Songs, but above all the Book of Ruth. Moreover, some episodes of the Gospels from the New Testament are recalled. But the most cited is an exegesis of the Bible: the *Zohar*. The narrator even possesses two copies of the *Zohar*: the abridged version offered by her lover, the other one bequeathed by her father, Imre, who received it from his father. It accompanies the great turning points of destiny. It is present at the farewells of the lovers at the airport: "Why are you giving me this book now, here?—Because we may never see each other again" (Santiago Bolaños 2010: 43).[22]

It should be pointed out that reading is presented as a gendered activity since all the men in the saga know how to and love reading, even the peasant great-grandfather of Extremadura, and yet his wife is illiterate. That is why the figure of the man, even if it is not in the foreground, remains significant. It is he who passes on the book; it is he who transmits the *Zohar*. The book correlates with the city of León where its compiler lived in the thirteenth century, Moses de León, to the point that the author does not refer to the city by name but by a systematic periphrasis: "the city of the author of the *Zohar*" (44).

This emblematic city ends up constituting a magnetic pole; it is indeed in León, land of the distant Sephardic ancestors of Imre, where Nostalgia's parents spend their honeymoon. This union symbolically seals a true homecoming: "Some of those names of towns and cities were stabbed in the soul; others came from the land of sweetness" (Santiago Bolaños 2010: 160).[23] Moreover, it is in León that Nostalgia builds a cemetery in the shape of a star.

---

[22] "¿Por qué me regalas este libro ahora, aquí? - Porque, quizás, no volvamos a vernos nunca."
[23] "Algunos de aquellos nombres de pueblos y ciudades eran puñaladas en el alma; otros, llegaban de la patria de la dulzura."

La canción de Ruth appears to dialogue with the *Zohar*, sometimes by allusion, sometimes by strict intertextuality, to clarify the narrative quest for revelation—"the light among the *darkness*" (emphasis added) (Santiago Bolaños 2010: 56).[24] The headings of the various chapters (called "treatises") indicate the path to knowledge of the origins, from the mysteries revealed to the final reparation: "Libro de los arcanos," "Secretum secretorum," "Discurso sobre los misterios del alma," etc. The thirteenth and last treatise is entitled "Comentarios al cantar de los cantares." Nevertheless, in the family under observation, the reparation remains pending.

If the *Zohar* offers points of reference, the real seminal writing is the Book of Ruth. However, the author only makes this explicit in the last chapter where she summarizes the fates of all the women in the saga. This time, the characters are seen through the prism of the Book of Ruth; the novelist invokes the story of the famous Ruth (great-great-grandmother of King David), born in the village of Moab. The figure of Ruth is that of a convert who adhered to the values of Judaism after the death of her first husband. Having become a widow, Ruth leaves Moab for good to accompany her desperate mother-in-law, Naomi, to Bethlehem. To survive on the way, she is forced to glean ears of corn after the harvest. Marifé Santiago Bolaños weaves together Ruth's path with that of the women of *La canción de Ruth*, who are so poor that they too glean in the fields. It was therefore under the same sign of desolation that little Catalina, an orphan, left the hostile land of Extremadura forever with her mother: "Daughter of a defeated man, whose mother and father were worth less than nothing, she left her village with a sad widow, whom no one invited to the table" (Santiago Bolaños 2010: 235).[25]

In a work whose hypotext is partly the Book of Ruth—Ruth the converted—it is appropriate to question the spiritual evolution of the protagonists. It appears that, apart from Catalina, who has remained frozen in her trauma, all the characters evolve. By filiation or affiliation, each somehow bears a Jewish mark. Does that lead to an ambiguity of identity? Let us examine two cases: that of Imre's parents and that of their granddaughter Nostalgia.

In Budapest, the parents adhered to the values of Judaism but without religiosity; it is in their exile in Madrid that their practice was reinforced. After their son's engagement to marry, they left for Israel without waiting for the wedding, "that way they would not have to attend an alien rite and their son would choose a future without impositions of tradition" (Santiago Bolaños 2010: 154).[26] Later, in Tel Aviv, an incurable disease having struck one of them, they commit suicide together; on their shroud, the wife embroidered a love chant from the Song of Songs.

Nostalgia, the narrator, is more difficult to characterize. Her education is secular and extensive: literature, science, art. She studies architecture just at the time of

---

[24] The full sentence says: "Cuando el ser Sacrosanto que creó el Universo quiso revelar su aspecto oculto, la luz entre las tinieblas."
[25] "Hija de hombre vencido, cuya madre y cuyo padre valían menos que nada, dejó su pueblo de la mano de una viuda triste, a la que nadie invitaba a su mesa."
[26] "Así no tendrían que asistir a un rito ajeno y su hijo elegía futuro sin imposiciones de la tradición."

student revolts and lives her love freely. Yet we know her quest for identity in a family where all effusion is cut short. Conversion signals emerge when the woman who dreamed of building the house of happiness finally designs a star-shaped cemetery, symbolically, in León where she goes with the *Zohar* in hand. Even if the author does not give the key to this evolution, it is obviously a sign of conversion to Judaism in the nascent state. Anyway, Nostalgia cannot be reduced to a single identity.

Intersecting Prisms

In the final analysis, for the novel's characters, the main issue is not only to locate their Sephardic motherland but also to be acknowledged as part of it. This mutual recognition is largely underway in twenty-first-century Spain both concretely and symbolically. For example, through a commemorative plaque, a poem, or a television series like "A Spaniard against the Holocaust" (2011) that recounts the trajectory of the aforementioned diplomat Ángel Sanz Briz, baptized the "Angel of Budapest" (Carcedo 2005).

One of the peculiarities of *La canción de Ruth* is that these "Sephardic returns," material or immaterial, intersect with other returns, in particular, the return of the "Children of Russia." Repatriation from the Soviet Union did indeed take place from the end of the 1950s and onward. Nevertheless, these returns, in a Francoist Spain, were generally accompanied by terrible emotional disappointments, due to social or even family rejection and professional downgrading. Angelina Muñiz-Huberman's novel, *Dulcinea encantada* (1992), exemplifies a case of final non-recognition leading to madness. That is why in Santiago Bolaños' novel, Basilisa, the narrator's aunt, after a frustrating trip to Madrid, returns to the Soviet Union for good like many "Children of Russia."

In this journey to the painful places of the twentieth century as represented in *La canción de Ruth*, fiction is the place from which the author questions the deadly pestilences that are civil wars, the deadly persecution of the Jews, social exclusion, and violence against women. But the most germinating humus of her writing is a double exile: the exodus of the Sephardim and that of the Republicans driven out of Spain by the same hateful obscurantism. In order to translate such a crushing of communities and destinies, the author chooses a fragmentary style of writing. In spite of all the chaotic times and places, Santiago Bolaños multiplies the spatiotemporal crossroads and junctions: significantly, she makes the family of Extremadura and that of Budapest converge and merge in Madrid during the Second World War. The characters of this *wandering Hispania*, which "for nearly five centuries have carried the Spanish wind in their eyes" (1992: 22),[27] always seem to be waiting to anchor in the real motherland, the *Matria*—land of "matriarchs" as Shlomo Avayou calls them, to whom we owe one of

---

[27] "Desde hace cerca de cinco siglos lleva el viento español en los ojos."

the most beautiful declarations of love to Sepharad: "Yes, she was mine and I was hers / and I don't think / I'll ever stop loving her."[28]

It is no less true that this extraordinary survival of hope makes the failure of the return all the more striking. In the novel, the unsuccessful return to the *Matria* of Basilisa symbolizes more broadly the non-return of a double diaspora, the Sephardic and the Republican, and denounces two stains on the historic fabric of Spain. There is no doubt that the long novel-poem that is *La canción de Ruth*, where some characters look from within Sepharad, others toward Sepharad, but where everything revolves around a narrator symbolically named Nostalgia, is a manifesto against amnesia.

Allow me in these final lines or finally to come back to my initial postulate that "non-Jewish" Spanish writers whose work is inhabited by Sepharad are perfectly positioned in the library of "Jewish literature." The Sephardic fervor conveyed by the Judeo-Spanish language, whispered in the ear from the cradle and passed down from generation to generation despite a five-century-long disconnection from the Iberian Peninsula, is still cited. Is it not equally extraordinary that, despite so many centuries of ostracism and lack of communication, songs like Ruth's still continue today to spring from the depths of Spain?

References

Avayou, S. (2016), *A Quién le tocó el fuego*, Self-translated form Hebrew, (ed.), Joan Margarit, Málaga: Los libros de la frontera.
Beckwith, S. N. (2020), "With Sepharad as a Void: Recent Reckoning with the Holocaust in Spanish Fiction," in S. Brenneis and G. Herrmann (eds). *Spain, the Second World War, and the Holocaust: History and Representation*, 536–51, Toronto: University of Toronto Press.
Bendahan, E. (2014), "El mundo literario judío como paradigma del exilio ¿literatura judía?," *El Judaísmo: Contribuciones y presencia en el mundo Contemporáneo, in Cuadernos de la Escuela Diplomática*, 51: 29–45.
Bendahan, E, ed. (2019), *Ahora Sefarad. Siete poetas en torno a la reflexión de la actualidad*, Madrid: Ars Poetica.
Carcedo, D. (2005), *Un español frente al Holocausto. Así salvó Ángel Sanz Briz a 5.000 judíos*, Madrid: Temas de Hoy.
Didi-Huberman, G. (2009), *Survivances des Lucioles*, Paris: Éditions de Minuit.
Duroux, R. and C. Keren (2013), "Retours sur dessins. Fred/Alfred Brauner 1938, 1946, 1976, 1991," in R. Duroux and C. Milkovitch-Rioux (eds.), *Enfances en guerre. Témoignages d'enfants sur la guerre*, 99–119, Geneva: Georg.
Gabbay, C. (2020), "Babilonia y Revolución en España: prácticas de escritura cosmopolita de una miliciana: Mika Feldman Etchebehere," in J. Kölbl, I. Orlova and M. Wolf (eds.), *¿Pasarán? Interacting in the Spanish Civil War*, 82–99, Vienna: NAP.
Gelman, J. (2012), *Dibaxu. Poesía reunida*, Barcelona: Seix Barral.

---

[28] Shlomo Avayou (Izmir, 1939). "Sí, fue mía y yo fui suyo, y no creo / que nunca deje ya de quererla," poem "Con Sefarad adentro," *A quién le tocó el fuego* (2016) quoted from Bendahan (2019: 28).

Muñiz-Huberman, A. (1992), *Dulcinea encantada*, México: Joaquín Mortiz.
Muñoz Molina, A. (2001), *Sefarad*, Madrid: Alfaguara.
Muñoz Molina, A. (2003), "Sépharade," Interview, Le Monde, 27 February.
Preston, P. (2012), *The Spanish Holocaust: Inquisition and Extermination in Twentieth-Century Spain*, London: Harper Press.
Rozenberg, D. (2006), "L'Espagne et le lien séfarade. Résurgences, Affirmations Identitaires, Retours," *Diasporas. Histoire et Sociétés*, 8: 137–52.
Sánchez, C. (2013), *The Scent of Lemon Leaves*, trans. J. Wark. London: Alma Books.
Santiago Bolaños, M. (2010), *La Canción de Ruth*, Madrid: Bartleby.
Santiago Bolaños, M. (2013), *Nos mira la piedad desde las alambradas*, Zaragoza: Olifante.
Santiago Bolaños, M. (2020), *Espejos de la nada. Marina Tsvietáieva y María Zambrano*, Madrid: Báltica.
Sierra Blas, V. (2009), *Palabras huérfanas, los niños y la Guerra Civil*, Madrid: Taurus.

Conclusion

Poetic Justice for the Lost Spain: Deciphering Jewish Keys in Modern and Contemporary Imaginaries

Cynthia Gabbay

There is no such thing as the so-called "Judeo-Christian" civilization. This confusion—expressed by a striking oxymoron—started when the Hellenized-Romanized cultures gobbled the Jewish written legacy, the Torah, without acknowledging the complementarity of its pair, the Oral Law (*HaTorah She BeAlpeh*)—an inapprehensible cultural phenomenon, founding of the cultural Jewish way of life. By discarding Jewish unwritten wisdom, the (under construction) Christian world ignored the knowledge required to carry out the hermeneutical process of reading, discussing, and incarnating the Text. This founding cultural appropriation of the Jewish legacy, mediated by a collage of plurilingual fragmented translations—which eventually became the "Old Testament" and was soon "replaced" by a "newer" and "updated" one—was at the origin of producing the Western colonizing culture, allegedly legitimized by an ancient de-seeded *savoir*. Christianity (the West) represented, and still does, a colonizing force over the Jewish people, which historically survived subjugated under the power of other cultures, and has been always forced to negotiate its own endurance.[1] This negotiation has given birth to a broad-spectrum Jewish cultural variability—from decolonizing cultural phenomena to political nationalism.

In modern times, the Haskalah revolution by the last three decades of the eighteenth century in Germany and Yiddishland—often misinterpreted as "the Jewish Enlightenment" (Litvak 2012)—has been identified as the first in Western history to have produced a corpus of Jewish secular thought and literature. However, this perspective might be erring on the side of Eurocentrism; instead, I propose to recognize the first modern *révolte* against Imperial Catholic persecutors, one that brought out a Jewish (secular)[2]

---

[1] Victor J. Seidler examines the attitude of the Western culture toward Jewish culture: "Christianity has refused to accept the fact that Christianity and Judaism exist as discrete and distinct traditions. There is a Christian attempt to perpetuate the myth that they exist as distinct civilisations that have been joined together through painful histories of power, humiliation and terror [. . .]. Too often, there has been a desire for Christianity to appropriate Judaism, for at some level it still exists *as* a way of justifying the Christian story" (2007: 4–5). For the problematics related to the mistaking notion of "Judeo-Christianism" see Seidler's introduction (2007: 1–27) and chapter 6 (2007: 66–72).

[2] I recognize here the problematics of referring to a *secular* Jewish literature, especially when talking of Sephardic literature, which simply should not be examined with the same hermeneutical

literature and thought, in a southern phenomenon initiated toward the Golden Age (a few decades before the sixteenth and seventeenth centuries) in Spain, Portugal, and Italy. This Jewish *dissidence*—that translated in *dissonance* in aesthetic terms—which spread to the Netherlands and the Eurocentrically called "New World," to Turkey, and the Middle East, was provoked by the 1492 (Spanish) and 1497 (Portuguese) Edicts of Expulsion; its *révolte* was strongly disseminated through generations by voices of *conversos, marranos* (also called *Crypto-Jews*), kabbalists, and heterodox thinkers, for which we can identify its more paradigmatic figure in Baruch Spinoza (1632–77) (Kaplan 2000).[3] This dissident literature—which in the research of the literature of the Spanish Golden Age is identified in the framework of "the *converso* situation" (la situación conversa) (Gilman 1972; Fine 2013: 499–526)—should be interpreted as a subaltern phenomenon which grew under political and cultural violence, and developed a knowledge of encrypting its own identity[4] in order to survive expulsion, persecution, and the tragedy of exile.

Key 1: Negotiating Survival

I consider that modern Jewish (secular) poetics broadly adopted this chameleonic knowledge when seeking to enter the Western literary and philosophical conversation. Therefore, the penetration of Christian ideas and practices in Jewish life answered

---

"secular" (Christianized) tools. Judaism cannot be deprived of its (complex) representation of the relationship between the Jewish people and G-d. *Secularism* is not about *agnosticism* but about the fact of dismissing the significance of an accompanying and illuminating distinguished interlocutor to discuss with. I argue that even when Jewish literature does not make references to "religious" or "liturgical" elements, the imprint of the relation with an authorial/authority voice, remains in the background and permeates the modern text.

[3] In my study of Antonio León Pinelo's work, *El paraíso en el nuevo mundo* (1656), whose author was of *converso* origin, I argue that his *epistemic disobedience* represented a fundamental encrypted retort to Christian theology and the West's epistemic perspective, especially regarding the Christian world's understanding toward other continents and cultures (Gabbay 2022c). *Epistemic disobedience* is, following Walter Mignolo, a "decolonial grammar" able to question and deconstruct the established cultural and systemic knowledge and, therefore, offers a "rewriting of History" (2010: 95).

[4] Dan Miron explains the complexity of a definition of a single Jewish identity: "Those who maintain that the term 'Jewish culture' should be replaced by the plural Jewish cultures seem to be closer to the historical truth. Also the 'Jewishness' of these cultures cannot be defined by extrinsic and fixed criteria, for they are Jewish because Jewish communities, as well as individuals at different times and places defined them as such. Non-Jewish host-societies contributed their share to the fluctuating process of Jewish self-definition by superimposing upon Jews their own projections of them as 'the other,' and they, as we know, did not differentiate between Jews who abided by the strictures of the rabbinical halakha and Jews who turned their back on them. Whereas Judaism (the very term is problematic and actually forced upon Jews from the outside—by Hellenistic defenders of paganism in ancient times and Protestant-German essentialist culture taxonomists in modern times) had probably never formed a single coherent cultural entity; its staple characteristic in modern times (since the second half of the eighteenth century) has been centrifugal splintering. True, this outward movement was from time to time slowed down and to some extent, even reversed—by events such as the emergence of modern (romantic), racial rather than religious anti-Semitism and its ever growing influence throughout the second half of the nineteenth century and the entire twentieth century; the advent of Jewish nationalism in the last decades of the nineteenth century" (2010: 403).

the need of negotiating survival.⁵ Modern as well as contemporary Jewish literatures are written then within frames of sociocultural coercion, negation, antisemitism, and (neo)liberalism—hence, a variety of forms of homogenization.

The massive participation of Jews in the Spanish Civil War, which anticipated the resistance against the Nazis (1938–45), both in the battle and in writing, must be interpreted in the continuity of that historical framework. At the same time, it is expected to find a similar cultural response engaging in *epistemic disobedience* toward the Christian pillars that allowed the growth of authoritarianism, fascism, and hatred racism in the twentieth century.⁶ From a cultural perspective, despite having been permeable to History, Judaism overcame colonization through the ages and therefore its culture is still distinguishable within the West. In effect, Judaic cultural manifestations are identifiable, even when they transit otherness, adopting chameleonic tactics of survival, embracing non-Jewish languages, and sharing knowledge with other nations.

Key 2: The Entanglement of Jewish Modes

As Anita Norich says, studying Jewish cultural phenomena represents "an interdisciplinary, multilingual, transhistorical field" (2008: 1); without this basic understanding, Jewish phenomena cannot be kenned. This volume has developed a variability of tools in order to decode *the entanglement of Jewish modes* in the literature of the Spanish Civil War, allowing us to identify *a proper Jewish literature related to the experience in Spain*. Given

---

[5] The extremely aggressive, radical, and demonizing writ of *herem* of the Jewish community of Amsterdam issued against Baruch Spinoza in 1656 (Nadler 2001: 1–15)—a practice that is in general temporal and therefore is not comparable to Christian excommunication—is, as I see it, a clear example of the way the Jewish discourse against dissidence was shaped under the pressure of political and cultural antisemitic violence resulting in tight "boundaries of identity" (Kaplan 2000: 108–42). In this particular case, the Talmud Torah Amsterdam congregation, composed by former Portuguese *conversos* and *Crypto-Jews*, needed to reestablish a visible Orthodox Jewish identity, compatible with a conditioned "co-habitation" within the Protestant society. In the fear of risking its survival in the Dutch territory, the *herem* adopted the ethos of Christian excommunication for the sake of a tightly homogenized identity—a characteristic foreign to a Talmudic culture. In recent years, but still unsuccessfully, factions within the Jewish community of Amsterdam have promoted the annulation of the *herem* against Baruch Spinoza. I interpret this move as an attempt to re-Judaize the history of the community—meaning, accepting epistemic disobedience as part of its own culture—as well as the figure of Spinoza. However, there still exist tendencies inside the same community that had recently come to declare war against the research on Spinoza's writing—see the Rabbi Yosef B. Serfaty's letter to Yitzhak Melamed declaring him *persona non grata* in November 2021. Nevertheless, after the international scandal this letter caused, the Ma'amad of the Spanish-Portuguese Jewish community of Amsterdam denied the effectiveness of its own Rabbi's declaration against the researcher Yitzhak Melamed and soon emitted a letter expressing its intention of dismissing the Rabbi. (See the details here: www.jta.org/2021/12/03/global/the-spinoza-scholar-who-was-banned-from-amsterdam-synagogue-is-now-invited-to-visit-it).

[6] In my study of contemporary Judeo-Spanish poetry in Latin America, I argue that the systemic implosion of the West that lead to the Shoah should be understood as a peak of the ecocide characteristic of the Anthropocene, which in the context of the human extermination also induced to the extinction of Jewish languages and knowledge (Gabbay 2022d). This extinction therefore implies *epistemicide*; hence, *epistemic disobedience* is expected in order to prevent the end of a culture.

the conditions of extreme variability, and as I pointed out in the introduction of this volume, the definition of "Jewish literature"—one that includes genres such as fiction, poetry, modern thought, memory, drama, epistle, and even translation—has produced a variety of debates; however, it would be impossible and unnecessary to reproduce them here. Dan Miron's understanding of Jewish literature as a *galaxy*—inhabited by a diversity of languages, forms, and registers—represents a suitable model to examine the dimensions of the Jewish imaginaries produced during and after the Spanish Civil War:

> There is no one single dominant Jewish literature; there is not even a "choir" of various Jewish literatures, because the basic harmony that sustains a polyphony is simply not there. There is rather a "complex," a wide, not always clearly defined, Jewish literary space, in which all sorts of literary phenomena, contiguous and non-contiguous, move, meet, separate, and put more and more distance among themselves. (2010: 414)

Also, because we understand the definition of "text" as a broad category (de Angelis 2020) that recognizes the semantic, the semiotic, and the materiality of the text as collaborative generators of *textualities* that become such through writing, reading, and interpreting, our volume studies texts in at least five linguistic codes: Spanish (Latin American and Peninsular), (Mideastern) Yiddish, (Canadian and American) English, German, and music. We have, however, identified other textualities in French, Hebrew, Russian, and Hungarian and we are aware that the texts offering Jewish imaginaries of the Spanish Civil War can be encountered in further languages, in philosophical modes, as well as in other aesthetic mediations such as photography, cinema, and the plastic arts.

Key 3: Poetic Justice

In this context, the volume explored the works of authors from Spain,[7] Canada, Argentina, Mexico, the USA, Germany, Morocco, Poland, and Ukraine, most of them exiles fleeing either the persecution of Jews in Europe or the Republican defeat in fascist Spain. One of them, Ruth Rewald, shared the tragic destiny of six million other Jews during the Second World War and knew no geography of escape (*geografía de fuga*) (Gabbay 2022a).[8] While authors like Ruth Rewald and Gerda Taro didn't survive, and the anti-fascist struggle in Europe was defeated by fascism and Nazism, their

---

[7] Besides the cases of exiles such as Max Aub and León Azerrat see the cases of the sisters Margarita Nelken and Magda Donato, both exiled in Mexico and closely related to Lan Adomián, as well as that of Irene Lewy Falcón, personal secretary of Dolores Ibárruri, "Pasionaria" and exiled in Moscow and Beijing.
[8] I call "geography of escape" (*geografía de fuga*) one of the archetypic mechanisms of the Jewish experience that consists in projecting into the imagination a geographical destiny and territory, different from the point of departure, and pursuing it when the inherited trauma is reignited due to traumatic situations of the present; in the case of Micaela Feldman, for example, this process is inscribed within her internationalist imaginary.

work, added to that of the hundreds of intellectuals and artists who participated and/ or wrote and created in the context of the war in Spain, conformed a cultural archive which endured beyond times like the ark of Noah crossing through the turbulences of History. Indeed, as Amelia M. Glaser pointed out, "the poetics of internationalism outlived the decade [1930s] of internationalism" (2020: 9). By the resilience of their individual paths, our reading of their work eventually implies proclaiming *poetic justice* over the misfortunes of History which led to the *genocide* and *epistemicide* in the heart of the West. *Poetic justice*, one that leads us to think of the Torah commandment "Justice, Justice Thou Shalt Pursue" (צֶדֶק צֶדֶק תִּרְדֹּף),[9] a *mitzvah* that was translated into secular Jewish socialist culture during the conformation of the socialist and anarchist Jewish movements in East and Central Europe, integrated by men and women "hesitating between the Torah and the red (or black) flag" (Biagini 2008: 11).[10] This tradition was internationalized toward the end of the nineteenth century, due to the persecution of the Jews and their consequent exile. The second and third generations of anarchist, socialist, and communist Jews were the ones to arrive in Germany, France, Italy, Spain, Palestine,[11] and the Americas and ally with anti-fascism, sharing within that international movement the common ideas on freedom and transnational solidarity. While the myth of a "Jewish-Bolshevik-Masonic complot against the West" nurtured throughout the twentieth century one of the most powerful antisemitic discourses, in fact, also adopted by Francisco Franco during the Spanish Civil War (Preston 2012), we believe that closely approaching the humanist work endured by the ones persecuted and blamed might help in deconstructing the demonizing antisemitic blood libel.

Amelia M. Glaser recalls that "volunteers from around the world in the Spanish Civil War were described as reciting the *Kol Nidre* prayer in the trenches" (2020: 2). If prayer is a form of poetry, Jewish and gentile poetry's presence in the trenches—a situation recalled also by the Argentine Fanny Edelman in her memories (1996: 66)—denotes the centrality of the relation between "the Letter and the Law" working together for justice, a concept that in Spanish, since the Middle Ages, is well known as "las Armas y las Letras,"[12] a semiotic marriage seeking *poetic justice*, especially in times of memory and postmemory. An unpublished interview with the Judeo-German-Australian poet Ludwig Detsinyi, known after the war as David Martin,[13] that was transmitted from

---

[9] The complete sentence in Deuteronomy 16:20 says: "Justice, justice shall you pursue, that you may thrive and inherit the land the Lord your G-d is giving you;"

צֶדֶק צֶדֶק תִּרְדֹּף לְמַעַן תִּחְיֶה וְיָרַשְׁתָּ אֶת־הָאָרֶץ אֲשֶׁר־יי אֱלֹקֶיךָ נֹתֵן לָךְ:

[10] A transhistorical similarity can be identified between the twentieth-century Jews fighting Catholic fascism in Spain—*hesitating between the Torah and the red (or black) flag*—and the Jewish pirates based in the Caribbean archipelago sabotaging the Spanish Imperial float, a few generations after their expulsion from Sepharad (Kritzler 2008).

[11] For the cases related to Palestine see the authors Hanan Ayalti (Russia-Palestine-France-Uruguay-USA), David Detsinyi (note 13), and in postmemory fiction, the Israeli author Ephraim Rachman (note 37).

[12] See Don Quijote's famous discourse on this topic in Miguel de Cervantes Saavedra, *El ingenioso hidalgo Don Quijote de la Mancha* (1605: I, 38).

[13] Detsinyi (1915–97) maintained intensive correspondence with the German researcher and editor Dirk Krüger and told the story of his participation in the SCW. Detsinyi wrote to Krüger: "'In Palestine I had received first aid training. And besides, I was a good linguist. I spoke fluent German,

Dirk Krüger—editor of Rewald's novel—to me, thanks to the generosity of Tabea Linhard, recalls how an anecdotal invention of the famous song "Am Rio Jarama— Februar 1937" (In the Jarama Front—February 1937) immediately became a poetic and musical "hit" of the SCW.[14] As Abe Osheroff, veteran of the Abraham Lincoln Brigade, says: "Poetry was everywhere. It became part of the climate in which the war was fought" ([1990] 2007: 11).

Regarding Rewald's text, *Vier Spanische Jungen*, Linhard mentions (this volume, ch. 9) the "obsolete" end of the story that imagined a Republican victory. Not only the Republic was defeated but also Ruth Rewald and her baby girl Anja were murdered by the Nazis. In contrast, Rewald's manuscript had a biography of its own. It completed a journey from France to the Moscow archives; ironically saved (when confiscated) from the Gestapo, it ended up in Germany, Rewald's land of origin. In its journey through space and time, the manuscript imagines an alternative history for Spain, from the point of view of a young generation, allowing a new reading of the past. So where injustice has been done, poetic justice shall prevail, re-epistemizing lost fields of knowledge.

Key 4: Tikkun Olam and Mosaic Enthusiasm

It is in that historical context that writers of Jewish origins semiotically inherited *Mosaic enthusiasm* (Gabbay 2020a: 35) which implies acting, playing, and writing against genocide and epistemicide; in the words of Michael Löwy "their thinking took shape around the Jewish (kabbalistic) idea of *Tikkun*, a polysemic term for *redemption* (*Erlösung*), restoration, reparation, reformation and the recovery of lost harmony" (2017: 7).[15] This

---

French and English. Italian to some extent and quickly learned Spanish. This was particularly needed in our multilingual XV brigade [Dimitroff Battalion] and in the medical section of the International Brigades. And I was born in Budapest, so I was actually Hungarian [. . .]. I was not a writer in the real sense of the word. Spain helped me to become one! I'm sure that the hunch and the hope of becoming one, one day [. . .] has something to do with my struggle in the Spanish freedom struggle—it was an addition to my political passion. [. . .] It was during this time that the poet Ludwig Detsinyi, later David Martin, was born. During that time, I wrote poetry as never before. Now and later I nailed poems of mine to trees and telegraph poles for the 'stretcher-bearers and first-aid men' to read. [. . .] I also remember for sure that one day I heard it [. . .] in the program of Radio Moscow [. . .] sung by Ernst Busch. I was stunned! Probably Ernst Busch found it [. . .] in one of the many brigade newspapers that printed it and set it to music [. . .]." In his unpublished text, Krüger adds a commentary on Detsinyi's account: " Detsinyi left Spain at the end of April 1938, arriving in London via Paris to join his parents. There, at the end of a great manifestation of solidarity for the Spanish people, and strengthened by developments in Germany, he realized the impossibility of continuing to write in the German language. Consequently, he switched to English and took up permanent residence in the town of Beechworth, Australia, via various intermediate stations as a journalist for British newspapers [. . .]. Even in his later work, he repeatedly dealt with the events in Spain" (Krüger and Martin, unpublished, 2015, courtesy of Dirk Krüger). Translation from German is mine.

[14] Listen online with music by Ernst Busch: www.youtube.com/watch?v=4yoAHUHafkQ (accessed on October 1, 2021).

[15] While Michael Löwy studied authors from *Mitteleuropa* who wrote at the intersection of German romanticism and Jewish messianism, a comparative assertion should be explored in relation to other Jewries. In my work, I nevertheless consider *Mosaic enthusiasm* in pursuit of Tikkun Olam a common Hebrew (Jewish) drive initiated in the figures of Miriam and Moses but inherited

labor at the intersection with their writing professions drove them to imagine *poetic justice*: the powerful tool which emerges at the crossroads of the Jewish wisdom devoted to "the Letter and the Law."[16] Mauricio Pilatowsky (this volume, ch. 4) shows through Max Aub's intellectual biography how Judaism was translated into modernity, putting the subject in an identity conflict with Jewish tradition and exacerbating his intellectual and humanist being. Therefore, following my own perspective, translating his *Mosaic enthusiasm* into a secular path for Tikkun Olam. In my own interpretation, one of the symptoms of this *modern conversion* results in what Pilatowsky identifies as Jewish intellectuals being "guardians of the text" who, incarnating *Western cosmopolitanism*, access an illusion of "universal citizenship" (Löwy 2017) negotiated within the Jewish diasporic condition; in effect, a variability allowed thanks to chameleonic tactics of survival.

Key 5: Literary Genres and Narratives of Caring

I started my research on the literature of the Spanish Civil War from a Latin American point of view. My first project of scope was devoted to the study of the memory of a heterogeneous group of Argentinian women of Jewish origins who took part in the conflict *in situ* (Gabbay 2020a). It comparatively explored the different literary genres their memory of Spain incarnated—an album of memories co-written by Adelina and Paulina Abramson in 1994, an autofiction by Micaela Feldman (Mika Etchebéhère) in 1976, a neo-picaresque Marxist memoir by Fanny Edelman in 1996, and a dialogical psychoanalytical

---

from the "micro-macro actions" of Na'ama and Noah, not because they ought to follow Adonai's instructions and reimagine a new world, but because they had to re-found a world in the wake of G-d's wrath, *because* of Adonai's destruction: they had to repair G-d's deeds in order to inherit the land and plant a vineyard. In this sense, I would call *Mosaic enthusiasm* a "seventh sense" constantly ignited in the struggle against *tohu va-vohu* (total chaos) and in negotiation with its divine author.

[16] European criticism has prioritized a list of Ashkenazi modern representative writers and thinkers who secularly worked on the inherited crossroads of the letter and the law such as Karl Marx, Rosa Luxemburg, Gustav Landauer, Franz Kafka, Franz Rosenzweig, Emma Goldman, Walter Benjamin, Martin Buber, Theodor Adorno, Hannah Arendt, and Emmanuel Lévinas. These authors produced a corpus that could be read as promoting *poetic justice* against antisemitism in European culture. Michael Löwy analyzes the works of some of these authors in their inner conversation at the intersection of messianism and libertarian (anarchist) utopia: "Uniting the *Tikkun* and social utopia, this configuration reinterprets the messianic tradition in the light of romanticism, and charges romanticism with a revolutionary tension—the result being a new modality of 'philosophy of history,' a new vision of the link between past, present and future. // The relationship between historical messianism and Marxist historical materialism varies in accordance with the authors, from complete incompatibility (Gershom Scholem and Gustav Landauer) to the narrowest of complementarities (Ernst Bloch and Walter Benjamin). [. . .] It cannot be denied that romanticism frequently leads to an idealization of the past, and that its critique of modern rationality often slides towards irrationalism; on the other hand, the confusion between the religious and the political sphere, between messianism and social movement, is not without considerable risks. Historical messianism—the revolutionary/romantic conception of the Central European Jewish intellectuals—does not always escape these dangers. But its great merit is in avoiding—or rather, explicitly rejecting—the two most catastrophic forms of combination between messianism and politics: first, the religious and totalitarian worship of the State; and second, the cult of the Supreme Guide" (Löwy 2017: 196–7).

autobiography by Marie Langer in 1989 (Gabbay 2020a: 42–50); all of them revealed that "the Spanish revolution"—for some of them—and "the fight for a Republican Spain"— for others—represented "the year zero" (Gabbay 2020a: 35; Rein and Thomàs 2018) of their political identities, which in all cases shaped their fiction and nonfiction writing where their Jewish/non-Jewish elaborations were translated in internationalist and cosmopolitan terms. Elsewhere, I compared the cultural contexts and texts written by Mika Feldman Etchebehere (1976) and Marie Langer (1989) and I analyzed how their writing corpora performed polysemic paths of individual journeys and *narratives of caring* moving between the poles of "Jewish belonging" and "internationalist becoming" (2020b). The variability of genres is constant across this open corpus of imaginaries. E. Helena Houvenaghel (this volume, ch. 10) shows in Angelina Muñiz-Huberman's *The War of the Unicorn* how the hybridity of genres is produced through the encounter of Jewish mysticism, the essay, and the novel. In most cases, the mobility between genres is outstanding in each of the mentioned authors. In the work of Marifé Santiago Bolaños (Duroux, ch. 11) the novel is built through poetry and song. In the avant-garde poems of the Inzikh group, experimentation plays with the representation of sound and silence (van der Meer, this volume, ch. 7). The Jewish literature of the SCW is produced through the extended fan of the essay, the song, the novel, the memoir, the poem, the short story, the autofiction, the chronicle, the epistle, or the prologue.

In Feldman's work, I have a special interest in the contraposition of her unresting inner voice and the tendency to *listening*, a particularity that I also identify through the voice of the narrator of the novel *Transit* written by Anna Seghers ([1947] 1987).[17] Following the analysis of Antonio Notario Ruiz (this volume, ch. 2), Jewish culture appears in contraposition to Christian culture through the element of *listening* against visual representation. In effect, Feldman performs the capacity of empathy through *listening*; the focus on dialogue (either with herself or with her *milicianos*) in her autofiction is outstanding. I have identified this capacity—directly related to a certain level of graphomania—also in Adelina and Paulina Abramson's *Mosaico roto*; but there, I allocated this "talent" to a possible Soviet spy training (Gabbay 2020a: 40). In the case of Jacob Glatstein (van der Meer, this volume, ch. 7), *listening* is put in the front of the poem "Stille Spanien" through the insistence on the element of *silence*.

Key 6: The Transhistorical Memory of Sepharad: A Holy War against the Modern Inquisitor?

A second project (Gabbay 2020c), also of comparative perspective, proposed to triangle Yiddish Mexican and American poetry,[18] Jewish poetry in Argentina,

---

[17] While the novel represents the early Second World War, it nevertheless depicts a scenario where the refugees and the recent history of the SCW are constantly present.
[18] My chapter also offers the translation of three Yiddish poems into Spanish, one of them co-translated with Miriam Trinh.

and Spanish poetry, all of them contemporary and related to the SCW. I studied Jewish authors such as Rubén Sinay (1918-90), César Tiempo (1906-80), Bernardo Kordon (1915-2002), Eduardo Samuel Calamaro (1917-2016), Aaron Kurtz (1891-1964), and Jacobo (Yankev) Glantz (1902-82) who wrote from the Americas, using the writing tool both as a means to add to the internationalist effort against the fascist rebellion in Spain and with the aim of interfering in their own local political realities, many of them involving Jewish politics. The research has rescued as one of the central Jewish imaginaries on Spain, the *memory of Sepharad*, which in the voice of Jacobo Glantz identifies the Francoist sabotage of the "alten land" (the old land) (1936: 23-4) with the same imperial and colonial crusaders who expelled the Jews from Spain in 1492 and invaded the so-called "New World" and its Indigenous peoples (Gabbay 2020c: 157-61). Glantz's (de)colonial perspective adds to the map of *cultural topoi* of the Spanish Civil War a Jewish dimension that merges past and present, identifying a continuity between the civilizing discourses of the Spanish Crown and Francoist crusaders. In another poem of his volume *Fanen in Blut—Shpanie 1936* (Flags in Blood—Spain 1936: 17-22), "In vandervaytkayt fun mayn folk" (In the Wide Wanderings of my People), Glantz depicts the struggle in Spain as if it were *a messianic time* when the Hebrews killed by the Inquisition awake from death in order to fight with the revolutionary militia against those incarnating traditional and Catholic Spain (Glaser 2020: 153), a call that in some of the letters presented by Deborah Green in this volume (ch. 5) appear through religious semantic fields—such is the case, for example, of a letter by Emmanuel Mink who wrote: "I was in pursuit of the *holy war* against barbarism."[19] Should we assume that Glantz's retrotopic perspective implies that an internationalist victory in Spain would have changed the understanding of the history of the Jews of Sepharad? *Poetic justice* indeed promotes epistemic repair of the past in the present time.

Key 7: Jewish Politics and Jewish Identity

From a Jewish political perspective, Glantz published his volume, *Fanen in Blut*, through the publishing house Gesbir, a "Society in support of the Jewish colonization in Birobidzhan," adding another dimension to the semiotic Jewish net around the Spanish war. Amelia M. Glaser (2020: 139-73)[20] examines how Jewish internationalist poetry used *passwords* (such as "no pasarán!" for example) in order to Judaize other

---

[19] There was also a Catholic perspective that identified the war in Spain as a theological war. Sebastián Pattin retrieved some testimonies of it: "Meinvielle stated: 'In the first place, let it be clear that, in Spain, a theological struggle is being waged. It is not simply a political or economic struggle, or even a cultural or philosophical struggle, but a struggle for Christ or for the Antichrist'" (translation from Spanish is mine). Julio Meinvielle's quote belongs to "De la Guerra Santa. Refutación del artículo de Jacques Maritain in La Nouvelle Revue Française," Criterio, August 19, 1937: 380. See Pattin 2019: 629.

[20] Glaser's monograph devoted chapter 4 to studying Jacobo "Yankev" Glantz's (bilingually titled *Fanen in Blut—Shpanyen 1936/Banderas ensangrentadas—España 1936*, Mexico), Aaron Kurtz's (*No*

minorities' struggles as well as to internationalize the Jewish battle for emancipation. Melina Di Miro (this volume, ch. 6) has shown how Alberto Gerchunoff and Samuel Glusberg alias Enrique Espinoza, leading Jewish intellectuals in Argentina, have used transhistorical rhetoric in order to bridge between their local Jewish condition, Jewish history in Spain, and anti-fascism. Gerchunoff relates academic puritanism with fascist Catholic rhetoric—subtly revindicating the superiority of the Talmudic-debate culture as an anti-academic spirit—and produces a paradoxical anti-Catholic statement when identifying Judaism with "true" Christianism, and using the equation that recognizes the undeniable Judaism in Joshua ("Jesus"). While his goal seems to have been Judaizing Catholicism, and therefore invalidating fascism, his texts conclude somehow in the erasure of the abysmal differences between the Catholic colonizing culture and its subaltern—or in Hebrew cultural terms it results in apologetics of the Christian delusional use of Judaism as its *kapara*.[21] Enrique Espinoza's rhetoric, on his side, builds—through the pun that confuses the words "Hebreos/obreros" (Hebrews/workers)—an imaginary identifying the Spaniard proletarians fighting fascism with medieval Jews set aside and tagged in European ghettos. There too, Espinoza rejects differentiating the Jewish people from other peoples and hence totally embraces internationalism. However, as opposed to Max Aub (Pilatowsky, this volume ch. 4), for example, Espinoza identifies with the Jewish people and Jewish cultural legacy. Moreover, he rejects a transhistorical connection between the Jews and Spain in favor of a "timeless connection" (*adhesión intemporal*) (Di Miro this volume, Espinoza 1938: 100) because he identifies Jews with Latin American *criollos*, who, like the Spanish proletariat, fought for their own freedom. His view then, even when using similar semantic fields and inhabiting close imaginaries (to those of Jacobo Glantz, for example), is detached from ethnicity and instead attached to a focus on the condition of a transnational subaltern. Unlike Mintz (Espinoza 1938) and, following E. Helena Houvenaghel's analysis, the metaphorical non-binary holy war between good and evil in Muñiz-Huberman's *The War of the Unicorn* (this volume, ch. 10), Espinoza rejects the identification of the struggle in Spain with a holy war. His point of view is then connected to those of the Jewish Canadian writers presented in this volume by Emily Robins Sharpe (ch. 8): the support of Republican Spain is directly related to the decolonial effort in Latin America, precisely (and paradoxically from a cultural point of view) *from* Spain.

---

pasaran!, New York, 1938), and Peretz Markish's (*Lider vegn Shpanye*, Moscow, 1938) Yiddish poetry books dedicated to the Spanish war.

[21] Traditionally, *kapara* represents the sacrifice undertaken in order to make atonement for one's sins. Through a specular ritual procedure, the sins of a person or of a nation are transferred to an animal which is then sacrificed and offered to G-d. The decolonial perspective I propose identifies Christian appropriation of the Jewish legacy, metaphorically understood as an act of *delusional kapara*, implying that, semiotically, Christianity acts as if through the sacrifice of the Jewish people (the persecution, the ghetto, the pogroms, the Shoah) it could be redeemed of the sin of colonizing other cultures.

Key 6: Neo-Sephardism and Orientalism

In the voice of the Argentinian poet Samuel Calamaro, the war in Spain linguistically bridges the centrality of the anti-fascist struggle for the Jewish people and the expulsion of Sepharad through an implicit relation: the use of old or baroque Spanish and its liaison to *neo-Sephardism* (Aizenberg 2003). *Neo-Sephardism* is an Ashkenazi Latin American movement that, through the cultural appropriation of the Sephardic legacy, succeeded in the integration of Jewish culture into the Argentinian melting pot (*crisol de razas*). My conclusion after studying these six paradigmatic cases (Kurtz, Glantz, Calamaro, Kordon, Sinay, and Tiempo) is that, by adding a transnational alternative to Benedict Anderson's proposal (1983), the anti-fascist struggle drew its semiotic forces from an "imagined community" that defended the Republic disregarding frontiers and national identities. This *anti-fascist imagined community*—which, just like national communities, also exists on the basis of the symbolic ties it creates—gathers around language in order to draw attention to the object of its interest: Spain. In this sense, in the poems of the Civil War studied and composed by the internationalist intelligentsia, Spain is objectivized by an *imaginative geography* (Said 2003: 49–73), based on a juxtaposition of outdated and updated positive knowledge where more than once, in both Yiddish and Spanish, recourse is made to orientalist visions of the peninsula. There, the need to conceptually occupy the peninsula through discourse is imposed, as a counterpart to the physical occupation carried out by the fascist enemy. I use here the concepts proposed by Edward Said, despite the fact that I am not dealing with a postcolonial reality as such; I consider that in the semiotic dimension of language and the imaginaries it promotes, cultural hierarchies are stipulated and power relations are imposed in the very act of the intellectual group that turns the subject of its imagination into an object. Thus, *neo-Sephardism* joins, in those poems, orientalist perspectives and subaltern visions of Spain, and together they impose femininity on the peninsula. This imposition of femininity in turn uncovers a patriarchal positioning of the subjects who speak in the poems; see for example the poem "Clamor por la noche de la caída de Bilbao" by Samuel Calamaro (1938: 39–44) where Spain is allegorically depicted as a raped child at the same time that the poem denounces the systematic rape of Republican women promoted by the fascist forces as a tool of indoctrination. The use of the precious old Spanish diminishes the feminist denunciation because it obliges to put extreme focus on the beauty of language, hence converting reading into a cruel act of criminal collaboration: in fact, there is no possible way of covering rape with beauty; the voice of the poet makes there a perverse turn. Indeed, Calamaro's octosyllables describe an abominable scene in which hordes of men "trample the pillows / and sheets of the girl" (pisotean las almohadas / y sábanas de la niña) (lines 19–20). The abuse is metaphorically suggested by images of torn objects, "smashed barrels" (despanzurrados toneles) (line 27), "[scavenged] gold from chests and satchels" ([hurgados] oros / de cofres y taleguillas) (lines 29–30), and "[torn] silks and [. . .] vanilla coifs" (rasgados cendales y [. . .] cofias de vainilla) (lines 31–2), using semantic fields and a vocabulary, here too, orientalist. The poem closes with an image that sexualizes the already inert body: "Oh, the cherry blossoms / of the girl's breasts, / and two peach blossoms!"

(lines 33–5). Meanwhile, the voice of Queipo de Llano resonating through the radio, suggested in Glantz's poem "In alten land" (1936: 23–4), proclaimed the rape of the red women as a "civilizing" punishment. In Calamaro's poem, the consequent "civilizing" practice is properly the central scene of the poem.

Poets were not mistaken when they understood the struggling fist as equivalent both to the gun and the pen; indeed, I consider that in language the imaginary and cognitive matter of culture is at stake and that, in fact, the great intellectual movement that took place around the Spanish Civil War largely projected the epistemological mechanisms of the Western tradition on Spain, and greatly influenced our postmodern perspective on the peninsula and the history of its tragic twentieth century. (Secular) Jewish poets also played a part in this step.[22]

Key 7: Gendered Metaphors and the Structure of Memory

I argue that, eventually, the internationalist imaginary adopted a gendered structure because of the significant role anti-fascist Spain played in collective memory. In public discourse, Spain was conceived, in Pierre Nora's terms, as a starred "realm of memory," "a refuge" (Nora 1996: 1) for both the internationalist struggle and the cosmopolitan imaginary: indeed, Spain remained in the collective memory as the "mother" (Molina Taracena 2020: 231–48), (hence, the womb, a refuge) of internationalist anti-fascism (see also Binns 2020: 19–34). In our terms, for the intellectuals of the Spanish Civil War, poetic language not only became an ark of memory where the language of the Spanish war was to be archived but also was transformed through time into a *nest* that every once in a while gives birth to new literature reincarnating the anti-fascist struggle in Spain. In a way, our knowledge about the Spanish Civil War builds a gender based imaginary defining it as a refuge for emancipating utopia, in other words, messianism, which in Judaism is related to the feminine presence of G-d on earth— or in Gershom Scholem's words "the hypostasis of God's 'indwelling' or 'presence' in the world" (1991:141): *Shekhinah*.[23] However, in Judaism, G-d's presence—unlike in Christianity—does not adopt anthropomorphic personifications, so when we talk about "feminine" we do not relate to a feminine physical figure, but to a feminine substance that *cares*, *accompanies*, and *illuminates* the Jewish people: in effect, it is visible only as *ziv* (radiance, splendor). In fact, from a Jewish imaginary point of

---

[22] As a contraposition of the Sephardic imaginary of the old land, a study could be carried out focusing on contemporary Spanish locations such as the cities of Madrid, Barcelona, or Valencia that appear in the center of the literature of several Jewish authors such as Feldman (1936), Ilya Ehrenburg (*No pasarán!*, 1936), and Mijail Koltsov (*Diary of the War in Spain*, 1937) for Madrid; H. E. Kaminski (*Ceux de Barcelone*, 1937) and Muriel Rukeyser (*Savage Coast*, [1937] 2013; and some of her testimonial poems, 2011) for Barcelona.

[23] Raphael Patai explains: "While Wisdom thus had all the prerequisites for developing into a veritable female deity, no such development took place within Judaism. Instead, post-Biblical Judaism created for itself a new concept of feminine divinity in the figure of the Shekhinah, who first appears in the Aramaic translation-paraphrase of the Bible, the so-called *Targum Onkelos*" (1968: 140). Scholem also denies any relation between Hochma (Wisdom/Sophia) and *Shekhinah* (1991: 149).

view, *Shekhinah* has been related to Spain since the Middle Ages. Jewish mysticism relates two modes of movement to the divine feminine presence: movement across the Heavens due to God's exile (*tzimzum*) and movement among the Jewish people, starting in the Tabernacle of the Temple and following the exiles after its destruction (*hurban*). *Shekhinah* is said to have accompanied the Jewish people in its paths to exile from Sepharad.[24] In this dialogue between the Jewish people and the feminine presence of divinity, a cultural *matrix* developed.

Key 8: Autofiction, Testimony, and Polyglossia

My third project, which is related to the imaginaries of the SCW and also consists of the preparation of a monograph, is focused on the case study of the Moisesville-born[25] Mika Feldman Etchebehere, who published both a French (Etchebéhère 1975) and a Spanish version (Etchebéhère 1976) of the autofiction *Ma guerre d'Espagne à moi/Mi guerra de España* (My Own War in Spain), inspired by her experience as captain of a POUM militia during the war (Gabbay 2016).[26] Unlike the genre of the autobiography or the memory—which in chapter 3 (this volume) Leonardo Senkman adjudicates principally to communist intellectuals that participated in the war—the genre of autofiction plays a defensive function, allowing for a relativization of the emotional and existential witness's risk. Indeed, Mika Feldman Etchebehere's testimony appears a few weeks after the dictator's death, at the peak of the Cold War, preluding the transition to democracy in Spain. My study focuses on linguistic and structural issues relating to Feldman's autofiction, also put in relation to her previous writings (Gabbay 2022a, 2020d). Her work is paradigmatic of a feminist anti-fascist cosmopolitan who follows

---

[24] Arthur Green says: "God and Israel are lovers, frequent partners in dialogue, sharers of the sufferings of exile, but they always remain distinct from one another. The God who suffers exile may be depicted as *shekhinah*, the long-suffering presence that accompanies Israel in their wanderings" (2002: 18).

[25] Moisesville was the first agricultural Jewish colony in Argentina (province of Santa Fe), founded by pioneers from Podolia (Ukraine) and Russia in 1890, and supported by the Baron Hirsch's Jewish Colonization Association. The spoken language of the Argentine *shtetl* was Yiddish; the schools of the Alliance Israélite Universelle introduced the instruction of Spanish, Hebrew, and French.

[26] The title of Feldman Etchebéhère's autofiction is reminiscent of the memoir *Ma guerre d'Espagne. Brigades internationales: la fin d'un mythe* by the disillusioned communist Sygmunt Stein, which was originally published in Yiddish in Paris in 1961 as *Der Birger-ḳrig in Shpanye: zikhroynes fun a militsyaner* (and was pre-published in *feuilletons* in *Forverts*, New York, 1956), a time when Mika Feldman—an Yiddish speaker herself—was already back in Paris (where she lived between 1930–6 and 1946–92). Feldman's title in French insists on the possessive form "à moi." One wonders if she read Stein's memoir and responded to it with her own text, where she shows the misfortunes of being a dissident anarcho-communist of the Partido Obrero de Unificación Marxista (POUM) under communist rule. (For a short history of the POUM, see Christ 2005.) Stein opens his memoir: "À l'origine, l'idée de partir en Espagne, où avait éclaté l'insurrection contre Franco, n'était pas motivée par l'envie d'aider la République, mais par la nécessité de m'aider moi-même. // Je ressentais alors l'un des plus grands chocs moraux de ma vie. [...] À cette époque j'habitais Prague, et j'y dirigeais le Gezerd, une organisation communiste qui faisait de la propagande dans la population juive en vue d'instaurer une République juive autonome au Birobidjan" (2012 :13).

the path of writing in order to pursue *poetic justice* after the defeat in the trenches. I argue that the account of her "depatriarchalization" (Gabbay 2022a, 2020b: 210–13) of the war experience in Spain not only vindicates the internationalist anti-Catholic struggle against Franco and the Falange but must be read in the cultural context of the intellectual anarcho-Marxist Jewish field from where it arises (Gabbay 2016). Moreover, the intricacies of Feldman's polyglossia and trilingual writing—in a different context, she also wrote in Portuguese under a disguised identity—demonstrate that her efforts devoted to translation, self-translation, journalism, and literature are to be read at the inherited intersection of "the wisdom on the letter and the law," paradigmatic of her inexhaustible *Mosaic enthusiasm*.

Key 9: Cosmopolitanism, Double Imposture, and Authorship

The most challenging element in Feldman's literary path is perhaps her *poetics of silence*—overlapped with the so-called "Jewish poetics of internationalism" (Glaser 2020: 140)—which have codified the Jewish experience through the suggestive negation of the author's past previous to the war, a phenomenon that provoked a *double imposture* through a polysemic use of pennames and pseudonyms, as well as the miswriting of the authorial signature (Gabbay 2022b). The characteristic silence and camouflaging of identity traits in the writings of Micaela Feldman are traversed by the antisemitic experience of the twentieth century denoted in her displayed *narrative of origins* (*discurso de origen*) which uses a password[27] ("rusos" [Russians]) to mention the heritage of revolutionary enthusiasm in which she mirrors her own path.[28] In the intersection of these Jewish modes also stands the arduous work of Feldman in rebuilding her memory of the war, forty years after the battle. This memory, which devotes also an important amount of work to *forgetting* and eliminating details of her biography, works toward the construction of *a cosmopolitan imagination*, *digestible* enough—eliminating traits of superpolyglossia[29]—for the gentile public. Through a genetic[30] and paratextual study[31] of her self-translated autofiction, I identified

---

[27] For the use of "passwords" in internationalist Jewish milieus see Amelia M. Glaser (2020: "Introduction," 1–38).

[28] In Argentina, following the East European mass immigration of Jews in the late nineteenth and early twentieth centuries, the term "Russian" denoted Jews and communists. This denomination is still commonly used today. In her autofiction, Mika says: "This war and this revolution are mine. I have dreamed of them since childhood, listening to the tales of the Russian revolutionaries who escaped the Czarist prisons and Siberia" (1976: 83–4). Translation is mine.

[29] *Superpolyglossia* refers to the ability of managing more than six languages, or popularly saying, "simply more languages than the average," a characteristic trait that in the twentieth century was commonly assigned to Jews. Silencing one's own superpolyglossia means then erasing traits of Jewish identity.

[30] Genetic studies are a research methodology that examines manuscripts and/or different versions of the literary published text.

[31] Paratextuality refers to the relation between a text and its satellites which includes: related reviews, interviews, titles, subtitles, prefaces, prologues, footnotes, afterwards, etc.

a structural *circumcision of the text*, especially in the French version of *Ma guerre d'Espagne à moi*: indeed, while translating her own text, the author eliminated passages in order to suit the monolingual pact (*brit*) of European cosmopolitanism of the twentieth century, hence forcing her multifaceted transnational identity into the framework of white cosmopolitanism (Gabbay 2022b). In this context, identity characteristics were erased; however, my research studies the modes by which Jewish traits are preserved: the voice of the narrator, which seems to reproduce an inner polyphonic Talmudic-like debate regarding her gender identity; the authority of her voice toward the masculinities she confronts as a captain; and her political and personal choices. Her self-translated autofiction—as well as her short stories published during the war (Etchebehere 1938a and 1938b) for the magazine of the anarcho-feminist group Mujeres Libres (Free Women) (Ackselsberg 1991)—result in some of the most particular and distinguishable literary items of the Spanish Civil War corpus because of the *horizontalism* of her perspectives (Gabbay 2020d) and the marginal voices she introduces in her accounts (Gabbay 2022a).

While Feldman worked toward apparent "assimilation" to European cosmopolitanism, her Jewish practices, by contrast, also contaminated the European field. Similarly, Glaser—who has provided an important key to the study of the Yiddish poetry of the Spanish war—"considers [...] [that the poets] were not merely describing other struggling peoples; they were bringing other peoples into fold, making them metaphorically Jewish" (2020: 2). In effect, transnational solidarity might have been also a means to Judaize the relation to otherhood, in a way, reclaiming their colonized modernity, vindicating the Jewish existence on earth, and in the case of Spain, especially reclaiming the loss of pre-modern Sepharad.

As shown previously (Gabbay 2020c; Duroux, this volume, ch. 11; Robins Sharpe, this volume, ch. 8), the imaginary reunion between Spain and Sepharad appears in the work of several authors. Sometimes it is through deep transhistorical *saudade*; other times, through the transhistorical overlapping of memories of pogroms and the punishment of the Inquisition (for the case of Peretz Markish see Glaser 2020: 146–56). In the case of Angelina Muñiz-Huberman's novel *The War of the Unicorn*, as shown by E. Helena Houvenaghel, the figure of Abraham Abulafia offers, through Jewish mysticism and wisdom, an allegorical answer regarding the victory of evil in twentieth-century Europe.

Key 10: Iterology, Overcoming Trauma, and Empathy

Following a theoretical premise by Michel Butor (1972: 4–19), I have identified the *iterology* of Mika Feldman, that is, the relation between Feldman's writing practices and her diasporic parkour (Gabbay 2022a). There, and through the series of letters guarded in French and Spanish archives, I have analyzed the imaginary emerged from her account of the traumatic results of the war in which she lost her companion, her friends, and *milicianos*, and where the shared socialist utopia was defeated. Her letters reveal the construction of an imagination depicting a diasporic network of solidarity and resistance spread like *a constellation of inner-exiles (insilios) and exiles* and reunited through the reparative nature of writing, which worked toward overcoming trauma, melancholy, and grief. Out of the management of trauma, three decades later, Feldman succeeded in producing *poetic justice* for her experience in Spain through a knitted elaboration of her *narratives of caring* (Gabbay 2020b: 212–17), similar to the case of Yiddish authors, on whom Amelia M. Glaser points out that "the passwords that gave Yiddish poets and readers entrée—imagined or real—into the experiences of other marginalized groups established a precedent for translating Jewish trauma into empathy" (Glaser 2020: 9). In the case of Mika Feldman, who wrote her experience in both French and Spanish defying her own trauma, *empathy* was indeed translated into feminist *caring*, which in a way became the materialization of utopia in writing. What I called a path from *Jewish belonging* to *internationalist becoming* (Gabbay 2020b: 207–9) is depicted and confirmed in Glaser's research as "a redemption narrative" that "offers a place for Jewish past and an internationalist future" (Gabbay 2020b: 143).

Key 11: Spanish Philo-Sephardism: Between Cultural Appropriation and Revisionism

The last twenty years[32] have seen in Spain the landing of a new literary tendency vindicating the Sephardic past, a tendency coming from canonic literature that perhaps differentiates itself from mainstream Spanish literature in that it winks to Central European tradition.[33] It is about philo-Sephardic literature or, in other words, Spanish literature inviting to recall the Sephardic peninsular past in the context of the history of Spanish philo-Semitism,[34] one that is also intricate with antisemitism (see Salah, this volume ch. 1).[35] In the context of the impact left by 1492 and the Inquisition

---

[32] During Franco's regime, Spanish literature was silent regarding Jewish topics (Díaz-Más 1999: 346–361).
[33] Also the academic Spanish world has seen several decades of intense research in Sephardic and Jewish studies. In the context of our topic here I recommend to explore the fascinating figure of Máximo José Kahn (Germany-Spain-Argentina), a Jewish writer of German origin that was living in Spain during the Civil War, and was later exiled both in Mexico and Argentina. For a broad perspective on his works relating to Judaism and Spain, see Martin Gijón (2012).
[34] Álvarez Chillida identifies the political agenda of philo-Sephardism at its origins which "looked to renew Spain's global influence and impact through a reconciliation with the Hispano-American republics (an objective of the thriving Hispano-Americanist movement) and with the aforementioned Sephardic communities in North Africa, the Middle East, and the Balkans. This would entail cultural policies to strengthen their ties to the 'Motherland'" (2020: 68). Opening the same volume, Brenneis and Herrmann say in its introduction that "the Spanish philosemitism celebrated by some Spanish intellectuals during the early twentieth century did not translate into a massive national effort to protect Sephardic Jews" (2020: 9). Therefore, while philo-Sephardism/philo-Semitism have been present in Spanish society for a long time, they still pertain apparently to a delimited intellectual group.
[35] The exacerbated and scandalized descriptions given by Rafael Cansinos Assens in Asher Salah's chapter regarding León Azerrat might deserve a proper section to be discussed. Cansinos Assens, educated in fierce Catholicism, but considered one of the most important twentieth-century Spanish Hebraists, philo-Semite also by conviction of his paternal *converso* origin, relates to young

on Jewish memory, the anti-Judaic Francoist imaginary (Preston 2012), and the Shoah, philo-Sephardic literature's most paradigmatic novel is, probably, *Sefarad*, by Antonio Muñoz Molina (2001). There, the author shows the contiguities and continuities of Europe in Spain and exposes the relationship between the national political realities. *Sefarad* has successfully identified the open historical corridor between Germany and Spain where Jewish and non-Jewish characters (one of them Walter Benjamin) paradoxically circulate across the so intimately Jewish and fiercely antisemitic Europe. Tabea A. Linhard says:

> Muñoz Molina joins different stories, and forms of exile, and forms of loss and absence, so that ultimately the "melancholy of a long exile" is all that remains. Although the author does not state this directly, it is not the sadness of melancholy but rather the promise of nostalgia that ends up unifying the different texts in that in one way or another narrate an impossible return to a home that no longer exists and the grief that results from this impossibility. (2014: 64)

In effect, the novel relies on semantic fields naming exile and nostalgia; through them, it seems to recall the lost Jewish Spain. In addition, other stories like the one presented in this volume (ch. 11) by Rose Duroux—herself a refugee child from the Republican exile in France—*La canción de Ruth* by Marifé Santiago Bolaños (2010), adopt similar semantic fields, this time, through the voices of various generations of women. The equation allowing the juxtaposition and comparison between the 1492 and the Republican exiles is given by the transhistorical similarities of both.[36] This phenomenon can be interpreted in different ways. From one side, its use in postmemorial Spanish (non-Jewish) fiction rings the bell of possible "cultural appropriation" (Young 2010: 1–31) of the Jewish memory when imitating—thematically or structurally—Sephardic narratives and, therefore, deepening the inequalities between those who inherited Spain and those who were expelled from it.[37] On the other hand, both *Sefarad* and *La canción de Ruth*, while they rely on the so-called Sephardic semantic fields of nostalgia and exile, also include, separately and together with the Sephardic voices depicted, a non-Jewish perspective of Spanish history. This literary strategy results in the representation of a reality where Jewish loneliness seems to be purged, despite

---

Azerrat using a racist discourse ("from that dark African continent," "devastating plagues," "one of those terrible plagues"), that, if one did not know Cansinos' philo-Semitism, one would not hesitate in identifying as antisemitic. I think his devotion to hatred discourses on Azerrat is paradigmatic of the way Spanish culture was traversed by an intricate relation between philo-Semitism and antisemitism. See also the example given by Rose Duroux in this volume of the philo-Sephardic and antisemite Ernesto Giménez Caballero.

[36] I have argued that the research on the Republican exile would benefit from Jewish memory studies perspectives in Gabbay 2022a, particularly relating to the 1492 exile.

[37] In contraposition to philo-Sephardic postmemorial fiction one could compare postmemory Jewish fiction of the SCW, as, for example: *Las hojas muertas* by Bárbara Jacobs (México, 1987), *Exil der frechen frauen*, by Robert Cohen (Switzerland/USA, 2009), *Tío Boris. Un héroe olvidado de la guerra civil español* by Graciela Mochkofsky (Argentina, 2006), and *Cholem ve Lochem BeEspamia* (Misha from Palestine) by Efraim Rachman (Israel, 2016).

Jewish historical and cultural particularity. A problem would arise if, on this ground, a romantic universalist veil depicting the persecution of cosmopolitan characters by the fascists would be misunderstood when obliviating that cosmopolitanism is a Western construction dedicated to enabling the "tolerance" of otherness: the *others*-inside-the-nation.[38] In effect, Robins Sharpe says: "'Cosmopolitan' has long been a euphemistic epithet for 'Jew'" (2020: 20). Nonetheless, the Jews of the twentieth century were not *cosmopolitans*, they were "simply" *Jews*—polyglot refugees, persecuted, lonely, diasporic *guardians of the text*, both desperate to live and driven by hope and determination, deterritorialized vision, and inherited enthusiasm. Cosmopolitanism is not Jewish; Western cosmopolitanism imitates twentieth-century Jews and in its imagination (expert in oblivion) forgets that the first cause of *galut*, diaspora,[39] and polyglossia was hatred and persecution. Twentieth-century Jews were not adventurers, *flâneurs*, or bohemians, they were survivors who embraced internationalism and transformed it into a lifebuoy. When Western culture romantically imitates their so-called "cosmopolitanism," the humiliation, initiated in the pogroms and "culminated" in the Shoah, is deepened. Western cosmopolitanism—that, for example, in the case of Mika Feldman (Gabbay 2022b), Jews adopted as a survival masquerade—is seemingly the modern fashion of cultural colonialism by osmosis. In my understanding, both *Sefarad* and *La canción de Ruth* have attenuated the erasure of the particularity of the Jewish condition and, therefore, the acceptance of their otherness allows an asymmetrical specular relation between the Jewish and the Republican exiles. Hence, a verisimilar representation is reached.

But does philo-Sephardic literature perform cultural appropriation of the representation of Jewish memory? I believe the answer is nevertheless not so categorical. Spivak closes her essay "Can the Subaltern Speak?" arguing that the subaltern does not have a voice (1994: 111). We know that a variety of Jewish figures paradoxically performed their voices the most, precisely during the twentieth century—to such an extent that Yuri Slezkine calls it "the Jewish century" (1994). However, to have a *voice* demands courage and requires fighting authority and disturbing hierarchies. To reach a voice does not mean necessarily the possibility to abandon subalternity but it does mean overcoming the inherited identification with those who do not have a voice (yet!) and transforming it into a *choice* to be representative of their shared subalternity. Because the subaltern Jew has a voice, then it can be "culturally appropriated." But

---

[38] Slezkine understands this imitation of *Jewishness* as the foundation of modernity: "The Modern Age is the Jewish Age, and the twentieth century, in particular, is the Jewish Century. Modernization is about everyone becoming urban, mobile, literate, articulate, intellectually intricate, physically fastidious, and occupationally flexible. It is about learning how to cultivate people and symbols, not fields or herds. It is about pursuing wealth for the sake of learning, learning for the sake of wealth, and both wealth and learning for their own sake. It is about transforming peasants and princes into merchants and priests, replacing inherited privilege with acquired prestige, and dismantling social estates for the benefit of individuals, nuclear families, and book-reading tribes (nations). Modernization, in other words, is about everyone becoming Jewish" (Slezkine 2004: 1).

[39] For a beautiful and precise definition of *diaspora*, see Feierstein 2019. 513–24.

Jewish voices bounce their existences between two extreme situations: solidarity[40] or rejection, and in between these extremes contagiously spread their thinking and their language among the societies and public discourse to which they "belonged." Philo-Sephardic contemporary literature could also be part of this contagious process, one that, from the positive side, has allowed, for example, the recognition of Spanish nationality for Sephardic descendants.[41] Just as eventually *neo-Sephardism*—through Ashkenazi cultural appropriation of the Sephardic legacy—has served in Latin America as a tool to integrate the Jewish community into the local societies, philo-Sephardic literature (and in the background, philo-Semitism) has opened a window to some kind of reparation toward the Sephardic diaspora. In *La canción de Ruth*, the use of a lullaby line in Judeo-Spanish, "Durme, durme, amor: / Agora es Sefarad" (2010: 154) functions as a "password" to *awaken* and open the door of the Sephardic world to the Spanish contemporary public. Jewish emancipation, however, one deprived of national frames, can only be imagined in the framework of language and in the utopian territory of the Jewish text.

Imagining a Conclusion

As Robins Sharpe shows (2020: 7), in the case of Canada, the Spanish Civil War allowed a very special leap for Jewish writing. This event, indeed, should be considered a trigger of a creolization turn in Jewish literature; it should also be recalled as Judaizing world literature. Maybe one of the most outstanding phenomena that have arisen through the study of the imaginaries of the Spanish Civil War has been that Jewish authors are particularly aware of the language issues in the war events, an issue that is common for refugees and immigrants in general. In texts by Simón Radowitzky, Max Aub, and Alberto Gerchunoff, for example, none of whom are native Spanish speakers but all of whom nevertheless wrote their best lines in Spanish, there is this feeling of an under-language that slips in between the words and the structure of the Castilian sentence. This *under-language*—a consequence of Jewish polyglossia—is an added mode identifiable in the Jewish literature of the SCW. In the case of Ruth Rewald—as Tabea Linhard has shown—polyglossia results in specific cases of (in my own words) miscegenation of Spanish and German. In all the cases presented in this volume, language is central to the discussion on Jewish imaginaries.

Because of the intertextual nature of our object of study, the literary and cultural study of the Jewish imaginaries of the Spanish Civil War is enriched when using keys that examine overlapping semantic fields. I propose to inverse and adapt Michael Rothberg's model of "multidirectional memory" (2009)—which entangles the thinking

---

[40] For a German version of radical philo-Semitism see the life and work of the anarchist Rudolph Rocker, who was also deeply impacted both by Jewish anarchist communities and by the SCW, and while remaining in the USA his contemporary works had an important impact on the anarchists in Spain (Rocker 1937).
[41] The Law 12/2015 of Spain promotes the nationalization of Sephardic Jews.

on the Holocaust with postcolonial genocides and oppressive political realities—through retrotopian metaphors (Sepharad, the Inquisition, orientalist perspectives of Spain) projected onto the Spanish Civil War that point at the schism between the Middle Ages and modernity: at the devastating point triggering Sephardic diaspora, its Jewish estrangement, and the era of European colonization. In these textualities, Roskies' Jewish "transhistorical memory" (1999: 13), which explains the mechanisms of the Jewish people when confronting devastation and tragedy, can be well identified as *transhistorical imagination*, especially in those writers who wrote about the war from abroad: metaphors recalling the (pre-)Sephardic past in Spain should be read as cognitive tools to place and confront the debacle of the Spanish war in the chain of Jewish history and tragedy. Indeed, Jewish memory not only responds to a divine mandate (*Zkhor*, Yerushalmi 1996); its nature is transhistorical; encoded from a non-linear perspective, it functions as a cultural tool to inscribe and confront catastrophe within a familiar framework already inscribed in the tribal memory as an event that repeats itself or is intrinsically related to an earlier catastrophe. This recognition allows the present to be written in a "genealogy of disaster" (Feierstein 2016: 102), so that it anticipates the nature of the coming trauma and thus predisposes a cultural strategy to cope with it.

Finally, the Jewish literature of the Spanish Civil War does not constitute a canon. Even though we have retrieved the intersection of several Jewish modes writing the war, as well as common lines and poetics, its imaginaries represent the testimony of a complex constellation of different genres, languages, registers, and references. It should be imagined indeed as a decentered galaxy (Miron 2010) or a rhizome. Let's understand it as *an open corpus*, seeking *poetic justice* through its alliances with other constellations. Nevertheless, the Jewish imaginary distinguishes itself from the general imaginaries of the Spanish Civil War, which lack the transhistorical dimensions and resonances of the catastrophe that represented the defeat, as well as messianic enthusiasm, the joy derived from an expectation of forthcoming cultural decolonization, mystical revelation, and political emancipation.

References

Abramson, P. and A. Abramson. (1994), *Mosaico roto*, Madrid: Compañía Literaria.
Ackelsberg, M. A. (1991), *Free Women of Spain: Anarchism and the Struggle for the Emancipation of Women*, Bloomington: Indiana University Press.
Aizenberg, E. (2003), "Sefardíes y neosefardíes en la literatura latinoamericana," in N. Rehrmann (ed.), *El legado de Sefarad en la historia y la literatura de América latina, España, Portugal y Alemania*, 49–58, Salamanca: Amarú.
Álvarez Chillida, G. (2020), "Antisemitism and Philosephardism in Spain (1880–1945)," in S. J. Brenneis and G. Herrmann (eds.), *Spain, the Second World War and the Holocaust. History and Representation*, 65–79, Toronto: University of Toronto Press.
Anderson, B. (1983), *Imagined Communities: Reflections on the Origin and Spread of Nationalism*, London & New York: Verso.

Biagini, F. (2008), "Yiddishland libertaire. Bref apercu historique," in A. Bertolo (ed.), *Juifs et anarchistes*, 11–16, Paris: Editions de l'Eclat.
Binns, N. (2020), *"Si España cae –digo, es un decir–"*. *Intelectuales de Hispanoamérica ante la República Española en guerra*, Valencia: Calambur.
Brenneis, S. J. and G. Herrmann. (2020), "Introduction," in S. J. Brenneis and G. Herrmann (eds.), *Spain, the Second World War and the Holocaust. History and Representation*, 3–26, Toronto: University of Toronto Press.
Butor, M. (1972), "Le voyage et l'écriture," *Romantisme*, 4: 4–19.
Calamaro, E. S. (1938), *Caramillo*, Buenos Aires: Tiempo Nuestro.
Christ, M. (2005), *Le POUM. Histoire d'un parti révolutionnaire espagnol 1935–1952*, Paris: L'Harmattan.
Cohen, R. (2009), *Exil der frechen frauen*, Zurich: Unionsverlag.
De Angelis, R. (2020), "Textuality," *Oxford Research Encyclopedia of Literature*, Available online: https://doi.org/10.1093/acrefore/9780190201098.013.1098 (accessed September 30, 2021).
Díaz-Más, P. (1999), "Judíos y conversos en la literatura Española," in Y. Stillman and N. Stillman eds., *From Iberia to Diaspora. Studies in Sephardic History and Culture*, 346–61, New York: Brill.
Edelman, F. (1996), *Banderas, pasiones, Camaradas*, Buenos Aires: Ediciones Dirple.
Espinoza, E. [Glusberg, Samuel]. (1938), *Chicos de España (1935)*, Buenos Aires: Perseo.
Etchebehere, M. [Feldman]. (1938a), "Altavoz de la 14ª División," *Mujeres Libres*, 11: 22–3.
Etchebehere, M. (1938b), "Claro obscuro de trincheras…," *Mujeres Libres*, 12: 21–2.
Etchebéhère, M. [Feldman]. (1975), *Ma guerre d'Espagne à moi*, Paris: Denoël.
Etchebehere, M. [Feldman]. (1976), *Mi guerra de España*, Barcelona: Plaza & Janés.
Feierstein, L. R. (2016), "Duelo y/o melancolía. Huellas religiosas y culturales en las representaciones, elaboraciones y duelos de la violencia en Argentina," in L. R. Feierstein and L. Zylberman (eds.), *Narrativas del terror y la desaparición en América latina*, 99–119, Buenos Aires: EDUNTREF.
Feierstein, L. R. (2019). "Diaspora," *Lo Sguardo – rivista di filosofia*, 29 (II): 513–24.
Fine, R. (2013), "La literatura de conversos después de 1492: obras y autores en busca de un discurso crítico," in R. V. Fine, M. Guillemont and J. Diego Vila (eds.), *La literatura de conversos después de 1492*, 499–526, Madrid/Frankfurt: Iberoamericana/Vervuert.
Gabbay, C. (2016), "Identidad, género y prácticas anarquistas en las memorias de Micaela Feldman y Etchebéhère," in *Forma. Revista d'estudis comparatius. Art, literatura, pensament*, Vol. 14, 35–57, Barcelona: Universitat Pompeu Fabra.
Gabbay, C. (2020a), "El onceavo mandamiento: memoria del fuego en la literatura judía y feminista de la guerra civil española," in E. Kahan, A. Raber, and W. Wechsler (eds.), *Hacer Patria. Estudios sobre la vida judía en Argentina*, 31–67, Buenos Aires: Teseo.
Gabbay, C. (2020b), "(Jewish) Women's Narratives of *Caring* and Medical Practices during the Spanish Civil War," in Miriam Offer (ed.), *Nashim: A Journal of Jewish Women's Studies and Gender Issues, 36, Jewish Women Medical Practitioners in Europe Before, During and After the Holocaust*, 205–33, Bloomington: Indiana University Press.
Gabbay, C. (2020c), "Una cuestión de espacio: promesas de liberación y utopía en la poesía yidis e hispana de la guerra civil española," in P. Molina Taracena (ed.), *Poesía de la guerra civil española: una perspectiva comparatista*, Chapter 9, 153–78, Bern: Peter Lang.
Gabbay, C. (2020d), "Babilonia y Revolución en España: Prácticas de escritura cosmopolita de una miliciana/ Mika Feldman Etchebehere," in J. Kölbl, I. Orlova and

M. Wolf (eds.), *¿Pasarán? Kommunikation im Spanischen Bürgerkrieg. Interacting in the Spanish Civil War*, 82–99, Vienna: New Academic Press.

Gabbay, C. (2022a), "Iterología de Micaela Feldman/Etchebehere tras la guerra civil española: entre el insilio melancólico y el exilio de imaginación cosmopolita," in C. Nickel and D. Santos Sánchez (eds.), *Women in Exile: Female Literary Networks of the 1939 Republican Exile*, Special Volume in *Journal of Spanish Cultural Studies* 23 (1), 51–70, https://doi.org/10.1080/14636204.2022.2033430.

Gabbay, C. (2022b), "L'autotraduction de Mika Feldman Etchebehere ou écriture à deux plumes pour un pacte cosmopolite," in C. Lavail and A. Taillot (eds.), special issue in *Crisol* 26, forthcoming.

Gabbay, C. (2022c), "La Fundación Cultural de un Nuevo Espacio Epistemológico: Los Escritos Enciclopédicos del Converso Ibero-Peruano Antonio León Pinelo (1590–1660)," *Revista Iberoamericana (Pittsburgh)*, 278: 145–63.

Gabbay, C. (2022d), "*Neojudezmo* en la lírica latinoamericana disidente: la construcción de registros intersticiales entre la autotraducción y el glosario," in M. L. Spoturno and R. Grutman (eds.), *Mutatis Mutandis* 15 (1)'s special issue, *Self-translation and/in Latin America and the Latina diaspora*, 65–94, https://doi.org/10.17533/udea.mut.v15n1a05.

Gilman, S. (1972), *The Spain of Fernando de Rojas*, Princeton: Princeton University Press.

Glantz, Y. (1936), *Banderas ensangrentadas—España 1936*
[פאנען אין בלוט – שפאניע 1936 לידער און פאעמען]. Mexico: Gesbir (Society of support for the Jewish colonization in Birobidzhan).

Glaser, A. M. (2020), *Songs in Dark Times. Yiddish Poetry of Struggle from Scottsboro to Palestine*, Cambridge: Harvard University Press, chapter. 4, 139–73.

Kaplan, Y. (2000), *An Alternative Path to Modernity. The Sephardi Diaspora in Western Europe*, Leiden: Brill.

Kritzler, E. (2008), *Jewish Pirates of the Caribbean: How a Generation of Swashbuckling Jews Carved Out an Empire in the New World in their Quest for Treasure, Religious Freedom, and Revenge*, New York: Doubleday.

Krüger, D. and D. Martin. (2015), "Ludwig Detsinyi / David Martin. Als Sanitäter im Spanischen Bürgerkrieg Schöpfer des weltberühmten Liedes 'Am Rio Jarama' – Februar 1937," [Written interview by correspondence], unpublished.

Kurtz, A. (1938), "*No-Pasarán*": *Lider, balades un poems fun Shpanishn folk in zayn kamf kegn fashyzm*, New York: Yiddish Cooperative Book League of the Jewish Section of the International Workers Order.

Langer, M. (1989), *From Vienna to Managua. Journal of a Psychoanalyst*, London: Free Association Books.

Linhard, T. A. (2014), *Jewish Spain: A Mediterranean Memory*, Stanford: Stanford University Press.

Litvak, O. (2012), *Haskalah: The Romantic Movement in Judaism*, New Jersey: Rutgers University Press.

Markish, P. (1938), *Lider vegn Shpanye*, Moscow: Farlag "Emes."

Martin Gijón, M. (2012), *La patria imaginada de Máximo José Kahn: Vida y obra de un escritor de tres exilios*, Valencia: Pre-Textos.

Mignolo, W. (2010), *Desobediencia epistémica. Retórica de la modernidad, lógica de la colonialidad y gramática de la descolonialidad*, Buenos Aires: Ediciones del Signo.

Miron, D. (2010), *From Continuity to Contiguity: Toward a New Jewish Literary Thinking*, Stanford: Stanford University Press.

Mochkofsky, G. (2006), *Tío Boris. Un héroe olvidado de la guerra civil española*, Buenos Aires: Sudamericana.
Molina Taracena, P. (2020), "La imagen de España como madre," in P. Molina Taracena (ed.), *Poesía de la guerra civil española: una perspectiva comparatista*, 231–48, Bern: Peter Lang.
Muñoz Molina, A. (2001), *Sefarad*, Madrid: Alfaguara.
Nadler, S. M. (2001), *Spinoza's Heresy: Immortality and the Jewish Mind*, Oxford: Oxford University Press.
Nora, P. (1996), "General Introduction. Between Memory and History," in A. Goldhammer (trans.), Realms of Memory. Rethinking the French Past, Vol. I, 1–20, New York: Columbia University Press.
Norich, A. (2008), "Introduction," in A. Norich and Y. Z. Eliav (eds.), *Jewish Literatures and Cultures. Context and Intertexts, Brown Judaic Studies*, Vol. 349, 1–7, Providence: Brown University.
Osheroff, A. ([1990] 2007), "Reflections of a Civil War Veteran," in J. Pérez and W. Aycock (eds.), *The Spanish Civil War in Literature*, 9–22, Texas: Tech University Press.
Patai, R. (1968). *The Hebrew Goddess*, Brooklyn: Ktav Publishing House.
Pattin, S. (2019), "Guerra española, guerra santa: apuntes a partir de una controversia conceptual en Argentina (1936–1937)," *Historia Contemporánea*, 60: 619–646.
Preston, P. (2012), *The Spanish Holocaust. Inquisition and Extermination in Twentieth-Century Spain*, London: Harper Press.
Rachman, E. (2016), *Cholem ve Lochem BeEspamia* (Misha from Palestine), Tel Aviv: Zivoni'im.
Rein, R. and J. M. Thomàs. (2018), "Introduction," in R. Rein and J. M. Thomàs (eds.), *Spain 1936. Year Zero*, 1–12, Brighton: Sussex Academic Press.
Roskies, D. G. ([1984] 1999), *Against the Apocalypse: Responses to Catastrophe in Modern Jewish Culture*, Syracuse: Syracuse University Press.
Rothberg, M. (2009), *Multidirectional Memory: Remembering the Holocaust in the Age of Decolonization*, Redwood City: Stanford University Press.
Robins Sharpe, E. (2020), *Mosaic Fictions: Writing Identity in the Spanish Civil War*, Toronto: University of Toronto Press.
Rocker, R. (1937), *The Tragedy of Spain*, New York: Freie Arbeiter Stimme. Available online: https://theanarchistlibrary.org/library/rudolf-rocker-the-tragedy-of-spain (accessed March 1, 2021).
Rukeyser, M. (2011), *"Barcelona, 1936" & Selections from the Spanish Civil War Archive*, Rowena Kennedy-Epstein, New York: Lost and Found, The CUNY Poetics Document Initiative II.
Rukeyser, M. ([1937] 2013), *Savage Coast*, New York: The Feminist Press.
Said, E. W. (2003), *Orientalism: Western Conceptions of the Orient*, London: Penguin Classics.
Santiago Bolaños, M. (2010), *La Canción de Ruth*, Madrid: Bartleby.
Scholem, G. (1991), *On the Mystical Shape of the Godhead: Basic Concepts on the Kabbalah*, New York: Schocken.
Seghers, A. ([1947] 1987), *Transit*, trans. J. Stern, Aix-en-Provence: Alinea.
Seidler, V. J. (2007), *Jewish Philosophy and Western Culture: A Modern Introduction*, New York & London: I.B.Tauris.
Slezkine, Y. (2004), *The Jewish Century*, New Jersey: Princeton University Press.

Spivak, G. C. (1994), "Can the Subaltern Speak?" P. Williams and L. Chrisman (eds.), *Colonial Discourse and Post-Colonial Theory*, 66–111, New York: Columbia University Press.

Stein, S. (2012), *Ma guerre d'Espagne. Brigades internationales: la fin d'un mythe*, Paris: Seuil.

Yerushalmi, Y. H. (1996), *Zakhor. Jewish History and Jewish Memory*, Seattle and London: University of Washington Press.

Young, J. O. (2010), *Cultural Appropriation and the Arts*, Oxford: Wiley Blackwell.

Contributors

Cynthia Gabbay is a Le Studium Researcher at the Rémélice Laboratory of the Université d'Orléans (France) and an Associate Researcher at Centre/Zentrum Marc Bloch (Humboldt University of Berlin). She is also a member of the international research group "The Impact of the Spanish Civil War in the Intellectual Life of Spanish America" at Universidad Complutense de Madrid. She has a PhD in Latin American and Romance Studies from the Hebrew University of Jerusalem (2012) and has completed several postdoctoral research stays in Jewish studies both in Israel and Germany. She coordinates the online series "*Simania*: Salon Readings" (LAJSA), where she also serves on the Board of Directors. Moreover, she is a coeditor of the scientific journal *Lingua Franca* (SHARP). Her first book was published as *Los ríos metafísicos de Julio Cortázar: de la lírica al diálogo* (Hispamérica/Eduvim, 2015). Cynthia Gabbay's fields of interest are semiotics, translation studies, metafiction, popular culture, and poetry.

Asher Salah is a Professor at the Bezalel Academy of Arts and the Hebrew University of Jerusalem (Israel). He has been a fellow at the Katz Center for Advanced Judaic Studies (Philadelphia) (twice), and (twice) at the Maimonides Center for Advanced Studies in Jewish Scepticism (Hamburg). His research deals with Jewish scholarship in early modern Italy, Sephardic studies, and Jewish cinema. His publications include *La République des Lettres: Rabbins, médecins et écrivains juifs en Italie au XVIIIe* (2007), *L'epistolario di Marco Mortara. Un rabbino italiano tra riforma e ortodossia* (2012), *Diari risorgimentali* (2017), and *Genealogies of Sepharad* co-edited with Daniela Flesler and Michal R. Friedman (*Quest. Issues in Contemporary Jewish History* 18, December 2020).

Antonio Notario Ruiz is an Associate Professor of Aesthetics and Theory of the Arts in the Faculty of Philosophy at the University of Salamanca where he also serves as Dean of the Faculty. He is also a piano teacher. He has published more than sixty collaborations in books and specialized journals. Director of the *Pensamiento y Sociedad* Collection of Ediciones Universidad de Salamanca, he is a member of the Research Group on Aesthetics and Theory of the Arts (GEsTA) at the Institute of Iberoamérica. He is also co-founder of the Sociedad de Estudios de Teoría Crítica and of *Constelaciones. Revista de Teoría Crítica* (www.constelaciones-rtc.net/).

Leonardo Senkman has a PhD from Universidad de Buenos Aires. He is an associated researcher at the Harry S. Truman Institute of the Hebrew University of Jerusalem. His topics of research are immigration, refugees and exiles to/from Argentina, antisemitism in Latin America, human rights violations, and Jewish Latin American writers. He has published more than 100 publications, among them, thirty books as either author or editor. Recent publications are: (as co-author with Luis Roniger) *Conspiracy Theories and Latin American History: Lurking in the Shadows* (London: Routledge, 2021); *César Tiempo. Los arrabales de un judío errante* (Buenos Aires: Leviatán, 2021).

Mauricio Pilatowsky Braverman is a Professor of Philosophy at UNAM-FES Acatlán, Mexico. His primary research and teaching interests are Jewish thought, Mexican imaginaries, and critical theory. He has been an invited professor at universities in Spain, Argentina, and Colombia. Some of his publications are the books *La autoridad del exilio: una aproximación al pensamiento de Cohen, Kafka, Rosenzweig y Buber* (UNAM, 2008) and *Las voces desterradas: reflexiones en torno al imaginario judío* (UNAM, 2014).

Deborah Green is a litigation and appellate attorney, an independent writer, and a native Yiddish translator. She is currently writing *Kaddish for the Fallen*, a nonfiction narrative describing Jewish participation in the International Brigades during the Spanish Civil War. Her Yiddish translations have been published in various anthologies including *Avrom Avinu Receives a Letter and Other Yiddish Correspondence* (Yiddish Book Center, 2019). She also participated in an international translation project for the newspaper, *Haynt, A Tsaytung Bei Yidn*. Ms. Green maintains a website, https://jewsfightingfascism.com/, where some of her translations may be found.

Melina Di Miro holds a PhD in Literature from the University of Buenos Aires. Her PhD dissertation studies the narrative of Samuel Glusberg and Alberto Gerchunoff. Di Miro has organized and participated in several conferences on Jewish Argentine literature and has published on this subject in international academic journals. She published several chapters in *Historia Comparada de las Literaturas Argentina y Brasileña* (Eduvim) and collaborates with the *Área del Espectáculo y Judeidad* (IAE-UBA). Di Miro is the coeditor, together with Susana Skura, of *El dibuk—Entre dos mundos. Un siglo de metáforas* (2019).

Golda van der Meer holds a PhD from the University of Barcelona in Linguistic, Literary, and Cultural Studies. Her recent research project focuses on the development of Yiddish modernist poetry in relation to the experience of exile during the interwar period. In addition, her research interests concern literary translations, gender and women's studies, minority languages, and avant-garde Yiddish poetry. She currently works as a Yiddish teacher and as a translator of Yiddish poetry. She is also a coeditor of the *Mozaika Magazine* and collaborates with the Jewish Film Festival of Barcelona.

Emily Robins Sharpe is Chair and Associate Professor of English at Keene State College in Keene, New Hampshire, USA, where she is also an affiliate faculty member of the Women's and Gender Studies and Holocaust and Genocide Studies programs. She is the author of *Mosaic Fictions: Writing Identity in the Spanish Civil War* (University of Toronto Press, 2020) and co-director of the Canada and the Spanish Civil War Project, a print series and virtual research environment (www.spanishcivilwar.ca).

Tabea Alexa Linhard is a Professor of Spanish, Comparative Literature, and Global Studies at Washington University in St. Louis (Missouri, USA). She is the author of *Fearless Women in the Mexican Revolution and the Spanish Civil War* (2005) and *Jewish Spain: A Mediterranean Memory* (2014), and the co-author of *Revisiting Jewish Spain* (2013) and *Mapping Migration, Identity, and Space* (2018). She recently completed *Unexpected Routes: Refuge in Mexico (1931–1945)* and is currently working on a new research project on female secret agents in the 1940s.

E. Helena Houvenaghel holds a Chair in Spanish Literature at the University of Utrecht. Her research area is exile literature (www.helenahouvenaghel.site). Founder and director of the interdisciplinary Fenix Network for Research on Female Exiles and Refugees (https://fenix.sites.uu.nl), she coordinates and serves as editor of Fenix's collective projects (e.g., *Spanish Exile in Argentina: A Gendered Perspective*; *Spanish Women Refugees' Transit in France*; *Spanish Women Writers in Mexican Exile*; *Angelina Muñiz-Huberman, a Non-Conformist Voice*; *Networks of Spanish Women Exiles in Argentina*; *Teresa de Ávila: Routes of a Polysemic Model of Femininity (1936–1986)*, forthcoming). She is also preparing the sixth Fenix congress: Redes y Rutas: Women of Jewish and Spanish Descent in Latin American Exile, 2022.

Rose Duroux is a Professor Emeritus of CELIS (Centre de Recherches sur les Littératures et la Sociopoétique) at the University of Clermont Auvergne. Her current research interests focus on contemporary exilic memory. She also studies refugee assistance during the Spanish War and the Second World War from the point of view of women and children. She has co-edited *Enfances en guerre. Témoignages d'enfants sur la guerre* (2013) devoted to the study of childhood in war. Also noteworthy is her publication "Return to Life of the Spanish Women Deportees from the Ravensbrück camp: The Help of Neutral Countries" (*Culture & History Digital Journal*, 2019).

Index

1492 30, 93, 184 n.3, 201, 208, 215, 216, 216 n.36
1936 1, 4, 6–7, 27, 29, 32–3, 41 n.3, 48, 50, 58, 62–3, 65, 77, 80, 113, 119, 120, 127, 133, 185, 188–9
1937 5–6, 7 n.8, 8, 8 n.10, 12, 27–8, 31, 36, 42–4, 45 n.5, 46, 52, 80, 90, 93, 95, 106, 120, 129, 132, 135, 140, 160, 160 n.5, 187, 190, 205
1938 4, 6, 28, 30–2, 42, 46–7, 66–7, 93, 96–7, 99, 102 n.3, 112 n.1, 120, 133, 136, 160, 170, 202, 205 n.13, 209 n.20
1939 1, 6, 23–30, 33, 36, 44, 47, 59, 62, 65, 68, 70, 92, 98–9, 127, 129–30, 132, 135, 139, 160, 189, 192, 192 n.17
1940 1, 33, 35, 131, 190

Abad de Santillán, Diego (1897–1983) 63, 63 n.8, 71
Abramson, Adelina ("Adelina Kondrátieva", 1917–2012) 10, 206–7
Abramson, Paulina ("Paulina Mariana Mámsurova", 1915–2000) 10, 206–7
Abramson, Samuel H. (1909–96) 147
Abulafia, Abraham (1240–91) 174–82, 214
Adomián, Lan (1905–79) 10, 12, 41–2, 44, 47, 52–3, 203 n.7
Adonai 96, 206 n.15, see also God
Adorno, Theodor (1903–69) 12, 206 n.16, 42–4
African American 29, 46, 142 n.1
agit-prop 11, 57
agnosticism 80–1, 201 n.2
  agnostics 78
Albacete 94, 104
Alcazarquivir (*Ksar-el-Kébir*) 26, 33
Algeria 80, 161

Algiers 35
Allan, Ted (1916–95) 10, 14, 145–7
allegory 173, 175
  allegorical/allegorically 174, 175 n.5, 176, 179, 210, 214
American (North) 1, 4, 35, 43, 94, 106, 137, 140, 143, 146, 152, 203, 207
  Anglo-American 130
  Yiddish-American 13
amnesia 198
anarchism 27–8, 72
  anarchist/anarchists 4, 12, 27–8, 30, 32–3, 56–73 n.20, 83, 129 n.5, 204, 206 n.16, 218 n.40
  anarchist-communist 61, 64
  Anarchist-Communist Federation 67
  anarcho-communist/anarcho-communists 57, 212 n.26 (*see also* Comintern, communist-anarchist)
  anarchist-feminist 72
  anarcho-feminist 214
antifascism/anti-fascism 8, 14–15, 36, 144, 146, 204, 209, 211
  antifascista/antifascistas 32, 66 n.16, 168
  antifascist/anti-fascist/antifascists/anti-fascists 1, 2, 4–6, 12–13, 29–31, 53, 60–1, 66, 67, 94–5, 99, 105, 122, 162, 164, 168, 170, 185, 203, 210–12
anti-Jewish 14, 99, 118, 150
antisemite/antisemites 101, 186, 216 n.35
antisemitic 3 n.4, 24, 30–1, 36, 45, 60, 97, 99, 111, 151–2, 154, 202 n.5, 204, 213, 216
antisemitism 5, 12, 25, 28–31, 53, 78, 82, 93, 97–9, 102 n.4, 106, 114, 132, 139, 143, 145, 150, 152–3,

155, 159, 162, 202, 206 n.16,
   215, 216 n.35
appropriation/appropriations   3 n.4, 77,
   82, 200, 209 n.21, 210, 216–18
   culturally appropriated   217
Arab/Arabs   1, 6, 32–3, 35
   Arabic   23, 29, 32, 34
Aragon   57, 67, 139, 148, 154
Arbeiter Fraind   61, 61 n.4
archival   159
   archive/archives   10, 13, 24, 62, 66,
      68, 204, 205, 214
   archived   211
Arendt, Hannah (1906–45)   164–5,
   206 n.16
Argentina   6, 10–13, 45 n.5, 57–8,
   59 n.2, 61–2, 64, 67, 68 n.20,
   70 n.23, 111–13, 115–17, 119,
   121–5, 203, 207, 209, 212 n.25,
   213 n.28, 215 n.33
   Argentine/Argentines   13, 56–62,
      70–1, 70 n.23, 111–13, 117,
      119–26, 204, 212 n.25
   Argentinian/Argentinians   13, 81,
      106, 206, 210
Ashkenazi   123, 143, 206 n.16, 210, 218
assimilate   78, 87
   assimilated   16, 165
   assimilation   130 n.8, 153, 214
Asturian revolution, the   121
asylum   31, 62, 76, 89, 158 n.1, *see also*
   refuge/refugee(s)
atheist/atheists   24, 78–9
Aub, Max (1903–72)   10–12, 23–4,
   76–90, 185, 203 n.7, 206, 209,
   218
Auschwitz   99, 159
Austria   10, 44, 94, 168, 185 n.4
   Austrian   167 n.14
authorial   113–14, 120, 125, 142 n.1,
   201 n.2, 213
authoritarian   111, 115, 119
   authoritarianism   114, 119, 121, 202
   authoritatively   117
authority   29, 78, 201 n.2, 214, 217
   authorities   33–4, 45, 78
authorship   7 n.8
autobiography   49, 186, 206, 212

autobiographical   60, 174
autobiographies   8, 58
autofiction   8, 206–7, 212–14
Ayalti, Hanan (1910–92)   5, 10, 204 n.11
Azaña, Manuel (1880–1940)   26, 31, 115
Azerrat Cohen, León (1910–197?)   10,
   12, 23–36, *see also* Ben-Krimo

balade/balades   129, 133, 135
   ballad/ballads   129, 133, 135–8
Barcelona   5, 7–8, 10, 27–31, 33, 44, 48,
   56, 64, 66–8, 99, 101, 102, 137,
   160, 211 n.22
Battalion, Dimitroff (Balkan)   205 n.13
Battalion, Mackenzie-Papineau
   (Canadian)   143, 146
Battalion, Palafox (Polish, Soviet and
   Spanish)   6, 95
Battalion, Tschapaiew ("Battalion of
   the 21 Nations")   157–8, 163,
   167–8
belonging   5, 8, 13–14, 60, 62, 144, 155,
   162, 164–5, 170, 193
   Jewish belonging and/to/into
      internationalist becoming   73,
      207, 215
   non-belonging/not belonging   73, 81
Benjamin, Walter (1892–1940)   42,
   206 n.16, 216
Ben-Krimo   12, 23, 27–33, 36
Berlin   41, 44–5, 52, 57, 168
Bible   24, 97, 195, 211 n.23
   Biblical   118, 146, 188, 195
biography   14, 23, 25, 27, 43, 169, 174–7,
   181, 205–6, 213
   biographical   175–6
border/borders   68 n.20, 69, 71–2, 82, 86,
   88, 97, 102, 138, 177
   "border-crossing attitude"   174
   borderline   23
Botvin (newspaper)   6, 106
Botvin, Naftali (1905–25)   95
Botvin/Botwin Company   93, 95, 101
boundaries   36, 170, 175
Brecht, Bertolt (1898–1956)   42, 44–5,
   47, 50–1
Brigade, Abraham Lincoln
   (Anglosaxon)   165, 205

Brigade, Dabrowski/Dombrowski (Brigade XIII, Polish)   95, 106, 157
Brigade, Garibaldi (Italian)   165
brigadista/brigadistas   44, 56–60, 68, 70
   brigadists   5, 11
   interbrigadists   185
brit   214
British   31, 33, 106, 124, 143–4
Budapest   187–9, 192, 196–7, 205 n.13

Calamaro, Eduardo Samuel (1917–2016)   10, 208, 210–11
Canada   10, 13–14, 142–5, 147, 149–51, 203, 218
   Canadian   14, 145–7, 150–2, 154–5, 203, 209
canción   14, 47, 184, 216–18
   cancionero   46
   cantar   196
   cante jondo   52–3
   cantor (synagogue)   52–3
"Capa, Robert" (artistic signature of Gerda Taro and Andre Friedmann)   6, 7 n.8, 146
Catalan   23, 27–9, 32–3, 48, 56, 129, 129 n.6
Catalans (magazine)   31
   Catalonia   1, 29–30, 57, 60, 64, 66, 176
Catholic   3, 33, 81, 87, 111, 113 n.2, 114, 116, 124, 147, 152–3, 200, 204 n.10, 208, 208 n.19, 209
   anti-Catholicism   9
   anti-Catholic struggle   213
   Catholicism   13, 93, 116, 215 n.35
Cervantes Saavedra, Miguel (1547–1616)   82, 82 n.14, 113, 115, 118, 204 n.12
child   135–8, 161, 168, 172, 184 n.2, 188–9, 192, 210, 216
   childhood   53, 63, 153, 213 n.28
   childish   72
   children   32, 84, 89–90, 101, 103, 121, 133, 136–7, 143, 157, 159, 163–4, 166–70, 187, 189, 191, 195
   "Children of Russia"   197
   children's novels   158
   children's book   169
   children's literature   169–70
   Spanish children   159, 187, 190
Christ   70, 116, 118, 208 n.19
   Antichrist   208 n.19
   Christian/Christians   5, 70, 78, 87, 116–18, 154, 200 n.5, 207, 209, 209 n.21
   Christianism   209
   Christianity   78, 85–6, 116–17, 200, 209 n.21, 211
   Christianized   201 n.2
   "Judeo-Christian"   36, 200
   "Judeo-Christianism"   200 n.1
   Pre-Christian Christianism, The (Alberto Gerchunoff's text)   116
Christian imagination   70
circumcision (of the text)   214
Cohen, Leonard (1934–2016)   142, 144
Cohen, Matt (1942–99)   14, 144, 150–1, 150 n.7
Cohen, Robert (1941–)10, 160 n.4, 216 n.37
Cold War   13, 43, 159, 212
colonial   25, 34, 36, 68 n.20, 144, 154, 208
   anticolonialism   143
   colonialism   12, 32, 143, 217
   colonization   150, 202, 208, 219
   colonizing   200, 209
   colony   59, 66, 187, 190
   Jewish colony   212 n.25
   decolonial   209, 209 n.21
   decolonial grammar   201 n.3
   postcolonial   210, 219
Comintern   9, 43, 47, 49, 58 n.1, 92
   anti-communist   111
   non-communist   117
   communism   4, 43, 45, 49, 97–8
   communist-anarchist   67 (*see also* anarchism, anarchist-communist)
   communist/communists   4–5, 9, 11–12, 32, 43–4, 56–60, 62–3, 65 n.12, 66, 67, 83, 89–90, 93–4, 96–9, 103–4, 106, 162, 186, 204, 212, 212 n.26, 213 n.28

Communist International   58, 58 n.1, 60
Communist Party   5, 28, 44, 50, 57, 60, 95, 98, 106 (*see also* PC)
Communist Youth Federation (FJC)   58
conversión/conversions   78, 87, 145, 197, 206
  converso   201 n.3, 215 n.35
  conversos   148, 201, 202 n.5
  "*converso* situation, the"   201
  to convert (verb)   177
  convert/converts (noun)   78, 93, 196
  converted   5, 86, 93, 151, 173, 176, 196
Córdoba/Cordoba   6, 121, 123, 153
cosmopolitan   11, 13, 15, 57, 60, 73, 129–31, 135, 144, 207, 211–12, 217
  anarchist   73, 211
  cosmopolitan imaginaries   11, 15, 129
  cosmopolitan imaginary   13
  "*a cosmopolitan imagination*"   213
  cosmopolitanism   9, 13, 69, 145, 206, 214, 217
  cosmopolitans   217
counternarrative   5
criollo/criollos   119 n.10, 123, 124, 209
crypto-Jews   201, 202 n.5

decipher   82, 177, 193
  deciphering   180
decode   202
  decoding   187
Detsinyi, Ludwig (*known as David Martin*, 1915–1997)   204–5 n.13
Deuteronomy (book *Devarim* in the Torah)   204 n.9
diaspora/diasporas   30, 70–1, 73, 77–9, 77 n.4, 151, 162, 186, 198, 217–19, 217 n.39, *see also galut*
  diasporic   70, 73, 76–7, 79, 86, 88, 191, 214, 217
  diasporic condition   90, 206
displacement   73, 162, 167
  displaced   162
dissent/dissents   56, 58, 62, 66, 67

dissonance/dissonances   50, 201
Di Yunge (aesthetic movement)   128
Dropkin, Celia (1887–1956)   129
Dujovne Ortiz, Alicia (1940–)   72
Durruti, Buenaventura (1896–1936)   64, 66
Dworkin Waddington, Miriam (1917–2004)   14, 149

Edelman, Fanny (1911–2011)   58–9, 62, 204, 207
Ehrenburg, Ilya (1891–1967)   5, 10, 211 n.22
Eisler, Hanns (1898–1962)   10, 12, 41–5, 47–53
El mono azul (magazine)   112, 124
emancipation   5, 72, 78, 125, 209, 218–19
  emancipated   13
  emancipating   211
  emancipatory   42, 85
empathy   159, 186, 207, 215
  empathetic   169
England   29, 89, 99, 164
  English   23, 50, 81–3, 128, 130, 133, 138, 139, 167, 203, 204–5 n.13
entanglement   202
  entangled   12, 26, 182
  entangles   218
enthusiasm   65–6, 213, 217
  enthusiastically   65
  messianic enthusiasm   219
  Mosaic enthusiasm   2, 205–6 n.15, 206, 213
epistemic disobedience   9, 201 n.3, 202, 202 n.5–6
epistemic event   2, 15, 150
epistemicide   202 n.6, 204–5
epistle   203, 207, *see also* letter/letters
  epistolaries   8, 11
  epistolary   12, 57–8, 62, 113
Espinoza, Enrique (1898–1987)   10, 13, 112, 119–25, 209, *see also* Glusberg, Samuel
ethnic   5, 9, 60–1, 70, 113–16, 118, 122, 124, 131, 144, 147, 169–70
  ethnicity   56, 61, 209
  interethnic   33
  multiethnic   57

exclusion/exclusions   78–9, 81, 87, 116,
    143 n.3, 173, 181, 197
  exclusionary   115
  self-exclusion   191
exile/exiles   2, 6, 9–14, 23, 29, 33, 36,
    41–2, 44–5, 52–3, 56–9, 62,
    67, 70–3, 76–8, 83–4, 87–90,
    112 n.1, 130, 130 n.8, 136–40,
    145, 149, 159–60, 164, 172–5,
    181, 185–6, 196–7, 201, 203,
    204, 212, 212 n.24, 215–17
  exiled   14, 45 n.5, 62, 67, 69–71, 76,
    89, 127, 138, 158 n.2, 159–60,
    164, 173, 188, 203 n.7, 215 n.33
  exiliados   186
  exilic   8, 12, 14, 138
  inner-exiles (*insilios*)   215
Exodus (book *Shemot* in the Torah)   117
exodus/exoduses   186, 187, 189–90, 197
expulsion   11, 26, 77, 123, 145, 150 n.7,
    173, 185, 201, 204 n.10
  Edict of Expulsion, the/Edicts of
    Expulsion   93, 201
  expulsion edict, the   30
Extremadura   96, 186–9, 191, 193–7

FACA   64
FAI   28, 64, 121
  CNT-FAI   66, 68
  FAI-CNT   64
Falange   4, 11, 118, 213
  Falangist film culture magazine   35
  Falangist newspapers   34
  La falange (newspaper)   34
fascism   3–4, 28–33, 41, 45–6, 48, 49,
    64–5, 67, 92–6, 98–9, 102, 106,
    111, 117, 130–4, 138–40, 143–4,
    147, 149, 152, 159, 162–5, 168,
    202–3, 209, *see also* antifascism/
    anti-fascism
  fascist/fascists   4, 6, 8, 11, 30–3, 94,
    96–7, 99–104, 127, 140, 145–8,
    164–5, 172, 203, 208–10, 217
    (*see also* antifascism/anti-
    fascism, antifascist/anti-fascist/
    antifascists/anti-fascists)
Feldman, Micaela/Mika/Mika
    Etchebehere, Mika Etchebéhère

    (1902–92)   10–11, 185, 203 n.8,
    206–7, 211 n.22, 212–15, 217
feminist   5, 7 n.8, 9, 56, 65 n.13, 72,
    142 n.1, 210, 212 (*see also*
    anarchism, anarchist-feminist;
    anarchism, anarcho-feminist)
  feminist *caring*   215
fiction   1, 4 n.5, 8, 13, 88, 119, 128,
    142, 144–5, 147, 152, 160, 173,
    175–6, 181, 186, 194, 197, 203,
    207, 216, *see also* autofiction
  fictional   23, 111–14, 125, 146,
    174–7, 181, 184–5, 192–3
  fictionalized   72, 145–6, 150
  nonfiction/non-fiction   8, 175, 207
  postmemory fiction   204 n.11
  semi-fictional   160 n.4
First World War, the   8, 185
FORA   64
forget/forgets   3, 31, 80, 178, 217, *see also*
    oblivion
  forgetfulness   3 n.4
  forgetting   3, 151, 213
  forgot   178
  forgotten   7 n.8, 63, 161, 169–70
  unforgettable   45, 83, 191
France   5–6, 10–11, 14, 44, 60, 68–9,
    80–1, 88, 99, 136–8, 151,
    159–60, 162, 164–5, 168, 172,
    189, 204–5, 216
  Francophone   143, 144 n.4
  French   23, 29, 33, 35, 60, 68 n.20, 70,
    80–1, 93, 99, 102
    Frenchmen   106, 119, 143, 161,
      175, 203, 212, 212 n.25–6,
      214–15
  French-British divide   144
  half-French   143
  non-Francophone   147
  non-French   143
Franco, Francisco (1892–1975)   4, 11, 25,
    31–5, 41, 46, 60, 77, 83–4, 88,
    118–19, 129, 143, 145, 147–8,
    150–1, 154, 172, 175, 185,
    187–91, 194, 204, 213
  Francoism   76, 148, 153
  Francoist/Francoists   25, 31, 36, 68,
    127, 148, 152, 189, 197, 208, 216

Francoist imaginary   216
Freud, Sigmund (1856–1939)   29, 79, 130
   Freudian   29, 191
Friedmann, Endre Ernő (1913–54)   6, 7 n.8, 146

galaxy (Jewish literature)   10, 162, 203, 219
galut   70, 73, 78, 217
García Lorca, Federico (1898–1936)   1, 26–7, 84, 142, 142 n.1
gender   5, 11, 14, 211, 214
   gendered   169, 195, 211
genealogy   123, 150, 193
   "genealogy of disaster"   219
Genesis (book *Bereshit* of the Torah)   195
genesis of the book   163
genocide   2, 99, 162, 166, 170, 181, 204–5, *see also* Shoah
   genocides   219
genre/genres   4, 4 n.5, 14, 41–2, 52
   argumentative   175
   of the autobiography/of autofiction   212
   combination of   181
   "of commitment"   11–13
   elegiac   58, 62, 160, 175
   epistolary   15, 36, 57, 62, 90, 112, 125, 174, 175
   fictional and philosophical   203, 206, 207
   generic hybridity   174, 181
   generic rules   174
   historical   8
   hybrid/hybridity of   177–8, 212, 219
   subgenre   143
   variability of   207
"geography of escape" (*geografía de fuga*)   73, 203, 203 n.1
   "imaginative geography"   210
Gerchunoff, Alberto (1883–1950)   10, 13, 112–19, 121, 123–5, 209, 218
German/Germans   1, 11–12, 14, 29–31, 42, 44–5, 51–2, 65, 80–1, 83, 103, 114, 124, 130, 146, 151–2, 158–9, 162, 164, 166–8, 185, 189, 203, 218
   anti-German   68

Germanist   158, 161
Germanized   166
Germany   5, 8, 10, 13–14, 34, 81, 86, 94, 97, 114, 160, 165, 169, 189, 200, 203–5, 216
   Italian-German   67
   Jewish German   2 n.1, 45 n.5, 162
   German Jewish   123
   German Jews   165
   Judeo-German-Australian poet   204
   Polish-German   6
   "Spanish-German language mishmash"   168
Gestapo   27, 161, 205
ghetto/ghettos   122, 153, 209
   Warsaw   209 n.21
Glantz, Jacobo (Yankev, 1902–82)   10, 131, 133, 208–11
Glanz-Leyeles, Aaron (1889–1966)   10, 13, 128–30, 132, 135–40
Glatstein, Jacob (1896–1971)   10, 13, 128, 130, 132–4, 139–40, 207
Glusberg, Samuel (1898–1987)   10, 13, 112, 209, *see also* Espinoza, Enrique
God   2 n.1, 86–7, 96, 103–4, 173, 176–8, 182, 211–12, *see also* Adonai
Goldman, Emma (1869–1940)   27, 31, 206 n.16
Greckol, Sonja Ruth (1946–)   14, 144, 154–5
Group, Thälmann (Germanic and Scandinavian; known as "Jewish militia")   8

Hebraic wisdom   116
"Hebreo, Barrio"   122
Hebrew/Hebrews   24, 53, 78, 87, 128, 177, 186, 203, 206 n.15, 208–9, 212 n.25
   Hebrew-Spanish poet   139 n.19
   Hispano-Hebrew poets   123
Heine, Heinrich (1797–1856)   44, 77, 84, 86–7, 90, 123
Hemingway, Ernest (1899–1951)   2, 167
Hernández, Miguel (1910–1942)   41, 47, 53, 84, 124
Hispanic   83, 121 n.11

hispanophilia   121 n.11, 123–4
  Hispano-Hebrew   123
  Hispano Marroquí   32
  Hispano-Mexican   14
  Hispano-Sephardic   26
  Jewish   123–4
  Spanishness   52
Hitler, Adolf (1889–1945)   31, 65, 98–9,
    114–15, 117–19, 123, 151, 154,
    163
Holocaust   3–4, 133–4, 145, 150, 162–3,
    189, 197, 219
  post-Holocaust   132, 163
holy war   101, 124, 208–9
homeland   57, 59–61, 70, 72, 84, 149
  Jewish homeland   97, 135
horizontalism   9, 214
Hungary   94, 189
  Austro-Hungarian   185
  Hungarian   164, 189, 191–3, 203

Ibárruri, Dolores ("La Pasionaria",
    1895–1989)   122, 203 n.7
identity/identities   1–2, 9, 13–14, 23, 26,
    46, 60–1, 68–9, 71, 79, 81, 88–9,
    111, 113, 124, 207, 210
  "Jewish identity"   115, 124, 131,
    142–5, 154–5, 157, 185–6, 191,
    194, 196–7, 201 n.4, 202 n.5,
    206, 208, 213–14, 213 n.29
imaginary   3 n.4, 6, 12–14
  anti-Judaic Francoist imaginary   216
  antisemitic   46, 53
  biological   112, 145, 173, 209, 211, 214
  cosmopolitan imaginary   13, 73, 211
  gender-based imaginary   211
  imaginaries   4, 9–14, 92, 129, 158,
    203, 207–10, 212, 218–19
  internationalist imaginary   73,
    203 n.8, 211
  Jewish imaginary   12, 69, 92, 159,
    211, 219
  Mexican imaginary   80, 83 n.12
  musical   57, 73, 78
  Sephardic imaginary   211 n.22
  spatial   31
imagination   8, 154, 176, 203 n.8, 210,
    214, 217

  collective, exilic   9, 23, 66, 70
  cosmopolitan imagination   213
  transhistorical imagination   219
immigrant/immigrants   61, 113, 116,
    128, 130–1, 138, 143–4, 218
immigrated   60, 132, 139, 143
immigrating   135
immigration   30, 116 n.4, 142, 144,
    213 n.28
imposture   213
Inquisition, the   118, 139, 145, 150–1,
    153–4, 173, 208, 214–15, 219
  pre-Inquisition   151
intellectual/intellectuals   3, 5–6, 8, 11,
    13, 24–6, 33–4, 36, 44, 57,
    68, 90, 111–13, 115, 119–21,
    124, 185, 204, 206,
    213–19
  intellectualism   12
  intelligence   34, 79
  intelligentsia   210
International Brigade/International
    Brigades   4–6, 11–12, 29, 46,
    50, 52, 58, 62, 66, 92–4, 101,
    103, 106, 143, 157, 159–60,
    162–9, 185, 205 n.13
  International Brigadista   44
internationalism   5, 57, 60, 63, 67, 73,
    204, 209, 213, 217
  internationalist/internationalists   1,
    3, 8, 57–8, 60–1, 63, 73, 92,
    207–11, 213, 215
interpretation/interpretations   45, 53, 73,
    78, 113, 117, 120, 123–5, 136,
    155, 175, 180, 206, 217
  interpreted   24, 119, 175, 201–2,
    216
  interpreters   6
  interpreting   173–4, 195, 203
intersect   167, 192
  intersected   197
  intersecting   189
  intersection/intersections   9, 12–14,
    112, 159, 205, 206 n.16, 213,
    219
intertext   175, 179
  intertextual   175, 218
  intertextuality   9, 195–6

Introspectivist/Introspectivists   13, 127 n.2, 130–2, 134
Inzikh (journal)   13, 127, 129–33, 135, 138–40
Inzikh (movement/poets)   14, 127–32, 134–5, 138, 207, *see also* Introspectivist/Introspectivists
Israel   3 n.2, 10, 79–81, 99, 135, 153, 182, 194, 196
   Israeli/Israelis   82, 153, 204 n.11
   Israelites   24, 87
Italy   165, 201, 204
   Italian-German   66–7
   Italian/Italians   1, 56, 59 n.2, 61, 65, 83, 94, 130, 164
iterology   214

Jacobs, Bárbara (1947–)   10, 216 n.37
Jew   24, 26, 30, 36, 73, 76, 79, 83, 87, 98, 99, 103, 116, 118, 122, 153, 173, 217
   Jews   1, 3–6, 12, 23, 25–6, 29–33, 35, 60–1, 64, 76–9, 86–90, 92–9, 103–6, 111, 116, 118–20, 122–5, 132, 138–9, 144–5, 152–4, 162, 164, 173, 185–6, 188–9, 192, 197, 202–4, 208–9, 217
Jewish Antichrist, a   24
Jewish authors   1, 5, 10, 143
   Canada's Anglo-Jewish   208, 211 n.22, 218
Jewish culture   9, 97, 162, 200 n.1, 201 n.4, 207, 210
Jewish experience(s)   1–4, 12, 14, 42, 76, 162, 203 n.8, 213
Jewish history   14, 145, 159, 162, 173, 209, 219
Jewish imagination   70
Jewish languages   1, 168, 202 n.6
   non-Jewish languages   5, 10, 162, 202
Jewish Library   1, 186
Jewish literature(s)   1–2, 9–10, 113, 162, 169, 184–5, 188, 198, 200–1 n.2, 202–3, 207, 218–19
Jewishly   4–5
Jewish memory   3, 216–17, 219
Jewishness   2, 5, 13, 26, 61, 73, 87, 97, 112–13, 116, 121–5, 131, 135, 153, 159, 161–2, 186, 201 n.4, 217 n.38

Jewish people, the   1–3, 94, 99, 101, 142, 146, 153, 174, 181, 200, 209–12, 219
Jewish poetic modes, Jewish modes   1, 9, 12, 202, 213, 219
Jewish poetics   9, 14–15, 131, 201, 213
   of internationalism   204, 213
Jewish refugees   11–12, 30–1
Jewish text(s)   9–10, 113, 169
Jewish volunteer(s)   3 n.4, 29, 47, 60, 92–5, 98–9, 103, 106, 157, 159, 162–3, 165
   non-Jewish Jew, a   60
journal(s)   5–6, 13, 24, 26, 28, 34, 119, 127, 129–33, 139–40, *see also* newspaper/newspapers
   journalism   11–12, 24, 26, 145, 213 (*see also* photojournalism)
   journalist(s)   4, 6, 11, 24, 34, 36, 89, 145, 157
   journalistic   7, 12, 26, 28, 35, 77, 113
Judaic   186, 202
   anti-Judaic   216
Judaism   1, 3 n.4, 13, 36, 44, 52, 58, 78, 81, 85–6, 96–8, 116–17, 152, 177, 196–7, 202, 206, 209, 211
   medieval anti-Judaism   3 n.4, 78
Judeo-Spanish   26, 168
   Ladino   188, 198, 218
July   4–7, 48, 80, 87, 93, 96, 99, 101, 113, 160, 189
justice   79, 87, 90, 116, 124, 175, 178, 204–5, *see also* "Letter and the Law", the
   injustice   83, 87, 89, 205

Kabbalah   175, 177, 181–2
   kabbalist(s)   174–80, 201
   kabbalistic   14, 182, 205
Kafka, Franz (1883–1924)   9, 42, 77, 84–6, 90, 205 n.16
Kahn, Máximo José (1897–1953)   10, 45, 185, 215 n.33
Kantorowicz, Alfred (1899–1979)   157–9, 162–3, 168–9
kapara   209, 209 n.1
key/keys   6, 66, 124, 134, 136, 142, 181, 189, 195, 197, 214, 218

Klein, Abraham Moses (1909–72)   14, 147–9
Kordon, Bernardo (1915–2002)   10, 112, 208, 210
Krüger, Dirk (1940–)   158–61, 169, 204–5 n.13, 205
Kurtz, Aaron (1891–1964)   10, 131, 133, 136, 208, 210

Langer, Marie (1910–87)   206–7
language/languages   1–2, 5, 10, 13, 23, 26, 34, 36, 43–4, 50–1, 58, 61, 70, 72, 79, 82–3, 86, 88, 90, 93, 97, 105, 112, 117, 125, 128–32, 134–6, 138, 140, 142, 155, 162, 164–9, 184, 186, 188, 192, 198, 202–3, 210–11, 218, 219, *see also* multilingual
   linguistic   9, 60, 116–17, 130 n.8, 131, 159, 166–9, 203, 212
   linguistically   167, 210
   metalinguistic   12
La Protesta (newspaper)   61, 63 n.8
Largo Caballero, Francisco (1869–46)   121
Latin America   59, 119 n.10, 121–3, 125, 185, 209, 218
   Latin American   8, 13–14, 62, 119–20, 122–4, 203, 206, 209–10
Leivik, H. (1888–1962)   128
"Letter and the Law", the   204, 206, 206 n.16, 213
letter/letters   8, 9, 11–12, 31, 42–3, 56–8, 62–73, 92–3, 99, 103–5, 113, 131, 138, 171, 176, 190, 208, 214, *see also* epistle
   dead-letter box   113, 161, 177, 208
Leviticus (book *VaYikrah* in the Torah)   117
libertarian   2 n.1, 30, 56–7, 60–1, 67, 69, 206 n.16
listener   50–1
   listened   42, 46–7, 95
   listening   12, 42–3, 45, 47
   "songs"   52, 53, 68, 121, 207, 213 n.28
lullaby   136, 186, 188, 218

Madrid   5, 7–8, 24–7, 29, 31, 34–6, 44, 47–8, 52, 94, 103, 124, 150–1, 153–4, 159, 170, 185, 187–8, 192, 194, 196–7, 211 n.22
manifesto   45, 93, 106, 129, 140, 198
maquis   186
Markish, Peretz (1895–1952)   10, 131, 133, 209 n.20, 214
Marx, Karl (1818–83)   43
   Hanns Eisler   79, 206 n.16
Marxism   80, 122
   Marxist   42, 53, 206 n.16, 206, 213
      anarcho-Marxist   213
masculine   146
   masculinity/masculinities   3 n.2, 13, 152–4, 214
Matria   197–8
   matriarchal   9
   matriarchs   197
matrix   9, 56, 212
Mayer-Serra, Otto (1904–1968)   41–2, 44, 46, 48–50
Medem, Gina (1886–1977)   4, 94–5, 106
Medina Onrubia, Salvadora (1894–1972, SM)   12, 56–8, 61–9, 71–3
melancholy   188, 215–16
   melancholic   71
melody/melodies   48–50, 52, 87, 187–8
   Hebrew   45 n.4
   melodic   48–9
   Sephardic   46–7
memory   1, 3, 5, 8–10, 12–14, 46, 53, 56, 58, 65, 95, 106, 140, 148, 159, 161, 169–70, 193–5, 203–4, 206, 208, 211–13, 218, *see also* Jewish memory
   memoir/memoirs   8, 11, 24, 57–8, 62, 92, 97–8, 152 n.9, 207, 212 n.26 (*see also* postmemory)
   multidirectional memory   219
   transhistorical memory   219
   transhistorical memory, tribal memory   207
Messiah   2 n.1, 116
   messianic   2 n.1, 9, 11, 86, 117, 176–7, 206 n.16, 208, 219
   messianism(s)   5, 116–18, 124, 205 n.15, 206 n.16, 211

Mexico   10–13, 41, 44, 59, 62, 69–72, 76–7, 80, 83, 88, 90, 122, 160, 166, 172, 203
   Mexican   7 n.8, 58–9, 62, 70–2, 80–1, 83, 115, 162, 207
Middle Ages   118, 122, 204, 212, 219
   medieval   14, 78, 118, 122, 152, 154, 175, 179, 209
migration   9, 11–12, see also immigrant/immigrants, immigration
   migratory wave   185
   temporal   57
militia/militias   4–5, 8, 33, 67, 208, 212
   anarchist   189
   militiamen   5–6, 11, 44, 48, 60, 94
   militiawomen   11
   pro-Nazi   189
minority/minorities   70, 118, 164, 173, 209
mistranslation(s)   159, 167
Mochkofsky, Graciela (1969–)   10, 216 n.37
Montevideo   57, 62–6, 72
Montreal   142, 145, 147, 152–4
Moors   68 n.20, 153, 168
Morocco   6, 10, 12, 24–9, 31–7, 165, 203
   Moroccan   23, 25–9, 32–6, 154, 168
Mosaic, see enthusiasm, Mosaic enthusiasm
Moscow   28, 44, 57, 98, 150, 161, 187, 190, 194, 205
mother(s)   27, 31, 33, 43–4, 61, 71–3, 80–1, 103–5, 137–8
   motherland   211
   mother tongue   184, 187, 188, 191, 193–4, 196, 197
Mujeres Libres   214
multilingual   154, 165, 168, 202, 205 n.13
   multilingualism   70, 169
   multilinguistic   57
Muñiz-Huberman, Angelina (1936–)   10–11, 14, 172–6, 180–2, 197, 207, 209, 214
music   4, 11–12, 41–9, 53, 142, 147, 203
   musical/musically   12, 28, 41–7, 51–3, 187–8, 205
      musicality   134

   musicalizing   47
   musician/musicians   1, 6, 41–3, 142
   musicological   42–3, 52
   musicologist   46–7
   musicology   41, 46
Muslim(s)   29, 32–3, 144–5, 151, 154
   anti-Muslim history   14
   anti-Muslim violence   150
Mussolini, Benito (1883–1945)   33, 115, 118, 121, 123
mystic   173
   mystical   2 n.1, 98, 174, 176, 179, 219
   mysticism   173, 176, 181, 207, 212, 214

Naftali Botvin/Botwin Company   6, 93, 95
narrative/narratives   5, 13, 56, 58, 72, 92, 118, 145, 151–4, 157, 163, 168, 174–5, 179, 184, 187, 191–4, 196, 216, see also counternarrative
   narrative of origins   213
   narratives of caring   207, 215
nationalism/nationalisms   77, 79, 81–3, 87, 90, 111, 112, 114–16, 118–19, 125, 143
   ethnonationalism   200
   nationalist(s)   4, 13, 29, 34, 35, 60, 80, 83
   nationalistic   85, 90, 111, 124, 158–60, 163–6, 168, 174–5
Naye Prese (journal)   8, 93–4, see also Yiddish journals
Nazi/Nazis   2, 12, 14, 24, 29, 34, 53, 78, 88–90, 95, 98, 99, 106, 124, 163, 166, 173, 192, 194, 202, 205
   anti-Nazi   70
   Nazism   8, 12, 29, 44–5, 53, 76, 88–90, 111, 117, 119, 134, 144, 147, 185, 203
   Nazi–Soviet Non-Aggression Pact   147, 160, 162–3, 166, 170, 189
Nelken, Margarita (1894–1968)   5, 10, 203 n.7

Neruda, Pablo (1904–1974)   2, 41 n.3
nest   211
newspaper/newspapers   23, 25, 27, 28, 32–5, 77, 93–4, 103, 111, 128, 166, *see also* journal(s); press
newsletter   56, 73, 88, 105–6, 157
New York   10, 13
  New Yorker   44, 57, 127–8, 130, 132–3, 135, 138, 153
Noah   2, 13
  ark of   15, 204, 206 n.15
¡No pasarán!/*No pasarán!* (They shall not pass!)   47, 67 n.18, 133, 208 n.20, 209, 211 n.22
North America   6, 71, 89, 153, 164
Nostalgia (name)   185, 187–8, 192–8
Nostalgia   14, 59, 71, 145, 149, 153, 185, 216
  nostalgic   60, 152–3, 186
novel (literary genre)   14, 23, 46, 72, 85, 112–13, 134, 139, 144–7, 150, 152–3, 157, 159, 161–3, 165–7, 169–70, 174, 185–91, 193–5, 197–8, 205, 207, 209, 214, 216
  novelist(s)   41 n.3, 181, 184 n.2, 185, 196
  novel-poem   188, 198

oblivion   3, 9, 36, 217
  obliviating   217
  oblivious   96, 148
open corpus   10, 207, 219
Orient   35
  oriental   25
  Orientalism   210
  orientalist   25, 36, 210, 219
Ortega y Gasset, José (1883–1955)   84
  Ortega   121

pacto del olvido   151–2
Palestine   5–6, 10, 29, 31, 33, 78, 89–90, 94, 102, 104, 204, 216 n.37
  Palestinian(s)   6, 32, 104, 167 n.14
Paris   4 n.6, 5–6, 10, 24, 57, 62, 69, 80–1, 94, 98, 103, 160
  Parisian   7, 81
Pasionaria, La (1895–1989)   203 n.7, *see also* Ibárruri, Dolores

password(s)   111, 209, 215, 213 n.27, 218
PC   57–8, *see also* Communist Party
peregrinations   191
persecution/persecutions   3, 11, 31, 42, 45, 53, 85, 87, 97, 99, 116, 118, 173, 186, 194, 197, 201, 203–4, 217
  persecuted   11, 28–31, 89–90, 101, 116, 129, 173, 204, 217
  persecutors (Catholic)   200
philo-Semitism   29, 186, 215, 218, 218 n.40
philo-Sephardic   14, 184, 215–18, *see also* Sepharad, neo-Sephardism
  philo-Sephardism   12, 185–6, 215
philosophy   135, 173, 181
  philosopher(s)   42–3, 59, 153, 181
  philosophical   172–5, 177, 179, 181, 201, 203
photographer(s)   5–7, 146
photojournalism   6
pilgrimage   11
playwright(s)   25, 27, 181
poem(s)   24–5, 28, 34–5, 44–5, 51, 77, 90, 111–12, 124, 128–39, 142, 147–52, 154, 197, 207, 208, 210–11, *see also* novel, novel-poem
poet(s)   1, 5–6, 9, 13–14, 24–7, 29, 35, 41–2, 44, 59, 71, 84, 86, 123, 127–35, 137–40, 142, 148, 154, 172, 180–1, 190, 204, 210–11, 214–15
  poetic, poetical   9–10, 13, 15, 24, 26, 36, 44, 112, 125, 127, 129–32
  poetical activism   134–5, 137, 140, 154, 181, 186, 195, 205, 211 (*see also* Jewish poetic modes)
  poetic justice   10, 14, 159, 170, 204–6, 208, 213, 215, 219
poetics   9, 134–5, 185, 204, 213, *see also* Jewish poetics
  of silence   219
poetry   2, 13–14, 24, 35, 42, 45, 87, 124, 127–38, 140, 142, 144–5, 147, 149, 154–5, 188, 203–5, 207
polyglossia   9, 212–13, 217–18, *see also* multilingual, multilingualism

superpolyglossia   213, 213 n.9
polyglot(s)   13–14, 36, 217
Popular Front   7, 47, 49–50, 119, 127
Popular Olympiad   8, 48, 99
postmemory   3, 13, 109, 204, 216
   postmemorial   216 n.37
POUM (Partido Obrero de Unificación Marxista)   212
practice(s)   196, 201, 202 n.5, 211
   anarchist practices   67
   Jewish practices   214
   religious practices   78
   writing practices   214
Prago, Albert (1911–93)   163
pray   103
   prayer(s)   96–8, 187, 189, 204
   praying   86
press   6, 8, 25, 27–8, 32–6, 46, 78, 98, 105, 130 n.8, 132, 145, *see also* journal(s); newspaper/newspapers
Preston, Paul (1946–)   3 n.4, 189
proletarian(s)   5–8, 49, 57, 73, 90, 123, 209
propaganda   27, 30, 32–3, 67, 72, 92–3, 99, 104–5
   propagandist   93, 104
Pyrenees   70, 189

rabbi(s)   24, 29, 88–90, 151, 178, 202 n.5
   rabbinical   201 n.4
race(s)   3, 28–9, 78, 116, *see also* antifascism/anti-fascism, anti-Jewish; antisemite/anti-Semites, antisemitism; Judaism, medieval anti-Judaism; Muslim(s), anti-Muslim
   racial/racially   29, 78, 124, 168, 201 n.4
   racism   143, 202
Rachman, Ephraim (1929–)   10, 204 n.11, 216 n.37
radio   47 n.7, 48, 88, 153, 205 n.13, 211
   radiophonic   27, 32
Radowitzky, Simón (1891–1956)   10–12, 56–73, 218
refuge/refugee(s)   11–12, 30–1, 44, 62, 68 n.20, 71, 76–7, 81, 88–9, 103, 116 n.4, 160, 211, 216–18

religion(s)   3, 42, 56, 61, 79–82, 87–8, 97, 116, 121
   religious   5, 23, 31, 43, 53, 70, 77–8, 80, 83, 85, 87, 90, 96, 98, 105, 116–17, 124, 151–2, 173, 176, 179, 201 n.2, 201 n.4, 206 n.16, 208
repair   206 (verb)
   epistemic   208
   repairing   2
   reparation   196, 205, 215
   reparative   218
repeats   134, 219
   repeated   23, 32, 50, 137, 190
   repeatedly   32, 121, 136, 142, 149, 154
   repetition   137, 187
   repetitive   173–4, 181
Republic/republics   4, 7, 25, 27, 30, 32, 36, 45, 57, 59, 62, 66, 93, 111–12, 115, 117, 119, 121–3, 125, 145–6, 153, 159, 162–3, 166, 185, 205, 210
   Republican(s)   2, 4, 6, 11–12, 14, 25, 27–34, 36, 44, 46, 48, 50, 58–9, 62, 64–8, 70, 73, 76–7, 80, 83, 88–90, 97, 99, 103, 111–13, 119–20, 123–5, 127, 131, 147–8, 152–3, 158, 160, 174–5, 180, 185–7, 189–90, 197–8, 203, 205, 207, 209–10, 216–17
   republicanism   33
resistance   6, 48, 53, 70, 98–9, 124, 130 n.8, 163, 191, 202, 215
revolt   175
   Franco's military   175
   student revolts   197
révolte   200–1
revolution(s)   4, 9, 11–13, 27, 57, 60, 64, 67, 72, 98, 104, 121, 147, 150, 200, 207
   counterrevolutionary   30
   revolutionary/revolutionaries   3, 5, 12, 24, 28–9, 36, 44, 53, 59–60, 65–8, 70, 99, 101, 103, 122, 128, 134, 140, 149, 208, 213, 213 n.28

Rewald, Ruth (1906–42)   10, 14, 157–70, 203, 205, 218
Richler, Mordechai (1931–2001)   14, 144, 152–3
ritual(s)   117, 193, 209 n.21
  ritualistic   195
Russia   5, 10–11, 14, 59, 61, 61 n.4, 65, 97
  China-Russia border   187, 189–90, 197
  Russian(s)   28, 56, 61, 65–6, 72, 95, 98, 103, 130, 190, 203, 213, 213 n.28

Saint Cyprien concentration camp   68–9
Santa Teresa of Ávila (1515–82)   173
Santiago Bolaños, Marifé (1962–)   10, 14, 184–5, 188–9, 191, 194, 196–7, 207, 216
Sanz Briz, Ángel (1910–1980)   192, 197
Schaul, Hans (1905–88)   157–64, 169
Schönberg, Arnold (1874–1951)   12, 42–4, 51
Second International Anti-Fascist Writers Congress in Defense of Culture   5
Second World War, the   13, 23, 33–4, 93
  pre-   98, 139, 150–1, 173, 190, 197, 203
secular   12–14, 79, 105, 160, 196, 200–1, 204, 206, 211
  secularism   201 n.2
  secularized   79
  secularly   206 n.16
Sefarad   24, 184 n.3, 216–17
Sefarad   186, 188, 218
Sefer Yetsirá   177
Seghers, Anna (1900–83)   1, 5, 166, 207
self-translation   9, 213, *see also* translation(s)
  self-translated   213–14
Sepharad   8, 14, 123, 145, 185–6, 188, 192, 194, 198, 208, 210, 212, 214, 219, *see also* philo-Sephardic, philo-Sephardism
  neo-Sephardism   210, 218
  Sephardic   12, 14, 26

Hispano-Sephardic   26
pre-Sephardic   219
Sephardic World Congress   30, 123, 173, 181, 185–9, 192, 195, 197–8, 200 n.2, 210, 211 n.22, 215–16, 218–19
Sephardim   30, 186–8, 197
shekhinah   211–12
Shoah   1–3, 13, 172, 186, 202 n.6, 216–17, *see also* Holocaust
shofar   117
silence   83, 104, 132–5, 139, 148, 151–2, 191, 194, 207, 213
  silenced   11, 133, 151
  silencing   177, 193, 213 n.29
  silent   68, 130, 132–4, 136, 139, 191, 215 n.32
Sinay, Rubén (1918–90)   10, 112, 208, 210
socialism   5, 13, 119, 121
  socialist(s)   4–6, 8, 42–3, 70 n.23, 80, 98, 116 n.6, 135, 204, 214
song(s)   24, 41–4, 46–53, 60, 133, 142, 169, 185, 187–8, 195–6, 198, 205, 207
  songbook   41, 44, 47, 50
Soviet   8, 49, 58, 67, 93–4, 97–8, 104, 190, 207
  Soviet Union   6, 44, 98, 106, 111, 197
space   6, 36, 58, 102, 123, 142 n.1, 151–2, 154, 186, 188, 193–4, 203, 205
  spatial   14, 162, 176
Spanish Civil War, the   1–4, 8–11, 13–15, 24, 27, 29, 36, 41, 45–6, 53, 56–8, 60, 73, 77, 88, 90, 92–4, 98–9, 111–12, 119–20, 123–5, 127–35, 138, 140, 142–5, 147–8, 150, 152–5, 158–9, 165–7, 169–70, 172, 174–7, 179–82, 185–6, 189, 191, 193, 202–4, 206, 208, 211, 214, 218–19
spiritual   29, 94, 98–9, 173–7, 196
stateless   56, 67, 69, 71, 77, 90, 162, 164–5
Stein, Sygmunt (1899–1968)   4, 92–3, 97, 104, 212 n.26
subaltern   15, 201, 209–10, 217

superpolyglossia 213
survival 1–2, 62, 170, 191, 194, 198, 201–2, 206, 217
synagogue(s) 26, 32, 43, 52–3, 100, 151

Talmud 202 n.5
  Talmudic 9, 202 n.5, 209, 214
Taro, Gerda (1910–37) 5–7, 146, 203
Tel Aviv 166, 196
Testament 117
  'Old', New 195, 200
  testimonial 4, 8, 211 n.22
    testimony(ies) 8, 11, 23, 57, 59–60, 68, 76, 163, 212, 219
textual 58
  textualities 4 n.5, 9–11, 13, 21, 109, 203, 219
Thaelmann/Thälmann, Ernst (1886–1944) 27, 158–9, 169
Tiempo, César (Israel Zeitlin, 1906–80) 6, 10, 112, 208, 210
tikkun, *tikkun olam* 2, 205–6
Toledo 151
Torah 97, 182, 200, 202 n.5, 204
Toronto 4, 149–51
transhistorical 14, 154, 202, 207, 209, 214, 216, 219
translated 2, 7, 92–4, 138, 166, 201, 204, 206–7, 215
translation(s) 9, 12–14, 50 n.10, 71, 92, 130–1, 133, 135, 139, 159, 166–7, 169, 200, 203, 213, *see also* mistranslation(s)
  translating 206, 214–15
  translator 6, 63 n.8, 83 n.12, 92, 135 n.15 (*see also* self-translation)
transmission 188, 195
transnational 5, 11 n.11, 13–14, 36, 56–7, 60–1, 142, 145–6, 150, 152, 154, 165, 184, 204, 209–10, 214
trauma 3, 9, 150, 152, 189–91, 193, 196, 203 n.8, 214–15, 219
  traumatic 2–3, 151, 153, 203 n.8
Trotsky, Leon (1879–1940) 4, 65, 135

Trotskyism 119
Tschapaiew–Das Batallion der 21 Nationen (newspaper) 157–8, 163, 167–8
Turkey 45, 89, 194, 201
  Turkish 192, 194
  Turks 82
tzimzum (God's exile) 212

Uruguay 10, 56, 58–9, 62, 64, 204 n.11
  Uruguayan 59, 71
USA 5, 10–11, 13, 52, 61, 106, 203–4, 218 n.40
utopia 2 n.1, 116, 118, 167, 172, 180, 206 n.16, 211, 214–15
  utopian 2 n.1, 118, 218

Valencia 5, 7, 27–8, 67, 152–3, 190, 211 n.22
Vienna 43–5
Vogel, Debora (1902–42) 129

wandering Jew 12, 56–8, 60, 62, 68–80
Weiss, Leo (known as Leo Katz, 1892–954) 7–8
West, the 3–6, 10, 116 n.6, 200–2, 204
  Western 1, 4, 11, 13, 42–3, 78, 164, 200–1, 206, 211, 217
witness/witnesses 2, 8, 144 n.6, 159, 212
woman 25, 57, 65, 72, 104, 121, 129, 150, 160, 165, 172 n.1, 187, 197
womb 115, 211
women 5, 6, 11, 13, 42, 58 n.1, 64, 67, 72, 79, 89, 101, 103, 128–9, 152, 187, 191, 193, 196–7, 204, 206, 210–11, 214, 216
world literature 2, 8, 11, 13, 128, 130, 132, 166, 169, 218

Yale Harrison, Charles (1898–1954) 10, 145, 147
Yiddishkayt 97
Yiddish language 1, 6, 12, 23, 29, 31, 61, 97, 129–31, 135, 136 n.16, 140, 168
Yiddish letters 92, 106

Yiddish literature 128–9, 131–2, 134
Yiddish poetry 128 n.3, 130 n.8, 132, 135–6, 140, 209 n.20, 214, *see also Inzikh*
  Yiddish poets 5, 127–34, 138–9, 215

Zambrano, María (1904–91) 59, 62, 70–1, 80 n.6, 181
Zion 35, 139 n.19
  Zionism 29, 31, 33, 79, 81
  Zionist 24, 102 n.5, 135
Zohar 194–7

www.ingramcontent.com/pod-product-compliance
Lightning Source LLC
Chambersburg PA
CBHW062134300426
44115CB00012BA/1917